PSYCHOLOGY LIBRARY EDITIONS:
NEUROPSYCHOLOGY

Volume 6

PERSPECTIVES ON COGNITIVE NEUROPSYCHOLOGY

PERSPECTIVES ON COGNITIVE NEUROPSYCHOLOGY

Edited by
G. DENES, C. SEMENZA AND P. BISIACCHI

Routledge
Taylor & Francis Group
LONDON AND NEW YORK

First published in 1988 by Lawrence Erlbaum Associates Ltd.

This edition first published in 2019
by Routledge
4 Park Square, Milton Park, Abingdon, Oxon OX14 4RN
605 Third Avenue, New York, NY 10017

Routledge is an imprint of the Taylor & Francis Group, an informa business

British Library Cataloguing in Publication Data
A catalogue record for this book is available from the British Library

ISBN: 978-1-138-48894-6 (Set)
ISBN: 978-0-429-45935-1 (Set) (ebk)
ISBN: 978-1-138-63905-8 (Volume 6) (hbk)
ISBN: 978-1-315-63742-6 (Volume 6) (ebk)

Publisher's Note
The publisher has gone to great lengths to ensure the quality of this reprint but points out that some imperfections in the original copies may be apparent.

Disclaimer
The publisher has made every effort to trace copyright holders and would welcome correspondence from those they have been unable to trace.

Perspectives on Cognitive Neuropsychology

Edited by

G. Denes, C. Semenza, and P. Bisiacchi

LAWRENCE ERLBAUM ASSOCIATES, PUBLISHERS
Hove and London (UK) Hillsdale (USA)

Lawrence Erlbaum Associates Ltd., Publishers
27 Palmeira Mansions
Church Road
Hove
East Sussex, BN3 2FA
U.K.

British Library Cataloguing in Publication Data

Perspectives on cognitive neuropsychology.
1. Man. Cognition. Neuropsychological aspects
I. Denes, G. (Gianfranco) II. Semenza, C.
III. Bisiacchi, P.
153.4

ISBN 0-86377-046-0

Typeset by Tradespools Ltd., Frome, Somerset
Printed in Great Britain by BPCC Wheatons Ltd, Exeter

Contents

List of Contributors

Barry, Christopher School of Speech Therapy, South Glamorgan Institute of Higher Education, Western Avenue, Llandaff, Cardiff CF4 2YB, U.K.

Bisiacchi, Patrizia Dipartimento di Psicologia Generale, Università di Padova, Italy

Burani, C. Istituto di Psicologia del C.N.R., Viale C. Marx 15, 00156 Roma, Italy

Cappa, Stefano F. Istituto di Clinica Neurologica, Via F. Sforza 35, 20122 Milano, Italy

Carreras, Mirko Clinica Neurologica, Università di Ferrara, Corso della Giovecca 203, 44100 Ferrara, Italy

Cermak, Laird S. Psychology Service, Veterans Administration Hospital, 150 South Huntington Avenue, 02130 Boston, Mass., U.S.A.

Davidoff, Jules Department of Psychology, University College of Swansea, Swansea SA2 8PP, U.K.

De Bastiani, Pierluigi Istituto di Clinica Neurologia, Università di Ferrara, Corso della Giovecca 203, 44100 Ferrara, Italy

De Bleser, Ria Department of Neurology, Pauwelsstrasse, 5100 Aachen, West Germany

Denes, Gianfranco Istituto di Clinica della Malattie Nervose e Mentali dell'-Università, Via Giustinini, 5-35128 Padova, Italy

Ellis, Andrew W. Department of Psychology, University of York, Heslington, York Y01 5DD.

Flores d'Arcais, Giovanni B. Unit of Experimental Psychology, University of Leiden, 2300 RA Leiden, The Netherlands

Friederici, Angela D. Max-Planck-Institut für Psycholinguistik, Postbus 310, NL-6500 AH Nijmegen, The Netherlands

Huber, Walter Department of Neurology, Pauwelsstrasse, 5100 Aachen, West Germany

Kremin, Helgard Unité 111 INSERM, 2 ter Rue d'Alesia, 75014 Paris, France

Lass, Uta Institute of Psychology, University of Göttingen, West Germany

Lüer, Gerd Institute of Psychology, University of Göttingen, West Germany

O'Connor, Margaret Psychology Service, Veterans Administration Hospital, 150 South Huntington Avenue, 02130 Boston, Mass., U.S.A.

Parisi, Domenico Istituto di Psicologia del C.N.R., Viale C. Marx 15, 00156 Roma, Italy

Patterson, Karalyn MRC Applied Psychology Unit, 15 Chaucer Road, Cambridge CB3 2EF, U.K.

Rosenthal, Victor INSERM-TLNP, Pavillon Claude Bernard, Hôpital de la Salpêtrière, 47 Boulevard de l'Hôpital, F-75634 Paris, France

Sartori, Giuseppe Dipartimento di Psicologia Generale, Università di Padova, Italy

Semenza, Carlo Dipartimento di Psicologia Generale, Università di Padova, Italy

Sergent, Justine Montreal Neurological Institute and Hospital, 3801 University Street, Montreal, Québec, Canada, H3A 2B4

Vallar, Giuseppe Istituto di Clinica Nerologica, Università di Milano, Via F. Sforza 35, 20122 Milano, Italy

Preface

Neuropsychology has evolved considerably in the last decade. Methods of research have changed, new topics of interest have emerged, and there has also been an ongoing debate as to the objectives of the field. This evolution has most radically affected the study of cognitive disorders—an area that has developed particularly rapidly in recent years and that currently evidences a tendency to become a field of inquiry in its own right, that of *cognitive neuropsychology.* Classically, neuropsychologists described syndromes and tried to correlate deficits with lesion sites. Cognitive neuropsychologists, on the other hand, tend to infer the functional characteristics of normal cognition from the exploration of the deficient and spared cognitive capabilities of brain-damaged patients, and they look for clinical evidence permitting to adjudicate between alternative models of normal cognitive mechanisms.

The contributors to this volume all share a fascination with the new perspectives for understanding how the mind works that have arisen from the study of impaired cognition. Yet, and this is very characteristic of the present state of the art in cognitive neuropsychology, they disagree on many important issues, even those pertaining to the most basic assumptions of their discipline. Scientists actively involved in newly created fields often tend to eschew such basic controversies, and they manifest in their work a greater consensus than actually exists. The editors of this volume felt, however, that the avoidance of discussion seldom leads to the clarification of ideas and that it would be more profitable for their discipline were the opposing views concerning its basic assumptions clearly spelled out and debated. Accordingly, the first part of the book is devoted to an attempt to define and clarify these basic issues and to the confrontation of alternative views.

The remaining sections of the book contain 12 chapters presenting original studies on several topics of particular interest in cognitive neuropsychology, including language comprehension, reading and writing, face recognition, and memory. Cognitive neuropsychology is a young field almost exclusively confined to specialised journal publications in which, quite understandably, one has to take a lot for granted in order to get quickly to the particular question under investigation. Up to now there is no handbook of the discipline, overviews are scarce; and very few edited books, whose function is to provide authors with supplementary space for a more thorough analysis of the research question being raised, are available. The present volume is intended as a contribution to fill in this gap by presenting studies that both explore impaired cognitive functions and address a broad range of experimental questions that may be of interest not only for specialists or advanced students in cognitive neuropsychology but also for cognitive scientists interested in language comprehension, reading, writing, memory, or face recognition.

The book is based on the main lectures and discussion papers presented at the First and Second European Workshops on Cognitive Neuropsychology, which took place in Bressanone (Italy) in January 1983 and 1984. It has been written with the assistance of a grant from Couriglio Nationale delle Ricerche.

G.D., C.S., P.B.

PART I: BASIC ISSUES

1 A Function for Cognitive Neuropsychology

C. Semenza and P. Bisiacchi
Università di Padova, Italy

V. Rosenthal
INSERM, Hôpital Salpêtrière, Paris, France

INTRODUCTION

The current neuropsychological literature reveals the considerable influence of concepts and methods imported from cognitive science on the investigation into the effects of the neurological impairment of cognitive skills. Quite significantly, the commitment of an increasing number of neuropsychologists to the information-processing paradigm has taken place, together with a substantial change of attitude on the part of many cognitive psychologists who tend, at present, to view neuropsychological research as a valuable and potentially instructive source of data. This *rapprochement* manifests itself most obviously in the several attempts to develop working models of particular cognitive (sub)systems on the basis of both neuropsychological and "normal" findings (see, for instance, Cohen, 1983; Coltheart, Patterson, & Marshall, 1980; Ellis, 1982; Garrett, 1982; Marcel, 1983; Patterson, Marshall, & Coltheart, 1985). Given these recent developments, it is tempting to conclude that *cognitive neuropsychology* is in the process of becoming a respectable partner of the other disciplines that make up cognitive science.

This state of affairs appears to have several far-reaching consequences that we shall try to explore in the present chapter. It seems to us that the commitment, in the late 1970s, of many research workers in psychology, linguistics, computer science, philosophy, and sociology to an integrated cognitive science has been greatly inspired by the belief that none of these traditionally independent sciences can, by themselves, cope successfully with the complexity of cognition (cf. Norman, 1981, for further details). Linguistics, psychology, or artificial intelligence may ultimately pursue different goals; yet, many, or most of the questions that they are currently investigating can usefully be viewed as information-processing problems and, as such, an important preliminary task is that the structure of these problems be first understood. To be sure, it would be somewhat eccentric to compare man and computer in terms of their internal structure and circuitry. However, as information-processing systems engaged in tasks such as pattern recognition or natural language processing, *man and computer systems face a number of common problems—the problems that are inherent in the realisation of such tasks* (see Andreewsky & Rosenthal, 1985; Marr, 1977).

In this chapter we shall inquire into the rationale for the study of the effects of neuropsychological disturbances of cognitive skills in the research programme of cognitive science.

THE TARGET: INTELLECTUAL SKILLS

Intellectual skills are probably the most typical instances of activities that cognitive scientists are attempting to explain. The notion of skill is all the more important for neuropsychologists because they are engaged in observing individuals who fail to perform skilfully some typically cognitive tasks. The significance of this concept for the understanding of cognition has generally passed unnoticed, though it may be argued that the clarification of the structure of cognitive skills is crucial for any further advance in cognitive science. Perception, language comprehension and production, or everyday thinking are most obvious instances of cognitive skills, or, more appropriately put, of clusters of skills. Most significantly, however, it seems that *it is a necessary condition for the effective realisation of such activities that they be carried out skilfully* (i.e. smoothly, effortlessly, and outside of awareness). This may not necessarily be the case for all acts of cognition, but skilfulness seems to be a basic property of all complex mental activities that demand the deployment of considerable intellectual resources. It should be noted, on the other hand, that skills are never perfect—their execution always admits of a certain *degree of failure*—so one may wonder whether imperfection does not constitute another intrinsic characteristic of skilfulness.

In his seminal work, *Personal Knowledge* (1962), the philosopher Michael Polanyi devoted considerable attention to the analysis of the concept of skill. He noted that "...the aim of skilful performance is achieved by the observance of a set of rules which are not known as such to the person following them" (p. 49). It does not mean that we cannot tentatively define, at least, some rules, but—as Polanyi observed—such definitions are of little, if any, practical help. His well-known example concerned how to ride a bicycle. "A simple analysis shows that for a given angle of unbalance the curvature of each winding is inversely proportional to the square of the speed at which the cyclist is proceeding" (p. 50). But can this help one to ride a bicycle? "You obviously cannot adjust the curvature of your bicycle's path in proportion to the ratio of your unbalance over the square of your speed; and if you could you would fall off the machine, for there are a number of other factors to be taken into account in practice which are left out in the formulation of this rule" (p. 50). The cyclist, of course, is not permitted to transgress this rule. But the implicit observance of a rule should not be confused with following it explicitly. Such rules are products of analyses carried out by external observers, yet the behaviour of an organism may not necessarily be governed by rules by which it is describable. These rules, in fact, may be only tacit.

The execution of skills is not improved by conscious knowledge of their particular components, but rather, as Polanyi noted, these particulars must remain beyond one's focal awareness. In the present vocabulary, we would say that skilful performance is necessarily *goal-directed* and *automatic*, for if one pays attention to the particular components of a given activity the entire execution is liable to collapse. Thus, for instance, if a pianist shifts attention from the piece she is playing to what she is doing with her fingers, the execution of the musical work is impaired and she may even have to stop. Or, consider Polyani's (1962, p. 56) description of stage-fright, "which seems to consist in the anxious riveting of one's attention to the next word—or note or gesture—that one has to find or remember. This destroys one's sense of the context, which alone can smoothly evoke the proper sequence of words, notes, or gestures." The particulars of a skill are *unspecifiable*[1] for two reasons. First, because the performance is generally paralysed if we focus our attention on particulars. Second, and most important, skills are *logically unspecifiable* for it can be shown that the specification of particulars "composing" a skill would contradict what is implied in the whole performance. In fact, none of such particulars will account for the inherent purpose of the performance.

Skills are acquired through extensive practice. The performance of people who first try to speak a foreign language is clumsy, slow, effortful, and demands a good deal of attention; quite interestingly, these individuals may be aware of some particulars of their performance (e.g. looking for words, consciously combining them according to rules they have learned, etc. . . .). Proficient speakers, on the other hand, are barely aware of what they are doing when they speak (even though they sometimes happen to commit word slips or mispronounce words). Whereas skilful performance

[1] Not necessarily in the sense of our being ignorant of them, for sometimes we are able to describe certain details of our performance.

is opaque and inaccessible to conscious inspection, unskilled performance appears to be at least partly transparent (though one may not put too much credence in such introspection). In this context, it is interesting to consider that some intellectual activities never attain the level of skill and remain apparently transparent. Formal reasoning, whereby, for instance, one has to find the appropriate conclusion from:

all x are y

some y are z

is always poorly performed unless concrete instances are substituted for x, y, and z.

Finally, as already mentioned, complex cognitive activities are best characterised as clusters of skills—such activities are never represented by a single task, but, instead, constitute a cluster of related tasks—and, as Kolers and Roedinger (1984) pointed out, it is probably in the very nature of skills that they are *transferable* between related tasks depending on the degree of overlap in the structure of such tasks.

The Means

The foregoing description of skills allows one to appreciate the difficulty faced by psychologists and computer scientists in their attempts to understand and model cognitive activities. Traditionally, psychologists proceeded by way of devising experiments so as to put constraints on (or simply manipulate) certain particular factors supposed to play a pre-eminent role in the execution of a given task. But if one considers seriously the above-mentioned characteristics of skills—especially the observation that the skilful performance of a task is not necessarily governed by the rules by which it may be described, that it is goal-directed, and it is not decomposable to specifiable particulars—it becomes clear that traditional methods of psychological research may not be the most appropriate for the investigation of intellectual skills.

The experience with machine translation in the 1960s will help to illustrate this point. This work was undertaken with a number of *a priori* linguistic and psychological concepts or, more precisely, with an *a priori* definition of the particulars of which a translation ought to consist. That this pioneer venture in artificial intelligence did not succeed was not due to the incorrect implementation of procedures nor to the unavailability of current high-level programming languages, nor could it be attributed to the weakness of the computer technology of the day. The failure of machine translation was due to the incorrect definition of the structure of translation tasks. The primary problem in effect does not consist in finding an appropriate theory and technology of implementation of the translation tasks but rather in conceiving an adequate *theory of these tasks*.

The emergence of cognitive science can be viewed as a consequence of the misadventures of the first generation of artificial intelligence models as well as of the growing interest on the part of psychologists and linguists in the digital computer as a tool for modelling intelligent behaviour. Obviously, however, for a domain of intellectual interest to become an autonomous scientific discipline it is necessary to define a conceptual framework within which to operate. It is generally assumed that cognitive science is defined by the information-processing paradigm—a paradigm that supposedly can be applied to the description of all cognitive activity. Yet, in actuality this may not constitute an adequate framework within which to define or conduct scientific activity. Indeed, the adequacy of this application has prompted a host of controversies regarding, for instance, the question of just how analogous to the human brain a computer may be considered to be (see Dreyfus, 1979). The problem is that information processing is merely a conceptual tool or method for describing behaviour. Although in physics and psychology, comparable statistical methods are often used, no one would claim that these sciences share a common conceptual framework. Neither information-processing analysis nor statistical methods constitute a proper level of scientific theory. And accordingly, information processing *per se* does not allow one to assume that, although studying language comprehension and natural language processing, psycholinguists and computer scientists are basically raising similar questions.

In order to address a proper level of cognitive theory it is thus necessary to define a framework that logically permits one to consider that whatever information-processing device is to be used it will not modify the structure of a given cognitive activity. Specifically, we submit that *before considering how* a given cognitive task is or ought to be implemented by a particular information-processing device, it is first necessary to develop a theory that *specifies the problems* that are *inherent* in the execution of that task. These inherent problems bear on the nature and the order of operations that a task necessarily implies, but not on how they may be carried out. In other words, a *task theory defines the succession of operative sub-goals that have to be necessarily attained in the execution of a given cognitive activity*. This theory does not, however, furnish a definition of processes that permit a system to achieve such goals nor does it describe the device by which these processes can be implemented. A task theory of a cognitive skill is not a psychological, artificial intelligence, linguistic, or biological theory proper—it is a *cognitive theory* that specifies of *what* a task consists and *why*. It is only at another level, at the level of *implementation theory*, that the specification of processes is necessarily device-oriented, and thus situated at a psychological or artificial intelligence level proper. It follows that one may conceive several alternative implementations for a task on the basis of the same theory of that task.

Implementation theories also depend on the characteristics of the device that must execute the task, because the processes that are conceived have to be "executable by the machine." That is, an implementation theory should necessarily be compatible with a *theory of the machine* that physically "executes the program"—which is a theoretical level proper to biological or electrical engineering explanation (see Rosenthal, this volume, for more detailed discussion of this epistemic hierarchy).

These considerations have relatively clear implications with respect to the study of cognitive skills. Most obviously, if the currently frequent confusion between the above-mentioned three epistemic levels is to persist, it is unlikely that a clear picture of any cognitive skill whatsoever will emerge in the foreseeable future. Recently, this confusion has led to long debates between the proponents of the biological and the mentalistic bases of cognition or to speculations about the supposedly modular or interactive architecture of cognition. Most important, however, it let cognitive psychologists define prematurely their business as the study of cognitive processes. Although cognitive psychology may indeed propose to clarify the processes underlying cognitive tasks, such a goal is unlikely to be attained without a clarification of what has to be processed—that is, prior to the development of an adequate theory of the tasks being studied. In a way, one has to understand what actually has to be done in order to determine how it is or has to be carried out. This argument is so obvious that, to the best of our knowledge, no one has attempted to contest its logical validity in the field of cognitive psychology. However, the problem itself has often been eschewed by promptly adopting an intuitive pseudo-theory of the activity under investigation. For instance, the standard pseudo-theory of the tasks of language comprehension postulates that, after the initial perceptual processing of a language stimulus (e.g. a sentence), it is necessary to access and activate in the mental lexicon the meanings of individual words of which the stimulus is composed, and then to combine these lexical meanings according to the structural arrangement of the corresponding words in the input-sentence. Accessing the meaning of a word represented in the mental lexicon amounts to comprehending this word, etc. . . . Of course, the present definition is rather schematic and does not take into account the alternative formulations of this theory, which are often enriched by intervening factors (such as context effects, etc. . . .). The point is, however, that this standard pseudo-theory, which is based on common sense intuitions about language that can be traced back at least to Plato, and derives, in part, from Treisman's (1960) conjecture about "dictionary store" or "mental lexicon," has not been submitted to critical examination (either conceptual or empirical). On the contrary, once this theory had been (uncritically) accepted, a myriad of "legitimate questions" arose, questions on which a great number of studies are currently focused: What is the internal organisation of the mental lexicon? How is an individual lexical meaning accessed in the mental lexicon? Are semantic and syntactic processes independent or closely interacting? How does contextual information affect the standard lexical meanings retrieved in the mental lexicon? All these questions are considered as central to cognitive psychology, but it would be vain to look for an attempt at the critical examination of the "well-foundedness" of the standard conceptualisation of language comprehension from which they arise.

This critique of current psycholinguistic research should not necessarily be interpreted as suggesting that the standard "task theory" of language comprehension is wrong—though it is likely to be so given its perfectly *a priori* character—but to make clear the necessity of undertaking research aimed specifically at the development of task theories of cognitive skills. One of the most obvious lessons of two decades of experience in artificial intelligence research is that without an adequate task theory of a given intellectual activity the enterprise of modelling that activity is hopeless, no matter how powerful a computer is used and independently of the degree of sophistication of the program that one intends to write. To date, no satisfactory task theory of any intellectual skill has come out of the psychological or psycholinguistic laboratories—an observation that may be sufficient to suggest that a critical revision of our intuitive task theories of object recognition, language comprehension, expert behaviour, and many other cognitive activities is needed.

For instance, it is important to understand what the *initial conditions* are that enable a "stupid" (at the outset) system endowed with brute computational power to engage in the execution of a given cognitive task. Consider, in this case, that no information-processing system can engage in the task of interpreting natural language prior to morpho-syntactic disambiguation of the input, i.e. segmenting the input into words and identifying their grammatical roles (e.g. nouns, verbs, prepositions, etc. . . .)—if only to determine whether a given English or French word occurs in an input-sentence as a noun, as a verb, or as a preposition, etc. This example shows one of the prerequisites for the understanding of natural language, or, better, the nature of a problem that is inherent in any task of language comprehension. Morpho-syntactic disambiguation can, on the other hand, be implemented in a variety of alternative ways, but the details of this implementation are irrelevant here.

The identification of the necessary conditions and of the obligatory sequence of operative sub-goals that are inherent in and define the structure of an intellectual task can benefit greatly from the investigation of *unskilled* performance on tasks normally carried out in a skilful manner, as well as from the study of the effects of *disturbances* that render normally skilful execution impaired or relatively unskilled.

Computer systems have been, by all standards, unequalled champions of unskilled performance—and handbooks of artificial intelligence abound with picturesque anecdotes reporting this type of exploit. However, unlike unskilled performance in human subjects in which the operative sub-goals involved have yet to be discovered, for a computer system they are necessarily defined from the outset. Hence, experimenting with ideas concerning a task theory of an intellectual activity by way of devising computer systems and finding out whether they succeed in carrying out that activity, and eventually why they might fail, is an appreciable tool for the development of cognitive theories.

A FUNCTION FOR COGNITIVE NEUROPSYCHOLOGY

The method with which we shall be specifically concerned in this chapter consists in studying the effects of disturbances that interrupt the usual sequence of operations underlying the execution of a task and possibly fractionate the processes involved. Such disturbances may not easily be produced in psychological laboratories but they can often be found in brain-damaged patients. Indeed, one of the most interesting characteristics of neurological impairments of cognition is the emergence in behaviour of phenomena that lend themselves to interpretation in terms of partial products—products that under normal conditions would not manifest themselves in behaviour as such, but would undergo further elaboration (see Deloche & Andreewsky, 1982; Saffran, 1982).

The reasoning behind this argument is plain. A cognitive theory of a task specifies an obligatory sequence of operative sub-goals that are inherent in the execution of that task. That is, given a sequence of operative sub-goals 1 to n, an operation permitting to attain a particular sub-goal k is a prerequisite for the execution of all subsequent operations necessary to attain the sub-goals situated between k and n. Likewise, the entire process cannot be triggered at an intermediate level k because, again, the operative sub-goals 1 to $k-1$ constitute a prerequisite for k to n. For instance, to consider an example that is relatively straightforward, the early visual processing of a script is a condition *sine qua non* for interpreting the text: It is impossible to read without being able to process, at least partly, the visual patterns of a written stimulus.

Consider now a situation wherein the execution of a task is prematurely interrupted (e.g. due to brain damage) so that the goal at which the entire process is directed cannot be attained. Suppose that this interruption does not affect the possibility of carrying out the primary operations that trigger the entire process of execution of a given task, but occurs somewhere at an intermediate level, at the level whereby a certain amount of processing has already been done. If the behaviour of a patient who sustains a disorder of this type manifests any effects of that incomplete processing, this behaviour cannot but display the partial, incomplete product of the task process realised up to the stage of interruption. This is not to suggest that such partial products are always manifest in the behaviour of brain-damaged patients or that these products necessarily reflect the result of the last operation that could have been accomplished. Rather, the argument is that if they do occur in the behaviour of a patient, they can only reflect the results of operations carried out up to the process stage attained at interruption and not of those that normally unfold after that stage. Normally it is necessary that such partial products undergo further elaboration; therefore, it is unlikely that they (spontaneously) emerge in the overt behaviour of neurologically intact subjects. The primary interest in the study of the behaviour of brain-damaged patients is hence related to the possibility of observing the effects of processes purporting to achieve operative sub-goals situated somewhere half-way through the information-processing course—effects that are not manifest as such in the behaviour of normal subjects. The analysis of such effects may help us to identify at least certain operative sub-goals that are inherent in the execution of a given cognitive task, and to find out the order in which they ought to be attained.

In fact, it may be reasonable to assume that the temporal unfolding of the sequence of operations inherent in some task somehow reflects the degree of their elaborative complexity. That is, the sub-goals that have to be attained earlier in the time course may also be less complex and the result of the corresponding processes may be less elaborate than those that normally should follow. If one is permitted to believe that the less complex the phenomena under investigation, the greater the possibility of imposing some structure on our observations, then the analysis of less elaborate products is naturally best suited for the determination of what pertains to inherent sub-goals and what reflects a particular implementation of processes purporting to attain these sub-goals. The performance on all intellectual tasks depends on both the inherent structure of these tasks and their implementation. Thus the data collected in psychological experiments somehow reflect the "double allegiance" of the parameters defining the performance.

Of course, brain damage does not occur at an abstract theoretical level but affects the workings of real systems, that is, systems that are implemented in a particular substratum. However, it is reasonable to consider the partial products emerging in the behaviour of brain-damaged patients as less elaborate than what normally occurs in skilful performance. In this sense, although the impaired performance on some task necessarily reflects both an interruption of the information-processing course at the stage of a particular operation inherent in a task and a local fractionation of processes at that level, the product of such performance is typically characterised by a lesser elaborative complexity than what may have emerged under normal conditions.

One of the basic claims defended in this chapter is that, in so far as the effects of neurological disturbances of cognition are relatively selective and occur under a variety of forms, the investigation of these effects can greatly contribute to disentangling the double allegiance of psychological data and to developing cognitive theories of different intellectual tasks. It should be recalled that the prima-facie motivation for the classical neurological concepts of aphasia, agnosia, alexia, etc. arose from the observation that a brain lesion often affects cognitive (and other) skills selectively and most neurological syndromes (e.g. Broca's aphasia) can be described by co-existing patterns of deficit and preservation (see Hecaen & Albert, 1978; Marin, 1982; Marin, Saffran, & Schwartz, 1976; Saffran, 1982). The observation of this variety of pathological symptoms, especially with respect to the degree of elaboration of "pathological products," allows one to consider that they reflect interruptions at different stages of the information-processing course.

Two related examples will help us to illustrate this proposal. Albert, Yamadori, Gardner, and Howes (1973) reported an observation of an alexic patient who could neither read single words nor respond to written commands. The patient was nevertheless able to single out correctly an odd word in a list of printed items (e.g. *cat*, *dog*, *pig*, *hat*, *wolf*), to match without error a written word (one out of three) to a spoken one, to match correctly written words (names of objects) to pictures of objects, and even to detect without difficulty nonsense words or misprints of English words (though unable to read them aloud). This behaviour may seem all the more startling because when the same words were presented without additional information (e.g. auditory, picture to match, etc.) the patient was unable to read them aloud or to "describe their meanings," and could not explain his own behaviour in the "Odd-Word-Out Test" (note that quite similar observations have been reported by Allport & Funnell, 1981, case A.L.; Caplan, 1972; and Kremin, this volume, case BER). If, however, one considers the comprehension of words in reading no longer in terms of "accessing a mental lexicon" (which is tantamount to an all-or-nothing phenomenon) but in terms of interpretive elaboration developing through inherent stages of *pre-understanding* and dependent on the availability of the full sequence of operations, then the pathological behaviour reported by Albert et al. (1973) can be accounted for in terms of the interruption of processing at a moment where only "bare pre-understanding" has been achieved. Such pre-understanding may be sufficient to single out an odd item in an array of words but insufficient for producing a definition of the meaning of any of these words (see Andreewsky, Rosenthal, & Bourcier, 1987).

A phenomenon quite similar in substance (though not in detail) has been reported to occur in a sub-set of patients with a lesion to the "visual cortex" (Weiskrantz, 1977; 1980). The patients report no visual experience in the blind field but react to visual stimulation in that field. They are able to locate briefly appearing targets in space, discriminate the orientation of visual stimuli in the frontal plane, respond to the onset and termination of movement, and show other visual capabilities in the supposedly "blind" regions. In a word, these patients are capable of detecting and attending to visual events, even though they cannot provide any detail of these events, and think that they are merely "guessing," not "seeing."

Both these phenomena might be readily explained as effects of an interruption that occurs midway through an information-processing course and cuts off whatever further elaboration normally takes place. That is, none of these effects can be considered as reflecting an arbitrary segment of processing isolated by the pathology in question because they could not arise without an early exploration of the purely visual aspects of the stimuli—exploration that logically constitutes the primary link in the chain of necessary operations. In both cases, then, what emerges in behaviour is a result of processes carried out prior to the interruption. This result is characterised by very poor elaboration, thereby suggesting that the interruption occurs quite early in the information-processing course. Observations of this type are all the more instructive because they can be contrasted with other syndromes in which slightly more elaborate products arise in behaviour. For instance, what emerges in the reading of deep dyslexic patients is clearly more elaborate than what has been described by Albert et al. (1973) with respect to their alexic patient. Unlike the latter, deep dyslexics are capable of reading aloud some categories of words presented singly (mostly the content words), though they often commit semantic, derivational, or visual errors (Coltheart et al., 1980). The occurrence of semantic errors (e.g. when a patient utters "king" for a written stimulus *queen*) is particularly interesting in the present context because they are generally very close to the target (as in the present example), showing thereby that deep dyslexic patients carry out a good deal of elaborative interpretation of written (meaningful) stimuli, considerably more than the above-mentioned alexic patient who could, at best, single out an odd word in a list. Accordingly, deep dyslexic disorders can be considered as consecutive to an interruption that affects more advanced stages of processing.

The claim that neurological impairments of cognitive skills can be appropriately viewed as disturbances that prematurely interrupt and possibly fractionate the information-processing course is, admittedly, critical to the validity of a cognitive neuropsychological approach. This particular argument, however, was not invoked (nor has it been since) in the well-known controversy concerning the relevance of neuropsychological findings for the understanding of normal functioning that took place during the 1970s (e.g. Bever, 1975; Fodor, Bever, & Garrett, 1974; Marin et al., 1976).

Objections

Basically, there have been three objections to the relevance of neuropsychological data for the understanding of normal cognitive activities. First, it has been contended that brain insult might cause a global decrease in cognitive resources, so observed focal effects could be due to spurious or secondary variations that say nothing about normal "functions." This allegation is, however, at variance with hundreds of observations reported in the neuropsychological literature showing that although neurological patients fail on certain tasks, they are quite often able to perform as well as normals on other tasks (cf. Marin et al., 1976; or Saffran, 1982). Even if brain damage actually causes a global shortage in available cognitive resources, its effects (e.g. deficits) nevertheless often manifest themselves selectively and with a good deal of consistency within and between subjects.

Likewise, it has been argued that there is no way to demonstrate that brain insult does not fractionate a particular cognitive subsystem arbitrarily. This is a curious argument in the light of what has been stated previously, and as Marin et al. (1976) put it: "Who is to say, *a priori*, that brain lesions will fractionate the language (or whatever SBR) process more arbitrarily than artifices of psycholinguistic experiment?"

The third, more insidious, objection has been to say that one cannot determine whether the performance of a neurological patient relies on the residual intact machinery or on subsystems created *de novo*. Note that this argument holds potentially devastating implications only with respect to the hypothesis of the existence of *perverse mechanisms* that might develop in response to brain injury, either on the level of neural substrata or on the level of processes.

The idea that neural structures can (rapidly) develop in adult neurological patients is to date poorly supported by neurophysiological evidence, although it cannot be dismissed entirely (see Geschwind, 1980; Marin et al., 1976, for further detail). Yet, to suggest the possibility of perverse structures commits one to a very peculiar vision of nature. The point is not whether perverse structures can develop in biological tissue, but whether they can emerge with incomplete or "twisted" cognitive functions and with such remarkable consistency across subjects.

Regarding the possibility of the generation of perverse processes, it should be recalled that most patterns of patient performance *emerge very soon* after the occurrence of brain injury (many of them manifest themselves at the very first neuropsychological examination) and quite often tend to stabilise and even improve. Hence, the first riddle is *how fast* can the replacement "software" develop after brain injury? Next, given that the development of cognitive skills in children is *relatively slow* and requires *extensive practice*, how can new "cognitive software" emerge *so promptly* in an adult neurological patient *whose possibilities of practice are*, at least in the beginning, *so gravely compromised*? If, furthermore, one considers that the overall functional state of the system reflects the history of its prior activity and evolution, it seems questionable whether procedures or subsystems that are drastically different from those employed premorbidly can emerge right after a brain lesion has been incurred.

In sum, none of these classical objections has the logical force to undermine the validity of neuropsychological research, and the recent renewal of interest on the part of cognitive psychologists in the investigation of neurological impairments of cognition may not merely be reflective of a passing trend. It may hence be useful to consider the epistemic specificity of cognitive neuropsychological research.

Specificity of Cognitive Neuropsychology

We have already mentioned the potential benefits to be gained from investigating the effects of premature interruptions of the information-processing course. Although neurological disorders are not the only types of disturbances that merit the consideration of cognitive scientists, we argued that they occur with sufficient consistency and variety to be suitable for the identification of the sequence of operative sub-goals that are inherent in the execution of a given cognitive task. Besides this argument and the obvious point of the utility of diversifying the methodological arsenal, we submit that cognitive neuropsychological research has the same epistemic status as the laboratory studies of normal subjects, and thus that its value is mainly heuristic.

In fact, the investigation of neuropsychological disturbances forces one to ask questions that are often very *different* from those arising with respect to normal subjects or artificial systems. Neurological diseases are *accidents of nature* that are *blind with respect to our epistemic perspectives*. Investigating such impairments of cognition can, therefore, *direct our attention* to the relevance of phenomena that we otherwise might overlook. This is not to say that we might not conceivably come across them in the course of the exploration of normally functioning systems, but rather that many phenomena manifest themselves more obviously through the working of impaired systems. It is quite frequent that the finding of an effect consecutive to brain injury prompts a series of new and potentially instructive explorations. Consider, for instance, that the description of deep and surface dyslexias by Marshall and Newcombe (1973) prompted a myriad of studies on reading and word recognition centred on many questions that previously had not been raised.

ALTERNATIVE VIEWS

The argumentation exposed on pp. 1–10 with respect to the rationale underlying a cognitive neuropsychological approach and the specificity of such an undertaking does not reflect a position to which the "members of the cognitive neuropsychological community" are unanimously committed. In fact, our arguments contrast with a number of statements on these issues that have been developed in the literature. We shall briefly consider some of these controversial points.

The Relationship between the Brain and Cognitive Processes

Cognitive neuropsychology has been characterised in the preceding section as a cognitive psychology centred on exploiting some effects of cognitive disturbances rather than as a neuroscience attempting to correlate mental acts and neural events. This may not be a generally accepted view, however. Thus, for instance, Caramazza wrote in his article "The logic of neuropsychological research and the problem of patient classification in aphasia" (1984, pp. 9–10): "Cognitive neuropsychology is the study of the relationship between the brain and cognitive processes. The goal is to propose a set of statements about the processing components that define normal cognition and the neuroanatomical (and neurophysiological) substrates of these processes in the normal brain."

This statement calls for a few comments. Traditionally, neurologists and neuropsychologists used to define their respective fields as the study of the relationship between the brain and psychological functions—a definition that has inevitably generated a confusion both in terms of methods and levels of explanation. During the late 1970s, many neuropsychologists tended to distance themselves from the traditional (basically descriptive) approach and to develop a specific level of neuropsychological explanation proper. This new-look neuropsychology was inspired by concepts that emerged in the framework of cognitive psychology (but also linguistics and artificial intelligence) and quite loosely depended on neurological considerations. Although, from the present standpoint, even this new approach lacked a sufficient conceptual consistency, it corresponded to a renewal of the "neuropsychological paradigm" and prompted many valuable studies. In this context, it seems all the more curious that Caramazza, who has been one of the most prominent architects of this renewal, is suggesting that the goals of cognitive psychology and neurophypsiology alike should be combined. We have already noted that the nature of operations inherently implied in the execution of some task is independent of the hardware by which this task is implemented, even though the details of that implementation are dependent on the properties of the hardware. That cognitive processes are implemented in the brain and that there must thus be a causal relationship between neural activity and mental processes seems self-evident. That ultimately neurophysiology should provide a set of constraints on implementation theories is certainly not a contested issue. What seems much less clear *today*, however, is how to map cognitive concepts onto neurophysiological theories. "The neurological study of brain function", Marin (1982, p. 54) noted, "has always been complicated by the enormous conceptual distance that exists between the basic physiological mechanisms or brain structure, and their ostensive behavioral manifestations." The classical approach of localisation of functions has been of little heuristic value for the understanding of mental processes. The weakness of this contribution cannot be explained by the fact that the localisations are not sufficiently precise, for, even if they were, it is one thing to determine the location of a device, and another to explain its function. This point notwithstanding, it is, at present, even questionable whether any "rough cognitive functions" can be localised in the brain with certainty (see De Bleser, this volume). Neurophysiological explorations are now likely to reach the level wherein brain functions "are generically reduced to codes of electrical signals, membrane excitability changes, or column aggregates that manifest themselves in cellular biophysical codes" (Marin, 1982, p. 53).

There is, however, an immense conceptual gap between the properties of bioelectrical neuronal circuitry or cellular microstructure and cognitive theories attempting to define what operations are inherently involved in face recognition, language comprehension, calculation, or expert behaviour. Neurophysiological and cognitive theories do not address the same level of explanation. As a distinguished neurophysiologist noted recently, one may develop a satisfactory theory of a given cognitive task (e.g. of addition) with no shred of understanding of how this task is actually carried out at a biophysical level (Marr, 1982). Thus, although we as yet have no clear idea of how the human brain executes additions, it was possible to develop a cognitive theory of addition quite some time ago that provided the necessary basis to conceive mechanical cash registers and electronic calculators. It is only at the level of a particular theory of implementation that both the theory of a given task and the theory of the device that is to carry out that task physically constrain the definition of processes by which the task may be executed. However, although the development of theories specifying how cognitive processes are implemented in the brain will require the convergence of cognitive and neurophysiological explanations, at the present time, given the lack of adequate cognitive (and presumably neurophysiological) theories, the question of software—hardware mapping constraints remains an interesting but speculative issue. This issue, furthermore, does not seem to bear on any presently important research question in cognitive science. For it is useless to inquire into the details of implementation of a process prior to attaining an understanding of *what* precisely has to be performed.

Subtractive Approach

The concept that comes up most prominently in discussions concerning the rationale behind (neuro)psychological studies of cognition is that of *modularity*. Roughly, it refers to the assumption that mental functions are implemented as a collection of smaller, functionally meaningful processing components (modules) that are as independent of one another as the task and the medium allow (see Fodor, 1983; Marr, 1982; Rosenthal, this volume). Following this formulation, modularity can be viewed as a functional relationship between processing components whereby autonomy prevails over interactivity. This has an important methodological ramification. If interactivity is so weak that, in the short run, it may be considered as having a negligible effect on the working of a given module, it becomes possible to study this module separately without paying constant attention to its interdependencies. Such a situation depicts what Simon (1962) called *nearly decomposable systems*.

Modularity has been elevated to a general principle of systems design by Simon (1962) and Marr (1982) who have argued with respect to complex systems that only modular ones could emerge through the evolutionary process. Fodor (1983), on the other hand, went on to posit that modular organisation is a necessary condition for the exploration of cognitive functions, and he tentatively suggested which cognitive functions are modular and hence amenable to scientific study, and which are not modular, and consequently may not be subjected to fruitful scientific inquiry.

These claims raise several problems (see Rosenthal, this volume), but two stand out. First, the authors reverse the epistemic hierarchy of levels of explanation suggesting that an implementation theory of a task (which is the proper theoretical level of the concept of modularity) determines the theory of that task. Putting it simply, that is to say that what has to be done is determined by how it is done. But there is a contradiction here. In so far as modules are defined, *inter alia*, as domain-specific special-purpose devices, the study of such devices may be interesting from a theoretical point of view only if they constitute functionally meaningful components of a task. But the determination of what is a functionally meaningful component of a given task depends on the theory of that task, not on its particular implementation. In other words, without a theory of a given task, the principle of modularity of that task is conceptually empty and has no empirical ramifications because anything may be viewed as a module.

Notwithstanding these conceptual problems, for many scholars modularity represents a paradigm assumption of the information-processing approach to cognition. It derives in part from a long-standing scientific tradition of decomposing complex entities (mechanisms, systems, etc.) into their basic functional components—a method that has often been shown to be successful in the physical sciences. For some neuropsychologists the concept of modularity has provided the basis for the *subtractive assumption* according to which brain damage may cause a "removal" of a process (or module) "x" without affecting the workings of the other cognitive processes (Caramazza & Martin, 1983; Marshall, 1984; Shallice, 1981). The primary research question, in this context, is to identify processing components that can be shown to act independently of each other. Hence the importance of the study of dissociations. A simple case is to find patients that show impaired performance on all tasks that involve a theoretically meaningful processing component *x* and demonstrate normal performance on all the other tasks. Given this combination of deficit and preservation, it is concluded that successfully performed tasks are carried out by processing components that can act independently of *x*, and, conversely, that deficient performance on a given task implies that it normally requires the involvement and correct action of *x*. An example often quoted in the literature is the case of agrammatic Broca's aphasics who are supposed to suffer from an impairment of the syntactic component of language processing (Caramazza & Berndt, 1978). Yet, the observations that are most suitable to this framework bear on cases of double dissociation in which, given two (theoretically meaningful) processors *x* and *y*, it is possible to demonstrate, for two groups of patients A and B, that A execute normally the tasks that implicate *x*, and fail on those that implicate *y*, and vice versa for B (see Shallice, 1979, for further details).

The subtractive approach currently occupies a prominent place in many fields of neuropsychological inquiry. It is applied on the basis of two assumptions:

1. Cognitive architecture is functionally modular.
2. There is a transparent relationship between an observed deficit (effect) D and processing components P that are supposedly "removed" as a consequence of brain injury, so a selective deficit D can be held as a demonstration that P normally exists.

The trouble is that the latter assumption is logically untenable. The identification of D does not imply that P corresponds to any actual process, let alone that it represents any separate processing component. P is merely a definition (generally quite loose) of processes that are supposed to be a part of a normal performance. Yet, for the observed effects there may be a cluster of alternative architectural solutions and impairments; therefore, if D occurs selectively it may be viewed as an independent phenomenon, but this in no way entails that P is an independent process. The interpretive framework of the subtractive approach is founded on a confusion between the dissociation of phenomena (which can actually be observed), the dissociation of processes (which are generally unspecified), and the definition of inherent operations (which, in fact, is based on an *a priori* conception of a given task). This framework is based on a wishful illusion of transparency that stems from arbitrarily mapping *a priori* concepts onto an interpretive situation.

Regardless of the fact that the definition of a selective deficit is not necessarily equivalent to the definition of a process that is impaired or suppressed, it should be borne in mind that a hypothesis concerning some of the processes normally involved in the execution of a particular task does not constitute a theory of that task. Even if such hypotheses are compatible with certain particular findings, the processes that they specify are merely possible solutions, which do not necessarily capture any inherent characteristic of the skilful execution of a given task. Consider, for instance, models of reading and word recognition that are based in part on the conversion of graphemes into phonemes (GPC, for short; see Coltheart, 1978, 1981; Morton & Patterson, 1980; Newcombe & Marshall, 1980). The hypothesis of a GPC processor is indeed compatible with several observations of deep and surface dyslexic patients whose reading behaviour may be interpreted as showing, respectively, the disruption of, or exclusive reliance on, the GPC route (though, admittedly, these observations can be accounted for without resorting to the GPC route). However, the GPC hypothesis appears functionally odd and rather ineffective as regards spelling to sound irregularities (which are, for instance, very frequent in English), for it implies a necessary process of correction that is solely motivated by the very fact of postulating the existence of the GPC as a necessary operation in reading. Furthermore, it certainly does not seem particularly helpful or satisfying in the case of scripts such as Hebrew in which a letter string (real word) can have several readings, each with a different pronunciation. Although the hypothesis of GPC is plausible as a local explanation of some data and may seem intuitively compelling if one considers exclusively the reading of very regular alphabetic scripts, it appears to be a typical instance of misunderstanding the notion of the necessary operations inherent in the skilful execution of a task. In fact, GPC does not represent a tentative solution to an information-processing problem but an attempt at locally accounting for a few experimental findings on the basis of *a priori* concepts. The only valid conclusion that can be drawn, given the patterns of deficit and preservation in the variety of acquired dyslexias, that respects the problem of spelling to sound irregularities (and variabilities) is that skilful reading necessarily involves some process of visual segmentation of the script. The specification of this process and even of the size of segments will depend on the nature of the other problems inherent in skilful reading.

FUNCTIONAL REORGANISATION DUE TO BRAIN DAMAGE

The arguments developed in pp. 10–16 concerning the eventuality of the postmorbid creation of new subsystems should not be interpreted as a denial of functional reorganisation after lesional occurrence. In fact, it seems unlikely that the performance of neurological patients merely represents a combination of intact and lacunae patterns of behaviour. To the contrary, it may be argued that their performance reflects a *reorganisation* that *highlights the particularities of the residual system* in its regular functions as well as in its hidden potentialities (see Marin et al., 1976; Saffran, 1982).

Investigating reorganised systems naturally has its positive and negative sides. On the one hand, if reorganisation is not considered as an intervening factor, it creates grounds for the misinterpretation of findings. The example of the GPC hypothesis illustrates this point. The observation that the reading aloud of surface dyslexics consists manifestly in letter-to-sound translation (see Marshall & Newcombe, 1973; Patterson et al., 1985) could be interpreted in support of GPC. The question, however, is whether the conversion of graphemes into phonemes by surface dyslexics corresponds to an operation inherent in skilled reading or reflects a functional shift due to reorganisation. We have already mentioned several arguments that lend support to the latter interpretation. The observation that surface dyslexic patients (who previously were skilled readers) read out words at a very slow rate and at the cost of painstaking effort makes it questionable whether GPC is a part of normal process, if only because the rate of normal reading would then depend on the rate of grapheme-to-phoneme conversion. Rather, the reading through GPC appears to reflect a potentiality (e.g. quite natural for "irregularly spelt" non-words) that can, under extreme circumstances, become the only available strategy.

Compensatory Effects

Notwithstanding the fact that it may sometimes be difficult to distinguish functional shifts from the effects due to overusing normal processes that predate the morbidity, we submit that the potential benefits of investigating brain-damaged patients are greatly enhanced by the occurrence of ing brain-damaged patients are greatly enhanced by the occurrence of reorganisation. Quite frequently, neuropathological reorganisation results in overusing unimpaired processes in order to *compensate* for a deficiency in other processes—and in this sense functional reorganisation emphasises certain particularities of the normal system. Compensation may occur passively or actively. The former may amount to selective reliance on processes that would normally interact with some others. For instance, the paralexic errors of deep dyslexics manifestly arise because no interactions with the process of visual segmentation of the script take place in these patients (see Coltheart et al., 1980). These errors may thus be viewed as effects of passive compensation, that is, over-reliance on residual operations.

Active compensation appears to represent the optimal (though presumably unconscious) strategy that, for a given configuration of deficit and preservation, consists of "overusing" those of the available operations that are likely to compensate best for the subject's deficiencies. *Compensation strategies* can easily be distinguished from functional shifts (discussed previously) as they rely on operations that can be shown to take place in normal subjects (i.e. they manifest themselves through errors that are similar in direction to those committed by brain-damaged subjects). Furthermore, these strategies may lead to normal performance on some tasks and poor execution on others. For instance, it has recently been shown that, in language comprehension, all mildly impaired aphasics are likely to over-rely on pragmatic factors. In matching pictures to sentences with "compelling pragmatic implications" (e.g. *The ball hits the window*; *The woman slips on the stairs*), aphasics frequently chose pictures of "pragmatically implied" actions (i.e. with respect to the above examples: a ball that breaks a window; and, a woman that falls on the stairs) but performed correctly on control items. It is significant to note that normal subjects also committed this type of error, though to a lesser extent (Rosenthal & Bisiacchi, 1984). The over-reliance on pragmatic factors thus appears to reflect the workings of a normal operation that in the intact system is usually counterbalanced by operations that are either inefficient or impaired in aphasics.

Little attention has been given to compensatory effects of functional reorganisation taking place after the occurrence of brain injury. In many cases, the discussion of the potential effects of reorganisation has been eschewed lest it supply arguments against the relevance of neuropsychological evidence. However, if one keeps in mind that it is unlikely that new subsystems emerge in adult neurological patients, the very existence of reorganisation after the occurrence of brain injury cannot constitute an argument against the possibility of drawing inferences pertaining to normal functions from the investigation of impaired performance. On the contrary, the example of a compensation strategy further supports our claim that functional reorganisation is likely to render identifiable normally discrete and hardly discernible operations. Briefly, the disruption or suppression of some processes due to brain damage causes adjustments in the workings of others. At worst, these adjustments may amount to functional shifts that, nevertheless, do not represent a radical modification of the nature of a given process. Thus, for instance, grapheme–phoneme conversion, observed in the behaviour of surface dyslexics, can hardly be viewed as a device created *de novo*, but rather, reflects operating under extreme conditions that force the system to resort to strategies that are otherwise seldom employed because they are highly inefficient. In other cases, functional reorganisation may manifest itself through modification of the relative weight of unimpaired processes. This has been illustrated through the example of a compensation strategy whereby operations based on some pragmatic factors are manifestly over-employed.

METHODOLOGICAL REVISION

It is quite natural that the emergence of the new paradigm of cognitive neuropsychology has many practical implications for a variety of issues ranging from the relevant research questions that should be formulated and the types of inferences it is permissible to draw, to the mode of conducting experimental studies. We have dealt with the first issue at some length throughout this chapter; therefore, it is not necessary to dwell on it any further. Suffice it to say, it is quite conceivable that the research questions that appear to be relevant for cognitive neuropsychology may not necessarily be identical to those that were raised in the classical neuropsychological framework. In the present section we shall deal with a few other issues that in our view merit particular attention.

The Selection of Testing Materials

One of these issues bears on the principles governing the choice of tasks and the selection of testing materials for brain-damaged patients. Most often in the past, neuropsychologists were interested in tasks that allowed the detection of deficits and spared capabilities, and, consequently, they selected testing materials on the basis of 100% correct performance of normal controls. Although this strategy remains perfectly defendable, it has been often overlooked that some "deficits" ascribed to neurological patients may, in fact, be due to compensatory effects reflecting overuse of normal operations. In order to find out whether this is actually the case, it is necessary to carry out a comparison of trends. The identification of tasks on which the performance of neurological and normal subjects is *compar-*

able in direction requires the use of the *same parameters for both groups*.

The most convenient parameter that allows one to conduct qualitative analyses is evidently a type of error, provided that the experimental task is chosen so as to permit some degree of imperfect performance by the normal subjects. That is, if one observes that normal subjects commit, say, 15% of errors, whereas a group of brain-damaged patients makes 50% of the same type of error, then it is likely that those errors arise through the utilisation of the same operation, and accordingly, it becomes possible to inquire into the operations that normally complete or counterbalance its action.

Patterns of Recovery

The exploration of patterns of recovery is another research strategy that has not received sufficient attention. Quite frequently patients showing an interesting constellation of deficit and preservation recover to a considerable extent in the first few months following the occurrence of brain damage. Longitudinal studies centred on the assessment of patterns of recovery are thus potentially instructive as regards the identification of the normal sequence of operations or at least with respect to some particular operations that may be prerequisite for others. For instance, if one assumes that the presence and correct action of x is a prerequisite for y to take place, then it follows that the latter operation cannot be recovered prior to x, the issue being amenable to empirical clarification through the observation of patterns of recovery.

The Logic of Demonstrations

Neuropsychological investigations may occasionally supply evidence that lends itself to types of inferences that are scarcely possible in regular laboratory studies—namely, that can be viewed as logical demonstrations of the (in)dependence of phenomena or of the viability of particular hypotheses.

Consider, for instance, the theories that attempt to explain in part the behaviour of deep dyslexics (especially the impossibility of reading aloud regular non-words) as an impairment of the grapheme–phoneme conversion (GPC) route. In these theories it is suggested that this route is a functional part of the normal apparatus of reading, and the condition *sine qua non* for reading aloud nonsense words (see pp. 16–21). If one finds a patient showing the patterns of deep-dyslexic reading, i.e. including the inability to read non-words, but who is able to sound correctly all individual graphemes, it can be considered to demonstrate that the availability of the so-called GPC route is not a sufficient condition for the reading of non-words.

A classical example of this type of demonstration can be found in a study conducted by Andreewsky and Seron (1975) that showed that in order to be agrammatic it is necessary to preserve a good deal of syntactic competence. They used sentences, presented visually, containing the same (syntactically ambiguous) word twice, once as a noun and once as a conjunction. Their agrammatic patients uttered this word when used as a noun but not as a conjunction, although in both cases the word has the same pronunciation. It is well known that agrammatic patients often omit function words. But how could the patients studied by Andreewsky and Seron determine *when* the word was used as a noun, and *when* as a functor? Thus, logically, this study demonstrated that in spite of being "agrammatic" the patients were able to carry out the morpho-syntactic disambiguation of sentences, thereby providing evidence that agrammatism cannot occur in an across-the-board fashion (viz. in order to behave "agrammatically" one has to determine the syntactic function of words in a sentence), and further, suggesting that it is preferable not to view syntactic processing in a unitary fashion.

Patient Classification

The issue of patient classification in neuropsychological research has been extensively debated in the recent literature. It is clear that utilising loose classification criteria for the constitution of experimental patient groups may often be inappropriate for a particular research study, which may in consequence fail to provide useful findings for the conceptualisation of normal functions. Thus, several authors have stressed the necessity of refining classification criteria so as to go beyond the method of grouping patients according to clinical diagnoses in which both anatomy (e.g. frontal lesion) and clinical syndrome (e.g. Broca's aphasia) are *fixed parameters* (see Caramazza, 1984; Saffran, 1982; Schwartz, 1984).

Organising patient groups around syndrome categories has been undertaken primarily for medical purposes, and, in this respect, it has undoubtedly proven to be useful. It was the only systematic basis for classification during the period of the first neuropsychological explorations, and for a century or so a good deal of information has been gathered from contrastive studies of groups defined according to syndrome-based categories. However, along with the substantial refinements in neuropsychological research, more subtle questions about the cognitive system are beginning to be raised. It thus becomes obvious that the inclusion of patients in experimental groups according to lesion site and the results of standard neurological examinations (which are determined by clinical rather than cognitive research purposes) is unlikely to enhance the discrimination of subtle but conceptually interesting effects.

The recent proliferation of single case studies (to be distinguished from the classical case reports) may be viewed as an attempt to remedy these shortcomings (see Shallice, 1979). These studies seem especially useful for detailed investigation of *privileged cases* that show previously unnoticed patterns of functional reorganisation, or in which the phenomena under exploration appear with particular clarity.

Regarding group methodologies, on the other hand, several valuable suggestions for alternative grouping principles have been proposed (see, e.g. Caramazza & Martin, 1983; Saffran, 1982). The methods of detailed investigation of small groups (patient–group methodology, Caramazza, 1984) and of *a posteriori* classification (Caramazza, Berndt, & Brownell, 1982) seem to be of particular interest. The latter method consists in running the subjects first, and grouping them *post experimentum* according to both *consistency of performance* and *similarity of individual performance profiles*. This leads to the constitution of groups that are homogeneous with respect to the questions being asked, and enables the investigator to probe for subtle deficits and preserved capabilities that can be distributed over different syndrome-based categories of patients.

The critique of the classical methods of patient classification does not necessarily imply that the use of syndrome-based groups cannot afford valuable observations. In fact, it is not patient classification *per se* that poses the principal problem, but it is rather the classical way of conducting experimental studies and of drawing inferences on the basis of the performance of syndrome-based groups that no longer appears to be defendable. The validity of neuropsychological observations is less dependent on patient classification principles than it is on the *similarity of individual performance profiles*. In this sense, we feel that there has been a tendency to go overboard in cognitive neuropsychology with respect to the dismissal of syndrome-based classification. It seems to us that the only viable solution that may prevent the rejection of valuable studies and allow one to check for the validity of the inferences being drawn and of the evidence supplied is to *disclose all the individual data* in experimental reports. Besides the benefit of avoiding unnecessary debates and contestable editorial decisions, the disclosure of individual data may permit one to come up with a fresh look at the data gathered by other investigators.

CONCLUDING REMARKS

Psychological investigations of cognition have been generally conducted under the assumption that one can reduce the complexity of mental functions to a series of rudimentary skills that can, furthermore, be studied by relatively simple, well-defined tasks. Since most real-life tasks are marred by undesirable (and uncontrollable) factors, it has been necessary to devise experiments so as to tap the basic functional mechanisms and nothing else. Although it is an open question whether the execution of such tasks actually relies on rudimentary cognitive skills, the experiments devised along these lines typically bear a *metacognitive character* in the sense that subjects are required to carry out tasks that are as devoid of pragmatic context as possible. That the execution of such tasks by trained undergraduate students may be free of the errors that typically occur when pragmatic factors are allowed to interfere has been somewhat rapidly considered as a demonstration that these tasks tap the rudimentary cognitive mechanisms.

However, assuming that subjects have to compensate for the absence of pragmatic constraints, metacognitive tasks are liable to mobilise more resources of cognition (e.g. in abstraction) than do tasks rooted in real-life situations. We have no appropriate metrics to assess the burden of metacognitive demands on the execution of tasks that normal (trained) individuals carry out smoothly, nor do we know to what extent impaired systems can respond to these demands. Yet, it is quite likely that the burden of metacognitive-processing demands is even greater for impaired systems, and this poses the problem of the interpretability of results consisting in the poor scores of brain-damaged patients and the entirely correct performance of normals. Specifically, given this type of result, it is quite impossible to infer whether the failure of some neurological patients to carry out the task bears any direct relationship to any local processing deficit (e.g. unavailability of necessary operations), or stems from a cognitive overload caused by metacognitive demands. Note, for example, that agrammatic patients that show a severe comprehension deficit on some metalinguistic tasks often demonstrate the understanding of structurally similar sentences in normal conversation.

This is not to argue that metacognitive tasks should simply be relinquished, as one can hardly imagine other tasks that would lend themselves so easily to experimental manipulation. Rather, the point is that diverging evidence from normal and neurological subjects can readily turn out to be a trap. If cognitive neuropsychology is to contribute to our understanding of normal cognition rather than merely supply a better taxonomy of neurological syndromes, then *the significance of any neuropsychological finding should be independently corroborated through an investigation of normal subjects*.

Converging evidence from normal and brain-damaged subjects is presumably the strongest condition for the scientific validity of cognitive neuropsychological research. Obviously, convergence does not mean reproducing the same results with both types of population. If one finds neuropsychological evidence for the existence of some particular processing structure (or operation) in normal cognition, such a structure or operation should have detectable effects on the workings of a normal system. Consequently, it should be possible to corroborate the significance of this neuropsychological finding through the investigation of normal subjects. Demonstrating convergence of normal and neuropsychological findings is the only way to disentangle spurious pathological variations from truly significant effects that may manifest themselves more obviously in the behaviour of deficient systems. And, naturally, it is the condition *sine qua non* for the generalisability of neuropsychological findings.

There are several available examples demonstrating that converging evidence can be successfully obtained. Consider once again the behaviour of the alexic patient on the Odd-Word-Out Test described by Albert et al. (1973). This observation appeared troublesome in the context of the mainstream theories of the day, because it could have been interpreted to suggest that lexical understanding is not an all-or-nothing phenomenon (and does not necessarily involve conscious awareness). Marcel's (1980) experiments on subliminal priming in normal subjects further corroborated this finding, as they showed that subliminal primes unidentified by the subjects facilitated the processing of related target words.

Or consider the study conducted by Blumstein, Milberg, and Shrier (1982) who found consistent priming effects in a lexical decision task even in those aphasics (e.g. Wernicke's, globals) who were otherwise severely impaired on semantic judgement and naming tasks. This result, suggesting that lexical decision taps mechanisms (or processes) that are different from those underlying overt semantic judgement or naming, corroborated the similar conclusion that emerged from experiments conducted by West and Stanovich (1982) with normal subjects.

In this respect, a failure to obtain converging evidence from neuropsychological and laboratory inquiries casts doubt on the validity of conclusions that may have been put forward on the basis of either of these inquiries. For example, the failure to find clear correlates between normal hemispheric asymmetries and the results of investigations of unilateral brain injuries, despite over 15 years of concentrated efforts, undermines the credibility of these studies suggesting that a careful re-examination of our notions of cerebral laterality is needed (see Hardyck, 1983).

Indeed, cognitive psychology and neuropsychology may no longer be permitted to ignore each other.

REFERENCES

Albert, M. L., Yamadori, A., Gardner, H., & Howes, D. (1973) Comprehension in alexia. *Brain*, *96*, 317–328.

Allport, A. & Funnell, E. (1981) Components of the mental lexicon. *Philosophical Transactions of the Royal Society of London*, *B295*, 397–410.

Andreewsky, E. & Rosenthal, V. (1985) Les avions ne sont pas des modèles des oiseaux, cependant.... In C. Bonnet, J. N. Hoc, & G. Tiberghien (Eds.), *Psychologie, intelligence artificielle et automatique*. Bruxelles: Mardaga, 191–202.

Andreewsky, E., Rosenthal, V., & Bourcier, D. (1987) A preliminary phase of language comprehension: Outline of a system's model. *Kybernetes, 16*, 27–32.

Andreewsky, E. & Seron, X. (1975) Implicit processing of grammatical rules in a classical case of agrammatism. *Cortex, 11*, 379–390.

Bever, T. G. (1975) Some theoretical and empirical issues that arise if we insist on distinguishing language and thought. *Annals of the New York Academy of Science, 263*, 76–83.

Blumstein, S. E., Milberg, W., & Shrier, R. (1982) Semantic processing in aphasia: Evidence from an auditory lexical decision task. *Brain and Language, 17*, 301–315.

Caplan, L. (1972) *Cueing in alexia without agraphia.* Paper presented at the 24th Annual Meeting American Academy of Neurology. St Louis, Missouri.

Caramazza, A. (1984) The logic of neuropsychological research and the problem of patient classification in aphasia. *Brain and Language, 21*, 9–20.

Caramazza, A. & Berndt, R. S. (1978) Semantic and syntactic processes in aphasia: A view of the literature. *Psychological Bulletin, 85*, 898–918.

Caramazza, A., Berndt, R. S., & Brownell, H. (1982) The semantic deficit hypothesis: Perceptual parsing and object classification by aphasia patients. *Brain and Language, 15*, 161–189.

Caramazza, A. & Martin, R. (1983) Theoretical and methodological issues in the study of aphasia. In J. B. Hellige (Ed.), *Cerebral hemisphere asymmetry: Method, theory and application*, New York: Praeger Scientific Publishers.

Cohen, N. J. (1983) Amnesia and the distinction between procedural and declarative knowledge. In N. Butters, L. R. Squire (Eds.), *The neuropsychology of memory.* New York: Guilford Press.

Coltheart, M. (1978) Lexical access in simple reading tasks. In G. Underwood (Ed.), *Strategies of information processing*. London: Academic Press.

Coltheart, M. (1981) Disorders of reading and their implications for models of normal reading. *Visible Language, XV(2)*, 245–286.

Coltheart, M., Patterson, K. E., & Marshall, J. (1980) *Deep dyslexia.* London: Routledge & Kegan Paul.

Deloche, G. & Andreewsky, E. (1982) From neuropsychological data to reading mechanisms. *International Journal of Psychology, 17*, 259–279.

Dreyfus, H. (1979) *What computers can't do.* New York: Harper.

Ellis, A. W. (1982) *Normality and pathology in cognitive function*. London: Academic Press.

Fodor, J. A. (1983) *The modularity of mind.* Cambridge, Mass: MIT Press.

Fodor, J. A., Bever, T., & Garrett, M. F. (1974) *The psychology of language.* New York: McGraw-Hill.

Garrett, M. F. (1982) Remarks on the relation between language production and language comprehension systems. In M. A. Arbib, D. Caplan, & J. C. Marshall (Eds.), *Neural models of language processes*. New York: Academic Press.

Geschwind, N. (1980) Some comments on the neurology of language. In D. Caplan (Ed.), *Biological studies of the mental processes*. Cambridge, Mass: MIT Press.

Hardyck, C. (1983) Seeing each other's point of view: Visual perceptual lateralization. In J. B. Hellige (Ed.), *Cerebral hemisphere asymmetry method, theory and application.* New York: Praeger Scientific Publishers.

Hecaen, H. & Albert, M. L. (1978) *Human neuropsychology.* New York: J. Wiley & Sons.

Kolers, P. A. & Roedinger, H. L. (1984) Procedures of mind. *Journal of Verbal Learning and Verbal Behavior, 23*, 425–449.

Marcel, A. J. (1980) Conscious and preconscious recognition of polysemous words: Locating the selective effects of prior verbal context. In R. S. Nickerson (Ed.), *Attention and performance VIII.* Lawrence Erlbaum Associates Inc., 435–457.

Marcel, A. J. (1983) Conscious and unconscious perception: An approach to the relations between phenomenal experience and perceptual processes. *Cognitive Psychology, 15,* 238–300.

Marin, O. M. S. (1982) Brain and Language: The rules of the game. In M. A. Arbib, D. Caplan, & J. C. Marshall (Eds.), *Neural models of language processes.* New York: Academic Press.

Marin, O. M. S., Saffran, E. M., & Schwartz, M. F. (1976) Dissociation of language in aphasia: Implications for normal functions. *Annals of the New York Academy of Sciences, 280,* 868–884.

Marr, D. (1977) Artifical intelligence—A Personal view. *Artificial Intelligence, 9,* 37–48.

Marr, D. (1982) *Vision.* San Francisco: W. H. Freeman.

Marshall, J. C. (1984) Multiple perspectives on modularity. *Cognition, 18,* 209–242.

Marshall, J. C. & Newcombe, F. (1973) Pattern of paralexia: A psycholinguistic approach. *Journal of Psycholinguistic Research, 2,* 175–195.

Morton, J. & Patterson, K. E. (1980) A new attempt at an interpretation or an attempt at a new interpretation. In M. Coltheart, K. E. Patterson, & J. Marshall (Eds.), *Deep dyslexia.* London: Routledge.

Newcombe, F. & Marshall, J. E. (1980) Transcoding and lexical stabilization in deep dyslexia. In M. Coltheart, K. Patterson, & J. C. Marshall (Eds.), *Deep dyslexia.* London: Routledge.

Norman, D. A. (1981) *Perspectives on cognitive science.* Hillsdale, New Jersey: Lawrence Erlbaum Associates Inc.

Patterson, K. E., Marshall, J. C., & Coltheart, M. (1985) *Surface dyslexia.* London: Lawrence Erlbaum Associates Ltd.

Polanyi, M. (1962) *Personal knowledge.* Chicago: The University of Chicago Press.

Rosenthal, V. & Bisiacchi, P. (1984) Exploring tacit integration in the language comprehension of aphasics and normals. *Proceedings of the 22nd Annual Meeting of the Academy of Aphasia.* Los Angeles, Cal.

Saffran, E. M. (1982) Neuropsychological approaches to the study of language. *British Journal of Psychology, 73,* 317–337.

Schwartz, M. F. (1984) What the classical aphasia categories can't do for us, and why. *Brain and Language, 21,* 3–8.

Shallice, T. (1979) Case study approach in neuropsychological research. *Journal of Clinical Neuropsychology, 1,* 183–211.

Shallice, T. (1981) Neurological impairment of cognitive processes. *British Medical Bulletin, 37,* 187–192.

Simon, H. A. (1962) The architecture of cognition. *Proc. Amer. Phil. Soc., 106,* 467–482.

Treisman, A. (1960) Contextual cues in selective listening. *Quart. Journal of Experimental Psychology, 12,* 242–248.

Weiskrantz, L. (1977) Trying to bridge some neuropsychological gaps between monkey and man. *British Journal of Psychology, 68,* 431–445.

Weiskrantz, L. (1980) Varieties of residual experience. *Quart. Journal of Experimental Psychology, 32,* 365–386.

West, R. F. & Stanovich, K. E. (1982) Source of inhibition in experiments on the effect of sentence context on word recognition. *Journal of Experimental Psychology: Learning, Memory and Cognition, 8,* 385–399.

2 Does It Rattle When You Shake It? Modularity of Mind and the Epistemology of Cognitive Research

V. Rosenthal
INSERM, Hôpital Salpêtrière, Paris, France

INTRODUCTION

This chapter is devoted to an inquiry into the nature and development of scientific knowledge in the field of cognitive science. By scientific knowledge I am referring to *rational* explanations of the structure and occurrence of phenomena that are considered interesting and pertinent by the scientific community. I take the issue of scientific knowledge to be primarily a matter of theoretical statements, not of empirical evidence, and consequently, I shall be concerned mainly with the definition of cognitive theories and the nature of explanation of cognitive phenomena. The present discussion will, of necessity, be restricted to a selected number of questions that I believe to be critical to the development of cognitive science, although, of course, this selective emphasis does not exclude the existence of other important issues.

Roughly, by cognitive science I mean the enterprise that consists of attempting to define the structure of so called intellectual tasks, whether performed by the human mind or an artificial device. Since human intellectual activities constitute the prima-facie model of cognitive achievement, and "machine cognition", is primarily modelled on our *understanding* of "natural cognition", it may be reasonable to focus the present inquiry on psychological explanations of cognitive tasks (at least to the extent that this may be possible).

Another reason to devote particular attention to psychological explorations of the mind is that cognitive behaviour has proven recalcitrant to explanation, even though the methods by which it has been studied are generally considered to be equivalent to those that led to the spectacular advancement of the natural sciences. A clarification of these difficulties seems to me to be all the more necessary because popular wisdom currently tends to link cognitive explanation with biological theory in order to remedy the "intrinsic weakness" of purely psychological explanations.

What do we mean by *explanation of cognitive functions*? On what grounds can we assume that a "function" is *explorable in its own right*? Are there any *limits of explorability* of cognitive phenomena, and how relevant is, in this respect, the issue of *cognitive architecture*? These and other related questions will guide the present inquiry into the epistemology of cognitive research.

A function appears to us as intuitively salient and "natural" by virtue of our ability to perceive (and even estimate) the *rightness* of the performance on which it relies (cf. Polanyi, 1962), and given the possibility of specifying its *purpose*. Thus, for instance, we grant language comprehension or object recognition the status of "natural cognitive functions" because we can readily estimate how rightly they are performed and whether their (at least implicitly acknowledged) purpose is achieved.[1] I shall not consider here the usual objection to the study of specific mental functions on the grounds that such a study ignores the unity of the mind. Suffice it to note that I do not see any contradiction between considering the mind as a single and integrated entity and its being endowed with several *logically specifiable* functions, which thereby can be studied independently by virtue of their being logically specifiable. In this, I am committed to the assumption, implicit to all the disciplines studying living organisms, that these organisms may be usefully viewed as systems endowed with machine-like equipment consisting of jointly functioning parts or organs.

It is logically possible to specify the purpose of any particular task or function as well as to estimate the rightness of a given performance because, as Polanyi (1962) noted, the teleological character of machine-like equipment is inherent in the conception of jointly functioning parts. The perception of teleological organisation constitutes the necessary condition for the recognition of rationality in the execution of any given task. Here is the way Polanyi (1962, pp. 331–332) described the achievement of a complex task:

[1] I am not suggesting that these "natural functions" are easily definable. As a matter of fact, in spite of their salience it is by no means easy to specify the general purpose of such functions and the criteria of rightness that ought to be satisfied. It often seems more appropriate to consider cognitive functions as clusters of sibling tasks, each task being more easily characterisable than the function to which it belongs. But even then, it is the specific claim of this chapter that a theoretically interesting definition of cognitive tasks (e.g. to say in what they consist) is a matter of scientific investigation, and that such a definition is neither easy to arrive at nor intuitively given. More on this later.

> Technology, embodied in rules of rightness, teaches a rational way to achieve an acknowledged purpose. Such rules devise a stratagem consisting of several steps, each of which performs a function of its own within a coherent, economic, and in this sense rational, procedure. The procedure may include the contriving of a machine, built of a number of parts, each of which has a function of its own within a coherent, rational operation. There is a specifiable *reason* for every step of the procedure and every part of the machine, as well as for the way the several steps and the various parts are linked together to serve their joint purpose. This chain of reasons is set out in the operational principles of the process or of the machine.

The purpose of a complex operation is achieved by a procedure consisting of several steps defined by particular *sub-goals*. Because there is a specifiable reason for every step of the procedure, there must also be a *logical order* in which each step has to be achieved. The *teleological structure of a task* is thus embodied in the logical order of sub-goals that it is necessary to attain in order to achieve the ultimate purpose of the task in question.

There is, however, an important distinction to be drawn between task structure and the procedures that permit the realisation of the task. The former pertains to the *theory of the task* whereas the latter pertains to the *theory of its implementation.* A task theory bears on what has to be done in order to achieve the purpose of the task and does not specify *how* to do it. There are several reasons for this but a few stand out. Once the structure of a task has been defined, it need not be done again (unless one decides to change the rules of the game), whereas there are *always* several alternative ways to carry out this task, even in the same particular device (see Marr, 1977).[2] Furthermore, the implementation of any given task depends not only on its structure and on the characteristics of a particular device but also on special demands such as speed, reliability, or economy, which are not necessarily compatible. Another reason is that you may be able to define a task without having the technological means to realise it. This brings us to the third, most important, reason—not only are the "whats" independent of the "hows", but the latter are always dependent on the former.

The foregoing distinction of theory types implies an epistemological *hierarchy*—you cannot specify how to implement a task without being able

---

[2] Thus, for instance, there is only one "task theory" of the Fourier transform and several alternative ways to implement a transform. The example comes from Marr (1977). A reader familiar with his writings will note, in spite of different terminology, a striking similarity between our respective approaches. My distinction between task theory and implementation theory is similar to what Marr called, respectively, "computational theory" and the "algorithm". Although I wasn't aware of this aspect of Marr's work at the time the present ideas emerged, I should acknowledge the influence of his writings (especially Marr, 1976; 1977; and Chapter 1 in Marr, 1982) on my subsequent thinking.

to define its teleological structure, though, of course, you may have the theory of a task and still be far from able to implement it. Because the implementation of a task depends on the theory of this task, the elaboration of the former cannot but follow the formulation of the latter. To put it plainly: You must first determine what to do and then try to solve the problem of how to do it.

In so far as the theory of a task is independent of the characteristics of the device that can or eventually will carry it out and given that it does not (and cannot) specify the demands imposed on any particular execution, a task theory is not a psychological, artificial intelligence, or biological theory proper. It is a *cognitive theory*, a theory that has to specify *in what* the task *inherently* consists. Implementation theory, on the other hand, involves a stratagem embodied in a sequence of processes that follow, step by step, the particular sub-goals of the operation (although they do not have to match them one by one). This stratagem is necessarily device-oriented and has to satisfy the specific constraints (e.g. speed, economy, or reliability) imposed on the required performance. It is only such a device-specific theory that may turn out to be a psychological or artificial intelligence theory proper.

The failure to perceive the distinction between task theory and implementation theory and the general trend to underestimate the imperative character of the previously mentioned epistemological hierarchy (whereby the teleological structure of a task has to be specified prior to the study of the nature of processes that carry it out) are, in my view, among the principal causes of difficulties encountered by cognitive psychology. Problems may also arise from the very narrow interpretation of the metaphor of the machine-like equipment of living organisms. There is a tendency to confound the observation that machines and organisms are built out of a number of parts or organs, each of which performs a function of its own, and the fact that the theory of any complex task is defined by a set of sub-goals. The definition of these sub-goals rests on the perception of a discontinuity in the structure of a given task, that is, of the phenomenal distinctness of each sub-goal relative to those that immediately precede or follow it. The heterogeneity of sub-goals is an obvious property of complex tasks and constitutes the critical characteristic of goal-oriented behaviour. It is this heterogeneity that imposes the necessity of devising a sequence of steps that are to be performed in an ordered fashion, because the achievement of a particular sub-goal k is the condition *sine qua non* for attaining $k + 1$. Thus, for instance, in the visual perception of objects, fixing a rough two-dimensional shape based on an exploration of each retinal "image" is a condition necessary for the development of a description of overall three-dimensional shape (Marr, 1982). Or consider language processing where the identification of the morphological constituents (i.e. words) of an input sentence is a prerequisite for applying real-world knowledge to sentence interpretation (see Part 2 for further detail).

Now, the heterogeneity of sub-goals ought to be distinguished from the structural and functional heterogeneity of a machine. Specifically, there in no way has to be a one-to-one mapping (or worse, isomorphism) between the parts of a machine and the sub-goals of the task that it is to perform. Although the functioning of the machine should necessarily be compatible with the task for which it has been designed, the problem of contriving such a machine is how to match the definition of the task with technological and economical constraints as well as with the particular demands imposed by the quality of the execution that is desired. Given the necessity of reconciling such heterogeneous (and often contradictory) demands, it is quite unlikely that particular sub-goals of a task map systematically onto distinct parts of the machine that carries out this task.[3] I shall return to this in the following sections.

It is quite conceivable that without further clarification the distinctions I have drawn so far might be shrugged aside as mere hairsplitting or beside the point. I shall therefore try to demonstrate the logical necessity of endorsing the epistemological hierarchy that has been defined and show the consequences of confounding different levels of explanation. The currently popular issue of modularity will help me to clarify these points.

PART 1

In his seminal article "The Architecture of Complexity", Herbert Simon (1982) suggested that complex systems might best be viewed as composed of (or assembled from) subsystems (components) endowed with functional autonomy. The autonomy of components and the unity of the overall system may be viewed as relative to the strength of within and between component interactions whereby strong interactions, taking place within components endow them with functional autonomy, whereas weak interactions occurring between subsystems naturally ensure the unity of the overall system, permitting the co-ordination of its various parts. (It may be supposed, with a reasonable likelihood of being correct, that in so far as the execution of complex tasks requires the achievement of heterogeneous sub-goals, it can only be carried out by a device whose structure is accordingly complex.) Simon argued that, both in terms of scientific explorability as well as the probability of emerging through the process of

[3] Needless to say, that in so far as the distinction between the theory of a task and the implementation of this task in a particular device holds for any type of complex achievement (whether in technology, biology, or business administration), the foregoing discussion is not restricted to "dumb" machines but applies to minds and computers as well.

natural evolution, complex tasks are most plausibly implemented by *nearly decomposable* systems—i.e. systems in which global interactions are sufficiently weak to be viewed as having negligible effects on the workings of any particular component. With reference to scientific explorability, it is clear that under the condition of near decomposability it is possible to study every subsystem separately without paying constant attention to its interdependencies. Given this argument, Simon went further to suggest that systems that are complex without somehow being decomposable may "to a considerable extent escape our observation and understanding" (p. 219).

Considering the difficulty of designing complex systems that are not composed of autonomous pieces of processes (modules) and the likelihood that such systems would either be inefficient or break down too easily, Simon proceeded to cast doubt on the possibility that integrated non-modular systems could have emerged in the course of natural evolution. Marr (1982), on the other hand, has tended to elevate *modularity* to a general principle of systems design, whether natural or artificial. Following this principle, the execution of any complex task has to be split up into separate pieces of processes and implemented as a collection of smaller sub-tasks "that are as nearly independent of one another as the overall task allows" (Marr, 1982, p. 102). Marr goes on to say:

> This principle is important because if a process is not designed in this way, a small change in one place has consequences in many other places. As a result, the process as a whole is extremely difficult to debug or to improve, whether by a human designer or in the course of natural evolution, because a small change to improve one part has to be accompanied by many simultaneous, compensatory changes elsewhere.

These two ideas:

> that only (complex) systems designed in a modular fashion are functionally viable; and, likewise,
> that it is only in virtue of their being modular that complex systems are potentially explorable

have become relatively popular in the last few years. Indeed, there is a tendency, currently, to consider modularity as something of a *raison d'état* in cognitive psychology—had not nature designed the cognitive system in a modular fashion it wouldn't be amenable to scientific explanation. Although this argument is quite moving, the alleged requisite relationship between the architecture of mind and the explorability of mental systems could surely benefit from further clarification.

Consider the possibility of contriving a machine assembled from functionally autonomous parts, each specialised in a particular sub-goal of the task that is to be executed. The principle of such a machine appears compelling, and it seems perfectly possible that such a device would work as long as the task is fairly simple and does not require highly elaborated results. But in practice it wouldn't be tenable as a general principle because, normally, the implementation of any task has to reconcile various demands that are not necessarily converging. More important, there is no logical necessity that every sub-task (defined by a particular sub-goal) be implemented by a separate piece of a machine or process, especially in tasks whose results are highly elaborate (as is the case of cognitive tasks) and in which there is no possibility of predicting, *a priori*, all the possible inputs and results that might be required. Briefly, there is no logical necessity that implementation processes be mapped onto task structure on a one-to-one basis, i.e. that any given process be specialised in achieving a particular sub-goal of the task being executed. On the contrary, it is perfectly conceivable that processes are not specifically individuated in view of attaining particular sub-goals of the task but rather are devised in view of the overall performance and participate in the execution of a cluster of different sub-goals.[4]

All this is not to say that processes or parts of a machine cannot be autonomous, must be equipotential, or cannot be specialised in some theoretically interesting way. Modularity might, indeed, appear to be interesting and *useful* from the point of view of cognitive theory if modules represented constant entities (in the sense that their operational principle wouldn't change from one implementation of a given task to another) and if they could be considered as meaningful embodiments of logically necessary steps of a task—i.e. if every specific process or part of a machine were individuated in view of achieving a particular sub-goal of a task and nothing else. But if by modularity one merely means autonomy and specialisation of processes, its relevance diminishes considerably for the cognitive scientist, if only because there is *little chance* that the understanding of the functioning of such a "module" would lead to the understanding of the task to whose execution this module actually contributes Briefly, modularity would present considerable interest for the cognitive scientist if, and *only if*, modules could be viewed as devices individuated in view of achieving particular sub-goals of a task (viz. if their function were meaningful from the viewpoint of the theory of such a task). But in so far as there is no logical necessity to implement complex tasks in such a fashion and, even, little probability that this will often be the case, the whole debate on modularity turns out to be beside the point.

[4] As a matter of fact this is how computer systems generally work.

Were Simon right in suggesting that only systems that are modular (in the sense previously defined) are scientifically explorable, given the implausibility of implementations whereby every specific process (or processing component) is individuated in view of achieving a particular sub-goal of the task, there would be little chance that attempts at understanding complex systems would ever be successful. But Simon does not appear to make the distinction between the task and the device that carries it out. For one thing, as long as you are unaware of the purpose of a machine and unable to define the task that it executes, you may not even be able to understand its operational principles. Suppose you are exploring and trying to understand the functioning of, say, a garbage-collecting robot but you are unaware of the purpose it serves—that is, you can observe it working in the passenger hall of an airport but do not know that it is actually collecting garbage and not just randomly picking up objects lying on the floor.[5] Because you are smart and educated, you will be able to find out the physical laws that the functioning of the machine does respect. Because you are an experienced empiricist, you will describe the movements of the machine, its shape, and, for example, the conditions in which the machine slows down, stops, etc. . . . (And because you just happen to be a passenger, you appreciate that the robot picked up a discarded pack of cigarettes lying near by, not your briefcase containing the text of your next talk on modularity.) Suppose that you will even be able to describe its electronic circuitry . . . But all this will not allow you to determine the exact purpose of the robot, explain why it picks up empty cans, cigarette butts, stray newspapers but not your briefcase, or your children, nor will it allow you to define what the task precisely consists of, and, as a consequence, you will be unable to explain the functioning of this robot in a way that does not trivially apply to everything. For, in fact, you need first to understand the notions of GARBAGE and GARBAGE-COLLECTING (which, suppose, you don't understand yet), notions that you cannot infer from the sole description of the robot's movements, shape, architecture, or electronic circuitry.

So far I discussed two levels of scientific theory, task theory and implementation theory, but for the clarity of the foregoing example it may be necessary to introduce a third hierarchic level of explanation, that of *machine theory*, which is proper to mechanical, electronic, or biological engineering. I have already noted that the implementation of a task depends on the theory of this task, a theory that has to solve the problems that are inherent in the realisation of the task no matter how it is performed and what carries it out. Likewise, although the algorithm has to be executable by the machine for which it has been defined, it depends

[5] Note that in order to understand the purpose of such a robot, it is necessary to grasp the concept of GARBAGE.

more on the theory of the task that it implements than on the hardware by which it is embodied. Notwithstanding that mechanisms are empirically more "accessible" than abstract theories, the mere exploration of a machine can neither provide one with the definition of the task being executed nor with the algorithm by which the task is implemented. Returning to our example, even if the robot were perfectly modular, assembled from functionally autonomous parts each of which achieves sub-goals that are inherent in garbage-collecting tasks, and even if you could observe the action of each part independently of its relationships with others, as long as you ignore the purpose of the overall activity of the robot (and presumably the notion of GARBAGE) you won't be able to explain the function of any of its parts in an enlightened manner. The decomposability (or modularity) of a system does not make it any more understandable.

The important point here is this: If you are interested in a functional explanation of cognitive tasks (and probably if you are interested in the explanation of any kind of functional achievement), your research programme should take into account the epistemological hierarchy that has been outlined, or one consistent with it. Again, according to this hierarchy, the theory of a given "machine" depends on the algorithm by which its task is implemented, and the algorithm depends, in turn, on the theory of this task (cf. Marr, 1982). First you need to determine *what* has to be performed, and *why* it is composed of such and such sub-goals; second you have to determine *how* it can be carried out, and only then can you try to define *by what* it can be executed.[6] This rule appears so obvious that I presume no one could seriously support an opposing view, e.g. reversing the hierarchy of theoretical levels. What rather is likely to occur is the adoption of naïve *a priori* conjectures regarding the upper level theories in order to focus the investigation on some particular problem pertaining to the lower (e.g. machine or behavioural) level.[7]

[6] Let me note here that the existence of an epistemological hierarchy does not imply that the lower-level theories (implementation and machine theories) are less important or otherwise easier to elaborate. The point is that you have to answer certain questions in a particular order and not which of these questions is more important or easier to deal with.

[7] The trouble is that the imperative character of this hierarchy may not appear as obvious in sciences that explore existing systems (e.g. psychology or physiology) as it has become in artificial intelligence (that creates new systems), particularly after the failure of the early work (on machine translation) that was based on naïve *a priori* conjectures regarding the task being modelled. It is always possible to explore a device without understanding its task but if you try to create a system without an adequate theory of what it has to do, it will simply not work. And, indeed, it turns out that the level of task theory is generally the most neglected in psychology and neurophysiology, current research being mostly concentrated at the level of implementation "without", as Chomsky (1980) noted, "appropriate prior understanding of the top level" (see also Marr & Nishihara, 1978).

In conclusion to this part, I have tried to show that modular architecture does not necessarily guarantee explorability and that the possibility of developing task theories *does not* depend on the organisation of the systems that carry out these tasks. Moreover, I have suggested that a distinction should be made between the specialisation of processes and modularity. It may be interesting from a theoretical standpoint to call "module" a specialised process individuated in view of attaining a specific sub-goal defined by the theory of the task to whose execution this process contributes. But there appears to be no convincing argument that complex tasks *have* to be implemented in this way. Design arguments supporting the thesis that only modular systems could have emerged in the course of natural evolution smack of anthropomorphism in so far as natural evolution is viewed as a process orchestrated by a human-like designer whose decisions are constrained by the limits of what is "humanly processible". But who is to claim that the task of a human designer, obliged to submit to the constraints of time, available means, and the limits of what is humanly processible, is comparable to millions of years of repetitiousness, prodigality, and variable stresses that have shaped the organism to survive and cope with its environment (cf. Marin, 1982)?

Most important, though, it is the lack of clarity in the definition of cognitive theories, and, *ipso facto*, in the debate on modularity, that incited me to dwell on the importance of an epistemological hierarchy in the explanation of cognitive tasks (which are similar, in this respect, to any instance of complex biological achievement). The acknowledgement of such a hierarchy should, in my view, reduce the relevance of architectural considerations for the development of cognitive theories. It is, however, one thing to show that arguments based on general principles in favour of the modularity of complex systems may not be defendable, and another to extend this line of reasoning to an examination of arguments for the modularity of specific systems. I shall thus turn, in the second part of this chapter, to such specific arguments and examine, with reference to the influential monograph of Jerry Fodor (1983), the putative properties of modules, and the virtues of implementing a skill in a modular fashion. An example showing what a task theory might look like will also be useful to this discussion.

PART 2

For more than half a century psychologists have been reluctant to engage in theoretical considerations unsupported by "direct empirical evidence" lest the spectre of old-fashioned speculative psychology be resuscitated. But outright empiricism inevitably exacts a price; and the price to pay has been embarrassingly high, for it amounted, half-way through this century, to an unprecedented theoretical impoverishment of the discipline. Although the advent of the so-called cognitive revolution tended to lessen the aversion of experimental psychologists to "purely theoretical" issues, even in the late 1970s the label of "theoretician" had a patently disparaging connotation and was unlikely to bring academic recognition. Given this backdrop, one cannot help but be struck by the impact of Fodor's monograph *The modularity of mind* (1983), which, although addressing a broad range of theoretical issues (and even a few among the most discredited in the past), has nevertheless managed to capture the attention of academic circles all over the world and to be widely debated. Even a cursory glance at the literature that followed the publication of this monograph reveals that theoretical psychology is shamelessly getting good press again.

Fodor proposes another, very different look at the problem of the architecture of mind—if only because he closely links it to a theory of mental functions. His arguments in support of some form of modularity of mind are based to a considerable extent on an exposé of a task theory of the initial steps in language perception/comprehension. And in contrast to the general theses on the inevitable modularity of complex systems, Fodor offers a tentative explanation of what might be gained by a certain type of system were it to be modular. More important still, Fodor appears, in most respects, to be committed to the epistemological hierarchy that has been defined earlier, and he does not make unduly strong or general claims regarding the allegedly necessary modular organisation of complex systems. Accordingly, the objections to the view that modularity constitutes a general principle of complex systems design are not all applicable to Fodor's arguments on the modularity of some particular mental processors.

Fodor is concerned mainly with "receptive" processing by the cognitive system, especially the processing of linguistic stimuli, although he uses occasional examples drawn from the field of visual perception. His definition of computational problems inherent in the processing of linguistic input hinges on the consideration of the respective virtues of top-down and bottom-up models, and takes, on several occasions, the accent of a crusade against the extreme versions of the former. That is, Fodor is committed to the idea that the cognitive system has to apply considerable "real-world knowledge" to input processing but stresses the necessity of defining *diachronically* the types of computations that gradually become applicable. In this respect it is insufficient to demonstrate that perception or language comprehension are corrected by top-down information because one has to show the temporal locus of these descending contributions. If one takes into account the observation that the cognitive system is able to process "unanticipated stimulus layouts" or to perceive novelty, and that "even if you know precisely what someone is going to say ...

there are simply too many linguistically different ways of saying the same thing" (p. 90), one has to admit that the reliability of input processing depends on the presence of bottom-up processes.

The paradox of models in which top-down information applies from the very outset is that they imply that the system already "knows" how things are. But "if you already know *how* things are, why look to *see* how things are" (p. 68). Briefly, in so far as not all incoming stimuli are redundant and given that the organism does the analysis of unredundant stimulus arrays (e.g. unpredictable sentences), input processing has to be *initially* data-driven. The only higher level knowledge involved in the initial processing of incoming input will thus be the "knowledge" of how to analyse the form of this input.

Still, it may be interesting to elaborate a bit further on this point. A system that does not know *a priori* what the stimulus is about cannot but explore those properties of the input that are lawfully determined and hence analysable in some lawful way. If cognitive processors are *computational* systems, they have access to input solely by virtue of the *form* in which it is couched. Thus, it is only this initial analysis of its form that renders input accessible to other, more fine-grained explorations. Imposing the requirement of diachronicity on the definition of computations is a way of recognising the problem of *compatibility* between input forms and the types of computations that can be applied to them. And this way of developing a task theory of input processing leads Fodor to a "trichotomous functional taxonomy of psychological processes; a taxonomy which distinguishes transducers, input systems, and central processors, with the flow of input information becoming accessible to these mechanisms in about that order" (pp. 41–42).

Transducers "are analog systems that take proximal stimulation onto more or less covarying neural signals" (p. 41). These systems are not computational to the extent that the character of their outputs "is determined, in some lawful way, by the character of impinging energy at the transducer surface". Since this energy is itself "lawfully determined by the character of the distal layout . . . it is possible to infer properties of the distal layout from corresponding properties of the transducer output. *Input analysers* are devices which perform inferences of this sort" (p. 45).

An illustration of this proposal will be found in the work of Marr (1976; 1979) and Ullman (1979) in the field of visual perception. Marr (1979, p. 206) shows that:

> . . . early visual processing must be limited to the recovery of localized physical properties of the visible *surfaces* of a viewed object, particularly local surface dispositions (orientation and depth) and surface material

properties (colour, texture, shininess, and so on). More abstract matters such as a description of overall three-dimensional shape must come after this more basic analysis is complete.

Consider two examples showing just what such computations may actually consist of. The primary exploration of the visual stimulus has to result in the constitution of a primitive description of a viewed object, which has been dubbed by Marr (1976) a *primal sketch*. Roughly, this description is inferred from intensity changes over the visual field. By contrasting points that tend to be places of locally high or low intensity, it is possible to capture directions, magnitudes, and spatial extents of intensity changes of the visible surfaces. This permits, given a set of appropriate algorithms, to make explicit two-dimensional geometrical relations and thus to fix a rough shape of the object being viewed. In a similar vein, Ullman's algorithm for inferring "form from motion" is based on the observation that transformations of intensity in the visual field are lawfully determined by the spacial displacement of a given object (Ullman, 1979). And to extend this reasoning a bit further, one may note that auditory stimulation could also be analysed by contrasting energy peaks of acoustic waves.

More generally, Fodor (1983) defines input systems as interfaces between transducers and central processors whose role is to infer as many properties of the input as possible without engaging the entire belief system of the organism. This may (and usually does) implicate "levels of encoding that are quite abstractly related to the play of proximal stimulation" (p. 41) and a considerable degree of complexity (see the following). Input analysers characterise the actual arrangement of "things in the world" thereby providing grounds for (top-down) operations of central systems. The important point here is that it appears to be most advantageous for the organism to infer as much information as possible through the exploration of the lawful characteristics of transduced inputs (whether from such parameters as intensity changes or energy peaks, from the immediate proximity of high or low intensity points, or from the morpho-syntactic structure of utterances) before taking recourse to descending higher-level knowledge (see also Marr, 1979; Marr & Poggio, 1977, for a similar suggestion). Elevating this observation to a general principle has, admittedly, several implications for the elaboration of task theories, implications that Fodor extends to the problem of the architecture of mind.

Fodor views the trichotomous taxonomy not only as a useful characterisation of computational processes that take place successively in the course of information processing, but also goes further to insist that the computational (and temporal) distinction between input analysers and central processors is co-extensive with the phenomenological distinction between perception and thought.[8]

> Roughly, endorsing this computational architecture is tantamount to insisting upon a perception/cognition distinction. It is tantamount to claims that a certain class of computational problems of "object identification" (or, more correctly, a class of computational problems whose solutions consist in the recovery of certain proprietary descriptions of objects) has been "detached" from the domain of cognition at large and handed over to functionally distinguishable psychological mechanisms. Perceptual analysis is, according to this model, not, strictly speaking, a species of thought (pp. 42–43).

But in so far as the trichotomous architecture is not an inherent characteristic of input processing (see footnote 8) it becomes legitimate to inquire what it buys for an organism to isolate input analysers from central processors. "Implicit in the trichotomous architecture", Fodor writes, "is the isolation of perceptual analysis from certain effects of background belief and set . . . this has implications for both the speed and the objectivity of perceptual integration" (p. 43). It may indeed. But it remains to be shown whether the speed and the objectivity of perceptual integration do require the encapsulation of input analysis in order to prevent the intrusion of higher-level knowledge. In this context, the most relevant question would be whether higher-level knowledge actually could interfere with input analysis were the input system not insulated from central systems. This question may best be dealt with by referring to Fodor's description of the typical characteristics of input systems, characteristics suggesting, in his view, that input analysis is carried out by a modular device.

(1) *Input systems are domain specific.* The more specific a stimulus domain, Fodor says, the more plausible the speculation that it is computed by a special-purpose mechanism. It is unlikely that the same principles that apply to the perception of cows, butterflies, or Bartok's Romanian dances also apply to the perception of language. "The computations which sentence recognizers perform must be closely tuned to a complex of stimulus properties that is quite specific to sentences" (p. 50).

The input processor for language, therefore, should be solely responsive to the properties of language and operate only in domains that exhibit these properties. On the one hand, this processor should be tuned to the specific visual or acoustic patterns of language. But on the other, in so far

[8] Fodor nevertheless admits the possibility that input analysers may be continuous with higher cognitive processes. "It is perfectly possible", he writes, "to imagine a machine whose computations are appropriately sensitive to environmental events but which does *not* exhibit a functional distinction between input systems and central systems" (p. 42).

as certain grammatical analyses are required very early in the time course, and given that morphology and syntax are couched in the very structure of utterances and thereby analysable through the application of form-exploring algorithms, it seems reasonable to suppose that the input processor for language is responsible for the exploration of those characteristics of sentences that are lawfully embodied in the input structure, and *ipso facto* can be carried out on purely formal grounds. It may not be necessary, here, to dwell on the logical necessity of early grammatical analyses (see the following). Suffice it to note that if one considers the argument that it appears to be most advantageous, from a computational point of view, to "squeeze" as much information as possible from the purely formal characteristics of the input before resorting to top-down interactions, Fodor's suggestion that the input processors for language are tuned to the specific properties of linguistic stimulation and contain algorithms for grammatical analyses of sentences makes perfectly good sense.

(2) *The operation of input systems is mandatory.* There is a good deal of evidence, Fodor observes, that input processors are automatically triggered by the very exposure to the stimuli to which they apply. If there is a possibility of executive control on central processes, one cannot help but run input analyses all the way through the input system.

> Input analysis is mandatory in that it provides the *only* route by which transducer outputs can gain access to central processes; if transduced information is to affect thought at all, it must do so via the computations that input systems perform (p. 54).

Briefly, it once more makes perfectly good sense to keep running the analysis as long as the system remains "ignorant" of what the input is all about.

(3) *Input systems are fast.* Input systems, in Fodor's account, are automatic, mandatory, and insensitive to the subject's utilities; they use only a small portion of information that might *in principle* bear on a given input—briefly they acquire speed at the cost of unintelligence. Input systems are fast, Fodor says, because they are bull-headed.

(4) *There is only limited central access to the analyses that input systems perform.* The lower the level of input analysis the less it is accessible to conscious report. Although there may be some, though very limited, access to higher levels of input analysis, it is only the *final* result that is "... fully and freely available to the cognitive processes that eventuate in the voluntary determination of overt behavior" (p. 56).

If one assumes that input processing goes from "bottom to top", with the stimulus gradually undergoing increasingly elaborate analyses, it appears understandable that the more its results become compatible with central cognitive processes the more they are accessible to conscious inspection and report. By basing his criterion of accessibility of input analyses on the feasibility of conscious report, Fodor misses the point; for it is not necessarily that you cannot report because there is no access to the information at some lower levels of analysis, it may well be that *up to some level there is nothing couched in a format appropriate for explicit report.* If, as Fodor suggests, the conscious report is mediated by central systems, the information to be reported by these systems must be couched in a format compatible with their know-how. Although interlevels of input analysis do indeed appear to be opaque to higher cognitive systems, this is not necessarily because input systems are encapsulated but may well be due to format incompatibility. But does it matter anyhow? Fodor claims that it does. More on this later.

(5) *Input systems are informationally encapsulated.* From the viewpoint of a task theory of language perception/comprehension, it is necessary to analyse very early on the structure of linguistic stimuli because this is the only way to obtain information permitting the application of higher-level knowledge. You have to be able to distinguish between *HOUSE THE POLICE* and *POLICE THE HOUSE*, or to determine when presented with ... *BEAR* ... whether you have to apply knowledge associated with a verb (to bear) or with a noun (bear), just as you have to distinguish between linguistic and non-linguistic stimuli. That is, you must determine what kind of knowledge is needed prior to trying to apply any knowledge at all (see the opening sections of Part 2). Briefly, if you consider that:

the recognition and primary analysis of linguistic forms cannot be knowledge-driven or context-driven because neither "real-world knowledge" nor context can determine forms and syntactic roles;

it is sufficient to supply linguistically acceptable sentences to run a good deal of grammatical analyses without any recourse to pragmatic or semantic knowledge; and

you need the result of grammatical analyses in order to determine what kind of knowledge could be applied;

there must be a stage in the processing of linguistic stimuli prior to which central processes cannot influence input analysis. It is only at this stage, once the elements of an input utterance are identified as particular items in the morphemic inventory of the language, that anything like "real-world knowledge" associated with these particular items can come into play. In fact, the identification of these items can be viewed as what actually satisfies the criterion of format compatibility.

The present argument may alone suffice to explain why input analyses are to a large extent impenetrable to cognitive systems. But Fodor prefers to resort to a different explanation. Input systems are cognitively impenetrable because they are informationally encapsulated. They somehow are physically insulated, lest the central systems attempt to meddle in their domestic affairs. And the informational encapsulation of input systems is, Fodor says, "the essence of their modularity".

Fodor's arguments supporting his notion of informational encapsulation of input systems are, in fact, arguments for relative two-sided impenetrability: Central systems can hardly influence input processing, and input systems can hardly (if at all) gain access to cognition. Further arguments, e.g. that encapsulation affords an interesting degree of autonomy (you are doing what you have to do and are neither bothered nor constrained by exogenous sources of information), do not really fare any better: Since the incompatibility of formats entails impenetrability, why insulate physically what is in any case impenetrable computationally?

There may be three rules, Fodor says, for evaluating the claims of the cognitive (im)penetrability of input systems:

1. It is insufficient to demonstrate top-down influences on perception or language comprehension—one has to demonstrate that the *locus* of top-down effects *is internal* to input analysis.
2. Evidence of some sort of cognitive penetrability of an input system does not, by itself, demonstrate its penetrability across the board—input systems are viewed as impenetrable to a considerable extent (or relatively impenetrable) but not as hermetically insulated.[9]
3. "The claim that input systems are informationally encapsulated must be very carefully distinguished from the claim that there is top-down information flow *within* these systems" (p. 76).

One may argue, Fodor concedes, that the effects of contextual facilitation in certain psycholinguistic experiments using the technique of priming run counter to the thesis of cognitive impenetrability of input analysers. The problem is reasonably serious: You present subjects with, say, letter strings briefly flashed on a screen and ask them to decide whether the stimulus is a (legal) word (the experiment is to be run with native speakers). The subjects have to answer "yes" or "no" as quickly as possible by pressing a corresponding "y" or "n" key, and you register reaction times. There is overwhelming experimental evidence that if you present *TABLE* shortly before *CHAIR* you will find a relatively small but persistent facilitation (i.e. shorter reaction time) for *CHAIR* than if it were preceded by, say, *SMOKE* (instead of *TABLE* or any other word "closely

[9] This point, which appears very interesting indeed, seems rather unwelcome for Fodor's thesis of the informational encapsulation of input systems.

related" to *CHAIR*). This finding could be a nuisance in so far as you *don't* need to consult your knowledge about chairs and tables (and heaven knows what else) in order to recognise that *CHAIR* is a morpheme in your language (and given that both the presentation and reaction times are generally very fast—fractions of a second—merely aggravates the case). Because such a lexical decision task does not require anything besides the determination of whether a stimulus is a morphologic entity in the language and because Fodor insists that the "*output of the language processing module* (viz. input system, V.R.) respects such structurally defined notions as *item in the morphemic inventory of the language*" (p. 92), the effect of contextual facilitation appears to contradict the notion of the cognitive impenetrability of input systems. Note that contextual facilitation occurs even for minimal stimulus durations that are processible by subjects (below some duration threshold of target exposure there is no reaction at all), so it is impossible to suggest that if stimulus duration were shorter there would be no such facilitation.

Fodor offers a solution to this problem by proposing that it is possible to reconcile the encapsulation of input systems with contextual priming because these systems may contain devices that simulate higher-level contributions. One such device, he suggests, could be the mental lexicon, a kind of morphological dictionary that does not contain knowledge about meaning or semantic interlexical relations, but in which items are connected on *purely associative grounds*—this solution buying speed and contextual facilitation (in experiments on priming) without cognitive penetrability of the input system.

> The present suggestion is that no . . . intelligent evaluation of the options takes place, there is merely brute facilitation of the reaction of "bug" consequent upon the recognition of "spy". The condition of this brute facilitation buying anything is that it should be possible, with reasonable accuracy, to mimic what one knows about connectedness *in the world* by establishing corresponding connections among entries in the mental lexicon. In effect, the strategy is to use the structure of interlexical connections to mimic the structure of knowledge . . . Associations are the means whereby stupid processing systems manage to behave as though they were smart ones. In particular, interlexical associations are the means whereby the language processor is enabled to act as though it knows that spies have to do with bugs (whereas, in fact, it knows no such thing). The idea is that . . . terms for things frequently connected in experience become themselves connected in the lexicon. Such connection is *not* knowledge; it is not even judgement. It is simply the mechanism of the contextual adjustment of response thresholds (pp. 81–82).

The idea of using higher-level knowledge "superficially" and "unintelligently" merits closer examination even though Fodor's suggestion of packaging an associative lexicon in the input system sounds desperately ad hoc. In this respect the question is what might it buy for an organism to have an associative (stupid) lexicon in the input system (given that it will not ultimately replace the obligatory use of higher-level knowledge)? On Fodor's account all it buys is an explanation of contextual facilitation of primed targets in lexical decision or naming experiments without resorting to top-down interactions (he thus saves the bathtub with loss of both baby and bathwater). Although the apparent contradiction is solved because input systems can prompt facilitation without being cognitively penetrated, the ad hocness of this solution does not make the story of encapsulation any more compelling.

Still, if one situates this problem in a teleological perspective there may be a way of providing a plausible explanation of why priming effects are compatible with the *relative* impenetrability of input systems. Consider the following points.

First of all, very often parsing cannot be fully achieved without taking recourse to higher-level knowledge. This fact is implicitly recognised by Fodor who quotes Hilary Putnam's poser: "Lincoln said, 'You can fool all of the people some of the time'" (p. 135). The sentence has two plausible readings and two underlying syntactic structures. Second, many instances of referential ambiguity (e.g. anaphora) cannot be solved by purely formal analyses. In the following example: "The soldiers fired at the prisoners, and we saw them falling", you can't determine the reference of *THEM*, and thus the complete syntactic structure of the sentence, without consulting knowledge of this type of situation. Third, many more spoken sentences are grammatically ill-formed or, even, ungrammatical, than is generally admitted. If stupidity buys speed, encapsulation doesn't buy intelligence. A stupid parser can analyse grammatical sentences but has no means with which to correct ungrammatical ones.

If input analyses precede a central system's knowledge-driven involvement, it is necessarily motivated *teleologically*. Although causal explanations in terms of format incompatibility, the paradox of fully top-down processes (you can't apply the knowledge relative to a given input before you know what it is about), etc. are certainly relevant to this matter, any plausible explanation of this precedence ought to specify its purpose or reason. I shall tentatively suggest that it may be this: Input analyses *enable*, *prepare*, and *facilitate*[10] cognitive involvement. In particular, consider the "frame problem" in artificial intelligence as an expression of the same general problem cognitive theories are *always* confronted with: How am I to determine those and *only those* domains of knowledge that are sufficient to cope with the present circumstances? The trouble is that everything I

[10] What I mean by "facilitate" will be explained later.

know in one field might *in principle* be related and relevant to everything I know in all other fields, so every piece of knowledge is *a priori* relevant and may be usefully applied to everything else and vice versa (this is, in a nutshell, Fodor's argument on the isotropicity of central systems—and I take it to be in principle correct). Note in this respect that I wouldn't want to (and obviously can't) consult everything I know about everything, not even everything I know about felines, in order to understand Muriel's lamentations about the damages occasioned by her cat.

The point I wish to make is that the work of input processors would be useless if central systems that supposedly take over the job were to act isotropically. The infinite connectedness of knowledge is likely to give rise to a never ending quest[11]. It may, however, be reasonable to suppose that input analyses induce a momentary restriction of the scope of applicable relevant knowledge (even if it is not definitive), thereby relieving the central processors from plunging straight into isotropy. How might this be done?

Relative impenetrability (viz. limited possibility of interactions between input processors and central systems) ought to be interpreted as impenetrability *up to a certain point*. This point may be reached as soon as the criterion of format compatibility is satisfied. In the present context this may be the determination of the lexical morphology of the input.

As soon as the criterion of format compatibility is satisfied it becomes possible to initiate *coarse-grained* and initially rather unintelligent interactions between the input analysis and central processing. The purpose of such interactions may be threefold: (1) to prepare for others, more fine-grained interactions—especially by restricting the scope of applicable knowledge; and thereby (2) to initiate central processing; and (3) to enable the input system to terminate parsing by providing cues that could not otherwise be derived from an analysis of input structure.

There must be, in effect, some presumably very crude relationship between the lexical morphology of a language and the domains of experience (domains of knowledge) with which lexical forms are normally associated. This relationship does not necessarily presuppose interlexical connections (e.g. in the input system), it merely requires that individual words (morphological entities) be somehow linked to the domains of real-world knowledge, domains with reference to which they are normally

[11] I follow here Fodor's opinion that current artificial intelligence devices, such as "frames", "scripts", etc., are in no way solutions to this problem. They are merely clever tricks that may somehow stimulate (if you don't ask too much) a well-centred, non-isotropic processing when applied to a severely restricted universe that lends itself to stereotypical definition.

employed. In accordance with Fodor's suggestion, such connections do not indeed constitute knowledge, or even judgement. They just serve to "inform" that a given target word *has to do* with some particular domain(s) of experience, thereby constituting the primary link between input analyses and central processors. This may be so because as soon as input analysers determine the lexical morphology of the input, its associative relationships within and between knowledge domains become available. The availability of these relationships may, by itself, be sufficient to trigger preliminary operations of the central systems, as these relationships determine, for an input sentence, which domains of knowledge have *a priori* the best chances of being relevant to the interpretative process.

The triggering of these preliminary operations plays, in this framework, a role similar to that subsumed under the traditional concept of activation of semantic networks, except that no such nets containing the semantic representation of lexical meanings appear to be necessary or even useful. My suggestion is, moreover, related in a certain way to the previously mentioned argument that what may be available to report is only what has been tackled by knowledge-manipulating systems. But for present purposes it may be sufficient to note that priming effects are, on this interpretation, merely a *by-product* of coarse, unintelligent interactions based on a crude relationship between lexical morphology and domains of real-world experience. Such associative relationships will not mimic the infinite connectedness of knowledge, they can only rely on frequent co-occurrences. And no associative lexicon packaged in the input system would be necessary to explain contextual facilitation in experiments on priming. Briefly, this is how a stupid relationship can yield smart and *useful* results. Indeed, these crude relationships between lexical morphology and domains of real-world experience permit the initiation of operations of central systems while at the same time severely restricting, from the outset, the scope of interpretative processes.

If you are buying the present suggestion you are committing yourself to an explanation of the purpose of input analysis (parsing, in itself, does not constitute this purpose) and to a tentative solution to the frame problem. Central systems are devices that constitute the essence of cognition; in particular, they are the means whereby the subject's knowledge of the world is applied to input interpretation. By input interpretation I mean a variety of phenomena ranging from object recognition or sentence comprehension to the reading of scientific experiments. But central systems do not communicate with the external world *directly*. They have "access" to input solely via the analyses performed by the input processors. This access depends on format compatibility—that is, the outcome of input analyses has to be couched in a form manipulable by the central processors. Variations of luminosity or acoustic waves do not represent forms accessible to the central processors, but 3D representations or lexical morphemes are "partial products" couched in a format compatible with knowledge-driven computations.

The problem of format compatibility is inherent in the notion of computational systems. If we assume that cognitive processors are computational systems, we also assume that they process information solely in virtue of the form in which it is couched (see also Fodor, 1983, pp. 39–40). For those acquainted with computer programming, the problem of format compatibility is self-evident, if only because the data must be couched in a form that the computer can "understand" (viz. compute).

One purpose of input analyses is thus to "re-write" the input in a form accessible to central systems.[12] It is precisely in this sense that I noted that input analysers *prepare* and *enable* cognitive involvement. Another purpose is to restrict—i.e. *facilitate*—knowledge interactions and thus make it possible to arrive at any interpretation at all. This bears on the frame problem, which constitutes the most serious and most clearly perceived difficulty in the artificial intelligence modelling of cognitive tasks. But this difficulty is by no means specific to artificial systems.

As was observed earlier, every piece of knowledge may, in principle, be connected to any other piece of knowledge, no matter how remote appear *a priori* their respective domains, and any such knowledge can, in principle, be relevant to the interpretation of a given input (viz. any attempt at interpretation can in principle give rise to isotropy). The infinite connectedness of knowledge and the isotropicity of central processes thus pose a serious problem: How is it possible to arrive at an interpretation at all, and to do so reasonably fast, given that infinite connectedness and isotropy can potentially generate endless computations? Were I to have operated isotropically on a recent safari, the reader would have probably been relieved of the task of pursuing the present considerations by a female lion, but I recognised her quickly enough to avoid becoming animal food. This, as it were, is food for thought, making more palatable the argument that if it were impossible to hit directly upon a few limited domains of knowledge that *a priori* best apply to a given problem (e.g. the most frequently associated in the real world), cognitive processes would have to be triggered isotropically. Localness is the leading characteristic of computations that will ultimately yield an interpretation, and if input systems were not to constrain severely the scope of applicable knowledge, perceptual information would never be

[12] It goes without saying that this "re-writing" cannot be viewed as purely mechanical translation. In fact, input analyses are fairly complex and imply a good deal of elaboration.

interpreted quickly enough to ensure the survival of the human species.[13]

This is not to say that the domains of knowledge circumscribed by input analyses are the most appropriate nor that other domains could not be involved in the process of interpretation. But in so far as input interpretation has to be triggered locally (i.e. within a restricted domain), the frame problem must of necessity be solved in order for any perceptual (linguistic or otherwise) task to be realisable. And in so far as interpretative processes have to be constrained and severely limited in scope *from the outset*, the only device that can do the job is the input system (as it is impenetrated by knowledge and thus uninformed of infinite connectedness and relevance). This is what I meant by noting that input analyses *prepare* and *facilitate* cognitive involvement.

My further suggestion is that coarse, necessarily unintelligent interactions are *sufficient* to restrict the scope of applicable knowledge and hence to ensure the localness of the interpretative process. Heaven knows how these interactions precisely operate. But the principle of very coarse interactions has been shown to permit the disambiguation of polysemous words in a computational experiment (Andreewsky, Rosenthal, & Bourcier, 1985), and there are reasons to believe that many cases of referential ambiguity can be solved in this manner (de Fornel & Rosenthal, 1987; Rosenthal & de Fornel, 1985).

(6) *Input analysers have "shallow" outputs*. This point has already been dealt with at considerable length in the preceding sections. Fodor is committed to the idea that the more constrained are the computations of a system, the shallower are their results. But he takes the shallowness of input analyses as a characteristic of encapsulated systems—informational encapsulation being in his view the most important aspect of modularity. And in so far as input systems are encapsulated, they cannot interface with cognitive processes everywhere, on pain of their ceasing to be functionally individuated systems. In fact, Fodor says, they can only transmit their end-products.

But these additional arguments for the encapsulation of input systems do not make Fodor's proposal of the modularity of these systems any more tenable. The (indeed quite reasonable) assumption that only the final stages of input analysis are interfacable with cognitive processes does not imply that the former is informationally encapsulated and *ipso facto*

[13] All this is not contradictory to the idea that interpretative processes are isotropic *in principle*, and indeed the history of science abounds in examples of solving specific problems in one field by analogy to other fields. One may even speculate whether we could develop civilisations and science if knowledge applications were non-isotropic. But, while being isotropic in principle, cognitive processes can yield an interpretation only when they operate *locally*.

modular. For it is sufficient to invoke the notion of format incompatibility to explain why the early stages of input processing are not cognitively penetrable. Likewise, the shallowness of input analysis does not, in and of itself, demonstrate encapsulation—suffice it to observe that analyses restricted (by format incompatibility, etc.) to the very lawful characteristics of input *structure* are necessarily shallow.

Fodor's next points, to the effect that: (7) *input systems are associated with fixed neural architecture* (*i.e. are hardwired*); (8) *exhibit characteristic and specific breakdown patterns* (see Semenza, Bisiacchi, & Rosenthal, this volume, for a related discussion); and (9) *their ontogeny exhibits characteristic pace and sequencing*; are far more speculative and do not provide any further support for his analysis of mental architecture. Consequently, I shall not be concerned with them here.

What rather deserves attention is Fodor's insistence that the issue of the modularity of input systems is amenable to empirical clarification. Admitting that most of the characteristics of input systems (i.e. fast, mandatory, domain specific, and yielding shallow outputs) are compatible with non-modular architecture, Fodor suggests that this clarification ought to bear on their informational encapsulation. Specifically, one should test whether input analyses are penetrable by top-down information. The trouble is that such a test cannot be conclusive. Because the incompatibility of format will suffice to prevent the premature occurrence of knowledge-driven interactions, observing the relative impenetrability of input systems,[14] and especially the impenetrability of the early stages of input processing, does not permit one to conclude that input systems are encapsulated. Finding impenetrability is not equivalent to demonstrating encapsulation. What one is left with, if Fodor's proposal of an empirical test were to be satisfied, is to shake the mind and check for a modular melody. If there is a rattle, modularity is in.

Notwithstanding this criticism, it should be recognised that Fodor's task theory of the initial steps in language perception/comprehension is roughly what one might expect a task theory to look like. It takes seriously the proposition that computations are determined by task structure and it defines a set of sub-goals that ought to be achieved in some orderly way. Specifically, it shows how the course of input processing is determined by the teleological structure of the task, thereby making, in some way, the elaborative growth of intermediate "products" reflect the task structure. This has several important implications for the way of conducting research in cognitive science, in general, and in cognitive neuropsychology, in particular, which Semenza, Bisiacchi, & Rosenthal discuss at considerable length in this volume. The trouble is that Fodor too readily infers from the

---

[14] See my discussion on point 5.

cognitive impenetrability of input analyses (task theory), which appears to be well supported, that input systems must be informationally encapsulated (implementation theory). If the trichotomous functional taxonomy of psychological processes does make sense in his theory of perceptual tasks—and I believe it does—it is in virtue of the usefulness of its characterisation of computational problems. But, as I pointed out earlier, this characterisation does not imply structural discontinuity.

The concluding sections of Fodor's monograph (1983) are a variation on the theme of explorability of natural phenomena. He writes:

> The condition for successful science (in physics, by the way, as well as psychology) is that nature should have joints to carve it at: relatively simple subsystems which can be artificially isolated and which behave, in isolation, in something like the way that they behave *in situ* (p. 128).

Input analysers are precisely subsystems of this type and this is why we already have considerable knowledge of input processing. But central systems are Quineian and isotropic, hence non-modular, and this is why, Fodor argues, we know very little, if anything, about cognitive processes other than input analyses. And, accordingly, this is very bad news for cognitive science.

> The limits of modularity are also likely to be the limits of what we are going to be able to understand about the mind, given anything like the theoretical apparatus currently available (p. 126).

Those who are sceptical may contemplate the state of the art in cognitive psychology and artificial intelligence. Although considerable progress has been accomplished in the fields of, say, visual perception or parsing, the research on central processes (e.g. thinking, memory, but in fact also language *comprehension*) has been, Fodor observes, a resounding fiasco.

If one needs another demonstration of the relationship between the architecture of mind and scientific explorability, and *ipso facto* of the co-extensiveness of computational character (encapsulated vs. Quineian and isotropic) and functional architecture (modular vs. non-modular), Fodor provides one: Input systems have proven to be explorable because they are modular, whereas central systems are recalcitrant to experimental methods because they are not modular. "Localness", he concludes, "... is the leading characteristic of the sorts of computations that we know how to think about" (p. 128), whereas isotropy is that sort of computation that nobody begins to understand.

Several objections may be raised with respect to this line of reasoning but a few stand out. I am not going to repeat the arguments to the effect that although the notion of the relative impenetrability of input systems appears to be convincingly supported, this is not the case for informational encapsulation. What deserves particular attention here is the definition of the computational character of central processors as Quineian and isotropic in an "across-the-board" fashion. This is, in effect, the only point of Fodor's that has been almost unanimously criticised in the literature (e.g. by Putnam, 1984; Schwartz & Schwartz, 1984; Shallice, 1984), with most discussants attempting to show that what appears to be isotropic (hence non-modular) *in principle* may, *in practice*, be computed locally. But because they assume that the modularity of a system is synonymous with its being explorable, this argument is a form of special pleading in order to extend the limits of explorability of cognitive phenomena. This is, in a sense, a modularity of despair.

I do not have any particular arguments with this critique of an "across-the-board" conception of isotropy because it is not inconsistent with my own suggestion that although central systems may indeed be isotropic in principle,[15] they have necessarily operated locally in all those cases for which they yield a solution (e.g. interpretation), because only local non-isotropic computations can ever yield solutions. And so far I have the impression that in a reasonable proportion of cases in our short lives we do arrive at an interpretation. Still, to the extent that central systems are isotropic in principle, Fodor may actually be right when he argues that they are not explorable as *independent entities*. In fact, if my suggestion is correct that input systems *prepare*, *enable*, and *facilitate* the operation of central processors (e.g. by restricting the scope of knowledge applicable *a priori*), one cannot consider the latter without defining how they interface with input analyses.[16] Which is a way of saying that one has to address the logic of the *whole task*.

Research in cognitive psychology has, in the past, often been devoted to a confrontation of general ideas (serial v. parallel processing, the respective weight of syntax and semantics, analytic v. holistic processes, modularity v. interactivity) rather than bearing on the definition of theories of

---

[15] The characterisation of central systems as Quineian and isotropic *in principle* refers to hypothetical states of affairs under which subjective experience is not relevant. However, when subjective experience is taken into consideration one is led to appreciate that the probability of relating things unconnected in experience is not equivalent to that of relating things connected in experience. And given the existence of unequal probabilities, the likelihood of central systems plunging into "full" isotropy is necessarily small. It is not that central systems cannot act isotropically. Rather, the point is that *in practice* they will seldom plunge into isotropy. Or, better, they will act isotropically only to a limited degree.

---

[16] I am restricting myself here to the discussion of those types of cognitive phenomena that are triggered by external stimulation, and I do not pretend that the present suggestion applies to all types of cognitive activities.

concrete tasks. If Fodor is right that we know almost nothing about central processes, it is not because the limits of modularity are also the limits of what we are able to understand about the mind, but, rather—to paraphrase his own statement—because of the currently dominant theoretical apparatus. I have tried to show in the present chapter that there actually exists a viable alternative to the theoretical apparatus Fodor is trying to present as the only one currently available. The earlier the stages of processing, the less elaborate their products, and the less elaborate the products the easier they may be conceptualised (even without any clear idea of the structure of the overall task being investigated).[17] It is thus not surprising that initial input analyses appear better understood than operations that follow them downstream in the time course. But if anything appears to be a condition of explorability, it is not modularity, nor even localness (as opposed to isotropy). It is the endorsement of the epistemological hierarchy whereby the theoretical conception of a task should come prior to other considerations.

[17] If only because we can observe the input, analyse it physically, and thus figure out the types of analyses that may be available from the outset.

REFERENCES

Andreewsky, E., Rosenthal, V., & Bourcier, D. (1985) Meaning without lexicon: A computational model for the resolution of lexical ambiguities. In G. Hoppenbrouwens, P. Seuren, & T. Weijters (Eds.), *Meaning and the lexicon*, Dodrecht: Foris Publications, 380–383.

Chomsky, N. (1980) Rules and representations. *The Behavioral and Brain Sciences*, *3*, 1–61.

de Fornel, M. & Rosenthal, V. Espace de travail et espace référentiel dans l'émergence du sens. *Cahiers S.T.S.*, *14*, 97–117.

Fodor, J. A. (1983) *The modularity of mind*. Cambridge, Mass: MIT Press.

Marin, O. M. S. (1982) Brain and language: The rules of the game. In M. A. Arbib, D. Caplan, & J. C. Marshall (Eds.), *Neural models of language processes*. New York: Academic Press, 45–69.

Marr, D. (1976) Early processing of visual information. *Phil. Trans. R. Soc. Lond.*, B *275*, 483–524.

Marr, D. (1977) Artificial intelligence—A personal view. *Artificial Intelligence*, *9*, 37–48.

Marr, D. (1979) Visual information processing: The structure and creation of visual representations. *Phil. Trans. R. Soc. Lond.*, B *290*, 199–218.

Marr, D. (1982) *Vision*. New York: W. H. Freeman.

Marr, D. & Nishihara, H. K. (1978) Visual information processing: Artificial intelligence and the sensorium of sight. *Technology Review*, *81*, 2–23.

Marr, D. & Poggio, T. (1977) From understanding computation to understanding neural circuitry. *Neurosciences Research Progress Bulletin*, *15*, 470–488.

Polanyi, M. (1962) *Personal knowledge*. Chicago: The University of Chicago Press.

Putnam, H. (1984) Models and Modules. *Cognition*, *17*, 253–264.

Rosenthal, V. & de Fornel, M. (1985) Traitement automatique des anaphores: Peut-on sortir d'un univers fermé? *T.A. Informations*, *vol. 26*(1), 11–23.

Schwartz, M. F. & Schwartz, B. (1984) In defence of organology. *Cognitive Neuropsychology*, *1*, 25–42.

Shallice, T. (1984) More functionally isolable subsystems but fewer "modules"? *Cognition*, *17*, 243–252.

Simon, H. A. (1982) *The sciences of the artificial* (2nd edition). Cambridge, Mass: MIT Press.

Ullman, S. (1979) *The interpretation of visual motion*. Cambridge, Mass: MIT Press.

3 From Models to Neuropsychological Data and Vice Versa

G. Sartori
Università di Padova, Italy

INTRODUCTION

In modern cognitive neuropsychology, data from pathology are used mainly for model-building purposes (see Coltheart, 1982). Patterns of associations and dissociations of symptoms permit us, according to this approach, to isolate processing components and to study their characteristics. In certain conditions, these data may be used to modify theories developed for explaining normal cognitive processes (e.g. Schwartz, Saffran, & Marin, 1980).

In analysing a neurological patient, a cognitive theory developed from studies on normal subjects is sometimes used. This is true, for example, in the field of reading research where neuropsychological investigations were preceded by extensive research on normals. It is assumed (cf. transparency assumption; see Caramazza, 1984a) that data on patients' performance, collected by means of experimentally conducted studies, may be interpreted in the framework of theories of normal cognitive processes and used as contributions to the modification of psychological theories. Schwartz et al. (1980), for example, reported a demented patient who was able to read aloud correctly those exception words that were not understood in visual comprehension tasks. This pattern of performance permits one to postulate the existence of a direct lexical route from orthography to phonology not mediated by meaning (e.g. Morton & Patterson, 1980) whose existence was never proposed by reading theorists working with normals.

Recently, cognitive neuropsychological research was attempted in fields for which detailed models of normal performance were not available. Models of writing and spelling (e.g. Morton, 1982), and calculation (e.g. Sartori, Roncato, Riumiata, & Maso, 1985) have been put forward using mainly data from pathological cognitive processes. The logic underlying the use of neurological data for model-building purposes, which makes extensive use of dissociations between symptoms or tasks and error analysis, is therefore of great importance and will be the argument of this paper.

Cognitive psychology and cognitive neuropsychology make strong assumptions about the modular organisation of the mind. In other words, a given complex mental process is thought to be constituted of more elementary components, one independent from the others. This basic assumption permits us to build computationally explicit models of cognitive processes that should be able to explain not only the whole range of normal performance, within a given domain, but also pathological behaviour, by means of appropriate functional "lesions" to the model. It has been argued, however, in the old times (e.g. Flourens, 1824) and more recently (e.g. Fodor, 1983) that not all cognitive processes may be studied with this way of theorising.

Caramazza (1984b) directly addresses the theoretical problem of relating neuropsychological data to theories of cognitive functioning.

His principal claims are based on the following assumptions:

1. "A set of observations E(i) ... constitute relevant evidence in support of hypothesis H... in model M provided that E(i) can be derived computationally from H in M..."
2. "A set of *pathological* observations E′(i) is evidence for M just in case it is possible to computationally derive E′(i) from M and L(i); where L(i) is a complex hypothesis about the locus of damage to a functional architecture...."

Caramazza observes that the postulated functional lesions L(i) within model M cannot be specified independently of E′(i), the neuropsychological data. E′(i) is, in fact, used to pin down those L(i) that, in M, permit one to derive E′(i). This framework is used by the author to show that studies with groups of patients are not useful tools for answering questions about models of cognitive functioning.

In the process that yields to the specification of model M, neuropsychologists use patterns of pathological data from several patients (E′(i)). Progressive adjustments on the characteristics of M lead to models from which, with the postulation of appropriate L(i), a large amount of pathological data may be derived. A set of E′(i) that constitutes a *double dissociation* is generally considered of great theoretical interest (e.g. Coltheart, 1985; Shallice, 1979) and in particular to have more relevance than a single dissociation. Caramazza thinks that these opinions about double dissociation are not well grounded. In particular, he claims that the assumption that double dissociation "does a better job of ruling out one of two alternative functional architectures than some other dissociations" is "unmotivated" on the grounds of the two assumptions stated above.

THESIS DEFENDAE

In this paper the issue of the relation of patterns of pathological performance to models will be discussed. In particular we will present arguments about the type of inferences one can make about the characteristics of model M from patterns of performance and from error analysis—an argument that has not been directly addressed by Caramazza (1984b). We will see that the relevance of double and single dissociation depends on the question one wants to answer about model M. If the question is "Can we identify separate processing components?" the answer could be yes in certain conditions. We will try to argue that in this case the answer depends on the type of model M one is assuming. If M is a stage model, the answer to the previous question is yes; but if it is a distributed memory model, the answer is no.

Within the framework of stage models we will show that a double dissociation has a more direct relation with models M. On the contrary, a single dissociation can be derived at least from two classes of models. This means that a *double dissociation* permits us, at least in certain conditions and for certain problems that will be specified, direct inferences that are not possible with a single dissociation; in other words, the first is more useful in model identification. We will show that what is mentioned is relevant only within stage models and not, for example, within distributed memory models. In this case, both double and single dissociations do not unequivocally isolate independent processes.

Other problems in relating models to data, such as error classification and partial impairment of performance, will be discussed.

We would like to distinguish within model M between *processing components* and *procedures*. Hereafter the term *processing component* will refer to an unspecified set of procedures, whereas *procedures* will denote a number of specified algorithms that perform the computation within a given processing component. A theorist may, in principle, make predictions from an architecture of processing components without specifying the procedures; this is frequently seen, for example, in neurocognitive theories of dyslexia. Error analysis seems more useful in specifying *procedures* than processing components. Error classification and error analysis seem to depend directly on model M and functional lesions L(i). Therefore, one error-classification system that is significant for a given model could not be significant for another.

DISSOCIATIONS

Double Dissociation

In this and in the following paragraph we will discuss the possibility of using single and double dissociation for drawing inferences of independence about underlying processing components. All the arguments are based on the assumption that model M is a stage model. In stage models, the information processed by a given stage does not pass to the following stage until all the computations are performed. Although the term *processing component* is general, the word *stage* refers to a processing component with the characteristics mentioned earlier.

Consider four patients performing two different tasks, A and B. Suppose patient 1 is perfect in both A and B, patient 2 is perfect in A and null in B, patient 3 is null in A and perfect in B, and patient 4 is null in both tasks. If we assume a model in which components are stages, it is clear that finding patients of type 1, 2, 3, and 4 is evidence for the existence of two distinct processes underlying tasks A and B. In practice, performance is rarely perfect or null but varies continuously within this range. Is the same conclusion also valid in this case?

Under some conditions, dissociations of performance may be explained as a consequence of the behaviour of a single processing component. It is frequently taken for granted that processes demand processing resources that are available in limited amounts. Those who think that many mental operations are automatic (e.g. Shiffrin & Schneider, 1977) generally believe, as well, that there are other operations that require processing resources. Suppose that a given stage has limited resources (e.g. Norman & Bobrow, 1975); in this case, reduction in performance could be the consequence of reduction of resources because of brain damage or computational difficulty of the task or stimulus degradation. It is therefore important to pin down those conditions in which dissociations may be unequivocally interpreted as evidence of separate processing components.

This has been done by Shallice (1979) who showed that finding patients of type 1, 2, 3, and 4 ensures that A and B are controlled by two different processing systems. This seems true not only when performance is perfect or null but also when there is a significantly large discrepancy in patient's performance (for example when a patient of type 3 is 70% accurate in task

A and 15% accurate in task B, whereas a patient of type 4 is 15% and 70% accurate, respectively).

We have just seen that a double dissociation ensures that two different processing stages are used in task A and B. But what can the double dissociation tell us about the structural organisation of these stages? Are they organised serially or in parallel?

It is clear that two stages that are in parallel can cause a double dissociation, but is the converse true? In other words, may every double dissociation be interpreted as evidence for two parallel stages?

Consider, for example, the double dissociation evidence for a serial organisation of stages X1 and X2. Suppose that X1 is the first stage and X2 the second. If the component X1 is greatly impaired, no activation of X2 can be observed, and therefore no overt behaviour is possible. But this contradicts the fact that patients of type 4 can be observed, and shows that a double dissociation cannot be produced by two independent serial stages.

Furthermore, consider the following example:

task A and B are multi-stage tasks, i.e. tasks that involve more than a single stage;
task A is performed by stages X1, X2; and
task B is performed by stages X1, X3.

In this case, the double dissociation does not ensure that all the stages are in parallel but rather *that at least two stages among those involved in performing tasks A and B are independent and that these stages are in parallel.*

Note here that a parallel circuit like the one underlying the double dissociation is equivalent to a logical disjunction (*or*).

Single Dissociation

A single dissociation is observed when patients of types 1, 2, and 3 or 1, 2, and 4 are reported. First, it is important to point out under what conditions a single dissociation between tasks or symptoms can be evidence for at least two independent processing components.

In fact, a single dissociation can be easily the consequence of resource confoundings. If task B is more difficult, it requires more computational resources than A; a patient, therefore, could show a better performance of A than B simply because B requires more resources than A and not because A and B have two underlying independent processing stages.

Intuitively, it appears that a single dissociation of tasks A and B that is interpreted as a consequence of independent processing components may be explained by a serial organisation of the dissociated stages (X1 and X2).

In fact, if both stages are intact, we will have a patient of type 1. If both stages or only X1 are disrupted, we will have a patient of type 2. Finally, a patient of type 3 will be observed if stage X1 is intact and X2 deteriorated (with the assumption that X1 is the first stage and X2 the second). A patient correctly performing B but not A will never be observed because information never arrives to X2 if X1 is impaired.

It is important here to note that a serial circuit that predicts a single dissociation is equivalent to the logical disjunction $\wedge$ (*and*).

But if two serial stages when systematically disrupted give rise to what here is called single dissociation, is it true that every single dissociation we observe will indicate that two stages are serial?

Assume that stage X1 performs a computation on stimulus set A and stage X2 on stimulus set B. Furthermore, assume that A is a sub-set (included in) B ($A \subset B$). To this relation, which is expressed in terms of set theory, corresponds the logical operator of implication (X1 can be X2). But this expressed in disjunctive normal form (logical operator $\wedge$, $\vee$, $\sim$ and can describe every circuit). In a serial circuit the information does not flow when X1 is disrupted and X2 is functioning (if X1 is the first stage and X2 the second). A parallel circuit can, on the contrary, easily handle the previously mentioned possibility. In conclusion, a single dissociation with one stage that processes a sub-set of the stimuli processed by the other stage cannot be explained by a serial circuit but by a parallel circuit.

An example of this exception to seriality of stages is the single dissociation of regular word and non-word reading in acquired dyslexia. It is possible to observe patients who can read regular words (which are processed both lexically and non-lexically in parallel) and non-words (which are read only non-lexically) with the same amount of accuracy and it is possible to find patients who can read regular words but no non-words. Until now, no one has observed the opposite dissociation (non-words good and regular words very poor), and probably a patient like this will never be observed. Two mechanisms for pronouncing letter strings have been hypothesised. The first, non-lexical, handles both regular words and non-words, whereas the second, lexical, handles all kinds of words—regular and irregular. But this latter mechanism processes a sub-set of the stimuli processed by the first mechanism. This is a case in which conclusions of seriality on the grounds of a single dissociation would be wrong. And, in fact, researchers have hypothesised two parallel stages for lexical and non-lexical reading (see Coltheart, 1978).

There is at least another case in which drawing a conclusion of complete independence on the ground of a single dissociation may be wrong. Let us assume that we have two tasks, A and B. To perform A only, stage X1 is involved, whereas to perform B, stages X1 and X2 are necessary. Let us assume, furthermore, that patients of type 1, 2, and 3 are observable. If we draw a conclusion of independence of tasks A and B and of stages that control those tasks, we will draw the conclusion that stage X1 is independent of stage X1 + X2. An example would be the following: Task A is matching upper and lower case letters, and task B is naming letters aloud. Although task A may be considered implicating only the letter-identification stage, task B contains at least identification plus articulation. Suppose that we find a patient who can perform upper and lower case matching but who cannot name letters aloud. Inferring that matching upper and lower case letters and naming aloud are performed by completely independent stages would be wrong.

The type of inference one can make from single dissociation seems to depend on the stages involved in each task. With respect to tasks A and B, there is the possibility that one or more stages are commonly used by each task or that no stages are in common. The first possibility has been mentioned before. The simplest case is when task A has stage X1, and task B has stages X1 and X2. *The single dissociation cannot be interpreted as evidence of complete independence between all the stages but as evidence that X1 is independent of X2.* Furthermore, the seriality of stages X1 and X2, with the first stage being the one in common to both tasks, is the consequence of a single dissociation of the two tasks.

When the two tasks have no stage in common, the inference of seriality could not be true if X1 and X2 are in parallel and only a one-way dissociation is observable for neuroanatomical reasons.

It is important to note that there can exist two stages with serial connections and with parallel accesses.

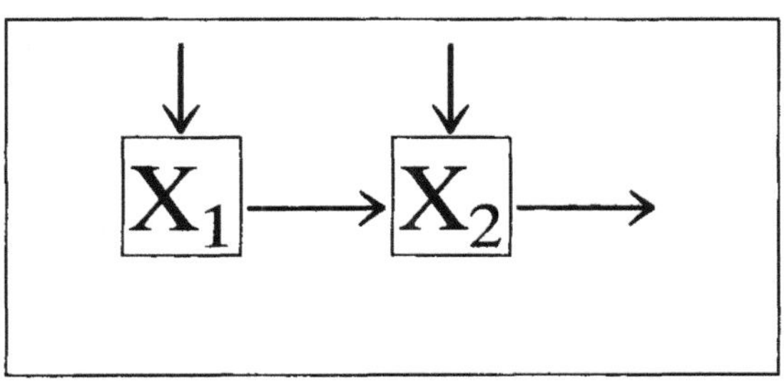

FIG 1 Diagrammatic example of two stages connected serially to one another that have parallel accesses.

In this case an accurate selection of tasks may identify this architecture. For this purpose we need tasks A and B with X1 in common, and tasks A and C with no common stages, and C with the stage that B has not in common with A. A single dissociation between A and B and a double dissociation between C and D permit us to identify this structure. This logic is used, for example, when researchers look for the role of articulation in reading. The articulatory stage is a late one and is preceded by a number of other stages in reading aloud. To verify if the failure in reading aloud may be attributed to an articulation deficit, an independent access to the articulatory stage is looked for and tested (generally repetition).

It is impossible to identify unequivocally two separate processing stages by means of a single dissociation. Sometimes, fortunately, it is possible to devise appropriate tasks so that the two postulated processing components may be accessed independently of one another by means of other tasks, as in the last example.

Processing Stages

Until now a processing stage has been considered, for simplicity, a unit. However, probably it should be split into three different parts (e.g. Caramazza & Berndt, 1983): (1) a set of procedures that perform the computation; (2) a code over which the computations are initiated; and (3) a working area where partial and final computation are stored.

If we consider two single-stage tasks (i.e. tasks that require only one processing stage) we can have two different codes and the same set of procedures (presumably an example of this case could be matching synonyms in auditory and visual presentation), or the same code and two different sets of procedures (performing sums with or without carriage). Some authors have hypothesised that every code has its own working area (e.g. Caramazza & Berndt, 1983). This assumption surely restricts the possible combinations in locating a functional deficit but requires some empirical evidence in support. A common general-purpose working area could be, for example, dynamically allocated by two different stages. Sharing a common working area could explain, for example, a resource-limited process.

If we observe a dissociation between single-stage tasks that have different codes and working space, this could be caused by any of the 2*2*2 = 8 possibilities. It is even more complicated when we want to interpret a dissociation between tasks with many serial stages (e.g. synonym-matching or homophone-matching tasks). Here the possible loci of impairment rise dramatically. On some occasions, however, it is possible to localise the functional deficit. Consider when two sets of procedures are applied to the same code, as in performing additions and subtractions. If we find a double dissociation between addition and subtraction and we make the "one code–one working area assumption", then the dissociation can be attributed to a selective impairment of the procedures.

In general, it seems that a successful fractionation in stages and within stages requires "pure tasks" (i.e. tasks that require the use of a few well-defined stages) and converging evidence coming from different tasks with and without common stages.

Problems of Minimisation

Generally models of cognitive functioning are considered to be satisfactory if they are the simplest (or most economical) of possible models.

Consider the following formulae (which correspond to models):

(X1 ∨ X2). According to what has been discussed previously, this corresponds to two stages with parallel accesses.
(X1 ∨ X2) ∨ (~ X1 ∧ X2), which corresponds to the diagram of Fig. 1, has two parallel stages with serial connections.

These two models are logically equivalent and a unique double dissociation does not permit us to distinguish between the direct activation of X2 and the one through X1.

The model in Fig. 1 can schematise the organisation of the memory system with X1 = short-term memory and X2 = long-term memory. The seriality of X1 and X2 is a common requirement by theorists of memory, but neuropsychological data have shown that X1 and X2 can be accessed independently of one another (patient K.F. by Warrington & Shallice, 1971). The use of a double dissociation captures only the parallel access of X1 and X2. This dissociation alone cannot, therefore, distinguish between the two representations. To identify the serial connection between X1 and X2, we can, however, devise two tasks with X1 as common stage and look for a single dissociation (as shown previously).

Partial impairment

An assumption underlying the concept of stages used here is that they function as switches (Sternberg's (1969) notion of stages). If the stage is functioning well, information is transmitted; otherwise nothing happens. Furthermore, the behaviour of a given stage is independent of the other stages' functionings. But under this conception how can a partial impairment (when the patient's performance is poor but not null) arise?

An easy answer to this question is derived from the assumption that at stage level or at level of stage components (codes, procedures, and working space) the representation is distributed (see the following paragraph).

Can we explain the degradation in performance without assuming the distributed representation of stage sub-components? Imagine that a stage can be represented by a set of sub-stages (e.g. stage A (X1, X2, X3, X4)), such as the input logogen system, which contains a number of logogens corresponding to the words. If the sub-stages are working in parallel, perfect accuracy will be observed in the perfect functioning of all the single sub-stages, whereas degraded performance will be observed in the total impairment of one or more sub-stages. In serial sub-stages, a single impairment is sufficient to abolish the performance completely.

Distributed Memory Systems

All the arguments previously presented are based on the assumption that two different stages are separate entities that perform a set of computations separately from one another. Recently (e.g. Hinton & Anderson, 1981), an alternative conceptual framework has received increasing attention. According to the distributed memory models, two different tasks, A and B, may not be performed by means of different stages, but rather by a single set of elements with different levels of activation. Suppose the existence of three elements x, y, and z (which may be, for example, groups of neurones); task A may be performed with such levels of activations as $x = 80\%$, $y = 20\%$, $z = 80\%$, whereas task B may be performed with $x = 20\%$, $y = 80\%$, $z = 20\%$.

The idea that functions are not housed in discrete elements but distributed over a number of elements that perform different functions is not new (e.g. Flourens, 1824; Lashley, 1950), and recent developments have permitted a computational approach to the problem.

Can a distributed memory model explain a double dissociation? Wood (1977) using a model by Anderson, Silverstein, Ritz, & Jones (1977) has shown that this is possible by simulating the effect of lesions to the model. This particular behaviour of distributed systems may be easily understood by using a simple matrix model as in Fig. 2.

Input vectors			*Matrix*				
A	B						
1	0		10	5	2	6	row 1
1	1		9	6	5	8	2
0	1		8	13	2	13	3
1	0		6	2	8	10	4
			24	14	16	20	*Threshold*
		A′	1			1	*Output vectors*
		B′	0			1	

FIG 2 A simplified version of a distributed memory model. The stimuli (A and B) activate a net of neurone-like units. Responses are coded as a profile of activations (A′ and B′).

Elements of this matrix model of distributed memory cf. Hinton, 1981 are: (1) input vectors, which represent the stimulus; (2) a matrix, which corresponds to the cognitive structure; (3) thresholds; (4) output vectors, which represent the response. Input and output vectors elements can assume values of 0 and 1. Each column of the matrix corresponds to a unit that has four input lines (which correspond to the rows). The output of a unit is generated by adding up all the values in its column that are in rows that have 1 as input. An input vector with 1 in a given row activates the elements of the matrix of the corresponding row, whereas no activation corresponds to a 0. A 1 is attributed to the output vector only if the sum of the activated elements of a given column (unit) is larger than the corresponding value in the threshold.

Take, for example, how the stimulus pattern A gives rise to the response A′. A activates rows 1, 2, and 4 of the matrix. The sums of the activated elements of columns 1, 2, 3, and 4 are respectively 25, 13, 15, and 24. The units with values above the thresholds (which are 24, 14, 16, and 20) are columns 1 and 4. From this follows the output vector 1, 0, 0, 1, which corresponds to A′.

If the lesion in a patient reduces the activity of the element in row 1, column 1 from 10 to 1, the patient performs B correctly but not A So if in another subject the lesions involve the elements in row 2, column 4 and row 3, column 4 by reducing their activity respectively from 8 to 4 and from 13 to 6, this person will perform A correctly but not B. This shows that a double dissociation, in principle, does not require two independent processing components. This conclusion, in fact, follows only if a stage model is assumed.

One important characteristic of distributed systems concerns single dissociation. Every single dissociation, in fact, has parallel inputs. Modular systems may, on the contrary, have both parallel or serial organisation. It is possible, however, to mimic this characteristic of modular systems by postulating the existence of series of stages that are in themselves distributed (see Hinton, 1981).

ERROR CLASSIFICATION

Single and double dissociations refer to patterns of selective decrease in the patient's performance. They are relevant to answer questions about the architecture of processing components (within stage models) but, as already mentioned, they do not permit us to draw inferences about the *procedures* of a given processing component.

Qualitative analysis of the patient's failure in performing a given task is a way of testing hypothesis about procedures. Whenever a wrong response is produced by a patient there must be a transparent modification of the relevant set of procedures that give rise to this error. But how can errors in performance be categorised? Take, for example, the error classification in dyslexia research; we find categories such as visually similar words, visually dissimilar words, morphological errors, semantic errors, etc. Even if one has the impression that categories could be defined at an empirical level, it seems that every error classification refers to a model for which a crucial processing component and its procedures must be specified at some level. For example, suppose that a patient is reading the word *andare* (to go) as *andato* (he has gone). This error could be classified as either *visual* or *morphological* (if semantic errors are scored only in the presence of a visual dissimilarity between stimulus and response). If one classifies it as morphological, there is the implicit assumption that there is a morphological processing of the printed word and that the procedures applied to the string yield, as a result, a root morpheme plus a suffix.

Consider another example in the field of number-processing disorders. Some authors (e.g. Sartori et al., 1985) have observed patients whose predominant errors in reading arabic numerals is of the type *507*→ "57". This "zero-deletion error" has been interpreted as syntactic in nature. This error classification, however, is grounded only if a model of the *procedures* used to build verbal numerals from arabic numerals is specified.

Suppose that reading *507* requires the following steps:

1. Count the number of digits in the arabic numeral. In this example the result is three.
2. Derive a number (semantic representation) by multiplying the first digit on the left by 100. If the second digit is 0, add the third digit to the previous result. The final result of this step is the representation $(5 \times 100) + 7$.
3. Produce the verbal numeral from the number by applying the following rule: Produce the word corresponding to the constituent numbers of the abstract representation from left to right. The final result will be "*cinque cento sette*" ("five hundred and seven").

In this model, syntactic rules are applied in steps 2 and 3, and the only way of producing "57" in response to *507* is to make a mistake in the first step by counting the constituent digits as 2 instead of 3 and consequently to activate, as second step, a rule other than the correct one. Therefore, within this model the "zero-deletion error" could not be a theoretically relevant category, and in any case, it is not a syntactic error.

An error category, therefore, can be meaningful for a given model M and meaningless for model M′, but meaningfulness can be verified in M only if the error can be derived from the sufficiently specified procedures by postulating appropriated malfunctionings.

Error classification is therefore model dependent and as errors depend on the characteristics of the procedures, their analysis is relevant to answer questions of the type "Can the set of procedures for processing component X(i) predict errors of the type e(i)?"

CONCLUSIONS

In relating models to performance breakdown, there are at least three distinct types of question a theorist has to answer:

1. Are separate processing components in model M essential to predict a dissociation?
2. If the answer to the previous question is yes, does a given architecture of these components predict the pathological performance E′(i)?
3. Is a postulated set of procedures capable of predicting a given error?

If a stage model is assumed, then single and double dissociations are relevant to answer questions of type 1. This is not true in the case of distributed memory models. In particular, with reference to question 1, a double dissociation between symptoms or tasks is always predicted by separate processing stages, and conversely, a double dissociation may always be interpreted as evidence for separation of at least two processing stages. And with reference to questions of type 2, the separated stages that give rise to a double dissociation always have a parallel access. If at least one stage is used in common by tasks A and B, a single dissociation means that two stages are in series. This conclusion needs to be tested against resource confoundings devising other tasks with independent access to the postulated processing components.

We have seen that a parallel circuit is equivalent to the logical disjunction, whereas a serial circuit is equivalent to a logical conjunction. Furthermore, neuropsychological data permit us to hypothesise the existence of inhibitory stages where information flows if a given stage is not functioning (the letter-by-letter reading strategy in pure alexia could be considered an example) are equivalent to the logical negation.

We know from propositional calculus and from the logic of circuits that every network can be represented by means of the previously mentioned logical operators (see Mendelson, 1970). It seems, therefore, that cognitive neuropsychological investigation, under the assumptions previously mentioned, can, in principle, give exhaustive representations of the cognitive network in terms of the processing components.

All the previous conclusions are valid only under the assumption that model M is of a stage type. Distributed memory models may predict both single and double dissociations without postulating separate processing components. Incidentally, it is interesting to note that methods developed in cognitive psychology are very powerful in studying serial stages (see Meyer, Schvaneveldt, & Ruddy, 1974; Sternberg, 1969) but not parallel stages. On the contrary, in cognitive neuropsychology double dissociation is a powerful tool for isolating parallel stages, whereas the identification of serial stages is not as easy and is limited by a number of constraints.

Errors are relevant to answer questions of the following type:

4. Can model M with certain processing components and procedures predict, assuming a certain set of functional lesions, the production of the type of error under consideration?

From this it follows that there is no way of classifying errors without relating them to model M and to functional lesions L(i). An open question is whether errors arise from the functioning of a sub-set of the original procedures, from the misapplication of a given procedure, or from a new procedure with a transparent relationship to M.

ACKNOWLEDGEMENTS

In writing this paper I have appreciated the observations on the topic by A. Caramazza, M. Coltheart, R. Job, and T. Shallice.

REFERENCES

Anderson, J. A., Silverstein, J. W., Ritz, S. A., & Jones, R. S. (1977) Distinctive features, categorical perception and probability learning: Some applications of a neural model. *Psychological Review*, *84*, 413–451.

Caramazza, A. (1984a) The logic of neuropsychological research and the problem of patient classification in aphasia. *Brain and Language*, *21*, 9–20.

Caramazza, A. (1984b) On drawing inferences about the structure of normal cognitive systems from analysis of patterns of impaired performance: The case of single-patient studies. *Brain and Cognition*.

Caramazza, A. & Berndt, R. (1983) A multi-component deficit view of agrammatic Broca's aphasia. In M. L. Kean (Ed.), *Agrammatism*. New York: Academic Press.

Coltheart, M. (1978) Lexical access in simple reading tasks. In G. Underwood (Ed.), *Strategies of Information Processing*. New York: Academic Press.

Coltheart, M. (1982) The psycholinguistic analysis of acquired dyslexia. *Philosophical Transactions of the Royal Society*, *298*, 151–164.

Coltheart, M. (1985) Cognitive neuropsychology and the study of reading. *Attention and Performance*, *XI*.

Flourens, P. J. (1824) *Recherches esperimentales*. Paris.

Fodor, J. (1983) *The modularity of mind*. Cambridge, Mass: MIT Press.

Hinton, G. (1981) Implementing semantic network in parallel hardware. In G. Hinton & J. Anderson (Eds.), *Parallel models of associative memory*. Hillsdale, N.J.: Lawrence Erlbaum Associates Inc.

Hinton, G. & Anderson, J. (Eds.) (1981) *Parallel models of associative memory*. Hillsdale, N.J.: Lawrence Erlbaum Associates Inc.

Lashley, K. (1950) In search for the engram. *Symposia of the Society of Experimental Biology*, *4*, 454–482.

Mendelson, T. (1970) *Logic of circuits*. McGraw-Hill. Shaum series.

Meyer, D. E., Schvaneveldt, R. W., & Ruddy, M. G. (1974) Functions of graphemic and phonemic codes in visual word recognition. *Memory and Cognition*, *2*, 309–321.

Morton, J. (1982) Disintegrating the lexicon: An information-processing approach. In E. Mehler, E. Walker, & M. Garrett (Eds.), *Perspectives in Mental Representation*, Hillsdale, N.J.: Lawrence Erlbaum Associates Inc.

Morton, J. & Patterson, K. (1980) A new attempt at an interpretation, or, an attempt at a new interpretation. In M. Coltheart, K. Patterson, & J. Marshall (Eds.), *Deep dyslexia*. London: Routledge & Kegan Paul.

Norman, D. & Bobrow, D. J. (1975) On data limited and resource limited processes. *Cognitive Psychology*, *7*, 44–64.

Sartori, G., Roncato, S., Riumiati, R., & Maso, A. (1985) Number processing and dyscalculia. *Cognitive Neuropsychology Conference*. Venezia, March 1985.

Schwartz, M., Saffran, E. M., & Marin, O. S. M. (1980) Fractionating the reading process in dementia: Evidence for word specific print-to-sound associations. In M. Coltheart, K. Patterson, & J. Marshall (Eds.), *Deep dyslexia*. London, Routledge & Kegan Paul.

Shallice, T. (1979) Case study approach in neuropsychological research. *Journal of Clinical Neuropsychology*, *37*, 187–192.

Shiffrin, R. M. & Schneider, W. (1977) Controlled and automatic human information processing: II. Perceptual learning, automatic attending and a general theory. *Psychological Review*, *84*, 127–154.

Sternberg, S. (1969) The discovery of processing stages: Extensions of Donders method. In W. G. Koster (Ed.), *Attention and Performance. Volume II*, Amsterdam: North Holland.

Warrington, E. K. & Shallice, T. (1971) The selective impairment of auditory verbal short-term memory. *Brain*, *92*, 885–896.

Wood, C. (1977) Variations on a theme of Lashley: Lesion experiments on the neural model of Anderson, Silverstein, Ritz and Jones. *Psychological Review*, *85*, 582–591.

4 Observations on Theoretical Models in Neuropsychology of Language

D. Parisi and C. Burani
Istituto di Psicologia del C.N.R., Rome, Italy

INTRODUCTION

Neuropsychology has made considerable progress recently and it is one of the few areas of psychological research where a sense of continuity and progress is clearly felt. The study of acquired dyslexias has been the starting point of the new cognitive neuropsychology (Coltheart, 1985), but the approach is rapidly being extended to the dysgraphias, developmental dyslexias, the agnosias, and other linguistic and cognitive disturbances (Ellis, 1982a; 1984).

The success of what we have called the new neuropsychology appears to be the result of four methodological choices:

1. The indepth and rigorous study of single patients (Caramazza, 1986; Shallice, 1979).
2. An explicit recognition of the feasibility of a completely functional approach to the study of mind, independent of the brain (Mehler, Morton, & Jusczyk, 1984).
3. A fruitful exchange of methods, data, and models between neuropsychology and cognitive psychology.
4. The use of "information-processing" models of cognitive abilities (Shallice, 1981).

However, recent literature gives the impression that the new neuropsychology has reached its azimuth and that its progress has slowed somewhat. We consider the case of the investigation of reading disorders as typical in this regard.

From the beginning, cognitive neuropsychology has aimed at explaining acquired dyslexias in terms of impairments to components of a functional model of skilled reading. This approach has been fruitful for both psychology and the neuropsychology of language. The adoption of a unitary approach to the study of both impaired and normal reading behaviour has produced convergent evidence for a theoretical account of the cognitive processes under investigation (Martin & Caramazza, 1986), leading to a specification of the current models of reading that were first developed to account for the performance of normal subjects in experimental tasks.

In the early investigations it was very fruitful to adopt "dual route" models of reading for interpreting abnormal reading behaviours. Patients were described who could read aloud words and non-words relying on just the extralexical route, and others who could read words almost perfectly through the lexical route although the extralexical route was seriously impaired. The reading performance of these patients constituted clear evidence for the theoretical partition—lexical v. non-lexical reading processes—in that they showed a functional dissociation between the two.

Within such an approach, additional acquired dyslexic syndromes were delineated and interpreted in relation to models of normal reading (Marshall & Newcombe, 1973; Patterson, 1981). The same happened later for the study of spelling disorders: Acquired dysgraphic syndromes were defined and related to dual route models of writing (Ellis, 1982b).

By now the gross distinction between lexical v. non-lexical reading and spelling has been demonstrated, and the principal syndromes accurately described. What appears to be more difficult is accounting for further patterns of disturbed performance. In the last few years accurate investigations of new cases and symptoms and attempts at giving an account also of "mixed" cases not clearly interpretable as any of the acknowledged syndromes have led to the specification of sub-components inside a single processing route.

When trying to describe sub-components, however, it became evident, at least to some investigators in the field, that it was possible to obtain the same symptoms from functional lesions at several different locations inside one route (Coltheart, 1984; 1986; Ellis, 1985). Hence, there is an acknowledgement on the part of these researchers of the difficulty in individuating the precise location of a given symptom in terms of the model.

The solution to this difficulty is sometimes found in the development of new experimental tasks, which should be more adequate for identifying the component(s) responsible for certain impaired performance. What is sought is a refinement of experimental tools and the collection of new data, whereas the validity of information-processing models as a theoretical tool is not questioned.

We think, instead, that even if the development of new more specific tasks is undoubtedly necessary, giving priority to the construction of experimental tasks and the collection of new data highlights the "data-driven" character of the theoretical models currently used in neuropsychology. To be more explicit, we think that the main reason for the difficulties encountered by the new neuropsychology lies mainly in point (3) mentioned earlier. It is unquestionable that the information-processing models represent clear progress with respect to the modelling tools previously available to psychologists. However, they are still very limited theoretical instruments. More specifically, we think that far more adequate instruments of investigation are provided by a computational approach. What we maintain and are going to discuss in the subsequent sections is the following: If psychology and neuropsychology are really to advance our understanding of the mind, information-processing models must be replaced by computational models.

SHORTCOMINGS OF INFORMATION-PROCESSING MODELS

Information-processing models have four basic shortcomings:

1. They are insufficiently specified.
2. Their name notwithstanding, they are static models.
3. They are too "data-driven".
4. They make acritical use of notions drawn from the discipline of linguistics.

In this section, we will discuss each of these points in detail. Our discussion will be limited to the cognitive neuropsychology of language.

1. Information-processing models are usually represented as labelled boxes connected by arrows. Two complaints can be raised with respect to these representations:

1. The content of the boxes is not sufficiently specified.
2. The "grammar" of the boxes-and-arrows models is not clear.

Quite often a box is assigned little more than a label to indicate its content and its role in a specific task or ability. Examples taken from current models of reading and writing are "Abstract Letter Identities" (ALIs) (Coltheart, 1981; Howard, 1986), "Visual (or Auditory) Input (or Output) Logogen System" (Morton, 1980); "Semantic/Cognitive System"

(Morton & Patterson, 1980); "Phonological (or Graphemic) Output Buffer" (Caramazza, Miceli, & Villa, 1986; Miceli, Silveri, & Caramazza, 1986; Morton, 1980).

Current accounts of the meaning of these labels still leave a number of theoretical questions open: What kind of information is contained in an ALI box or in a Visual Logogen Box? How are the systems of ALI(s) or Visual Input Logogens internally organised? What is in the cognitive system? and so on.

Although some components like the Cognitive System have seldom been discussed in detail, attempts to go beyond simple definition or labelling and to describe the content and role of other boxes have been made (for a good example of discussion of the role of the Output Phonological Buffer, see, e.g., Caramazza et al., 1986). However, these attempts have been too sparse and unsystematic.

In any case, what appears to be necessary is to go further "inside" each box and to give really detailed descriptions of how they function. This must be specified with reference to the type of task in which the box is employed, because it is not obvious that a given component functions in the same way independently of the task in which it is involved.

Sometimes, the lack of detail and explicitness in the description of a component is circumvented by introducing an additional box to explain certain behaviour (e.g., Caramazza et al., 1986; Howard, 1986). This way of proceeding has received so many objections that the deprecatory term "boxology" has been created to refer to it. But if one avoids constructing circular or excessively powerful models, the proliferation of boxes cannot be considered an evil in itself in so far as it is an attempt to distinguish sub-components and sub-processes, memory requirements, and so on. (An example of good "boxology" in this sense is Ellis's (1982b) model of single word processing in different tasks: reading, writing, repetition, copy.) The real issue is not the proliferation of boxes, but the lack of detail as to their content and functioning.

At a more general level, the "grammar" of the box-and-arrows models, i.e. the rules according to which these models should be constructed and interpreted, remains fuzzy. What "can" be in a box? What "can" a box do? Are there different types of boxes? What does an arrow stand for? Are there different types of arrows?

Looking at the published models of reading and writing one is confused at the variety of functions that appear to be implicitly assigned to boxes. "Visual Analysis" seems to be a process, the process of analysing and extracting visual features from the stimulus, whereas "Abstract Letter Identities" and "Visual Input Logogens" appear to be a store of permanent information about how single letters and words should, more or less abstractly, look like. However, Input Logogens are also characterised as "evidence-collecting devices" or "word detectors", and the component that produces ALIs is also characterised as a system of letter identifiers/detectors "...which are abstract in the sense that a single identifier responds to all fonts and cases of a particular letter..." (Coltheart, 1986). Hence, these components appear to be active processing mechanisms rather than stores of permanent information. On the other hand, "Phonological (or Graphemic) Input (or Output) Buffers" seem to be temporary stores of information.

The general problem appears to be that a variety of different aspects that should be clearly separated one from the other are confused within a box: permanent information used by the system to carry out the task, procedural knowledge about how to proceed in carrying out the task, the actual process of task execution, and temporary memory resources necessary for the task. Again, sparse suggestions for clarification have been advanced. Caramazza et al. (1986) suggest a distinction between "computational components" that "take as input one type of representation and give as output a different type of representation" and "buffer systems ... that hold representations of a particular type for further processing". Howard (1986) attempts to specify a memory requirement (Graphemic Buffer) for the functioning of the ALI box.

Some attempts have been made outside neuropsychology to specify some of these components. For example, the role of "Buffer Memory" has been analysed by Schaffer (1973, 1975, 1976) in relationship to typing and copy typing tasks. More specifically, Schaffer distinguishes two buffer memories in copy typing: an input buffer where a word is represented "...as a spelling string of letter tokens" and an output buffer where the word is represented as a "...string of response commands" (Schaffer, 1976, p. 383). However, Schaffer's proposals do not seem to have been taken into account in neuropsychology—and then, it is not obvious that memory requirements do not vary with different tasks.

In any case, these attempts at specifying the proposed theoretical models do not go much beyond the statements made earlier. A number of ambiguities remain and the processing steps and memory requirements are not sufficiently detailed.

Observations of the same kind apply to arrows in boxes-and-arrows models. An arrow may indicate a flow of information from one stage of a process to a successive stage, or it may indicate what must be done next, or the fact that one box (a process box) uses the content of another box (a permanent information store box), or finally it may indicate a procedure for transforming the content of one box into the content of another box.

2. A second limitation of information-processing models is that, their name notwithstanding, they are quite often static models. They do not really describe a process, i.e. a dynamic sequence of steps that leads from a

starting point to an end point, but only "components", "stages", "structures" that are part of a process. Even in the case in which a model specifies the "levels" that are involved in the execution of a task or the displaying of an ability, (a) it is not clear if these "levels" are to be interpreted as distinct sequential phases of a process, and in any case, (b) the operations that cause the process to go from one level to the successive level are not described.

An example of a rather static model that purports to be a model of a process and that has been applied to the study of aphasics' performance is Garrett's model for the production of sentences (Garrett, 1982). Garrett's model postulates various stages or levels in the process of producing a sentence (message level, functional level, positional level) and it describes the representations that are to be found at each level. However, the model does not say anything about the actual operations the speaker must execute in order to go from one stage to the successive one. It refers only to operations with such labels as "lexical identification", "selection of functional structures", "retrieval of lexical forms", etc.

This insufficient specification of the processing steps is likely to invalidate even the proposed subdivision of processing levels. Garrett supposes that there is an initial stage where the message to be conveyed is constructed. The process of message construction is based on "inferential processes" and is completely non-linguistic. Then, "procedures applied to the Message level representation construct the first language specific level of representation" (Garrett, 1982, p. 67), which is the functional level representation. As already noted, these procedures are not described but only labelled: (1) determination of the functional level structures; (2) meaning based lexical identification; (3) assignment of lexical items to functional structures.

Now, if we turn our attention to the actual process of producing a sentence, it is clear that the "message", i.e. the meaning of the sentence to be produced, cannot be considered as something given. In producing a sentence a speaker starts with a store of knowledge and one or more goals. On the basis of what the speaker knows and his current goals, a "message" is constructed, i.e. a sub-set of knowledge items is extracted or generated from the knowledge store. The problem is that this process of message construction cannot be separated from the process of assigning a lexicon (at least a content-word lexicon) and a syntax to the sentence. If one tries to develop a detailed procedural model of the *process* of producing a sentence, one may arrive at the conclusion (as we did, see Parisi & Giorgi, 1986) that (1) the syntax in a sentence-production system is distributed in the lexicon so that assignment of syntax and assignment of the (content-word) lexicon to the sentence to be produced cannot be separated (see also Bresnan, 1982); and (2) it is the syntax that is distributed in the lexicon that guides the "message-construction" process, so that the "message" level and the "functional" level cannot be separated. There is no separate, non-linguistic, level of message construction because it is the linguistic knowledge contained in the lexicon, including syntax, that ensures that the knowledge extracted or generated from the knowledge store (the "message") will constitute the meaning of a well-formed sentence of the target language.

This example shows that a model described statically as a set of "levels", "stages", "components" is not necessarily a partial but correct description of the actual process. When the static model is turned into a real processing model, the levels and components that have been postulated may turn out not to be those that really occur.

3. A third shortcoming of current models in neuropsychology is that they are too "data-driven". The theoretical models are developed *post factum* to account for observed behaviour, and successively modified on the basis of new data and empirical analyses. In this way, the scientific enterprise becomes overwhelmingly inductive and the advantages of the hypothetic–deductive method are largely missed. Theoretical models should be developed and elaborated on the basis of considerations of logic, consistency, completeness, and elegance in addition to suggestions from empirical evidence. Empirical evidence plays a role in verifying specific predictions based on the models and in suggesting ways of modifying these models.

Even experimental tasks can be improved upon using a non-data-driven approach. In order to construct the revealing tasks that are necessary to analyse the variety of impaired performance and that many feel to be still lacking, one must develop in advance a detailed theoretical model of the process underlying the target performance. This model should guide the researcher in discovering and constructing such tasks.

4. Finally, a fourth defect of the models used in the neuropsychology of language is that they very often appeal to notions and models drawn from linguistics. Quite obviously this happens only when linguistics has something to offer. For example, most work on dyslexias and dysgraphias does not rely very much on linguistics because this work is especially concerned with differences and relationships between oral and written language, and linguistics traditionally has not had much to say about oral v. written language. However, examples of use of notions derived from linguistics can be found also in the domain of reading and writing models. For instance, Venezky's (1970) correspondence rules for English orthography are generally used for describing the mechanism that translates graphemes into phonemes (Grapheme/Phoneme conversion system). Moreover, recent extensions of work on dyslexias and dysgraphias to the morphological organisation of the mental lexicon—or, better, lexicons—show the

usual reliance on linguistic notions like root, suffix, derivational v. inflexional endings, etc. (Caramazza, Miceli, Silveri, & Laudanna, 1985; Patterson, 1980).

A much heavier borrowing of concepts and models from linguistics occurs when the linguistic disturbances of interest touch on aspects of language that have actively been studied by linguists. This is typically the case for grammatical disturbances that neuropsychology is inevitably led to analyse and interpret in terms of the morphological and syntactic concepts used by linguists (Caplan, Baker, & Dehaut, 1985; Grodzinsky, 1984; Kean, 1979; Lapointe, 1983, 1985).

We have discussed elsewhere (Parisi, 1985, 1986) why linguistics should not be considered a theoretical tool by the neuropsychologist. Linguistics is concerned with linguistic competence, i.e. knowledge of language independent of the different tasks and abilities in which language is actually used. This implies that linguistic concepts and models cannot predict and explain some of the most useful and informative data the neuropsychologist is confronted with: dissociations of disturbances among different tasks and abilities. Linguistics can only assume a disruption of the underlying common competence, which would predict associations but no dissociations of observed disturbances. To predict and explain dissociations one must construct a model of what makes different tasks and abilities different—and this is outside the scope and interest of linguistics.

But even in the cases where linguistic concepts and models could be used, that is, in explaining associations of symptoms, these concepts may be of limited value. Linguistic concepts are purely descriptive, and they are used within static structural models that are developed on a restricted and very empirical basis: linguistic intuitions. Because neuropsychology deals with processes, it needs different types of concepts and models. A concept should be defined in terms of what an entity labelled with that concept actually does within a procedural model. A model must be a model of a specific process, i.e. a sequence of steps that produces a well-defined result. In other words, to analyse and explain the language disturbances he is confronted with, the neuropsychologist should use a variety of performance models and the concepts he needs should be defined within such models.

HOW TO OVERCOME THE SHORTCOMINGS OF INFORMATION-PROCESSING MODELS BY USING COMPUTATIONAL MODELS

We have discussed four limitations of theoretical models currently used by neuropsychologists. These limitations must be overcome for neuropsychology to make further progress, and we think that to overcome these limitations, information-processing models have to be replaced by computational models. In this section we will discuss some aspects of computational models that might contribute to overcome the limitations of information-processing models.

What takes place in the mind are processes. When someone uses his mental abilities to do something—in real life, in a laboratory, or in a hospital—a sequence of operations, i.e. a process, takes place in his mind. The best way to describe (understand) a process that takes place in a goal-directed system like the mind is to devise a computational model of the process. A computational model is a procedure that directs the system from the initial conditions (the input) to the end result of the process (the output) via a sequence of steps. (This is a very general description of a computational model that does not say anything on whether the "procedure" is implemented as a traditional sequential system or as a parallel connectionist system.) To be able to do something is to possess a procedure for doing it. Possessing (knowing) a procedure is a piece of more or less permanent information that a system can possess. This procedural knowledge is stored somewhere in the system. Executing the procedure, applying it in specific circumstances, however, requires two additional mental "resources". At certain points the procedure uses more static, "declarative" type of information, which is also permanently stored in the system. Furthermore, to execute the procedure a system must possess temporary stores where partial results can be kept for the time necessary for further processing.

To construct a procedural model of some specific task, activity, or ability, one must therefore specify:

1. A procedure that can accomplish the task.
2. The permanently stored "declarative" information that is used at various points of the procedure.
3. The working memory where the information being processed can be temporarily stored for the time interval necessary for its processing and which gives continuity to the process.

To specify a procedure (point (1) above), one must first specify the "performance range" of the procedure, i.e. what the inputs and the outputs of the procedure exactly are. For example, what physical variation of the input words a procedure for recognising spoken words can tolerate? Will a proposed procedure for producing sentences produce sentences containing pronouns, or is its output more limited? After the input and output performance range of the procedure has been specified, one must specify each step that comprises the procedure. One must describe precisely the operation (or operations) of each step and the information on which such an operation (or operations) must be carried out. This information can be permanently stored information or temporary information that results from previously executed steps of the procedure or, of course, input information.

Permanently stored "declarative" information (point (2) above) is specified by stating what its actual contents are and how the information is formally represented and organised. The same holds for information stored in the temporary working memories (point (3) above), with the additional requirement in this case that the properties of the memory store itself must be specified: How much information does it hold? for how much time? in which sensory-motor code? can the information be revived? how? etc.

A procedural model can be described at different levels of abstraction and detail. A natural way of progressing is to start from a gross description of the model and then progressively increase the detail and articulation of its parts until one can translate the model into a computer program. Expressing a procedural model in the form of a computer program and actually running the program has the obvious advantages of making sure that the model is complete, consistent, and sufficiently clear and detailed. This is why procedural and computational models tend to be equivalent.

We believe that constructing and using procedural/computational models can contribute to eliminating the four shortcomings noted above of the information-processing models currently used in neuropsychology.

First, procedural models, expressed as computer models, necessarily possess the precision and high level of detail that we found lacking in current neuropsychological models. Otherwise the model (the program) will not simply run on the computer. More specifically, for procedural models it is possible to specify their "grammar", i.e. a methodology for constructing and interpreting them. This is exactly what we have briefly attempted to do.

Second, procedural models are explicitly dynamic models of a process, specifying what is done, when, and with what results, for each step of the process. This ensures that in principle all the aspects of the process (activity, task, use of an ability) are covered by the model and that the proposed model, being a procedure, is actually capable of producing the expected performance.

With reference to the third defect of information-processing models, i.e. their data-driven character, it is obvious enough that computational models do not have this character. Quite to the contrary, the necessity of constructing complete and detailed models that actually run on a computer, enhances the hypothetical–deductive character of theory construction with greater reliance on logical considerations.

Fourth, procedural models make it possible and preferable not to borrow concepts and ideas from linguistics. Concepts used within procedural models are defined in terms of what an entity labelled with a given concept does in order to produce a desired performance. Because the properties of a performance vary with each performance, different concepts are necessary for procedural models describing different tasks or abilities (e.g. producing spontaneous speech, orally describing pictures, reading sentences, comparing oral sentences with pictures, judging the acceptability of oral sentences, reading single words, judging if an auditory stimulus is a word, etc.).

Such concepts are to be defined as part of the construction of a procedural model for each of these different tasks or abilities. Linguistic concepts, on the other hand, are defined within a single, uniform, abstract, competence model and, therefore, they are in principle not appropriate for describing and interpreting different tasks and abilities.

One must admit that the actual situation in computational linguistics is very often quite different in that many parsers and, more generally, computational models of language comprehension and production are based on grammars and do not attempt to define the concepts they need within the computational model itself. However, this is even less justified than the borrowing of concepts from linguistics in experimental psycholinguistics and neurolinguistics. In fact, computational linguistics has available richer and more powerful methodological and conceptual resources (from computer science, artificial intelligence, and the actual implementation of theories as computer programs) than experimental approaches and it should be able to define all the concepts it needs using these resources.

CONCLUSIONS

We have indicated some limitations of information-processing models currently used in cognitive neuropsychology and have made some suggestions as to how these limitations can be overcome if information-processing models are replaced by procedural/computational models. This is not to say that computational models do not have their own problems Perhaps the most serious problem of computational models is that even when a desired human performance, or its impaired version, has been successfully simulated on a computer, one can never be certain that the computer program performs in the same way as the human.

However, there are at least two ways in which one can deal with this problem. One is to enlarge progressively the performance range of the computational model so that more tasks and more detailed aspects of each task are reproduced by one and the same integrated model. If the performance range of a model is very restricted so that separate models are necessary for each task, it is quite possible that the computer and the human performance differ. On the other hand, there is likely to be more convergence if a computational model is able to reproduce detailed aspects of many different human abilities.

Another way to make computational models more likely to reproduce human mental processes is to integrate the computational approach with the experimental and clinical approaches to the study of mental processes. Computational models must be sufficiently sophisticated to generate predictions about intermediate stages and results in a complex task (Pylyshyn, 1980), about the real time properties of a process, and about possible malfunctioning in both normal and pathological systems. This would allow a fruitful interaction between computational and experimental/clinical work and would ensure that computational models not only reproduce the human behaviour but also the internal processes that generate this behaviour.

REFERENCES

Bresnan, J. (1982) *The mental representation of grammatical relations*, Cambridge, Mass: MIT Press.

Caplan, D., Baker, C., & Dehaut, F. (1985) Syntactic determinants of sentence comprehension. *Cognition*, *21*, 117–175.

Caramazza, A. (1986) On drawing inferences about the structure of normal cognitive systems from the analysis of patterns of impaired performance: the case for single-patient studies. *Brain and Cognition*, *5*, 41–66.

Caramazza, A., Miceli, G., Silveri, M. C., & Laudanna, A. (1985) Reading mechanisms and the organisation of the lexicon: Evidence from acquired dyslexia. *Cognitive Neuropsychology*, *2*(1), 81–114.

Caramazza, A., Miceli, G., & Villa, G. (1986) The role of the (output) phonological buffer in reading, writing, and repetition. *Cognitive Neuropsychology*, *3*, 37–76.

Coltheart, M. (1981) Disorders of reading and their implications for models of normal reading. *Visible Language*, *3*, 245–286.

Coltheart, M. (1984) Acquired dyslexias and normal reading. In R. N. Malatesha & H. A. Whitaker (Eds.), *Dyslexia: A global issue*. The Hague: Martinus Nijhoff Publishers.

Coltheart, M. (1985) Cognitive neuropsychology and the study of reading. In M. I. Posner & O. S. M. Marin (Eds.), *Attention and performance XI*. Hillsdale, N.J.: Lawrence Erlbaum Associates Inc.

Coltheart, M. (1986) Functional architecture of the language-processing system. In M. Coltheart, R. Job, & G. Sartori (Eds.), *The cognitive neuropsychology of language*. London: Lawrence Erlbaum Associates Ltd.

Ellis, A. W. (1982a) *Normality and pathology in cognitive functions*. London: Academic Press.

Ellis, A. W. (1982b) Spelling and writing (and reading and speaking). In A. W. Ellis (Ed.), *Normality and pathology in cognitive functions*. London: Academic Press.

Ellis, A. W. (1984) *Reading, writing and dyslexia: A cognitive analysis.* London: Lawrence Erlbaum Associates Ltd.

Ellis, A. W. (1985) The cognitive neuropsychology of developmental (and acquired) dyslexia: A critical survey. *Cognitive Neuropsychology*, *2* (2), 169–205.

Garrett, M. F. (1982) Production of speech: Observations from normal and pathological language use. In A. W. Ellis (Ed.), *Normality and pathology in cognitive functions.* London: Academic Press.

Grodzinsky, Y. (1984) The syntactic characterization of agrammatism. *Cognition*, *16*, 99–120.

Howard, D. (1986) Reading without letters? In M. Coltheart, R. Job, & G. Sartori (Eds.), *The cognitive neuropsychology of language.* London: Lawrence Erlbaum Associates Ltd.

Kean, M.-L. (1979) Agrammatism: A phonological deficit? *Cognition*, *7*, 69–83.

Lapointe, S. G. (1983) Some issues in the linguistic description of agrammatism. *Cognition*, *14*, 1–39.

Lapointe, S. G. (1985) A theory of verb form use in the speech of agrammatic aphasics. *Brain and Language*, *24*, 100–155.

Marshall, J. C. & Newcombe, F. (1973) Patterns of paralexia: A psycholinguistic approach. *Journal of Psycholinguistic Research*, *2*, 175–199.

Martin, R. C. & Caramazza, A. (1986) Theory and method in cognitive neuropsychology: The case of acquired dyslexia. In H. Julia Hannay (Ed.), *Experimental techniques in human neuropsychology.* London: Oxford University Press.

Mehler, J., Morton, J., & Jusczyk, P. W. (1984) On reducing language to biology *Cognitive Neuropsychology*, *1* (1), 83–116.

Miceli, G., Silveri, M. C., & Caramazza, A. (1986) The role of the phoneme-to-grapheme conversion system and of the graphemic output buffer in writing. In M. Coltheart, R. DXOB, - «('⅝B& bo. Sartori (Eds.), *The cognitive neuropsychology of language.* London: Lawrence Erlbaum Associates Ltd.

Morton, J. (1980) The logogen model and orthographic structure. In U. Frith (Ed.), *Cognitive processes in spelling.* London: Academic Press.

Morton, J. & Patterson, K. (1980) A new attempt at an interpretation, or, an attempt at a new interpretation. In M. Coltheart, K. Patterson, & J. C. Marshall (Eds.), *Deep dyslexia.* London: Routledge & Kegan Paul.

Parisi, D. (1985) A procedural approach to the study of aphasia. *Brain and Language*, *26* (1), 1–15.

Parisi, D. (1986) Grammatical disturbances of speech production. In M. Coltheart, R. Job, & G. Sartori (Eds.), *The cognitive neuropsychology of language.* London: Lawrence Erlbaum Associates Ltd.

Parisi, D. & Giorgi, A. (1986) GEMS: A model of sentence production. In *Proceedings of the II European Conference of the Association for Computational Linguistics.*

Patterson, K. E. (1980) Derivational errors. In M. Coltheart, K. Patterson, & J. C. Marshall (Eds.), *Deep dyslexia.* London: Routledge & Kegan Paul.

Patterson, K. E. (1981) Neuropsychological approaches to the study of reading. *British Journal of Psychology*, *72*, 151–174.

Pylyshyn, Z. W. (1980) Computation and cognition: Issues in the foundation of cognitive science. *The Behavioral and Brain Sciences*, *3*, 111–132.

Schaffer, L. H. (1973) Latency mechanisms in transcription. In S. Kornblum (Ed.), *Attention and performance IV.* New York: Academic Press.

Schaffer, L. H. (1975) Control processes in typing. *Quarterly Journal of Experimental Psychology*, *27*, 419–432.

Schaffer, L. H. (1976) Intention and performance. *Psychological Review*, *83* (5), 375–393.

Shallice, T. (1979) Case study approach in neuropsychological research. *Journal of Clinical Neuropsychology*, *1*, 183–211.

Shallice, T. (1981) Neurological impairment of cognitive processes. *British Medical Bulletin*, *37*, 187–192.

Venezky, R. L. (1970) *The structure of English orthography*. The Hague: Mouton.

PART II: LANGUAGE COMPREHENSION

5 Automatic Processes in Language Comprehension*

G. B. Flores d'Arcais
Max-Planck-Institut für Psycholinguistik, Nijmegen, The Netherlands; Unit of Experimental Psychology, University of Leiden, Leiden, The Netherlands

INTRODUCTION

Several fundamental issues in contemporary cognitive psychology theories have come to be expressed in the form of dichotomies that either represent alternative forms of information processing or indicate two essential phases of the cognitive processes. Most contemporary human information-processing theories can be characterised in terms of these alternatives. Issues such as top-down v. bottom-up; serial v. parallel processing, on-line v. off-line, hierarchical v. heterarchical, and automatic v. controlled, are all basic problems for the characterisation of the most important theories within cognitive psychology.

In this paper I will discuss the issue of automatic v. controlled processes in language comprehension and concentrate mainly on the first. The question is, of course, very broad, and the literature available is extremely large; this paper does not aim at an extended review of the literature.

After a brief general overview of the notion of automatic processing I will concentrate mainly on two areas of psycholinguistic research. The first topic will include a broad range of results from studies on *lexical access*. For example, evidence from studies on lexical access of polysemous or

* The last version of this paper has been written in 1983. Except for a couple of references added before publication, no major changes have been made since. The author's view on many of the issues discussed in this paper would be somewhat different if the paper had been written in 1987.

homographic words speaks in favour of a process in which the different senses of a lexical unit are automatically activated whenever that entry is accessed, but only part of the information that had become available as a result of the access is used for the appropriate response: Only one meaning is used for further processing. The second area I will discuss is *syntactic processing.* I will look at evidence from automatic syntactic processing taking place even in the absence of direct subsequent use of the information made available at the first stage. Finally, I will examine the possible implications of these data for developing a theory of language processing that is capable of making some contribution to cognitive neuropsychology at large.

AUTOMATIC AND CONTROLLED PROCESSES

The distinction between automatic and controlled processes constitutes a very central theoretical issue in contemporary cognitive psychology, and is well known through the theoretical and empirical contributions of LaBerge and Samuels (1974), Posner and Snyder (1975), Schneider and Shiffrin (1977), LaBerge (1981), to quote only a few seminal papers. The two terms *automatic* and *controlled* are used to identify two different types of processes of information taking place in succession or simultaneously. The distinction can be made clear through the following quotation from Schneider and Shiffrin (1977, p. 1):

> "Automatic processing is activation of a learned sequence of elements in long-term memory that is initiated by appropriate inputs and then proceeds automatically ... Controlled processing is a temporary activation of a sequence of elements that can be set up quickly and easily but requires attention, is capacity limited ... and is controlled by the subject".

Different properties of automatic processes have been described in the theoretical accounts provided on the issue. According to Posner and Snyder (1975), three fundamental criteria can be used to establish whether a process is automatic or not. An automatic process occurs (1) without intention; (2) without giving rise to any conscious awareness; and (3) without producing interference with other ongoing mental activities. Another essential characteristic of an automatic process is that it does not require special resources and in principle does not reduce processing capacity.

Briefly, automatic processes are unavoidable, without capacity limitations, without awareness, highly efficient and resistant to modification.

Controlled processes, on the other hand, are taken to be characterised as resource demanding, having a limited capacity, in principle conscious or accessible to awareness, and under the strategic control of the subject and, therefore, also highly flexible and modifiable.

Several terms are used in the literature for labelling the two processes. *Controlled* is in part, but not completely, synonymous with *strategic* or *conscious*, or *attentional*. Several other theoretical accounts can be directly related to the present one. For example, Turvey (1974) draws a distinction between *tacit* and *explicit identification* of a pattern, which is essentially the same dichotomy as automatic and controlled.

The defining criteria for automatic processes can provide useful elements for deciding whether a given process can be taken to be automatic or controlled. For example, the existence of given effects without any access to *conscious awareness* can be considered a criterion for defining a process as being automatic.

The defining criteria can also allow specific predictions, some of which have been tested in appropriate experiments. For example, if a task is carried out completely automatically, then it should not require any specific allocation of processing capacity. Performance on a concurrent task, under strategic control, should then remain unaffected whether the automatic task is simultaneously executed or not.

A number of issues have been debated and are still open on the topic. One of the most important is the issue of *dualism* v. *continuity* of the two processes. Although it is usually recognised that many psychological tasks are carried out with a contribution of both processes, the notion of two clearly *different* processes is preferred.

The idea that automatic processing does not put any demand on capacity resources is not without discussion. It has been recognised that capacity can be reduced while task-required automatic processes are being executed. Moreover, automatic processing can interfere with ongoing controlled processes (Shiffrin, Dumais, & Schneider, 1981) and automatic processes can be initiated by controlled procedures.

Another important point is whether automatic processing is to be taken as the first stage in a sequence, or as an activity simultaneous with controlled processes. Although most models assume the first stages of processing as being automatic, and the processes more related to perceptual integration and response selection as being under the control of strategic components, some approaches also allow the possibility for processing at the two levels, the automatic and the controlled one, from the very beginning.

EARLY AND RECENT MODELS IN COGNITIVE PSYCHOLOGY

A very superficial look at the development of the models and theories of processing within cognitive psychology during the last twenty-five years shows a clear increase of attention paid to automatic processes in the early stages of information processes. The change has been accompanied—and logically so—by a shift of the locus of selection in the models: from early selection, characterised by precategorical filters, to late selection, from more *active* to more *passive* devices for information processing. Of course, this is an oversimplification. Next to active type of models like Neisser's (1967) analysis-by-synthesis in the 1960s, in the same period one encounters already Morton's logogen (1969, 1970), perhaps the prototype of a passive model. Still, *parallel* processing in most early models was restricted only to the very early stages of information processing, whereas the main stages of processing were organised strictly *serially*.

Because the amount of information available to the processing system is, initially at least, normally very large, some selection has to take place, either already at the level of the interface between sensory information and more central levels of information processing or at some point during the process of information transformation. Accordingly, a very essential feature of *any* theory of information processing is the position and the role assigned to a *selective mechanism*, which either has to allow only a limited amount of the information available to the system to be processed for the response requested or, as much compelling evidence seems to require, demands a choice of a given response for execution among the information already processed and available. In models of which Broadbent's filter (1958) is a kind of prototype, this selective mechanism is precategorical, whereas the alternative class of models requires postcategorical selective operations, which may even take place very far "down" in the flow of information through the system, just before response execution.

Most early models of cognitive psychology were characterised by serial organisation of the stages of processing and by early selection. The classic example of this type is, of course, Broadbent's (1958) *filter* model. Notice that by locating selection *early* in the processing of information, one restricts the range of domain of possible automatic computations. If, for example, in a dichotic-listening task a model such as Broadbent's filter prescribes that information sent to the rejected channel not be allowed to reach a stage of perceptual processing, no computation of the rejected information is possible, either automatically or under strategic control, because this information is not allowed to go further than a sensory buffer. In order to allow more space to automatic processing one has to move any selective control mechanism further down from the input to the output side.

In contrast to the typical serial models of early cognitive psychology, during the 1970s a trend has emerged towards models characterised by parallel processing at several levels. An important contribution to this change has come from the framework of *levels of processing* introduced by Craik and Lockhart (1972), which has stimulated an impressive amount of empirical and theoretical work. The basic assumption of this approach is that input stimulus information is processed simultaneously in various ways and at different depths, at many levels. For example, a written word can be processed at the level of the physical properties, at the acoustic and at the semantic level. Each of these represents a processing level, characterised by different depths of processing. Processing at these various levels does not take place in an autonomous, independent way, but the computation taking place at one level affects processing at the other levels. Moreover, the beginning of processing at one level does not require completion of the computation at the "lower" level. The results of processing at each level are at the disposal of the system for computation at other levels.

Although the idea of levels of processing has never become a theory, it has had a very large impact on research in cognitive psychology. As a result, the models have become more interactive and characterised by late selection. This type of approach has important consequences for the issue of automatic processing. Although the notion of processing at different levels in parallel is logically independent of the issue whether processing takes place automatically or under strategic control, both theoretical demands and an impressive amount of evidence obtained within the level of processing framework indicate that the notion of parallel processing is easier to interface with the notion of automatic computation. Interactive models postulate simultaneous computation and availability of information at different levels. Also, no decision is required by some control unit as to which level of information has to be processed at any given moment. Thus, much processing is taking place that will not be demanded for the response. The selection of material for the response is based on information processed at different levels and possibly characterised by different codes.

A different issue is the question of autonomy v. interaction. A parallel model can be characterised by the contribution of different autonomous components or modules and their output, which becomes available for appropriate selection. Or, alternatively, processing in parallel at various levels can be highly interactive. Although much of the research in the context of the levels of processing framework in the 1970s has been characterised by interactive models, recent evidence within psycholinguistics (e.g. Frazier, Clifton, & Randall, 1983) seems to give strong support to an autonomous, modular point of view.

Recent models in cognitive psychology tend to be heterarchical, as compared to the early "pipeline", hierarchical type of models. Information is taken to be processed at different levels either fully in parallel or in cascades (McClelland, 1979). These ideas are all consistent with the notion of automatic processes followed, or accompanied, by controlled processes.

A basic assumption in automatic processing is that during the initial phases of information handling the whole stimulus input is analysed in parallel without attentional effort up to the level at which perceptual identification occurs. This assumption has not remained unchallenged, for example from the feature-integration theory by Treisman and Gelade (1980).

EVIDENCE FOR AUTOMATIC PROCESSING

Critical evidence in favour of the hypothesis of automatic processing comes from studies on *selective attention*. Within a psycholinguistic framework of particular interest are several studies on dichotic listening, such as experiments carried out with shadowing of one out of two concurrent messages.

Lewis (1970) presented simultaneously pairs of words to the two ears in a dichotic-listening paradigm: The words of the rejected channel were either unrelated, or associatively or semantically related to the words on the attended channel. Shadowing latencies to material presented on the attended channel were slower for words semantically related to the words presented on the rejected channel, although these words had not been consciously identified.

Ambiguous sentences in the attended ear can be interpreted according to the sense specified by a word presented on the rejected channel, even if this word is not consciously perceived by the hearer. Evidence comes from Lackner and Garrett's (1972) dichotic-listening experiment, and, perhaps more dramatically, from Von Wright, Anderson and Stenman (1975), who conditioned GSR to a specific word in the attended message and were able to obtain the GSR when the conditioned word was presented, without subjects' awareness, in the rejected channel. Words semantically related to the conditional stimulus word elicited a sizeable GSR when presented in the attended, but also in the unattended message.

That semantic information can become available without awareness should not be a surprise. After all, there is much evidence that people are capable of correctly identifying the category to which a character belongs—for example *letter* or *digit*—before they may be able to identify the character itself (Brand, 1971; Ingling, 1972; Posner, 1970). So, we know something *about* the identity of an event before we know the identity of the event itself.

Availability of semantic information without the subject's awareness has been demonstrated in a variety of studies with different tasks, in lexical decision, word naming, Stroop colour naming, tachistoscopic recognition, etc.

There is, for instance, a considerable body of evidence that some knowledge of the meaning of a word might become available even when the reader is not able to recognise or openly report it. For example,

Wickens (1972) showed that an observer may have some knowledge of the meaning of a *masked* word even though he might not be able to name it. The results of this study are perhaps not so impressive because the task was not the most appropriate for the question investigated (the dependent variable consisted of semantic differential ratings of two words given for recognition, one of which was in 50% of the time related in meaning to the first). More recently, however, stronger evidence has become available from studies such as Allport (1977), Broadbent and Broadbent (1977), Marcel (1980, 1983a, 1983b) and several others, one of which will be reported in some detail further on.

There is an extensive literature on the so-called subliminal perception of words, or of the effect of emotionally loaded words on perceptual recognition (see, e.g. Broadbent, 1971; Dixon, 1981). For the present purpose the most important questions obviously are: How and why can one be slower at naming an emotionally loaded word if one has not yet recognised it? And if one had already recognised it, why does it take longer to start uttering it than to name an emotionally neutral word?

Again, the results of studies on inhibitory effects of emotional words on word recognition are indications of early processing of semantic information before the words become consciously available for response. For a more extended presentation of empirical evidence on this point, and a more complete discussion, see Dixon (1981).

LEXICAL ACCESS

In this section I will briefly review a couple of the many studies available in contemporary literature on lexical access, which offer strong evidence for the automatic character of the process of accessing the meaning of a word.

One of the questions faced in many studies concerns the availability of one or both meanings of a "lexically ambiguous" word. (In this respect, psycholinguistic literature often fails to differentiate between cases of polysemy and homophony or homography; on the other hand, the distinction, which is not always easy to draw, is probably not so important for a psychological theory of lexical access.)

Two main questions have been repeatedly investigated: First, whether one or both or more meanings of the "ambiguous word" are accessed, and second, what the effect of the context is.

Basically, two classes of models can be distinguished. One class is characterised by *selective access* of meaning, the other by *multiple access* of meaning. In selective access models, the context constraints the lexical retrieval process in such a way that only one contextually appropriate meaning is accessed. In multiple access models, all senses of the word are accessed and the interpretation is selected on the basis of contextual information.

Psycholinguistic literature has in storage results favouring both types of models. For what concerns words in isolation, for example, Schvaneveldt, Meyer and Becker (1976) found evidence for single access, while Warren, Warren, Green and Bresnick (1978) obtained results favouring the multiple access position.

Studies of lexical ambiguity in sentence context have yielded not unequivocal results. Strong evidence of a biasing effect of context was obtained in Lackner and Garrett (1972) dichotic study, which showed that presentation of a word on the rejected channel had the effect of disambiguating the interpretation of a lexically ambiguous sentence administered on the selected channel. On the other hand, Foss and Jenkins (1973), besides finding higher latencies in phoneme monitoring tasks on a word following a lexically ambiguous word, failed to obtain any decrement in the ambiguity effect as the result of a biasing context.

Marcel's (1980) experiments with polysemous words and masking, described in a following section of this paper, allows the conclusion of a strong version of the selective model: Facilitation in lexical decision appears to hold for words related to one meaning of polysemous words, namely the meaning related to the prior context. When the prime is masked after a very short exposure, on the other hand, both meanings become available, as indicated by the facilitation effect on lexical decision for both readings of the ambiguous word.

Two important studies have provided interesting evidence on the issue. A paradigm used by Tanenhaus et al. (1979) consisted of measuring word-naming latencies with a variable time delay. In their experiment lexically ambiguous words in which the two readings corresponded to different grammatical classes, such as *noun/verb* (e.g. the word *watch*), were used in sentential context biasing either the noun or the verb meaning. Target words related to either the noun or the verb meaning (for example *clock* or *look*, respectively) were presented with different delays following the sentence-final ambiguous words. At 0 msec delay, regardless of context, both readings were facilitated. However, already at 200 msec delay the facilitation was obtained only for targets that were related to the sense of the ambiguous words determined by the context.

Essentially the same results were obtained by Swinney (1979) with another interesting experimental paradigm in a cross-model lexical-decision task. The subjects of Swinney's study listened for comprehension sentences containing lexical ambiguities and had simultaneously to take lexical decisions on *visually* presented letter strings. When the visual words were presented *simultaneously* with the end of the ambiguous words, without any delay, *both* readings of the ambiguous word were facilitated, even when the context strongly biased one of the meanings. However, at a distance of only four syllables from the end of the ambiguous words, this facilitation had disappeared, and only the words related in meaning to the contextually appropriate word were facilitated.

For example, consider the following passage used by Swinney (1979, p. 650): "Rumor had it that, for years, the government building had been plagued with problems. The man was not surprised when he found several spiders, roaches, and other *bugs* in the corner of the room."

Of the two readings of the ambiguous word *bugs*, the context here exemplified biased one reading (in the control sentence, the word used instead was *insect*). The words presented for lexical decision were either *ANT* (contextually related), *SPY* (contextually inappropriate but related to the other meaning), or *SEW* (unrelated). When one of the three words was presented visually *simultaneously* with the end of the word *bugs*, lexical decision on *both* the words *ANT* and *SPY* were facilitated as compared to *SEW*. However, when the target words were presented only a few syllables after the end of the word *bugs*, then only the contextually appropriate *ANT* was facilitated.

The results of the Tanenhaus et al. (1979) and Swinney (1979) studies thus suggest that both (all) meanings of an ambiguous word are *momentarily* available, and that this is also the case when the context strongly biases only one meaning of the ambiguous word. On the other hand, this availability of both (all) meanings of the ambiguous word is rapidly lost, and only the contextually appropriate meaning remains available after a brief interval of time (in the Swinney study after an interval of the order of 700–1000 msec).

Both the Tanenhaus et al. and the Swinney studies, together with Marcel's (1980) results, converge in suggesting an early, automatic activation of all meanings of a word whenever this is encountered, independently of the presence of a context. *Multiple access* of meanings seems therefore to take place *automatically* at the presentation of a word, while *selective access* of the contextually appropriate meaning seems to be a process taking place within a short delay after the onset, or following the offset, of the critical word.

Notice that one of the main criteria for automatic processing, namely the absence of awareness, seems to be fulfilled in these studies. In Swinney's (1979) first experiment, only 3 of the 84 subjects noticed any ambiguity in the contextually embedded prime words. If the contextually unbiased meaning had become available and had a facilitatory effect on the lexical access of the simultaneously visually presented word, this is not likely to be an effect of a conscious presence of the semantic–lexical information corresponding to the contextually "rejected" meaning.

LEXICAL ACCESS AS AN AUTOMATIC PROCESS

In all tasks designed to explore word recognition, such as lexical-decision tasks, word naming, threshold determination for tachistoscopically presented strings and similar, a phenomenon has consistently been found—namely, that the prior presentation of a word associatively or semantically related to the *target* word affects the speed and the accuracy of the response on the latter. This effect has been called *priming*; the word that affects the performance on the second is usually called the *prime*.

Different explanations have been proposed to account for the facilitation effect found. A typical suggestion is the notion of an automatic "spread of activation": Whenever a word contacts its representation in memory, the activation aroused in that particular location would "spread" along the memory network and activate to a larger or smaller extent the word representations that are associatively related to the accessed word. This spread of activation is taken to come about automatically.

According to a "classic", widely accepted model, proposed by Posner and Snyder (1975), this first, automatic process of spreading of activation, which is entirely preconscious and does not require any resource of the attentional system, would be followed by a second process controlled by the attentional system, which in the case of priming would act by building up expectancies about the target words that might be presented following the prime, etc. At this level, "wrong" expectancies should obviously also lead to inhibition instead of facilitating the recognition process of the target, because the wrong expectation would interfere with the incoming target. To put it differently, if an unrelated word is presented as the target, then the expectations based on the prime have first to be taken away. In Posner and Snyder's model this second process initiates with some delay as compared to the automatic component: in lexical-decision experiments, typically not earlier than with a 400–500 msec delay after the onset of the prime.

It is not the purpose of the present paper to evaluate the merits and the advantages of the dual model. I will in the first place concentrate on the automatic operations underlying the word-recognition process. To the theoretical notion of "spreading" of activation I prefer the notion of availability of semantic information whenever a word entry is accessed in the mental lexicon. According to this idea, when a word unit is accessed, the information within the semantic–conceptual domain(s) of which the word is part become(s) available for retrieval. This process of making the semantic information available to the system can be taken as a change in the level of activation of the logogens of the various units within a given domain. In the present formulation, this process is taken to be entirely automatic and unconscious.

That the facilitation effect of a prime on a related target is an automatic process is well documented. For example, Fischler (1977) embedded pairs of related words in lists of otherwise unrelated word pairs and found facilitatory effects of primes on targets for the few related pairs. Because the material was certainly not such as to encourage conscious attention on the relation prime–target, it is reasonable to conclude with Fischler that the facilitation found is likely to be the result of an automatic activation. Neely (1977) obtained facilitation for targets related to the prime when the conscious attention of the subject was deliberately directed to words other than the prime.

Shaffer and LaBerge (1979) found effects of words flanking a target on the ease of semantic categorisation of the target. Even when the flanking words are detrimental to performance, they are apparently accessed, and the information made available in this way affects the experimental task. These results thus also offer evidence for automatic semantic processing of words.

However, the strongest evidence for automatic word recognition is probably that coming from recent studies in which the prime was presented so briefly, and/or masked in such a way that the word could not be reported, nor did the subject seem to have any idea of what it could have been. Still, these studies showed a facilitatory effect of the prime word on the successive target (Allport, 1977; Fowler, Wolford, Slade, & Tassinary, 1981; Marcel, 1980, 1983a, 1983b).

Let me briefly report on one of Marcel's experiments. He presented sequences of three words, or letter strings (LS)—LS1, LS2, and LS3—and required lexical decisions to be taken at LS1 and LS3. On critical trials LS2 was a polysemous word such as *PALM*, and LS3 was related to one of its meanings (e.g. *WRIST*). LS1 was either related to the same meaning (e.g. *HAND*) or was related to the second meaning of LS2 (e.g. *FREE*) or, finally, was unrelated (e.g. *CLOCK*). (Notice that this example, provided by Marcel (1980), is perhaps not the best, for *CLOCK* might have some relation to *WRIST* via the related concept *WATCH*!)

The conditions of presentation were as follows: (1) LS2 was left unmasked; (2) LS2 was "pattern" masked (with a pattern of letters dispersed on the visual field); or, finally, (3) LS2 was "energy" masked (with random visual noise). This distinction is based on Turvey (1973): "Pattern" masking should allow semantic access but prevent awareness of the word, whereas "energy" masking seems to erase dramatically sensory information in such a way that no graphemic nor lexical/semantic representation can be reached, which is what was found in Marcel's experiment as well.

The results for the other two conditions were rather interesting: In absence of masking, the prior context affected the selection of one meaning of LS2—as indicated by the facilitation of LS3. But with pattern masking of LS2 *both* meanings of LS2 were accessed, irrespective of context. To exemplify the result, without masking, the sequence *HAND PALM* facilitated only the lexical decision on *WRIST* and not on *TREE*, but *with* pattern masking, both *WRIST* and *TREE* were facilitated. Marcel (1980) concludes that "unconscious" perception is taking place and would account for his data. This would include a process of lexical/semantic access of unlimited capacity and would precede conscious perception.

These results were interesting but not foolproof. For example, Fowler et al. (1981) were able to find some facilitatory effects on words prior to the masking: This finding is obviously at odds with Marcel's conclusions.

At any rate, Marcel's results are relevant for several issues: On the one hand, they allow some specific conclusions as to the locus and effect of context on lexical access; on the other, they are interesting with respect to the question of automatic v. strategic control of the processes of lexical activation. But for the present purpose, they offer at least strong evidence on the hypothesis of very early activation of semantic information, prior to access to conscious awareness.

There is, on the other side, also some evidence to the contrary. For example, Henik, Friedrich, and Kellog (1983) showed that the priming effect is related to the nature of the task to be performed on the prime word. If the task on the priming consisted of a letter search, then the priming effect on the target was reduced as compared to the condition in which the prime had to be named. Obviously, if early, automatic access of the prime word had taken place, the nature of the task to be performed on it should not have any effect on the size of the priming effect. On the other hand, several explanations of the results by Henik et al. are possible, which are not inconsistent with the notion of automatic access, such as the possibility of post-access effects of having to shift to non-semantic aspects of the prime word.

The work so far discussed has two implications. The first concerns the automatic character of processing. The second is related to the pre- or subconscious character of processing. The two are, of course, independent issues. Recent debates on the second question (e.g. a forum discussion in *Behavioral and Brain Sciences*, 1986, as peer comments to Holender, 1986) indicate much disagreement on the question of whether processing of words can take place at the pre- or subconscious level. Careful recent work on word recognition (e.g. Cheesman & Merikle, 1985) showed no evidence for subconscious perception of words when very severe criteria for the detectability of words are taken.

AN EXPLORATORY STUDY ON WORD AND PICTURE NAMING

There is a large amount of evidence from literature on dyslexia of patients' decodification of words that they are not able to read. The most dramatic demonstration of this fact can be found in the reports of several cases of deep dyslexia (see, e.g. Coltheart, Patterson, & Marshall, 1980): The fact that a subject reads "chair" when presented with the word *TABLE* obviously implies access to the meaning of the target word that the patient is not capable of reading.

In this section I will report on an exploratory study with few dyslectic subjects that provided some evidence for automatic access of words that these subjects did not seem capable of reading. One of the experiments consisted of a picture–word interference task of the type used by Rayner and Posnansky (1978), Rosinski (1977), and Lupker (1979). The task required simply to name a picture upon which a word was superimposed. This word could be either the name of the picture, a word of the same semantic category of the name of the picture, a word of another semantic category, or, finally, a non-word. According to the evidence available, when one presents a picture with a noun superimposed on it, one obtains—except in the case of noun–picture correspondence—picture-naming latencies that are usually longer than the latencies for naming pictures without any word. The other experiment consisted in presenting a target word flanked by another word that could be the same as the target, semantically related, or unrelated to it, as in the study by Shaffer and LaBerge (1979).

An important feature of the present study was that we chose for each subject the words and the pictures depending on the previous performance of the subjects on a simple word- and picture-naming task. In our study we asked our subjects, four dyslexic with known—but not uniform—problems in word recognition, to perform in two tasks, a picture-naming and a word-naming task. The subjects were first tested with a rather large series of words and pictures. In this task it was first established which words the subjects could and which they could not name, and which pictures the subjects could and could not name. Of course, such tests hardly yield very clear results: Some words are read correctly on the first trial, some only after one or more wrong attempts. Paraphasic errors are not infrequent, etc. We adopted a rather liberal criterion: Even when the word was read after a couple of unsuccessful attempts, it scored as "recognised". Not surprisingly, several pictures could also not be named: Our subjects showed the same difficulty in naming words and in naming pictures.

The test phase consisted of two tasks, carried out on different times, at several days' interval from the first test. The first task was a picture naming, in which each subject received pictures that he or she had been able to name previously, with a word superimposed, which the subject was requested and trained to ignore. The pictures were presented on a display, and the subjects spoke their response into a microphone. The data consisted of first the success or failure to give a name to the picture, and in the first case, of the correct or erroneous naming and of the latencies.

The second test consisted in a word-naming task in which the target was flanked, above and below, by two strings of letters that made a non-word or a word that was either identical to the central target, or a word of the same category, or a non-related word. Again the data consisted of the type of answer (none, correct, incorrect) and in the latency of response.

The results showed an effect of words that the subjects had not been able to read on their performance on picture naming and on word naming. In the picture-naming task, when the words superimposed on the picture belonged to the same semantic category as the pictures to be named, they interfered with naming performance more than when they belonged to another semantic category. In the word–word experiment, a facilitation effect was obtained for the cases in which the target to be read was of the same semantic category of the flanked words that the subject had not been able to read. Of course, nobody can guarantee that in the test phase the presentation of the words that the subjects had not been able to name would remain unrecognised again. But at any rate the data show an interesting effect that can allow the hypothesis that the semantic system has been appropriately addressed even in cases in which overt word recognition does not seem to take place.

These results speak again in favour of an automatic access of semantic information in the mental lexicon even in absence of overt recognition of the words. The results are also consistent with evidence of semantic errors in deep dyslexia patients.

The present results are very consistent with evidence of an automatic associative priming effect in a lexical-decision task obtained by Milberg and Blumstein (1981) in Wernicke patients. These subjects failed to perform in tasks requiring metalinguistic judgements on words or open semantic decisions, but their performance in a lexical-decision task showed that some semantic processing had taken place on words upon which at a conscious level the patients seemed unable to operate.

AUTOMATIC SYNTACTIC COMPUTATION DURING LANGUAGE COMPREHENSION

In this section I will present some evidence on *automatic* computation of *syntactic information* during the process of language comprehension. This will be introduced within the framework of the debate on the autonomy of syntax in psycholinguistics.

The questions asked in this framework have been the following. Does sentence comprehension include a stage at which syntactic information is processed *independently* of other sources of information, such as semantic or pragmatic? A positive answer to this question would imply that syntactic processing is based purely on syntactic cues, and that decision about syntactic analysis is made without any aid from semantic information. Clear support for this position comes from experiments by Forster and associates (Forster & Olbrei, 1973; Forster & Ryder, 1971). The evidence in favour of an alternative position, an interactive view according to which language comprehension is the result of a continuous interaction among different levels of information and processing, is, on the other hand, rather abundant (see on this point, e.g. Flores d'Arcais & Schreuder, 1983). During the last years much empirical work has provided again evidence for an autonomous, albeit less radical, position.

The whole issue has found a revival in recent papers (Forster, 1979; Holmes, 1979) and can be articulated with several questions. The questions that I have tried to answer in a series of experiments, and that are relevant for the present discussion, are the following:

1. Is syntactic computation an *obligatory* or an *optional* stage in language processing?
2. Are the results of syntactic computation *always* used during language comprehension, or employed only in absence of other information, or, finally, as a kind of information to be used only as a "back-up" device when the linguistic task at hand becomes prohibitive?

Several contemporary models of language comprehension are based on the assumption that syntactic computation is not an obligatory stage in sentence processing. Already in 1970, Bever argued that the listener closely attends to syntax only if semantic cues are not available: He or she extracts meaning information whenever possible on the basis of relations directly available from lexical semantic constraints and from the surface structure of the sentence.

In Riesbeck and Schank's (1978) model of sentence understanding, syntactic processing *follows* semantic and conceptual operations, and is an *optional* stage of processing. Still within A.I., among other models, Wilks's (1978) translation program manages to get along without syntax at all, and the input is transformed directly into conceptual structures.

In a series of experiments, some of which are reported in Flores d'Arcais (1982), I have tried to look into the question of whether language comprehension involves full and obligatory computation of the information, and whether the results of this computation are always used in understanding. In these experiments, essentially, syntactic, semantic, and pragmatic violations were introduced into the experimental sentences to see whether and to what extent they affect language comprehension, how easily they are detected, and whether they affect processing even when they are not explicitly recognised as such. For the issue discussed in the present paper I will report on two types of experiments, the first of which involved recording eye fixations during reading of sentences with syntactic, semantic–pragmatic, or other violations, the second of which consisted of reading sentences presented on a display word-by-word, left-to-right, with presentation rate monitored by the subject. Let us briefly consider the two types of experiments. Eye-movement and eye-fixation recordings during reading can be taken as indicators of the amount of attention devoted to each point in a sentence, and have been used in a variety of successful studies (e.g. Carpenter & Just, 1977; Just & Carpenter, 1978) to make inferences or test hypotheses about cognitive processes underlying reading.

In my experiment the sentences were presented visually on a screen, while the position and duration of eye gazes of the subject were recorded. The sentences were either "normal", or contained syntactic or semantic violations, or, finally, non-words or words containing a clear spelling error, and the subjects were simply asked to detect any error or violation in the sentence, and signal the discovery by pressing a button. At the end of the sentences, an appropriate question about the content of the sentences was presented in a proportion of the trials to ensure that subjects were reading for comprehension.

The data obtained were of two types, namely failures to detect errors and latencies in detecting them. The results were rather clear. In the first place, the subjects were very good at detecting non-words and semantic violations, but rather poor at detecting syntactic violations. This result is consistent with the outcome of other experiments and can be taken as an indication that the process of sentence comprehension is not strongly affected by syntactic violation.

The recordings of the eye-fixation durations showed that all words containing an error, be it syntactic, semantic, or other, were fixated significantly longer than control words. In turn, words that represented syntactic violations were fixated significantly shorter than words that were the locus of semantic and spelling errors.

A more interesting result emerged from a *separate* analysis of the number and duration of the fixations on the words of the sentences containing syntactic violation, for the cases in which the subjects had reported an error, and for the cases in which no error had been reported. In both cases the words containing an error were fixated significantly *longer* than control words. Thus, even when a subject is not capable of reporting the errors, and therefore does not seem *aware* of the presence of syntactic errors in reading sentences, he seems to spend a significantly longer time on these syntactic errors and fixates them longer.

The second experiment required the subjects to read sentences by getting one word at a time on the display, from left to right (a technique developed by Aaronson and Scaraborough (1976) and used since then in a variety of experiments to measure processing load during sentence comprehension). The sentences were 50% correct and appropriate or (50%) could contain a syntactic, semantic, or pragmatic violation, or a spelling error. The subjects had to react with an oral signal spoken into a microphone whenever they noticed "something strange or an error". The words were obtained by pressing on a key and remained visible on the display, thus "building up" a sentence from left to right. The subjects were trained to go through the sentences very quickly. The data in this experiment consisted of the times between the pressing responses, which can be taken as indicators of the time needed to process each word in the sequence. The evidence available from the literature indicates in general that the between-word latencies for words following points of large processing loads (for example, following ambiguous words) tend to be higher.

The results of our experiment indicate a relatively low proportion of detection of syntactic errors. Still, even when the errors were not reported, there was a significant increase in inter-word latencies for the two words following the violation. Even when a syntactic violation is not consciously reported, it seems to affect reading behaviour.

These results suggest that syntactic information is being computed even when it is not used explicitly for comprehension. While a subject is making sense out of the input signal, extracting the meaning in the best way possible, at some level the subject is also processing syntactic information. It is possible that the results of this processing remain below the level of awareness in normal conditions, but constitute a resource to which the listener or reader can always apply, when and if necessary. In the experimental situation used, some "syntactic module" notices the anomaly and the eye looks longer and more frequently at it, even when the reader in the process of comprehending the sentence does not seem to require all the linguistic information available and does not seem to have to decode the syntactic information in its totality.

The results thus support the hypothesis of a level of *automatic computation* of syntactic information that runs in parallel with processing at other levels. Notice that this hypothesis does not imply that syntactic information is only and always processed at a shallower level: Local and non-local syntactic cues are likely to be continuously used in constructing a representation of the meaning of the incoming signal. The hypothesis only suggests that full syntactic computation proceeds in an automatic way, that its output interacts with other levels of processing in producing a meaningful representation of the incoming signal, but that the specific output of this computation is not necessarily used and does not have to reach the level of awareness.

The picture that emerges from this study is that computation of the information available from the input material takes place at different levels in parallel, and all of the results of these processes become available. This normally ensures a redundancy of information from which to select in order to construct an internal representation of the sentence or of the text presented. The processor selects among information arriving from these different sources, and uses whatever is more easily and more efficiently available. The results of the experiment indicate that while syntactic processing is carried out automatically, the *results* of such computations are not always *used*, or are used only to a limited extent. The amount and the depth of such use is likely to be related to the difficulty of the linguistic task. As several experiments, including work in our laboratory, have shown, when faced with an easy, pragmatically and syntactic canonical sentence, the listener is able to extract the correct meaning by using only *superficial* cues such as word order, and relying on *strategies*, such as minimum distance principles, widely studied both with normal adults and children and with pathological subjects. However, when faced with more complex structures or with unexpected pragmatic relations, then the listener might have to "back up" to several sources of information, and in this case syntactic cues become very important in uniquely specifying the interpretation of the signal. Syntactic information is therefore *always* available as a result of an automatic computation, but is *used* more or less depending on the presence or absence of other evidence that might be of easier access, or as a control on the output of other computations that have taken place simultaneously.

SELECTION OF A RESPONSE FOR OUTPUT

So far I have argued that language comprehension includes some level of *automatic processing* of lexical/semantic and syntactic information. I have also proposed that processing takes place in parallel at several levels, and that the system can rely on the results of computations that have taken place at different levels, in a redundant matter.

An essential problem connected with any model characterised by automatic processing is the selection of the appropriate response for output, or, put more generally, the question of which of the different types of information made available within the system will be selected for the response to be executed. Where and what is the type and the locus of the control of the appropriate response?

Several alternatives are here possible. Consider first "passive" models: Here one can simply assume that the system will select for the response the strongest evidence available, or as an alternative, that what will be selected for the response is the information made available to some output buffer earlier, thus in a racehorse type of model. More "active" types of models, on the other hand, should include some selection or control mechanism capable of monitoring the choice of a response by using an appropriate criterion—for example matching the response with the input, or keeping track of the demands of the task.

The first type of model does not need to include an output-monitor mechanism. Execution of the response is contingent on the availability of a value that has exceeded a certain threshold value. Within this framework, the response is executed without any need for checking with the input or controlling the appropriateness of the response as related to the task. An example of this solution is the classic logogen in its original form (Morton, 1969, 1970).

The second type of model requires, on the other hand, a selection and a control of the response to be executed before output on the basis of the demands of the task or in comparison to the input format. In this respect, several recent theoretical suggestions have been made, such as Allport's (1977) *comparator*, Becker's *verification* stage (Becker, 1976), or Rumelhart's (1977) *blackboard*.

Essentially these models assume that a word-detector (a logogen) is in itself not capable of yielding a *unique* logogen output. The logogens generate different structural descriptions that must then be checked against the representation of the input in memory. Only then can a response be selected for execution.

Of course, these models have to take into account a series of important questions. For example, one has to solve the problem of the *compatibility of the codes*. The input code, the mental representation code, and the code of the information made available for response are certainly not in the same format. How can these three be compared?

The models deal with these problems in different ways, and it would be beyond the limits of the present conclusion to try to review them here. For the present purpose, it is important to claim that the material processed by the system is not entirely used for the task at hand, and that selection and control of the processed and available information represent processes to be distinguished from that of automatic computation of information.

CONCLUSIONS

The notions discussed in the present paper have relevant consequences for theory and research on aphasia, and in general, on neuropsychological disturbances. If linguistic information can be taken to be processed automatically (but not all processed material is used for the response), one can ask whether the malfunctions found in patients rather than being a question of lacking, insufficient, or wrong computation at a given processing level (for example a malfunction of an autonomous syntactic computation module) might be a matter of inappropriate control at the output level, or of insufficient ability to use response material already processed.

One should distinguish between availability of information and use of information for the task at hand. Because automatic procedures are so effortless and deeply rooted in the processing system, it is not unlikely that they are rather resistant and hence less vulnerable. Processing information under strategic control, on the other hand, requires effort, is bound to limited capacity, and is less deeply acquired (Shiffrin & Schneider, 1977). Lowering in performance as a result of poorer control can be easily brought about by task demands, stress, tiredness, etc. These experimental or natural conditions in a way "simulate" certain patients' behaviour. Seldom in aphasia research is a given performance found to drop to zero, as it should be if a "connection" route was really "cut". Some of the difficulties of patients with linguistic material are similar to those of normals in conditions of tiredness or stress. Close attention to speech production shows that errors produced in speech by normals are similar or identical to those produced by Broca's aphasics (Stemberger, 1984).

Recent work in aphasiology seems to indicate that language perception and comprehension systems might still be intact in patients showing severe grammatical disturbances. For example, it has been shown that agrammatic patients can be sensitive to grammatical structure (Linebarger, Schwartz, & Shaffran, 1983) and seem to possess a more or less intact language perception system even when their performance in ordinary tests of sentence understanding is very poor. Thus, sentence-comprehension disturbances do not necessarily reflect a loss of capacity to recover syntactic structure. Similarly, the semantic deficit in Wernicke aphasics might not be at the level of accessing the semantic organisation underlying words, but could reflect difficulties in the access or use of semantic information (Milberg & Blumstein, 1981).

Performance in a given task, in normal life or in the laboratory, does not necessarily reflect processing limitations, but is bound to several variables, such as tasks, demands, etc. most of which can be taken to affect controlled or strategic aspects of processing, and not the automatic, effortless level of basic linguistic operations such as those that are required in accessing the mental lexicon or in computing the syntactic structure of a sentence.

On the basis of these arguments it is perhaps possible to propose that at least some of the difficulties in language comprehension of agrammatics, or, in general, in language processing in the various forms of aphasia, may concern not so much processing but rather use and control of the results of computation that has taken place in an automatic and unconscious way. In the present form, this statement is, of course, very vague, and is put forward as a proposal to be developed further in considerable detail. If taken in a radical form, this hypothesis would require substantial revisions of the traditional views of aphasic disturbances as representing impairments of specific components of the language system. The position, on the other hand, is not without resonance in contemporary cognitive neuropsychology (see, e.g., Linebarger et al., 1983; Milberg & Blumstein, 1981). Recent evidence from aphasiology, such as the one quoted in this section, as well as data from normal speakers, suggest that along these lines it should be possible to find fruitful and viable experimental hypotheses.

REFERENCES

Aaronson, D. & Scarborough, H. S. (1976) Performance theories for sentence coding: Some quantitative evidence. *Journal of Experimental Psychology: Human Perception and Performance*, *2*, 56–70.

Allport, D. A. (1977) On knowing the meaning of words we are unable to report: The effect of visual masking. In S. Dornic (Ed.), *Attention and performance VI*. Hillsdale, N.J.: Lawrence Erlbaum Associates Inc.

Becker, C. A. (1976) Allocation of attention during visual word recognition. *Journal of Experimental Psychology: Human Perception and Performance*, *2*, 556–566.

Bever, T. (1970) The cognitive basis for linguistic structures. In J. R. Hayes (Ed.), *Cognition and the development of language*. New York: John Wiley & Sons.

Brand, J. (1971) Classification without identification in visual search. *Quarterly Journal of Experimental Psychology*, *23*, 178–186.

Broadbent, D. E. (1958) *Perception and communication*. London: Pergamon Press.

Broadbent, D. E. (1971) *Decision and stress*. London: Academic Press.

Broadbent, D. E. & Broadbent, M. H. P. (1977) General shape and local detail in word perception. In S. Dornic (Ed.), *Attention and performance VI*. Hillsdale, N.J.: Lawrence Erlbaum Associates Inc.

Carpenter, P. A. & Just, M. A. (1977) Reading comprehension as eyes see it. In M. A. Just & P. A. Carpenter (Eds.), *Cognitive processes in comprehension*. Hillsdale, H.J.: Lawrence Erlbaum Associates Inc.

Cheesman, J. & Merikle, P. M. (1985) Word recognition and consciousness. In D. Besner, T. Gary Waller, & G. E. MacKinnon (Eds.), *Reading research: Advances in theory and practice. Vol. 5*. Orlando: Academic Press.

Coltheart, M., Patterson, K., & Marshall, J. C. (Eds.) (1980) *Deep dyslexia* London: Routledge & Kegan Paul.

Craik, F. I. M. & Lockhart, R. S. (1972) Levels of processing: A framework for memory research. *Journal of Verbal Learning and Verbal Behavior*, *11*, 671–684.

Dixon, N. F. (1981) *Preconscious processing*. Chichester: John Wiley & Sons.
Fischler, I. (1977) Associative facilitation without expectancy in a lexical decision task. *Journal of Experimental Psychology: Human Perception and Performance*, *3*, 18–26.
Flores d'Arcais, G. B. (1982) Automatic syntactic computation in sentence comprehension. *Psychological Research*, *44*, 231–242.
Flores d'Arcais, G. B. & Schreuder, R. (1983) The process of language understanding: A few issues in contemporary psycholinguistics. In G. B. Flores d'Arcais & R. J. Jarvella (Eds.), *The process of language understanding*. Chichester: John Wiley & Sons.
Forster, K. I. (1979) Levels of processing and the structure of the language processor. In W. E. Cooper & E. C. T. Walker (Eds.), *Sentence processing: Psycholinguistic studies presented to Merrill Garrett*. Hillsdale, N.J.: Lawrence Erlbaum Associates Inc.
Forster, K. I. & Olbrei, I. (1973) Semantic heuristic and syntactic analysis. *Cognition*, *2*, 319–347.
Forster, K. I. & Ryder, L. A. (1971) Perceiving the structure and meaning of sentences. *Journal of Verbal Learning and Verbal Behavior*, *9*, 699–706.
Foss, D. J. & Jenkins, C. M. (1973) Some effects of context on the comprehension of ambiguous sentences. *Journal of Verbal Learning and Verbal Behavior*, *12*, 577–589.
Fowler, C. A., Wolford, G., Slade, R. & Tassinary, L. (1981) Lexical access with and without awareness. *Journal of Experimental Psychology: General*, *7*, 123–134.
Frazier, L., Clifton, C., & Randall, J. (1983) Filling gaps: Decision principles and structure in sentence comprehension. *Cognition*, *13*, 187–222.
Henik, A., Friedrich, F. J., & Kellog, W. A. (1983) The dependence of semantic relatedness effects upon prime processing. *Memory and Cognition*, *11*, 366–373.
Holender, D. (1986) Semantic activation without conscious identification in dichotic listening, parafoveal vision and visual masking: A survey and appraisal. *Behavioral and Brain Sciences*, *9*, 1–22.
Holmes, V. M. (1979) Some hypotheses about syntactic processing in sentence comprehension. In W. E. Cooper & E. C. T. Walker (Eds.), *Sentence processing: Psycholinguistic studies presented to Merrill Garrett*. Hillsdale, N.J.: Lawrence Erlbaum Associates Inc.
Ingling, N. (1972) Categorization: A mechanism for rapid visual processing. *Journal of Experimental Psychology*, *94*, 239–243.
Just, M. A. & Carpenter, P. A. (1978) Inference processes during reading: Reflections from eye fixations. In J. W. Senders, D. F. Fisher, & R. A. Monty (Eds.), *Eye movement and the higher psychological functions*. Hillsdale, N.J.: Lawrence Erlbaum Associates Inc.
LaBerge, D. (1981) Automatic information processing: A review. In J. Long & A. Baddeley (Eds.), *Attention and performance IX*. Hillsdale, N.J.: Lawrence Erlbaum Associates Inc.
LaBerge, D. & Samuels, S. J. (1974) Toward a theory of automatic information processing in reading. *Cognitive Psychology*, *6*, 293–323.
Lackner, J. R. & Garrett, M. F. (1972) Resolving ambiguity: Effects of biasing contexts in the unattended ear. *Cognition*, *1*, 359–372.
Lewis, J. L. (1970) Semantic processing of unattended messages using dichotic listening. *Journal of Experimental Psychology*, *85*, 225–228.
Linebarger, M. C., Schwartz, M. F., & Saffran, E. M. (1983) Sensitivity to grammatical structure in so-called agrammatic aphasics. *Cognition*, *13*, 361–392.
Lupker, S. J. (1979) The semantic nature of response competition in the picture–word interference task. *Memory and Cognition*, *7*, 485–495.
Marcel, A. J. (1980) Conscious and preconscious recognition of polysemous words: Locating the selective effect of prior verbal context. In R. S. Nickerson (Ed.), *Attention and performance VIII*. Hillsdale, N.J.: Lawrence Erlbaum Associates Inc.
Marcel, A. J. (1983a) Conscious and unconscious perception: Experiments on visual masking and word recognition. *Cognitive Psychology*, *15*, 197–237.

Marcel, A. J. (1983b) Conscious and unconscious perception: An approach to the relations between phenomenal experience and perceptual processes. *Cognitive Psychology, 15*, 238–300.

McClelland, J. L. (1979) On the time relations of mental processes: An examination of systems of processes in cascades. *Psychological Review, 86*, 287–330.

Milberg, W. & Blumstein, S. E. (1981) Lexical decision and aphasia: Evidence for semantic processing. *Brain and Language, 14*, 371–385.

Morton, J. (1969) Interaction of information in word recognition. *Psychological Review, 76*, 165–178.

Morton, J. (1970) A functional model for memory. In D. A. Norman (Ed.), *Models of human memory*. New York: Academic Press.

Neely, J. H. (1977) Semantic priming and retrieval from lexical memory: Roles of inhibitionless spreading activation and limited capacity attention. *Journal of Experimental Psychology: General, 106*, 226–254.

Neisser, U. (1967) *Cognitive psychology*. New York: Appleton-Century-Crofts.

Posner, M. I. (1970) On the relationship between letter names and super-ordinate categories. *Quarterly Journal of Experimental Psychology, 22*, 279–287.

Posner, M. I. & Snyder, C. R. R. (1975) Attention and cognitive control. In R. Solso (Ed.), *Information processing and cognition: The Loyola symposium*. Hillsdale, N.J.: Lawrence Erlbaum Associates Inc.

Rayner, K. & Posnansky, C. (1978) Stages of processing in word identification. *Journal of Experimental Psychology: General, 107*, 64–80.

Riesbeck, C. K. & Schank, R. C. (1978) Comprehension by computer: Expectation based analysis of sentences in context. In W. J. M. Levelt & G. B. Flores d'Arcais (Eds.), *Studies in the perception of language*. Chichester: John Wiley & Sons.

Rosinski, R. R. (1977) Picture–word interference is semantically based. *Child Development, 48*, 643–647.

Rumelhart, D. E. (1977) Toward an interactive model of reading. In S. Dornic (Ed.), *Attention and performance VI*. Hillsdale, N.J.: Lawrence Erlbaum Associates Inc.

Schneider, W. & Shiffrin, R. M. (1977) Controlled and automatic human information processing: I. Detection, search and attention. *Psychological Review, 84*, 1–66.

Schvaneveldt, R. W., Meyer, D. E., & Becker, C. A. (1976) Lexical ambiguity, semantic context, and visual word recognition. *Journal of Experimental Psychology: Human Perception and Performance, 2*, 243–256.

Shaffer, W. O. & LaBerge, D. (1979) Automatic semantic processing of unattended words. *Journal of Verbal Learning and Verbal Behavior, 18*, 413–426.

Shiffrin, M. & Schneider, W. (1977) Controlled and automatic human information processing: II. Perceptual learning, automatic attending and a general theory. *Psychological Review, 84*, 127–190.

Shiffrin, R. M., Dumais, S. T., & Schneider, W. (1981) Characteristics of automatism. In J. Long & A. Baddeley (Eds.), *Attention and performance IX*. Hillsdale, N.J.: Lawrence Erlbaum Associates Inc.

Stemberger, J. P. (1984) Structural errors in normal and agrammatic speech. *Cognitive Neuropsychology, 1*, 281–313.

Swinney, D. A. (1979) Lexical access during sentence comprehension: (Re)consideration of context effects. *Journal of Verbal Learning and Verbal Behavior, 18*, 645–659.

Tanenhaus, M. K., Leiman, J. M., & Seidenberg, M. S. (1979) Evidence for multiple stages in the processing of ambiguous words in syntactic contexts. *Journal of Verbal Learning and Verbal Behavior, 18*, 427–440.

Treisman, A. M. & Gelade, G. (1980) A feature-integration theory of attention *Cognitive Psychology, 12*, 97–136.

Turvey, M.T. (1973) On peripheral and central processes in vision: Inference from an information-processing analysis of masking with patterned stimuli. *Psychological Review*, *80*, 1–52.

Turvey, M.T. (1974) Constructive theory, perceptual system and tacit knowledge. In W.B. Wiener & D.S. Palermo (Eds.), *Cognition and the symbolic processes*. Hillsdale, N.J.: Lawrence Erlbaum Associates Inc.

Von Wright, J.M., Anderson, K., & Stenman, U. (1975) Generalization of conditioned GSRs in dichotic listening. In P.M.A. Rabbitt & S. Dornic (Eds.), *Attention and performance V*. London: Academic Press.

Warren, R.E., Warren, N.T., Green, J.P., & Bresnick, J.H. (1978) Multiple semantic encoding of homophones and homographs in contexts biasing dominant and subordinate readings. *Memory and Cognition*, *6*, 364–371.

Wickens, D.D. (1972) Characteristics of word encoding. In A.W. Melton & E. Martin (Eds.), *Coding processes in human memory*. Washington, D.C.: Winston.

Wilks, Y. (1978) Computational models for language processing. *Cognitive Psychology: Language*. Milton Keynes: Open University Press.

6 Autonomy and Automaticity: Accessing Function Words during Sentence Comprehension[1]

A. D. Friederici
Max-Planck-Institut für Psycholinguistik,
Nijmegen, The Netherlands

INTRODUCTION

Cognitive psychology has shown considerable interest in the influence of existing knowledge on the perception of sensory input. A number of studies have focused on how prior knowledge affects the comprehension of linguistic stimuli. There is clear evidence that contextual information does influence recognition of words in particular, however, when stimuli are degraded (e.g., Cole, 1973; Marslen-Wilson & Welsh, 1978). An interactive model has been put forward in order to account for facilitatory effects of relevant contextual information upon the recognition of spoken words (Marslen-Wilson & Tyler, 1980).

Forster (1979), in contrast, had suggested that lexical processing is autonomous and thereby unaffected by top-down processes. And, indeed, there are findings that seem to indicate that access of word meaning is not affected by knowledge-based processes (Seidenberg, Tanenhaus, Leiman, & Bienkowski, 1982; Swinney, 1979). Whereas Swinney (1979; Onifer & Swinney, 1981) interprets his results so as to support the *autonomy* claim, Seidenberg et al. (1982) interpret their data so as to reflect meaning access as an *automatic* process. Although their findings are compatible with the autonomy hypothesis as well, the authors stress that automaticity does not ensure autonomy. They assume that automaticity is probably a necessary condition for autonomous processing, but not a sufficient one.

[1] This paper was formulated in 1983. Meanwhile, quite a number of papers focusing on the issue of lexical access were published; these will not be discussed in this paper.

Automatic processes, for learned operations, can be characterised as those that remain basically unaffected by conscious attentional processes, once they have reached their "automatic" status (Posner & Snyder, 1975; Schneider & Shiffrin, 1977; Shiffrin & Schneider, 1977). Such overlearned, automatic processes may be very fast and, therefore, normally unaffectable by slower knowledge-based (top-down) processing. By contrast, autonomous processes are in principle cognitively impenetrable (Fodor, 1983; Pylyshyn, 1980). Thus, although it may seem as if we were looking at the same phenomenon, it could well be that automaticity and autonomy are interrelated only during development (e.g. language), but functionally independent once autonomy has been established.

On the basis of these considerations one could hypothesise that these two phenomena—although not independent during language development—can be affected selectively in the adult language-user. Thus, for the latter case, we would predict that loss of automaticity does not necessarily result in a loss of autonomy. It would seem then that automaticity is a necessary condition for the establishment of autonomous processes, but not for the presence of these.

The purpose of the work reported in this chapter was to explore these issues more directly by comparing processing devices of different groups of language-users at a developmental level, and in normal as well as in pathological adult language-use. The experiments investigated the effect of different contexts upon the recognition of open and closed class items. The distinction between the open class—being those major grammatical category elements that carry mainly referential meaning—and the closed class—consisting of the minor grammatical categories that carry primarily structural information—roughly corresponds to the content/function word dichotomy.

A number of attempts have been made to base the distinction of two word classes on theoretical linguistic grounds. None of the descriptions, however, satisfactorily classifies all elements of a particular language. The phonological distinction (Kean, 1979) between non-clitic elements (nouns, verbs, adjectives) and clitic elements (function words and bound morphemes) categorises prepositions into two different classes depending on their syllabicity: one, syllable prepositions cluster with non-clitic elements, and two, syllable prepositions with non-clitic elements. In a syntactic description that defines a difference between those elements that are heads of phrases and those that are not, prepositional forms cluster with major category words when heading a phrase and with minor category elements when they are not head of a phrase. The semantic approach (Klosek, 1979) distinguishing those elements that carry meaning from those that do not, has its problems not only in classifying prepositions that, when used to indicate location, cluster with meaningful major category items but also in categorising those nouns that do not carry a particular meaning (e.g. thing, cause, etc.) that consequently cluster with other minor category elements.

Behavioural data from different studies (Friederici, 1982; Garrett, 1980) suggest that the observed computational difference between different word classes or categories does not map onto either of the linguistic distinctions mentioned earlier. Rather they show an essential difference in processing lexical information and syntactic information independent of an item's class membership. Although there are some exceptions to the equation of lexical/syntactic information and open/closed class distinction, we will for the purpose of terminological simplicity none the less stick to the diction of the distinction between the open and the closed class. The open class refers to that part of the lexicon that contains information about form and meaning, whereas the closed class refers to a particular sub-part of the lexicon that represents the syntactic information carried by the closed class forms.

RECOGNITION OF OPEN CLASS WORDS AND CLOSED CLASS WORDS

Those studies that investigated the effect of context on the recognition of words, with either single word priming (Meyer & Schvaneveldt, 1971), syntactic priming (Goodman, McClelland, & Gibbs, 1981; Tyler & Wessels, 1984), or sentential context (Marslen-Wilson & Tyler, 1980), have focused their research on contextual effects on the recognition of open class items (nouns) only.

The claim, however, has been made that there are distinct recognition devices for items from the open and closed class (Bradley, 1978). Bradley has reported a number of processing differences in the way words of these two classes are retrieved from the lexicon. In a lexical-decision task, decision times for open class words were a function of the frequency of occurrence of these items, whereas no such relationship was observed for the closed class words. Further, differential interference effects for non-words derived from the two classes, as well as differential visual hemifield effects (Bradley & Garrett, 1983) were reported.

Replications and extensions of these important findings, however, in English and other languages have not borne out the original findings altogether. The frequency effect, for example, has not been reliably observed in English (Gordon & Caramazza, 1982) nor in Dutch (Kolk & Blomert, 1982) nor in French (Segui, Mehler, Frauenfelder, & Morton, 1982), but only in Spanish (Garcia-Albea, pers. comm.). In all but the latter replication experiment no systematic differences across the frequency range of the two classes of items were found. Recognition latencies of open class as well as closed class words demonstrated sensitivity to frequency of occurrence. Interference effects, though observable in English, Dutch, and French, are reported to be subject to strategic influences.

Although one may question the experimental support for the notion of two distinct recognition devices for the open and closed classes, there are still a number of reasons to retain the general hypothesis of two different access devices for lexical and non-lexical information. To name a few, in the analysis of errors in spontaneous production it was shown that open and closed class items are involved in different types of speech errors. The finding that lexical and grammatical formatives behave differently has been interpreted as an indication for processes at different levels of sentence representation (Garrett, 1975, 1980). Additional evidence for a computational distinction of the two vocabulary types has been provided by neuropsychological data. Deep dyslexic patients, for example, read open class words more easily than closed class words (Marshall & Newcombe, 1966; Morton & Patterson, 1980). Agrammatic aphasics as well seem to have particular difficulties in processing closed class but not open class elements (Bradley, Garrett, & Zurif, 1980; Caramazza & Zurif, 1976). At the developmental level it was found that children acquire some of the function-word knowledge much later than some of the content-word knowledge (e.g. Flores d'Arcais, 1981). Although the interpretation of these findings is not unequivocal, it is obvious that the two vocabulary types behave differently in a number of respects.

If it is true that the two classes of words are processed at different levels, one might propose that contextual constraints that are effective for recognition of open class words will not necessarily generalise to the recognition of closed class elements: Semantic context may affect recognition of lexical items, but not the recognition of grammatical items; syntactic context, on the other hand, may primarily affect retrieval of syntactic features of words such as grammatical class or category. Note that these hypothesised contextual effects do not violate the autonomy principle because they can be described as intra-level effects (Fodor, 1983).

THE EXPERIMENTS

A series of experiments were conducted in order to investigate the effect of context on the recognition of open and closed class elements. I will review and discuss the findings of those experiments that have already been published individually (Friederici, 1983a, 1983b, 1985). According to the considerations outlined earlier the main prediction was that a normal listener's recognition of open class words will be affected by semantic context, but that semantic context will not affect processing of closed class items.

The available data from normal listeners do not allow a clear determination of whether the observed effects are due to fast automatic processes or, rather, due to the autonomy of different language components. Children at different age groups were therefore tested in the hope that developmental changes would provide some insight into those underlying processes that are highly automatised in normal adults. It was, however, not predictable whether the two phenomena—automaticity and autonomy—would be separable given the consideration of a common developmental history. Yet another possibility to gain insight into those phenomena was explored. On the basis of the assumption that the two phenomena may have a selective effect on adult language-users, two groups of adult aphasics were tested as well. Investigations from two additional groups, using similar experiments, provide evidence for development of processing differences and indicate that the end point is autonomous subsystems.

Method and Material

The experiments discussed here all used the same method, a word-monitoring task. This task had been shown to be sensitive to the temporal course of comprehension processes in normal listeners (Marslen-Wilson & Tyler, 1980), in children (Tyler & Marslen-Wilson, 1981), as well as in aphasics (Swinney, Zurif, & Cutler, 1980). In such a task, the subject is requested to listen to a sentence and to monitor for a target word that is specified prior to the presentation of the sentence. The subject is instructed to press a decision key as soon as he or she hears the target. Reaction times and error rates are recorded.

The experiments varied word class as well as context. Different types of items from the open class, such as nouns and adjectives, and items from the closed class, such as determiners, conjunctions, and quantifiers, served as targets. Prepositions, for the reasons discussed above, were treated as a separate category. Sentences containing the target were preceded either by a semantically related (1) or a semantically unrelated (2) context sentence, for example (target word is in italics):

1. Der verarmte Spieler entschloß sich, ins Kasino zu gehen. Der Mann hoffte *Geld* zu gewinnen.
2. Der verliebte Student entschloß sich, ins Grüne zu fahren. Der Mann hoffte *Geld* zu gewinnen.

The stimulus set consisted of 100 pairs of test sentences; the second sentence of each pair contained a monitoring target word. There were 50 target sentences, each belonging to two pairs, preceded by either a semantically related or unrelated context sentence. The general distinction between open and closed class items was used in order to investigate lexical v. syntactic processes. Thus the 50 targets were selected under the following constraints: 10 words each were taken from the two word classes, from the open class (the experimental set consisted of nouns and adjectives), and from the closed class (the experimental set included determiners, conjunctions, and adverbs). Additional items were taken from three different "categories" within the closed class set (10 items each) in order to investigate possible effects of lexical information upon the processing of closed class elements. The same phonological form of a closed class item—a preposition—appeared in three different functional roles, i.e. as a lexical preposition, as an obligatory preposition, and as a verb particle. Because these different prepositional forms varied only their function but not their form, separate analyses were carried out for the across-class (open/closed) and within-class (prepositional form) distinction. However, for purpose of brevity the presentation here will be restricted to the general open/closed class difference. A discussion of the subtle within-class difference would go beyond the scope of this paper (for details, see Friederici, 1985).

PROCESSING OPEN AND CLOSED CLASS ITEMS DURING SENTENCE COMPREHENSION: EVIDENCE FROM NORMAL ADULTS

In a first experiment 48 normal subjects (24 male and 24 female students) who were paid for their participation were tested in order to explore the general features of on-line recognition of open and closed class elements in sentences. Subjects heard the 50 targets only once, two groups of subjects were used to provide observations on each target in semantically related and unrelated contexts.

Monitoring reaction times for open and closed class items in different contextual conditions are displayed in Fig. 1. The data clearly show different context effects for the two classes of items. Open class items are recognised faster when preceded by a semantically related context (338 msec) than when preceded by an unrelated sentence (369 msec). No such effect was found for the recognition of closed class words (319 msec, 328 msec). Over conditions closed class items were recognised faster (324 msec) than open class items (349 msec). The results for the open class items are compatible with the view that context facilitates word recognition. Whether the context effect observed in this study depend on automatic word-association effects (Stanovich & West, 1983) that are unaffected by knowledge-based processes (Seidenberg et al., 1982), or on lexical inferences drawn from the words given in the context sentence, or

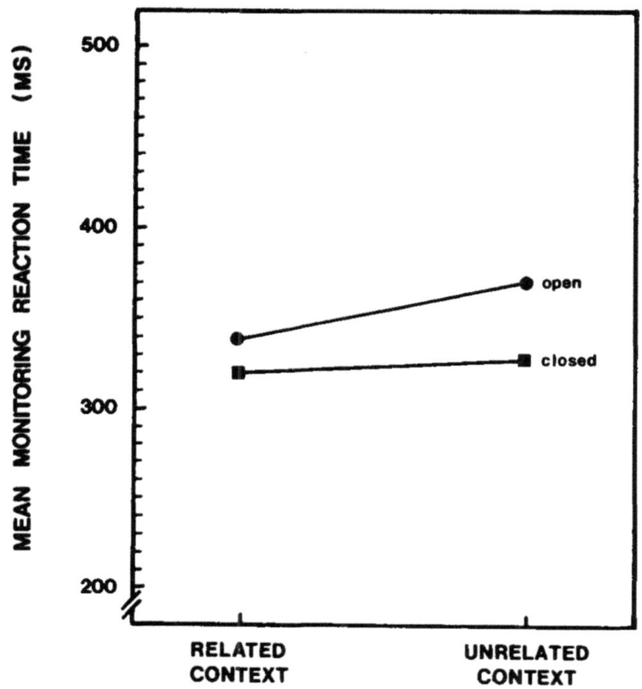

FIG. 1. Mean monitoring reaction times (in msec) for open and closed class items: normal listeners.

on syntactic and interpretative knowledge projected from the meaning of the whole sentence (Marslen-Wilson & Tyler, 1980) cannot be decided conclusively from the data obtained here.

Whatever the proper analysis of the context effects here, it is open to discussion whether the different information sources work at distinct autonomous levels of processing in a serial, in an autonomous but simultaneous, or in an interactive way. We may assume that syntactic parallel is used to build up expectations about the incoming item's form class, whereas semantic-interpretative knowledge is used primarily to build up expectations about the meaning of the incoming item. Depending on the semantic information given in a sentence, the interpretation of a sentence would have to rely more or less heavily on the correct processing of the syntactic information given. However, because a listener would not know in advance to what extent interpretation of a particular sentence will require syntactic analysis, the most efficient way to deal with that would be to compute automatically all the syntactic information available. And indeed, there are findings suggesting that syntax is processed automatically, independent of whether the semantic information is sufficient to build clear representations of the sentence's meaning (Flores d'Arcais, 1982).

The findings for the closed class items—at least for those that do not carry referential meaning—are different from the open class results. Recognition of closed class items is not affected by semantic context. Both classes of items were recognised equally fast when semantically related context was given; in semantically unrelated context, however, closed class items were responded to faster than open class items. By using the concept of a particular set's size, it was argued that the intrinsically small set of closed class allows search procedures to be (terminated) faster than those in the open class set. When sufficient semantically related context is available to limit the number of plausible open class items, both classes may be recognised equally fast. Note that this non-difference is not a floor effect: Reaction times are even faster when the sentential context allow for predictions of a specific word category such as, for example, prepositions.

A similar lexical-search theory in which it is assumed that priming occurs when the subject uses context to narrow the size of the search set has been proposed for the context of a single lexical item (e.g. Becker, 1979; Forster, 1976). Forster (1981) argues, however, that the context of a sentence fragment would not allow the application of such a strategy, because set size would still be too large to gain any advantage for word recognition. He denies the possibility that—in reading at least—lexical recognition derives any benefit from inputs from higher levels, either syntactic or semantic. Studies that measured auditory word recognition on-line suggest that information of higher levels is not only used post-access, but rather during access (Marslen-Wilson & Tyler, 1980) or even pre-access as well as during access (Grosjean, 1980). Although post-access effects are compatible with a strong autonomy position, during-access and pre-access effects are not. A weak autonomy position could hold that the different levels work in parallel with a continuous output to the higher levels, but also to a general processor that is able to take input from the different linguistic levels. This general processor continuously builds up expectations about the incoming information. Words may be recognised earlier in context because expectations could be met even before the entire word is perceived. Thus word recognition can be facilitated during access by syntactic and semantic information. The syntactic level itself, however, is autonomous in so far as it does not take semantic input from either the semantic level or the language processor.

The results reported so far support the view of a syntactic level working relatively independent from the semantic information, those closed class items that carry primarily structural information and are processed at a level that is not affected by semantic context.

CHILDREN'S SENSITIVITY TO CLOSED CLASS WORDS: THE DEVELOPMENT OF AUTOMATIC PROCESSES

The process a normal listener uses to recover the lexical, semantic, and syntactic information for sentence comprehension will presumably undergo developmental changes as the linguistic knowledge grows. Once the bulk of linguistic knowledge has been acquired, there may be even further developmental differences in how this knowledge is used. In describing these changes, we aim not only to get some insight about when particular linguistic knowledge is acquired but also to understand the processes underlying its use.

At a developmental level, the studies of Tyler (1981) seem to suggest that although there are no overall differences in how children of different ages use syntactic- and interpretative-knowledge sources during sentence comprehension, younger children are guided primarily by pragmatic and inferential processes. Other studies have consistently stressed developmental differences between syntactic processes on the one hand and semantic/pragmatic processes on the other (e.g. Slobin & Bever, 1982). Swinney and Cutler (1979) and Flores d'Arcais (1981) have shown that the acquisition of function words—or at least some aspects of them—develops much later than the children's content-word knowledge. Flores d'Arcais pointed out that there are developmental differences in the knowledge and the use of function words. Although children at a given age may understand a function word in context, they may not perform correctly on more abstract tasks.

It is not implausible to assume that this developmental lag reflects some essential underlying differences in how children process function words. It may well be that the ability to access these items automatically develops much later than the ability to use these items in production and comprehension. If this assumption were valid, we would expect children's recognition of function words to be dependent on semantic context.

Two versions of the experiment described above were conducted. Older children (8, 9, 10, and 11 years) were presented with stimulus material previously used with adult listeners. For younger children (5, 7, and 8 years) we used a version in which wording of the sentences was changed so that it was more appropriate for younger listeners. A more detailed description of these experiments was given elsewhere (Friederici, 1983b). Error data (Table 1) as well as monitoring reaction times (Fig. 2) show clear developmental differences. Five- and seven-year-olds made more errors than eight-year-olds. Children from all age groups more often failed to respond to closed than to open class items. Performance of open class word recognition was generally quite good, such that semantic context did not reveal a significant effect. Semantic context, however, did affect

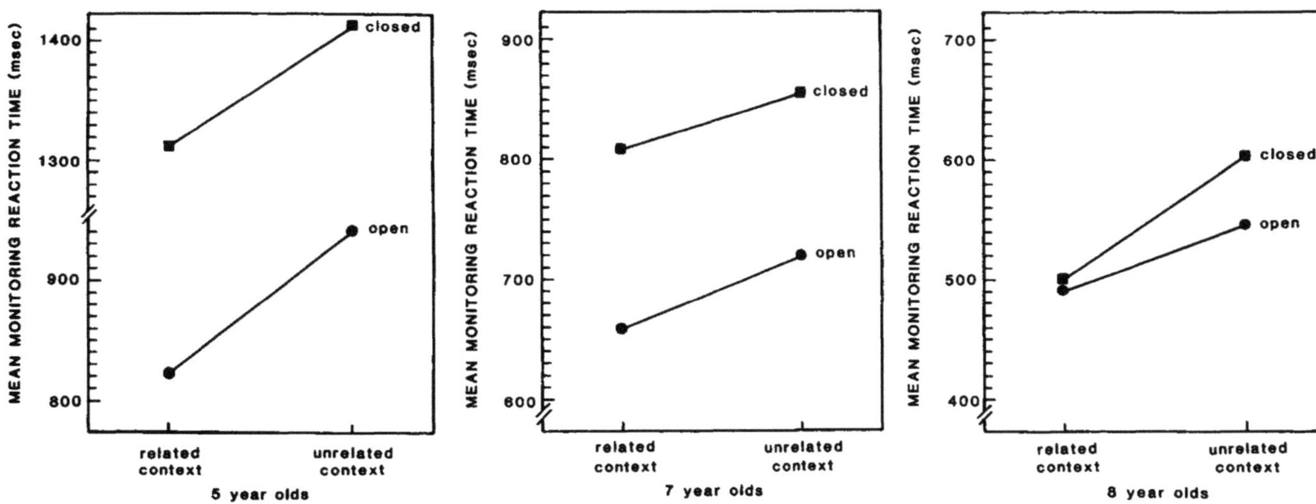

FIG 2. Mean monitoring reaction times (in msec) for open and closed class items: 5-, 7-, and 8-year-olds.

TABLE 1
Absolute Errors (out of 100 Trials) for Different Age Groups (5, 7, 8): Open and Closed Class Items

Word Class	*Context*	*Years* 5	7	8
Open	Related	0	7	2
	Unrelated	5	2	8
Closed	Related	28	28	18
	Unrelated	55	43	26

recognition of closed class items significantly. Children's responses to closed class elements were more likely to be wrong when these items were preceded by an unrelated context sentence than when preceded by a semantically related context sentence.

When looking at the reaction time data, the following picture emerges. Five-year-olds, generally, respond more slowly than seven-year-olds, and seven-year-olds show slower reactions than eight-year-olds. In agreement with a selective increase of errors for closed class words, children of five and seven years respond slower to closed than to open class words; this difference, however, disappears by the age of eight years. Context had a significant effect upon the recognition of open class elements in all three age groups: Open class words were recognised faster when preceded by a semantically related context sentence. Semantic context also had a significant effect upon the recognition of closed class items for the five-year-olds, but not for the seven- and eight-year-olds. It appears not only that children at a younger age generally have more difficulties in processing closed class items on-line but also that processes involving those items that carry structural information are penetrable by ongoing semantic–interpretative processes, suggesting that these syntactic processes are not yet automatic.

When considering the results from older children (Table 2 and Fig. 3), we see that the ability for rapid automatic identification of closed class items develops only very slowly. By the age of eight years the reaction-time difference between the two classes has disappeared. Semantic context had an effect on the recognition latencies of the open class words only; however, at this age, children still make more errors in reacting to closed than to open class words.

At the age of nine years, finally, children's reaction-time latencies are similar to that of older children and adults in that they react faster to closed than to open class items. They differ, however, from adults in that their recognition of closed class elements is not yet independent of possible semantic interpretations of the sentential context—a pattern

TABLE 2
Absolute Errors (out of 120 Trials) for Different Age Groups (8, 9, 10, 11): Open and Closed Class Items

		Years			
Word Class	*Context*	*8*	*9*	*10*	*11*
Open	Related	1	1	2	1
	Unrelated	2	2	0	0
Closed	Related	12	9	8	12
	Unrelated	28	21	11	8

that can still be seen in the 10-year-olds. The remaining developmental difference between these two age groups is that the reactions of nine-year-olds to closed class items are far less reliable than to open class items, especially to closed class items in sentences preceded by unrelated context.

It is only at the age of 11 years that children show the same pattern of performance as adults. They reacted faster to closed than to open class items, showed facilitation of recognition for open class items in a semantically related v. a semantically unrelated context and did not demonstrate any contextual effect on the recognition of closed class elements. Their overall reaction-time latencies, however, were still slower than that of normal adults. And unlike adults, they still demonstrated a particular—although minor—insecurity to react to closed class items in sentences, as indicated by the error (miss) rate.

From these results we may conclude that the ability to respond automatically to the syntactic environment as provided by closed class elements only develops around the age of nine years. The findings, however, also suggest that the development of rapid, accurate processes associated with automaticity is a necessary condition for syntactic processes to become autonomous. As the child develops, reaction latencies to closed class elements, in particular, get shorter and independent of semantic constraints, suggesting that their ability to process syntactic aspects becomes *automatic* and at the same time more and more *autonomous* from semantic-interpretative variables. Their error behaviour, however, indicates that it will take some more time before autonomy of syntactic processes is fully established. Final conclusions about the relation of these two phenomena cannot be drawn from these developmental data alone.

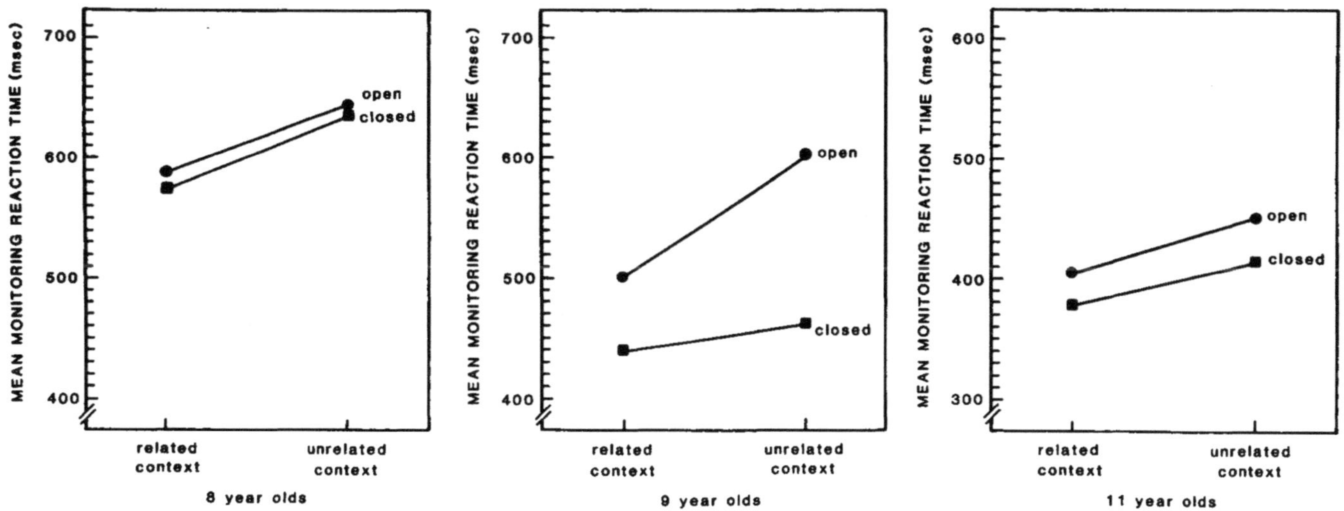

FIG 3. Mean monitoring reaction times (in msec) for open and closed class items: 8-, 9-, and 11-year-olds.

BROCA'S APHASIA: LOSS OF AUTONOMY OR LOSS OF AUTOMATICITY?

Agrammatism as seen in Broca's aphasia has been described as a general syntactic deficit (Berndt & Caramazza, 1980), and alternatively, as a loss of a specialised retrieval system for closed class elements (Bradley, Garrett, & Zurif, 1980). Under the assumption that such a specialised retrieval system is a necessary condition for autonomous syntactic processes, the breakdown of such a system would cause the loss of autonomous processes. On the other hand, one could also assume that this specialised retrieval system only guarantees automaticity of a given processor. On the basis of these considerations it has been proposed that Broca's aphasia can be attributed to the loss of automatic syntactic processes (Friederici, 1983a). This proposal is partly compatible with a recent suggestion by Blumstein, Milberg, and Shrier (1982) that Broca's aphasia is due to a general loss of automaticity—be it for syntactic or lexical processes.

Given these assumptions it seemed that automatic and autonomous processes may be observable as separately disturbed in Broca's aphasia. In an experiment that used the method and materials described earlier a group of seven agrammatic Broca's aphasics was tested. Seven Wernicke patients were used as the aphasic control group. Fourteen normal subjects who were roughly matched in age and education were used as non-aphasic controls. All patients were right-handed and suffered from a cerebrovascular lesion in the left hemisphere. Patients were classified according to the test scores of the Aachen Aphasia Test (Huber, Poeck, Weniger, & Willmes, 1983). For a more detailed description of the patients, see Friederici (1983a).

Error data (Table 3) and monitoring reaction times showed clear differences between the two aphasic groups. Pattern of performance for Wernicke's aphasics (Fig. 4) was basically similar to that of normal controls (Fig. 5), although their overall reaction latencies were slower. They reacted faster to closed than to open class items and showed a significant

TABLE 3
Absolute Errors (out of 100 Trials) for Aphasic Groups: Open and Closed Class Items

Word Class	*Context*	*Agrammatics*	*Wernicke's*
Open	Related	2	4
	Unrelated	5	1
Closed	Related	15	14
	Unrelated	14	15

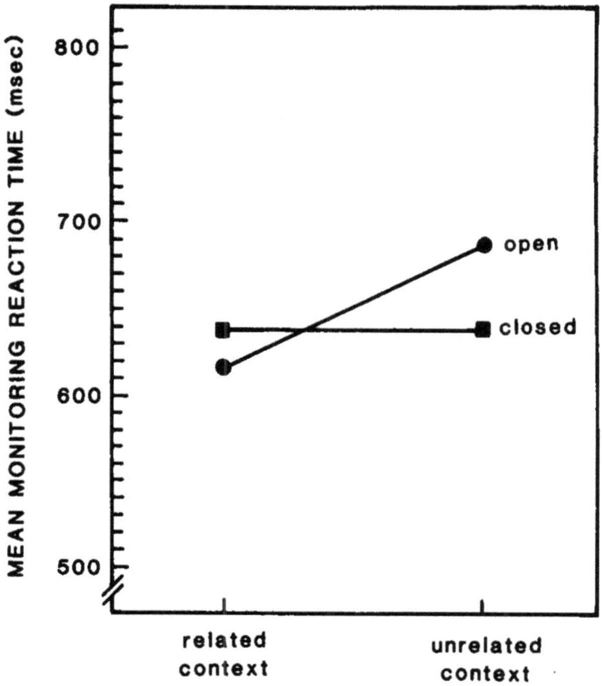

FIG. 4. Mean monitoring reaction times (in msec) for open and closed class items: Wernicke's aphasics.

context effect for the recognition of the open but not for the closed class. Agrammatic Broca's aphasics (Fig. 6), in contrast to normal adults and aphasic controls, reacted significantly more slowly to closed than to open class items, although their rate of accuracy did not differ from that of the aphasic controls. Unlike children, however, who show similarly slow reaction times for the closed class (around the age of seven years), Broca's aphasics do not demonstrate any context effect for the recognition of closed class items—neither in the reaction time nor in the error pattern. It is interesting to note that these patients, like normal adults, show a selective effect of semantic context upon the recognition of open class items. Agrammatic Broca's aphasics, like normal adults, process closed class items *independent* of semantic variables—just very slowly.

These findings suggest that what is lost in agrammatism is the ability to access automatically closed class elements; the process as such, however, still appears to be autonomous in that it is unaffected by semantic factors. Thus autonomy seems to be retained whereas automaticity for this special process seems to be lost. This interpretation, however, as it stands, can only explain the agrammatic deficit if we assume that such a specialised

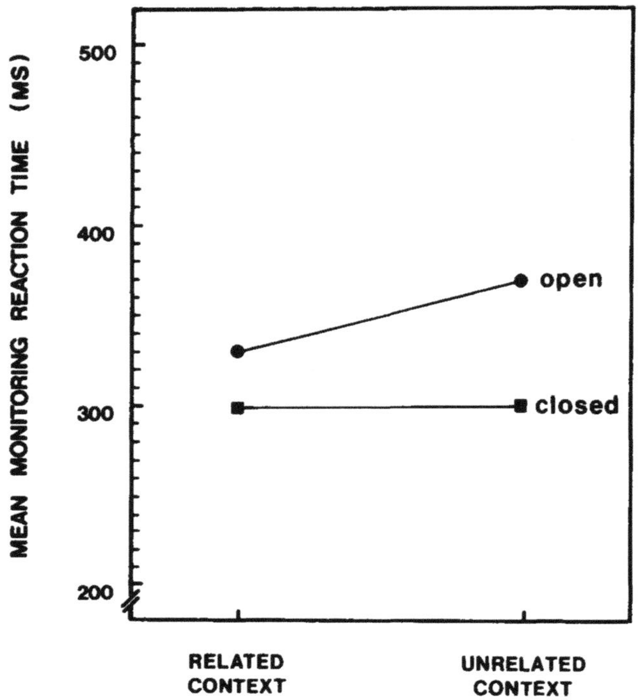

FIG. 5. Mean monitoring reaction times (in msec) for open and closed items: normal controls.

retrieval system is a necessary condition for normal sentence parsing. And indeed, there is considerable evidence showing that these patients are deficient, in particular, when it comes to retrieval and use of the structural information of closed class elements during sentences comprehension. This suggests that the retrieval system that guarantees fast and automatic access to closed class items and their structural information is a necessary condition for normal parsing and, furthermore, that its loss will result in agrammatic comprehension.

CONCLUSION

In this chapter the attempt has been made to describe the relation between autonomy and automaticity of syntactic processes. Although the two phenomena seem to be closely related during language acquisitions, findings from pathological language-use indicate that they can be disturbed independently. The data suggest that once autonomy of syntactic processes has been established, automaticity is no longer a necessary condition for the autonomy of the processes as such. Automaticity, however, seems to

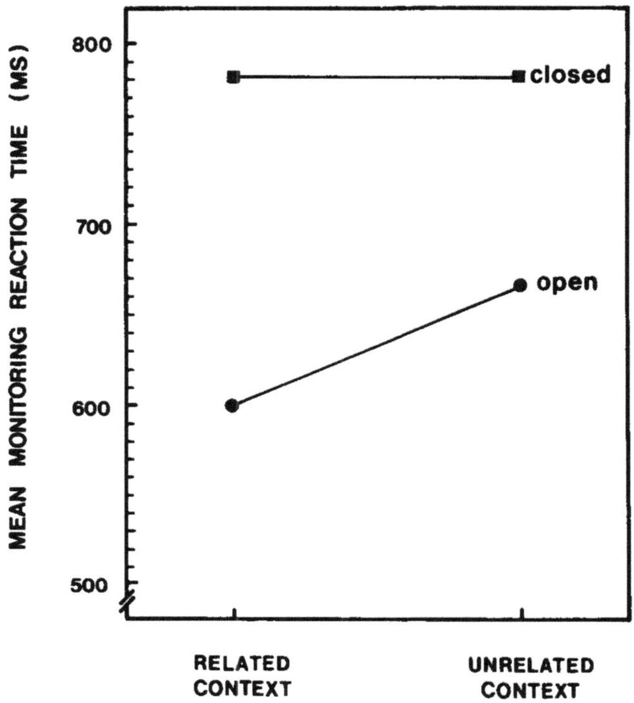

FIG 6. Mean monitoring reaction times (in msec) for open and closed class items: agrammatics.

be essential for the adequate retrieval and on-line use of all syntactic aspects given in a sentence. Loss of automaticity does not necessarily affect the architecture of the system, that is the autonomy of certain subsystems; it may, however, have severe effects on the ability to access specific information from a given subsystem and to use it during sentence parsing.

REFERENCES

Becker, C. A. (1979) Semantic context and word frequency effects in visual word recognition. *Journal of Experimental Psychology: Human Perception and Performance*, *5*, 252–259.

Berndt, R. & Caramazza, A. (1980) A redefinition of the syndrome of Broca's aphasia: Implications for a neuropsychological model of language. *Applied Psycholinguistics*, *1*, 225–278.

Blumstein, S. E., Milberg, W., & Shrier, R. (1982) Semantic processing in aphasia: Evidence from an auditory lexical decision task. *Brain and Language*, *18*, 301–315.

Bradley, D. C. (1978) Computational distinction of vocabulary type. Unpublished Ph.D. Thesis, MIT.

Bradley, D. C. & Garrett, M. F. (1983) Hemispheric differences in the recognition of closed and open class words. *Neuropsychologia, 21*, 155–159.

Bradley, D. C., Garrett, M. F., & Zurif, E. B. (1980) Syntactic deficits in Broca's aphasia. In D. Caplan (Ed.), *Biological studies of mental processes*. Cambridge, Mass: MIT Press.

Caramazza, A. & Surif, E. B. (1976) Dissociation of algorithmic and heuristic processes in language comprehension: Evidence from aphasia. *Brain and Language, 3*, 572–582.

Cole, R. A. (1973) Listening for mispronunciations: A measure of what we hear during speech. *Perception and Psychophysics, 11*, 153–156.

Flores d'Arcais, G. B. (1981) The acquisition of meaning of the connectives. In W. Deutsch (Ed.), *The child's construction of language*. London: Academic Press.

Flores d'Arcais, G. B. (1982) Automatic syntactic computation and the use of semantic information during sentence comprehension. *Psychological Research, 44*, 231–242.

Fodor, J. A. (1983) *The modularity of mind*. Cambridge, Mass: MIT Press.

Forster, K. I. (1976) Accessing the mental lexicon. In R. Wales & E. Walker (Eds.), *New approaches to language mechanisms*. Amsterdam: North Holland.

Forster, K. I. (1979) Levels of processing and the structure of the language processor. In W. E. Cooper & E. C. T. Walker (Eds.), *Sentence processing: Psycholinguistic studies presented to Merrill Garrett*. Hillsdale, N.J.: Lawrence Erlbaum Associates Inc.

Forster, K. I. (1981) Priming and the effects of sentence and lexical contexts on naming time: Evidence for autonomous lexical processing. *Quarterly Journal of Experimental Psychology, 33a*, 465–495.

Friederici, A. D. (1982) Syntactic and semantic processes in aphasic deficits: The availability of prepositions. *Brain and Language, 15*, 249–258.

Friederici, A. D. (1983a) Aphasics' perception of words in sentential context: Some real-time processing evidence. *Neuropsychologia, 21*, 351–358.

Friederici, A. D. (1983b) Children's sensitivity to function words during sentence comprehension. *Linguistics, 21*, 717–739.

Friederici, A. D. (1985) Levels of processing and vocabulary types: Evidence from on-line comprehension in normals and agrammatics. *Cognition, 19*, 133–166.

Garrett, M. F. (1975) The analysis of sentence production. In G. Bower (Ed.), *The psychology of learning and motivation: Advances in research and theory*, Vol. 9. New York: Academic Press.

Garrett, M. F. (1980) Levels of processing in sentence production. In B. Butterworth (Ed.), *Language production*. London: Academic Press.

Goodman, G. O., McClelland, J. L., & Gibbs, R. W., Jr. (1981) The role of syntactic context in word recognition. *Memory and Cognition, 9*, 580–586.

Gordon, B. & Caramazza, A. (1982) Lexical decision for open and closed class items: Failure to replicate differential frequency sensitivity. *Brain and Language, 15*, 143–180.

Grosjean, F. (1980) Spoken word recognition processes and the gating paradigm. *Perception and Psychophysics, 28*, 267–283.

Huber, W., Poeck, K., Weniger, D., & Willmes, K. (1983) *Aachener Aphasie Test*. Göttingen: Hogrefe.

Kean, M.-L. (1979) Agrammatism: A phonological deficit? *Cognition, 5*, 9–46.

Klosek, J. (1979) Two unargued linguistic assumptions in Kean's "phonological" interpretation of agrammatism. *Cognition, 7*, 61–68.

Kolk, H. H. J. & Blomert, L. (1982) On the Bradley-hypothesis concerning agrammatism: The non-word interference effect. *Brain and Language, 21*, 47–67.

Marshall, J. C. & Newcombe, F. (1966) Syntactic and semantic errors in paralexia. *Neuropsychologia, 4*, 169–176.

Marslen-Wilson, W. D. & Tyler, L. K. (1980) The temporal structure of spoken language understanding. *Cognition, 8*, 1–71.

Marslen-Wilson, W. D. & Welsh, A. (1978) Processing interactions and lexical access during word recognition in continuous speech. *Cognitive Psychology*, *10*, 29–63.

Meyer, D. M. & Schvaneveldt, R. W. (1971) Facilitation in recognizing pairs of words: Evidence of a dependence between retrieval operations. *Journal of Experimental Psychology*, *90*, 227–234.

Morton, J. & Patterson, K. (1980) Little words—No! In M. Coltheart, K. Patterson, & J. C. Marshall (Eds.), *Deep dyslexia.* London: Routledge & Kegan Paul.

Onifer, W. & Swinney, D. A. (1981) Accessing lexical ambiguities during sentence comprehension: Effects of frequency and contextual bias. *Memory and Cognition*, *9*, 225–236.

Posner, M. I. & Snyder, C. R. (1975) Attention and cognitive control. In R. L. Solso (Ed.), *Information processing and cognition: The Loyola symposium.* Hillsdale, N.J. Lawrence Erlbaum Associates Inc.

Pylyshyn, Z. W. (1980) Computation and cognition: Issues in the foundation of cognitive science. *The Behavioral and Brain Science*, *3*, 111–132.

Segui, J., Mehler, J., Frauenfelder, U., & Morton, J. (1982) Word frequency effect and lexical access. *Neuropsychologia*, *20*, 615–627.

Seidenberg, M. S., Tanenhaus, M. K., Leiman, J. M., & Bienkowski, M. (1982) Automatic access to the meaning of ambiguous words in context: Some limitations of knowledge-based processing. *Cognitive Psychology*, *14*, 489–537.

Shiffrin, R. M. & Schneider, W. (1977) Controlled and automatic human information processing II. Perceptual learning, automatic attending and a general theory. *Psychological Review*, *84*, 127–190.

Schneider, W. & Shiffrin, R. M. (1977) Controlled and automatic human information processing. I. Detection, search and attention. *Psychological Review*, *84*, 1–66.

Slobin, D. I. & Bever, T. G. (1982) Children's use of canonical sentence schema. A non-linguistic study of word order and case inflection. *Cognition*, *12*, 229–265.

Stanovich, K. E. & West, R. F. (1983) On priming by a sentence context. *Journal of Experimental Psychology: General*, *112*, 1–36.

Swinney, D. A. (1979) Lexical access during sentence comprehension: (Re)consideration of context effects. *Journal of Verbal Learning and Verbal Behavior*, *18*, 645–660.

Swinney, D. A. & Cutler, A. (1979) *Effect of sentential stress and word type upon children's comprehension.* Paper presented at the Midwestern Psychological Association, Chicago.

Swinney, D. A., Zurif, E. B., & Cutler, A. (1980) Effects of sentential stress and word class upon comprehension in Broca's aphasics. *Brain and Language*, *10*, 132–144.

Tyler, L. K. (1981) Syntactic and interpretive factors in the development of language comprehension. In W. Deutsch (Ed.), *The Child's construction of language.* London: Academic Press.

Tyler, L. K. & Marslen-Wilson, W. D. (1981) Children's processing of spoken language. *Journal of Verbal Learning and Verbal Behavior*, *20*, 400–416.

Tyler, L. K. & Wessels, J. (1984) Quantifying contextual contributions to word recognition processes. *Perception and Psychophysics*, *34*, 409–420.

7 Sentence-processing Strategies of Broca's Aphasics and Normal Speakers as Reflected by Gaze Movements

W. Huber
Department of Neurology, Pauwelsstrasse, Aachen, West Germany

G. Lüer and U. Lass
Institute of Psychology, University of Göttingen, West Germany

INTRODUCTION

Many experimental studies have shown that Broca's aphasics with agrammatic speech output also have difficulties in comprehending sentences. Superficially, these difficulties seem to be related to the same underlying linguistic deficit as their expressive language disorders. The exact nature of such a systematic supramodal disturbance is an issue of ongoing debate (e.g. Berndt & Caramazza, 1980; Goodglass, 1976; Kean, 1977; Kerschensteiner et al., 1978; Linebarger, Schwartz, & Saffran, 1983; Zurif, 1980).

There are two general objections to theories that try to equate expressive and receptive disturbances. First, there is only weak evidence that the aphasic syndrome can be qualitatively delineated as clearly in receptive as in expressive linguistic behaviour. Second, there is much counter-evidence from general psycholinguistic studies against the assumption of homologous processing in language production and comprehension. It is certainly not sufficient to consider the process of sentence comprehension a reversal of the production process.

Normal sentence comprehension is instead characterised by specific heuristics or strategies that enable the language-hearer to spare himself a full grammatical analysis of the perceived utterance (cf. Bever, 1974; Clark, 1978; Forster, 1979). By means of these heuristics, the hearer may rely only on the meaning of individual lexical items or on superficial string information that is directly mapped onto logical or thematic functions.

From both sources the hearer infers a reference situation that best fits his general word knowledge, communicative expectations, and—in an experimental setting—the specific task demands that are put upon him.

There is a growing number of studies that try to interpret the comprehension "errors" of aphasic patients within such a framework of linguistic strategies (Blumstein, Goodglass, Statlender, & Biber, 1983; Caramazza & Zurif, 1976; Heeschen, 1980; Lonzi & Zanobio, 1983; Saffran, Schwartz, & Marin, 1980; Scholes, 1978; Schwartz, Saffran, & Marin, 1980). The results of these studies indicate that Broca's aphasics rely heavily on semantic and pragmatic information that is derived from major lexical items. If such a key-word strategy results in an ambiguous understanding, as in sentences with semantically reversible subject–object relations, Broca's aphasics either perform at chance level (Caramazza & Zurif, 1976) or follow an elementary syntactic-mapping strategy that takes the initial noun phrase (NP) of a sentence to designate the agent (Heeschen, 1980). The consistency with which such a simple mapping strategy is pursued may vary greatly from one patient to the other as the results of Schwartz et al. (1980) suggest. High inter-individual variability might explain some of the contradicting results reported in the literature.

Marked differences between understanding reversible active v. passive sentences—as predicted by the first NP-mapping strategy—were found by Goodglass (1968), but not by Parisi and Pizzamiglio (1970), Lesser (1974), and Vermeulen (1982). Object topicalisation in reversible active sentences greatly affected the performance of German-speaking aphasics (Heeschen, 1980; Huber, in press), but not of Japanese patients (Kudo, Tateishi, Kashiwagi, & Segawa, 1982). Such differences in results may, of course, also have been influenced by intervening variables such as differences in overall severity of aphasia, in task demands, or in the underlying syntactic systems of the individual language studied.

There is also a general methodological shortcoming in the type of neurolinguistic studies referred to so far. Information based on error analysis permits only rather indirect conclusions about the levels of processing that are specifically impaired and/or observed in aphasia. Therefore, we decided to assess eye movements during sentence processing as a means of obtaining more direct information. In normal subjects, gaze patterns were found to reflect cognitive processes during reading of texts or during metalinguistic sorting tasks (cf. Just & Carpenter, 1977; Rayner, 1978; Reusser & Groner, 1981; Senders, Fisher, & Monty, 1978). In the present study, we wanted to examine the relationship between linguistic output and the processing that precedes it when subjects are asked to search an array of written words for a correct sentence, and to point out that sentence to the examiner. Our dependent variables were frequency, duration, and alternation of gaze. We hypothesised that for normal controls the strength of these variables would indicate which words were chosen for a solution and what was linguistically most favoured during processing.

Aphasic subjects are most likely to fail in this type of anagram task and respond with a linguistically inadequate or fragmentary sentence. The gaze pattern during the scanning of the written material preceding a response may either predict the type of erroneous response given later or be unrelated to the response but nevertheless systematically dependent on the linguistic features of the multiple choice stimuli presented during scanning. Only in the first case can an underlying deficit be directly inferred from the error analysis. In the second case, however, in which a discrepancy between systematic gaze behaviour and type of errors is assumed, a distinction would have to be made between at least two stages of solving the task, namely recognition of lexical–semantic and morpho-syntactic features and utilisation of these features for sentence construction. It is quite possible that Broca's aphasia affects processing in these two stages differently, thus reflecting the global clinical finding that language comprehension is relatively less impaired than production.

The influence of three specific linguistic features was controlled in the study. We know from studies of normal language acquisition in children that the processing of sentences is determined by strategies that begin with a search for the source of an action, the "agent" (cf. Bever, 1974). On semantic grounds, animate nouns are most likely to be considered as agents. Consequently, in production as well as in comprehension, noun phrases are most easily identified as a grammatical subject if they contain an animate as opposed to an inanimate noun (Bates & MacWhinney, 1981; Clark, 1965; Jarvella & Sinnott, 1972). In a sentence-anagram task, Saffran et al. (1980) demonstrated that the performance of Broca's aphasics was also constrained by the animacy contrast. The patients tended to order the elements correctly only when the agent was the single animate element of the anagram. In constructing the items of our task, we made sure that the nominal elements allowed for an agent v. non-agent interpretation.

The second feature is the grammatical category of the words. It is a classical issue in the aphasia literature that word category has a differential impact on the linguistic behaviour of Broca's aphasics (cf. the recent discussion by Bradley, Garrett, & Zurif, 1980, but cf. also Gordon & Caramazza, 1982). Therefore, the stimulus words used in our task were strictly controlled with respect to the distribution of major and minor grammatical categories. We expected that the gazes of Broca's aphasics would be more frequent and more extensive while scanning nouns and verbs than while scanning minor category words, like auxiliaries and particles.

Finally, it seemed to be an open question with respect to normal as well as to aphasic linguistic behaviour whether in the assigned task the sentence structure would be conceptualised in a linear or in a hierarchical way. We expected that the varying degrees of syntactic coherence among the constituents of the target sentence would be reflected by different values found for the eye-movement variables. If Broca's aphasics rely exclusively on key-word strategies, neither linear nor hierarchical processing of sentence structure should be demonstrable.

METHODS

Subjects

Included in the study were 10 patients with Broca's aphasia, 10 normal control patients, and 21 students. The sample characteristics are given in Table 1.

All aphasic subjects were outpatients receiving speech therapy. The etiology was vascular in all cases. Median duration of aphasia was 16.5 months (range 2–75). The lesions assessed by computerised tomography were restricted to areas supplied by frontal and/or medial branches of the left middle cerebral artery. The number of patients available was rather limited as patients with corrected vision, hemianopia, and occulomotor deficit could not be considered.

Unfortunately, only two aphasic control patients, one with mild Wernicke's aphasia and one with amnesic aphasia could be studied. Both patients had a CVA with CT-lesions in the superior temporal gyrus. They were males, 40 and 53 years old. Duration of aphasia was five and eight months. Several authors have claimed that patients with Wernicke's and amnesic aphasia show primarily lexical–semantic rather than syntactic impairments in both expressive and receptive tasks (e.g. Caramazza & Berndt, 1978; Scholes, 1978). A dichotomy between syntactic and lexical disorders in Broca's v. Wernicke's aphasia has been particularly claimed for sentence-anagram tasks (von Stockert, 1972; von Stockert & Bader, 1976). Therefore, the gaze movements of the two aphasic control patients

TABLE 1
Sample Characteristics

	Sex			Age (yrs)	
	n	*F*	*M*	*Md*	*Range*
Broca's	10	4	6	47.5	26–69
Normal Controls	10	5	5	48.5	32–62
Students	21	10	11	23.0	20–32

may be related to other linguistic features of our stimuli than is the case in patients with Broca's aphasia.

Baseline language performance of the aphasic patients was assessed by means of the Aachen Aphasia Test (AAT) (Huber, Poeck, & Willmes 1984; Willmes, Poeck, Weniger, & Huber, 1982). Each AAT profile was assigned to a clinical type of aphasia using a non-parametric discriminant analysis (ALLOC). Classification probabilities were 100% for each of the 10 patients with Broca's aphasia as well as for the two aphasic control patients.

Median and ranges of the AAT performance values in the Broca's group are given in Table 2. The spontaneous speech of two Broca's patients consisted only of one- and two-word sentences. In the remaining eight patients, speech output was characterised by moderately severe agrammatism with frequent omissions of function words and inflectional endings and with simple sentence structures without subordination of finite or infinite clauses. The percentile ranks in Table 2 are based on the performance of the whole AAT standardisation sample of 376 aphasic patients. As the percentile ranks of the individual patients show, reading comprehension was moderately impaired for three patients, only slightly for six patients, and was within the normal range for one patient. We assumed that these values were high enough to detect a systematic influence of linguistic features on the gaze behaviour of the patients when solving the sentence-anagram task.

The control patients were taken from the neurological wards. They had no signs of CNS involvement. Their educational and professional background was comparable to the aphasic patients.

Material

There were two experimental items. Their linguistic structure is shown in Fig. 1. From an unordered circular array of sentence constituents subjects were asked to construct a sentence, and they were told that there was only

TABLE 2
AAT Performance of Broca's Aphasics

Md/range *n = 10*	*Spontaneous Speech* *(ratings 0–5)*	*Sub-tests* *(percentile ranks)*	
Communication	2.0 (1–4)	Token Test	62.5 (28–94)
Articulation	3.0 (2–5)	Repetition	60.5 (23–72)
Automatised Speech		Written Language	66.0 (40–90)
Elements	3.5 (3–5)	Naming	71.0 (49–89)
Semantic Structure	3.0 (3–4)	Comprehension	76.0 (45–99)
Phonemic Structure	3.0 (2–5)	Auditory	80.5 (32–99)
Syntactic Structure	2.0 (1–2)	Reading	73.5 (32–93)

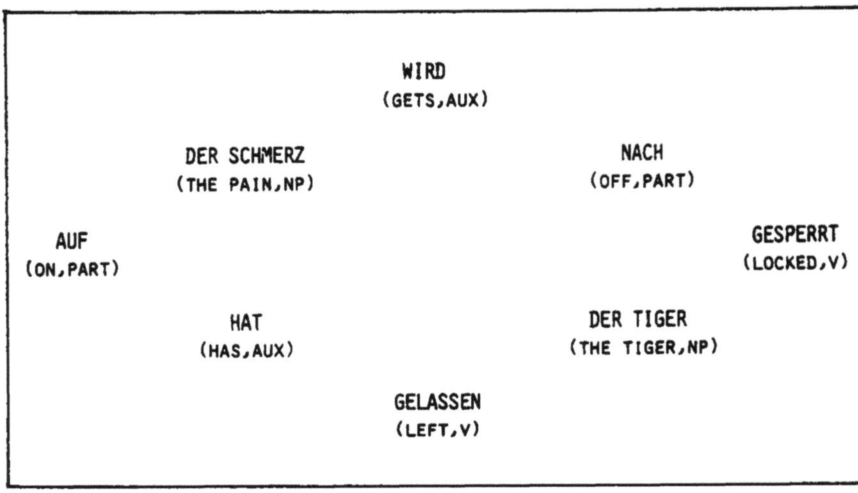

item 1. target sentence: DER SCHMERZ HAT NACHGELASSEN
distractor sentence: DER TIGER WIRD *AUFGESPERRT
(* semantically inadequate)

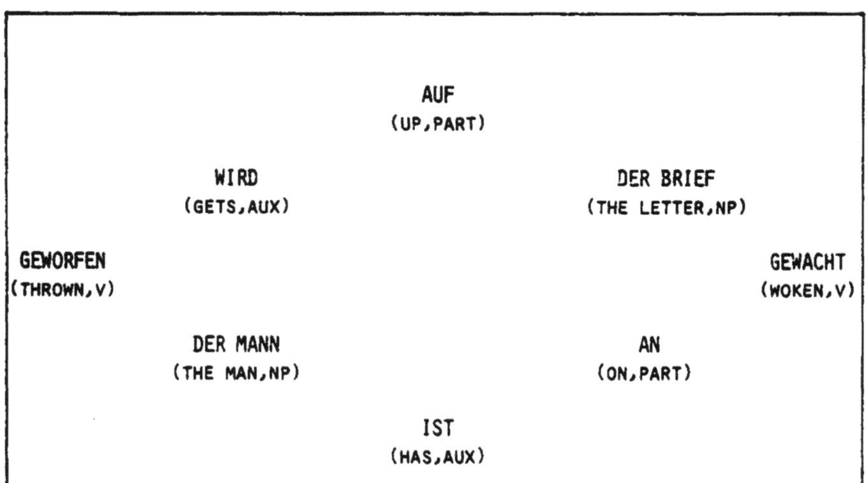

item 2. target sentence: DER MANN IST AUFGEWACHT
distractor sentence: DER BRIEF WIRD *ANGEWORFEN
(* semantically inadequate)

FIG 1 Experimental items.

one solution. In both items the target sentence had the same phrase structure, but they differed in semantic and thematic structure. The grammatical subject was inanimate in item 1 and animate in item 2.

The remaining distractor constituents allowed for a formally correct but semantically incorrect alternative sentence. All other combinations of target and distractor constituents led to linguistically inadequate solutions. In both items, the distractor sentence contained semantically inadequate verb particles. For example, in item 1, only the verb particle *ein* (English *up*) instead of *auf* (English *on*) would lead to a correct second solution, namely "Der Tiger wird eingesperrt"/"The tiger gets locked up'.

The linguistic design of the two items made it possible to control the influence of three linguistic contrasts on syntactic processing, namely major v. minor grammatical category, linear v. hierarchical sentence structure, agent v. non-agent interpretation of noun phrases. The target and the distractor sentence had the same syntactic structure. Thus, each anagram included four major grammatical categories (2 NP, 2 V) containing content words, and four minor categories (2 AUX, 2 PART) that are made up of function words. We expected that the contrast in grammatical category would possibly affect duration and frequency of gaze.

In Fig. 2, the sentence structure and two possible types of processing are given. During searching and control as reflected by eye movements, the sentence may be conceptualised syntactically, i.e. according to its constituent structure, which branches hierarchically to the right. In building up larger sentence constituents from the anagram given, a verb participle (V) and a verb particle (PART) would be the first constituent pair to be considered as they are structurally most closely linked together. Alternatively, processing may be linear starting with a noun phrase (NP) and an auxiliary (AUX), which are most likely the first and second constituent of a well-formed declarative sentence within the multiple choice set given. For each type of processing, different gradations of preference among pairs of constituents would hold as also shown in Fig. 2. These gradations should be reflected in frequency of gaze alternations.

In each item, the two noun phrases if taken by themselves allow for contrasting agent v. non-agent interpretation. Only *the tiger* in item 1 and *the man* in item 2 but not *the pain* and *the letter* can be taken as referring to a possible agent. The possible agent NP belongs to the target sentence only in item 2, thus allowing for a successful application of the agent-first strategy. We therefore expected that the second item would be solved faster and more accurately than the first. However, the second item turned out to demand as much overall decision time as item 1, presumably because of elliptic versions of the distractor sentence ("Der Brief wird geworfen/der Brief ist auf"), which had to be excluded as possible

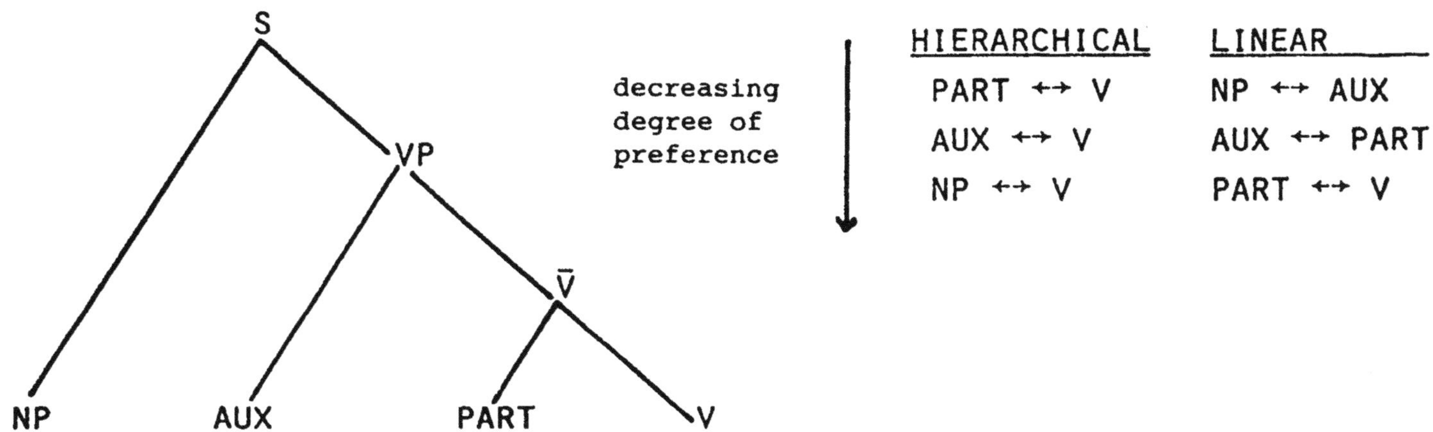

FIG. 2 Sentence structure and types of processing.

alternatives. This task ambiguity was not anticipated when we constructed and pretested the item.

The order of constituents as presented on the display screen was systematically varied between the two items so that possible preferences in direction of gaze could be controlled (cf. Ehrlichman & Weinberger, 1978). The differences we found with respect to overall gaze direction were determined essentially by the linguistic structure of the items, as we demonstrated in detail elsewhere (Huber, Luër, & Lass, 1983).

Procedure

In a pretraining session, patients became acquainted with the kind of sorting task we used. During the experimental session, two warm-up items were given whose critical linguistic features were, of course, different from those of the two experimental items.

Before the multiple choice set was shown, the constituents were presented individually. The subject had to read them aloud or—with the aphasic subjects—the examiner read them aloud. By this procedure, we wanted to minimise the influence of word length, lexical familiarity, reading difficulties, etc.

All stimuli were presented on slides and the duration of projection was determined by the subjects themselves. The subjects were told to push a button when they felt sure about the correct solution. The aphasic subjects could give the solution either verbally or by pointing.

The complete testing session, including calibration of eye properties of the individual subject, lasted about 30 to 40 minutes. Calibration was determined by requiring subjects to fixate in a random order 28 spots that were regularly distributed over the display screen.

The subject was seated 190cm away from the screen (100cm × 75cm) with the head held steady. All stimulus words were written in capital letters with a height of 2cm. Viewed from the subject's position, the midpoints of the eight constituents were separated from one another by a visual angle of 6°. Thus, during fixation of one constituent, adjacent constituents were out of focus. One gaze was defined as an uninterrupted sequence of fixations upon the same constituent position, defined as an ellipse (22.5cm × 14.3cm) around the constituent. Furthermore, only gazes with a minimum duration of 100 msec were used as unit of analysis. Such "global" measures of fixations are assumed to reflect higher level cognitive processes (cf. Just & Carpenter, 1976; Kliegl, Olson, & Davidson, 1983).

The eye movements were measured by tracking the corneal reflection centre with respect to the pupil centre via a video camera (cf. Young & Sheena, 1975). The x and y co-ordinates were calculated every 20msec. The co-ordinates were recorded and monitored by computer (system DEBIC 80).

RESULTS

As expected, the task was rather demanding for the aphasic subjects. On the average, it took them about 100sec to find a solution. Normal control subjects needed about 30sec and students only 10sec. The differences in overall decision time will be analysed later.

None of the aphasic subjects found the correct solution to item 1, and only one aphasic subject to item 2. All non-aphasic subjects solved item 1 correctly; but with item 2, an elliptic version of the distractor sentence was given by four control patients and two students.

Among the aphasic responses no consistent error type was found. Most of the aphasic patients were not confident about their response even after they pushed the button indicating that a solution had been found. Their responses were interrupted by hesitations and self-corrections, and very often they started scanning again in order to search for another solution. This high uncertainty and the inaccuracy of the responses made us wonder whether their scanning would exhibit any systematic effects at all.

In contrast, the non-aphasic subjects always uttered the recognised sentence immediately after pushing the button and usually showed confidence in their solution. We expected that the high accuracy of the normal responses could be predicted from the gaze behaviour, i.e. constituents of the target sentence would be looked at longer and more frequently than the constituents of the distractor sentence. This will be discussed later. The succeeding sections address the question of possible influence of the three specific linguistic contrasts that were built into the multiple choice set of constituents: animate/inanimate NP, major/minor grammatical category, linear/hierarchical sentence structure.

The data of each section were statistically analysed by means of ANOVA procedures (BMDP4V, Dixon & Brown, 1977). The ANOVA designs were set up according to Kirk (1968) with groups as the plot-factor and task parameters as the split-factors. Due to unequal variances, ANOVA and subsequent *t*-tests were always conducted with corrected degrees of freedom.

Overall Decision Time

We compared the overall decision time between the two items in order to detect a possible difference in task difficulty. The mean values are given in Table 3.

A split-plot ANOVA was administered to the groups as plot-factor and items as split-factor. There was no significant interaction and no significant main effect of the split-factor, i.e. the overall decision time for the two items did not differ significantly. There was, however, a significant main effect of the plot-factor and significant simple main effects on each level of

TABLE 3
Overall Decision Time

Means in Sec *Standard Deviation*	*Item 1*	*Item 2*
Broca's $n = 10$	108.6 (72.3)	98.1 (60.7)
Control $n = 10$	21.9 (25.7)	37.9 (39.4)
Students $n_1 = 17$[a] $n_2 = 21$	6.6 (4.4)	14.2 (13.1)

[a]Note: Four students could not be considered in item 1 because of technical problems.

the split-factor. Pair-wise comparisons between groups showed that the aphasics needed significantly more decision time than each of the two other groups for item 1, and significantly more than the students for item 2 (*t*-test, alpha level adjusted to 5/3%).

This result shows that the greater task ambiguity of item 2 did not lead to a significant increase in total decision time, i.e. the overall task difficulty was comparable for the two items. However, the different gradations among groups in items 1 and 2 may indicate that the normal control subjects had relatively more difficulties in finding out for item 2 what the distractor sentence was and recognising that it had to be excluded. Indeed, four of them gave as a solution an elliptic version of the distractor sentence.

As can be seen from the standard deviations in Table 3, there was a considerable amount of inter-individual variability. This might cover up systematic effects when the data are further split up. We therefore decided to investigate relative instead of absolute gaze values.

Processing of Target v. Distractor Sentence

In Table 4, relative gaze durations and gaze frequencies are summed up for all the constituents of the target and the distractor sentences. Group differences were assessed separately for the target sentence of each item by one-way ANOVA. In item 1, the aphasics differed significantly from each of the two other groups as was shown by significant main effect and subsequent pairwise comparison (*t*-tests) both for frequency and duration (aphasics v. controls, $P = 0.000/0.0001$; aphasics v. students, $P = 0.46/0.002$). In item 2, no differences between groups were found.

TABLE 4
Processing of Target v. Distractor Sentence

Means in % *Standard Deviation*	*Gaze*	*Item 1* *Target*	*Item 1* *Distractor*	*Item 1* *T v. D* *P-value*[a]	*Item 2* *Target*	*Item 2* *Distractor*	*Item 2* *T v. D* *P-value*[a]
Broca's	Duration	30.9	60.1 (13.7)	0.038	45.3	54.7 (6.4)	0.042
	Frequency	45.1	54.9 (7.5)	0.068	44.6	55.4 (6.3)	0.024
Controls	Duration	66.5	33.5 (16.7)	0.016	39.6	60.4 (17.2)	0.066
	Frequency	61.5	38.5 (9.0)	0.007	38.2	61.8 (14.5)	0.004
Students	Duration	64.1	35.9 (23.1)	0.023	45.3	54.7 (15.3)	0.179
	Frequency	57.0	43.0 (21.1)	0.204	44.5	55.5 (11.7)	0.039

[a] Distribution-free permutation test (Monte Carlo solution).

As the values for target and distractor sentences were completely numerically dependent, possible differences were assessed by means of distribution-free permutation tests (Willmes, 1982; Willmes & Pyhel, 1981) and not by *t*-tests. The *P*-values found are given in Table 4.

The target sentence of item 1 was processed more intensively than the distractor sentence by the non-aphasic subjects. This was to be expected from their invariably correct solutions. In item 2, however, the constituents of the distractor sentence were looked at more often and longer. This preference was also found in those subjects who gave the target sentence as the solution. Obviously, their gaze pattern indicates that the rejection of the distractor solution was more demanding in item 2 than in item 1. The gazes of the aphasic subjects were more attracted to the distractor constituents in both items, but for different reasons in each, as we will point out in the next section.

Processing of Animate v. Inanimate Noun Phrases

The distribution of relative gaze durations and frequencies are illustrated in Fig. 3. The Broca's aphasics processed the constituents containing an animate noun that can be interpreted as an agent more intensively in both items. The same result was found for the two non-aphasic groups, but only in item 2 where the possible agent NP had to be integrated into the target sentence. This differential impact of the NP-contrast proved to be statistically reliable.

The data were analysed by a split-plot ANOVA separately for each item. Parallel results were found for duration and frequency. In item 1, pairwise comparisons (*t*-tests) between groups—subsequent to significant interaction and significant simple main effects—yielded significant differ-

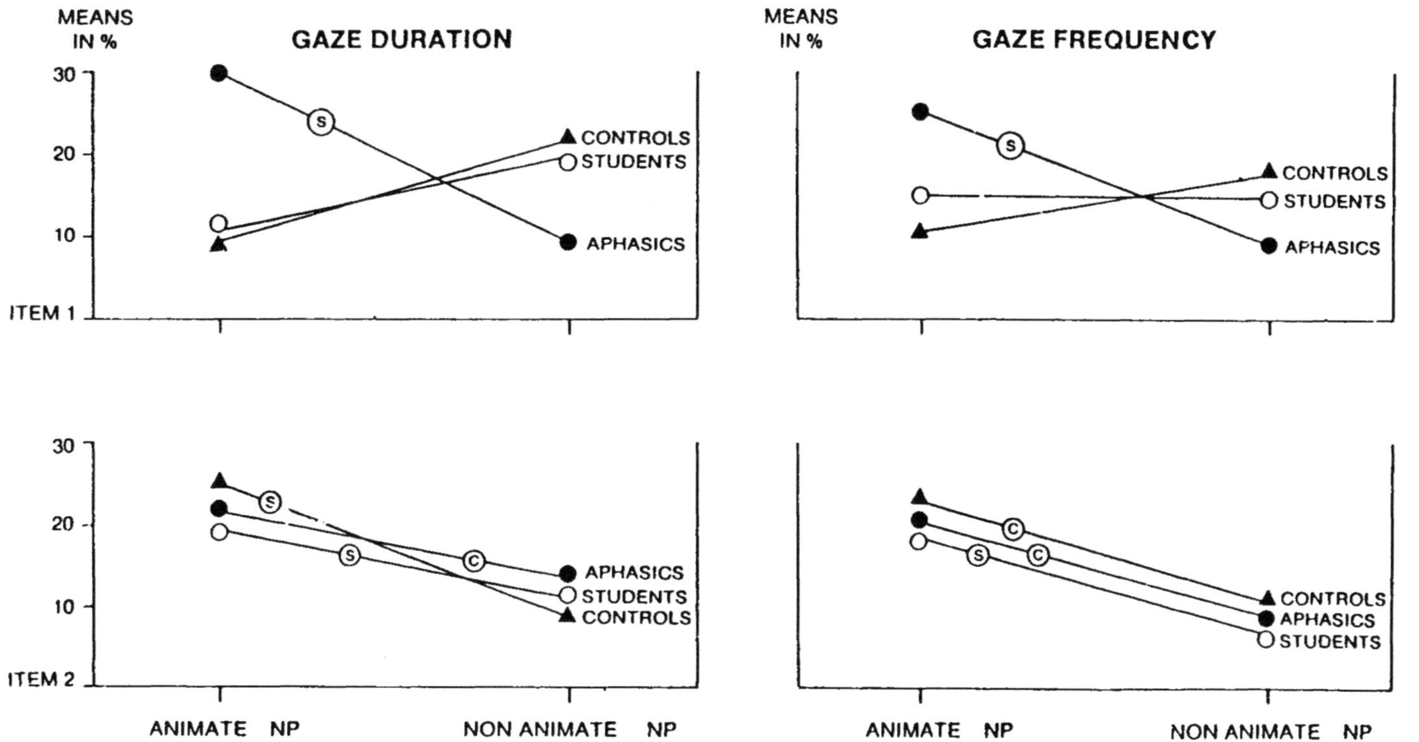

FIG. 3 Processing of noun phrases (NP) (s = significant, c = close to significant simple main effect, split-plot ANOVA, $\alpha = 5/3\%$.

ences between the aphasics and each of the non-aphasic groups for the processing of the animate NP. Significant differences between the two NPs (levels of the split-factor) are indicated in Fig. 3. In item 2, only the main effect of the split-factor was found to be significant, but not that of the plot-factor nor the interaction. Simple main effects revealed significant or close to significant differences between the two NPs as marked in Fig. 3.

The strong preference for animate NPs clearly shows that even the aphasic subjects scanned the constituents in a systematic way, although the aphasic responses given later did not reflect this. In item 1, the preference for the animate NP may imply the preference for the distractor sentence (cf. p. 145) as it contains the animate NP as subject. In item 2, however, the two effects are clearly independent of each other. Therefore, the preference for the distractor constituents of item 2, most likely reflect the intrinsic processing difficulties not only in the non-aphasic but also in the aphasic subjects. Again, this could not be inferred from the aphasic responses.

Processing of Major v. Minor Grammatical Categories

In Fig. 4, the values are summed up for NP and V as opposed to AUX and PART. In both items 1 and 2, the aphasic subjects processed the major categories containing content words more intensively than the minor categories. The control groups did not show differences with respect to the two types of grammatical categories in item 1, whereas in item 2, they also processed the major categories more intensively. These observations proved to be significant as indicated in Fig. 4.

Category differences were analysed by permutation tests as the values were completely numerically dependent. Group differences were again assessed by one-way ANOVA, yielding significant differences only in item 1. The relative gaze durations of the aphasic group were significantly longer than those of the two non-aphasic groups (*t*-tests, $P = 0.004$ and $P = 0.011$), and with respect to gaze frequency, the aphasics differed significantly from the control patients ($P = 0.013$).

So far, we have seen that the contrasts animate/inanimate NP and major/minor category had a strikingly similar impact on gaze movements, although in different ways for aphasic and non-aphasic subjects. Both, the gaze preference for major constituents and for the animate NP may reflect that the search for a solution and/or its control, after a sentence is conceptualised, is primarily guided by lexical–semantic information. The Broca's aphasics were restricted to semantic processing in both items whereas the non-aphasic subjects relied on it only in item 2, the solution of which was somewhat equivocal and therefore more demanding.

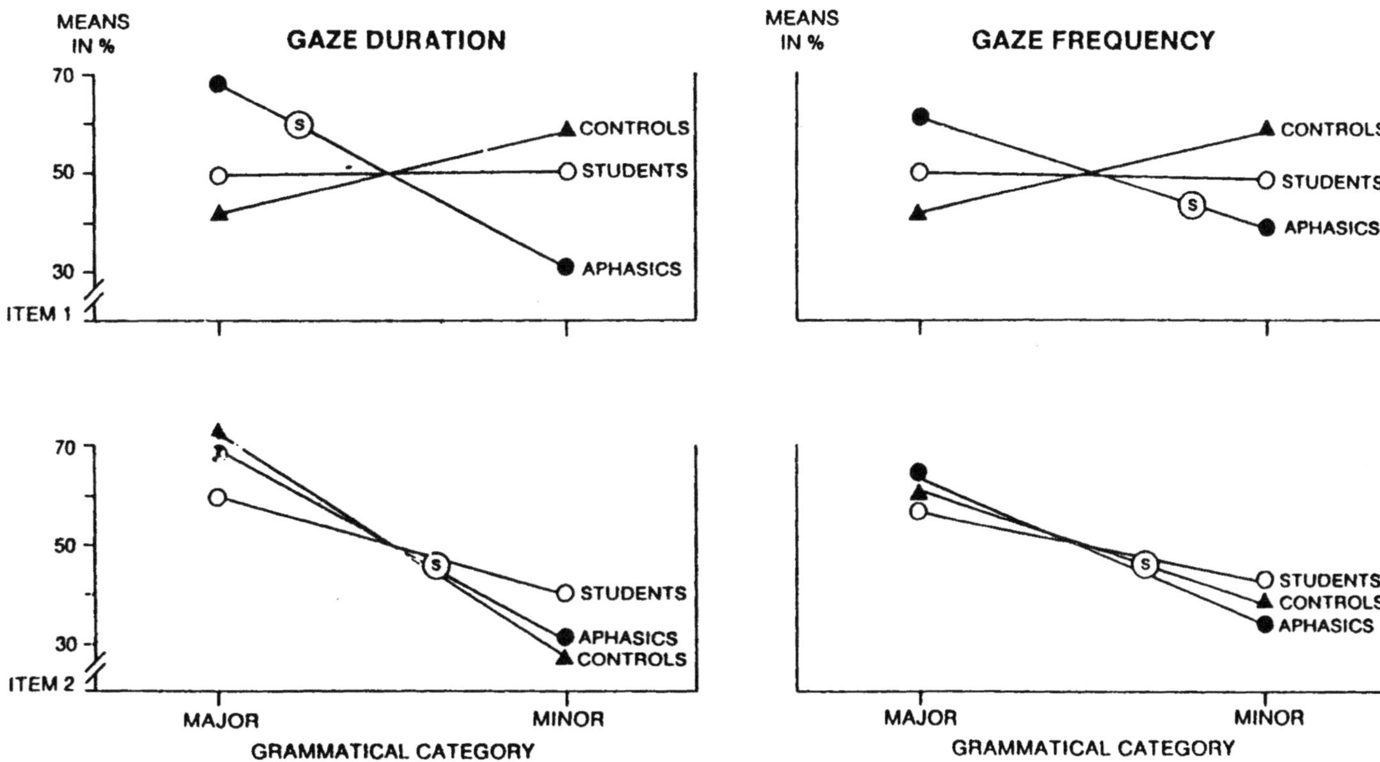

FIG. 4 Processing of grammatical categories (s = significant, distribution-free permutation test).

This finding of primarily semantic processing changed our expectations on the possible influence of sentence structure. If gazes are only attracted by the semantic information of lexical items then no evidence should be found for either hierarchical or linear sentence processing as stated in Fig. 2. We investigated this question in two steps. First, we analysed duration and frequency of gaze with respect to all four grammatical categories contained in the multiple choice set. Second, we considered gaze alterations between these grammatical categories.

Processing of Sentence Structures as Reflected by Duration and Frequency of Gaze

Gaze durations and frequencies were summed up for constituents of the same grammatical category. Both the target and the distractor sentence had the same constituent order, namely NP–AUX–PART–V (cf. Figs. 1 and 2). In item 1, the values found for the students' group decreased from left to right (cf. Table 5), indicating a linear processing of phrase structure. In the aphasic group, however, noun phrase (NP) and verb (V) were the two categories that were looked at longest and most frequently. Such a preference for both major grammatical categories was found for all three groups in item 2.

The data were again statistically analysed by split-plot ANOVA. The differential pattern of item 1 yielded significant group differences with

TABLE 5
Processing of Single Sentence Constituents

	Duration		Frequency	
Item 1	*Overall*	*Pairwise Comparisons*	*Overall*	*Pairwise Comparisons*
Aphasics	Sign	NP V PART AUX	Sign	NP V PART AUX
Controls	Non-s	AUX NP PART V	Non-s	AUX NP PART V
Students	Non-s	NP AUX PART V	Non-s	NP AUX PART V
Item 2				
Aphasics	Sign	V NP AUX PART	Sign	V NP AUX PART
Controls	Sign	NP V AUX PART	Sign	NP V AUX PART
Students	Sign	NP V AUX PART	Sign	NP V AUX PART

Note: Constituents are ordered with decreasing gaze values from left to right. Underlining indicates non-significant differences: solid line $\alpha = 5\%$, dotted line, alpha-level adjusted (Holm, 1979).

respect to the processing of the auxiliary verb (AUX). The aphasics looked at it for significantly shorter periods and less often than the two non-aphasic groups (*t*-tests, subsequent to significant simple main effect, aphasics v. controls, $P = 0.001/0.005$, aphasics v. students, $P = 0.001/0.006$). For item 2, no group differences were found.

With respect to the split-factor, we found significant main effects and several simple main effects as reported in Table 5. Because of complete numerical dependency, permutation tests were again used for pairwise comparisons between the levels of the split-factor, i.e. the grammatical categories. The *P*-values were judged according to Holm's (1979) sequentially rejective test procedure. The results are indicated in Table 5. In item 1, a differential distribution across the groups was found. NPs and in part also Vs were looked at with longest duration and highest frequency by the aphasics. No significant differences were found for non-aphasic subjects, although they processed V, the final constituent of the implied sentence structure numerically less intensively than the two initial constituents NP and AUX. In item 2, the distribution was similar across the groups, which is a consequence of the results reported earlier. The two constituents of the major grammatical categories are processed more intensively than the two minor ones.

Processing of Sentence Structure as Reflected by Gaze Alternations

In Table 6, the gaze alternations between two different grammatical categories in both directions are summed up. Alternations between identical categories were always among the least frequent ones. Their mean values are not included in Table 6, but add up to 100%.

Gazes jumped back and forth most frequently between NP and V in each group when processing item 2, thus indicating a semantic-processing strategy that relied on major grammatical categories. This was also the case for the Broca's aphasics in item 1. The students, however, had here in item 1 their highest frequency of alternations between the two initial sentence constituents NP and AUX, which most likely reflects a linear processing strategy. The control patients—quite unexpectedly—compared most often the finite auxiliary verb (AUX) and the verb particle (PART) that immediately follows the auxiliary (AUX) in the implied sentence structure.

The data were analysed by split-plot ANOVA and subsequent pairwise comparisons using permutation tests. The results of the comparisons that are most pertinent to decisions on alternative types of processing are reported in Table 7. Alternations between NP and AUX, NP and V, and PART and V are taken to indicate conceptualisation and/or control of the sentence structure in a linear, semantic, or hierarchical fashion, respect-

TABLE 6
Gaze Alternations (Means in %, Standard Deviations)

	Broca's				Controls				Students			
	NP	*AUX*	*PART*	*V*	*NP*	*AUX*	*PART*	*V*	*NP*	*AUX*	*PART*	*V*
NP	—	14.1 (7.3)	15.6 (8.2)	33.9 (12.7)	—	18.2 (19.4)	15.7 (12.4)	16.0 (18.3)	—	29.5 (26.3)	14.5 (16.9)	14.4 (14.6)
AUX	13.7 (5.9)	—	12.8 (6.3)	8.1 (6.9)	24.7 (18.8)	—	31.2 (26.7)	10.8 (11.9)	15.2 (13.1)	—	20.2 (24.8)	7.4 (9.4)
PART	11.5 (6.0)	10.7 (8.0)	—	11.0 (5.8)	11.0 (18.8)	9.5 (11.1)	—	6.3 (6.9)	13.5 (10.3)	11.7 (12.0)	—	5.5 (10.2)
V	25.6 (9.7)	15.0 (7.9)	11.1 (7.5)	—	28.7 (17.3)	13.2 (13.7)	7.3 (7.8)	—	23.1 (14.1)	15.6 (16.0)	14.4 (17.5)	—

Note: Values for item 1 above, for item 2 below, the diagonal.

TABLE 7

Pairwise Comparisons Between Gaze Alternations (*P*-values, two-sided, Permutation Test) and Corresponding Hypothesis on Type of Processing

Item	*Group*	*Gaze Alternations*	*Processing Type*	*Gaze Alternations*	*Processing Type*	*Gaze Alternations*	*Processing Type*
		NP–AUX v. PART–V	*Linear v. Hierarchical*	*NP–AUX v. NP–V*	*Linear v. Semantic*	*NP–V v. PART–V*	*Semantic v. Hierarchical*
1	Broca's	0.527	—	0.002	Semantic	0.007	Semantic
	Controls	0.156/0.009[a]	Linear[a]	0.844/0.273[a]	—	0.159	—
	Students	0.004	Linear	0.098	—	0.015	Semantic
2	Broca's	0.496	—	0.022	Semantic	0.003	Semantic
	Controls	0.072	—	0.668	—	0.004	Semantic
	Students	0.901	—	0.128	—	0.127	—

[a] When alternations between AUX and PART instead of between NP and AUX are taken to reflect linear processing.

ively. As the *P*-values of Table 7 and the corresponding means in Table 6 show, Broca's aphasics relied solely on semantic control whereas non-aphasic subjects made use of both linear and semantic control. It should be stressed, however, that complete gradations as assumed in Fig. 2 could not be established from the statistical analysis of the data.

DISCUSSION

Our task required subjects to construct a sentence on the basis of selection and combination of written constituents from a multiple choice set. Finding the target sentence implied excluding a semantically inadequate distractor sentence. The phrase structure of the two sentences was identical in both experimental items. However, the two items differed with respect to the distribution of animate v. inanimate NPs. In item 1, the animate NP functioned as subject NP of the distractor sentence, while it was the subject of the target sentence in item 2. These differences had a differential impact on the eye-movement behaviour of each subject group: patients with Broca's aphasia, non-brain-damaged control patients, and students. The eye-movement behaviour also reflected item differences with respect to processing the structure of the sentence, although the two items contained constituents with parallel grammatical categories and sentences with identical phrase structure. The two non-aphasic groups were found to be more sensitive to the item differences. The aphasic groups processed both items basically in the same way, which was very similar to the processing of item 2 by the two non-aphasic groups. Thus, the aphasic patients were restricted to processing strategies that are only part of the heuristic repertoire of normal speakers.

Semantically Based Strategies in Broca's Aphasia

The Broca's aphasics looked longer and more frequently at the animate than at the inanimate NP irrespective of its grammatical adequacy as a subject NP (cf. Fig. 3). They generally seem to rely on an agent-first strategy when they conceptualise a sentence, i.e. they look for an NP that can be interpreted as an agent, and they do not give up this initial approach even when no adequate integration into a sentence is possible, as their durations and frequencies of gaze in item 1 showed.

As can be expected from the agrammatic speech output of Broca's aphasics, they processed significantly less intensively the minor grammatical categories in comparison to the major categories in both items (cf. Fig. 4). However, this does not necessarily reflect a deficit in the knowledge or availability of these categories. If minor categories were totally irrelevant for Broca's aphasics, one would expect much lower values than the ones we found: About 30% of total gaze duration and frequency fell on minor categories. The two patients, one with Wernicke's and one with amnesic aphasia, whom we were able to study in addition to the group of Broca's aphasics, also showed a clear preference for major categories in both items. Thus, this finding can hardly be interpreted in terms of a deficit that is specific to Broca's aphasia.

It seems more plausible that the gaze preference for major categories reflects a semantic-processing strategy. The assumption of such a strategy can easily explain the strikingly high frequencies of gaze alternation between noun phrase (NP) and verb participle (V) in both items (cf. Tables 6 and 7).

This strategy might reflect the absence of syntactically conditioned processing of the implied sentence structure, either hierarchically or linearly. Therefore, the possibility of an aphasic deficit in syntactic processing cannot be ruled out. This deficit hypothesis could be rejected only if in a similar, but semantically less demanding, task, Broca's aphasics would exhibit gaze movements that are governed by syntactic coherence among sentence constituents.

Influence of Intrinsic Task Demands

The differential impact of the two task conditions (item 1 and item 2) on the gaze behaviour of non-aphasic speakers led to more intensive processing of the target sentence in item 1, but of the distractor sentence in item 2 (cf. Table 4). This cannot easily be related to differences in overall task difficulty as the decision times for item 2 were not significantly higher than those for item 1 (cf. Table 3). Rather, we would argue that the difference is directly linked to the processing of both the target and distractor sentence in the two items. In item 2, the target sentence was less equivocal to process than in item 1, as the identification of the animate subject NP was semantically cued. However, the rejection of the distractor solution was more demanding in item 2 than in item 1. This is shown by the error data of the control patients: Four of them responded with an elliptic version of the distractor sentence.

The difficulties intrinsic to the distractor sentence in item 2 also seem to have influenced the aphasics' behaviour. The Brocas', too, scanned the constituents of the distractor sentence longer and more frequently than the target constituents (cf. Table 4). In item 1, however, the aphasic subjects differed from the non-aphasic, as they again processed the distractor sentence longer than the target sentence, which was a consequence of their reliance on the possible agent NP. The Brocas' adherence to the agent NP was less pronounced for item 2 than for item 1 (cf. Fig. 3), presumably because the critical NP, *der Mann*, in item 2 refers to a less prototypical source of action than *der Tiger* in item 1.

Semantic and Linear Processing in Non-aphasic Subjects

The two non-aphasic groups did not adhere to an agent-first strategy throughout the task. The animate v. non-animate contrast had no significant effect in item 1, whereas the significant effect in item 2 may be confounded with the function of the animate NP as target subject (cf. Fig. 3).

Most interestingly, both non-aphasic groups also processed major grammatical categories more intensively than minor ones in item 2, but not in item 1 (cf. Fig. 4 and Table 5). Like the aphasics, they relied on a processing strategy in item 2 that was based primarily on semantic information of lexical items. The frequency of gaze alternation also indicates that they compared primarily NP and V for finding a solution (cf. Table 6).

In item 1, however, the gaze alternations of students can be also interpreted in terms of a linear conceptualisation and/or a serial left-to-right visualisation of the implied sentence structure NP-AUX-PART-V (cf. Fig. 2). The relative frequencies of gaze alternations decreased from about 30% for the two initial constituents NP and AUX, to 20% for AUX and PART, and to 6% for PART and V (cf. Table 6). Furthermore, NP and AUX were significantly more often compared than NP and V (cf. Table 7). The control patients most frequently compared the two minor categories AUX and PART in item 1. This might indicate that the complete sentence structure was less clear for them and that they, therefore, concentrated on the verb phrase of the intended sentence: $(_{VP}AUX(_{V}PART\ V))$. This was again done in a linear left-to-right fashion. Linear left-to-right processing by the control patients also took place in item 2, for in addition to the semantically conditioned comparisons between NP and V, there was a high portion of gaze alternations between the two initial constituents NP and AUX (cf. Table 6).

Contrary to our expectations, gaze alternations were not much attracted by those constituents that were most closely linked together according to the phrase structure of the target sentence (cf. Fig. 2). Therefore, hierarchical syntactic processing may not play an important role for solving the anagram task. However, one could likewise assume that only those pairs of constituents that are not directly dominated by a common higher category are processed most intensively because their syntactic coherence is less obvious. Thus, high frequencies of gaze alternations between NP and AUX may not exclusively reflect linear processing by the non-aphasic subjects. Besides being the two initial constituents of the target sentence, they are also structurally the least coherent ones. Morphological markedness could be a further reason why NP and AUX were frequently compared. In German, the grammatical subject and the finite verb/auxiliary generally show morphological agreement in person and number.

How can the processing differences of non-aphasic subjects with respect to sentence structure be explained? In keeping with the already given assumption of varying relative intrinsic difficulties between items 1 and 2, it appears that the lack of semantic cues for finding the target sentence in item 1 triggered syntactic processing. The greater task ambiguity of item 2 might have induced a primarily semantic-processing strategy. Alternatively, the semantic strategy can be viewed as a consequence of the successful applicability of the agent-first strategy in item 2.

Underlying Mechanisms of the Aphasics' Processing Difficulties

The specific aphasic behaviour in item 1, namely the preference for the animate NP and for major categories, can be seen as a variant of normal language behaviour. The aphasics' processing difficulties lay in the reliance on the agent-first strategy whether it led to success or not. This reliance apparently prevented the aphasic subjects from switching between linguistic strategies. An alternative explanation is that it is an underlying deficit in syntactic knowledge in Broca's aphasics that prevents them from switching to a syntactic-processing strategy.

A general weakness of the supramodal deficit hypothesis is its implication that language comprehension is organised in a way parallel to language production. This assumption is too strong, as many studies on normal as well as pathological language behaviour have shown (cf. Introduction). But the alternative assumption of restricted but essentially normal processing heuristics does not predict the kind and frequency of errors we found. In item 1, the agent-first strategy of a semantically based sentence processing would lead at least to a combination of the major categories of the distractor sentence, namely "Der Tiger (wird) gesperrt." Only one out of the 10 Broca's aphasics gave such a response. In item 2, the preserved heuristics of the Broca's aphasics should likewise lead to correct responses or to a fragmentary version of the target sentence, namely *"Der Mann (ist) gewacht."* But such a response occurred only twice among the 10 subjects. The general finding was that the particular eye-movement pattern predicted the solution given in non-aphasic but not in aphasic speakers. We found similar discrepancies in a study in which subjects had to recognise sequences of changing objects from a multiple choice of pictures or words (Lass, Huber, & Lüer, 1984).

There are various lines of interpretation for such a discrepancy. First, the eye-movement behaviour of aphasics might reflect the normal generation of hypotheses during linguistic problem solving, with the aphasics being, however, incapable of testing the hypotheses. These two phases of processing might be reflected in the temporal sequence in which certain gaze fixations and alternations occur. Unfortunately, we have so far no methodology available for a full temporal analysis of the eye-movement data. Second, in the aphasic patients, their own inner verbalisation after recognising a solution might have been so defective that they were able to give only erroneous responses even though their reasoning during problem solving was quite normal. It is, however, not clear whether inner verbalisation after finding a solution does in fact take place. Furthermore, it cannot be ruled out that the aphasics' difficulty was one of problem solving. Our control data from the standard aphasia examination showed that the reading comprehension of the patients was quite good compared to the aphasic population in general, though not normal (cf. Table 2). This third explanation may relate the specific aphasics' processing difficulties to an assembler problem, i.e. aphasic patients cannot keep track of decisions made stepwise during problem solving and/or cannot integrate the individual decisions to one solution. In other words, specific linguistic features can be detected but not fully exploited. This may be particularly characteristic for Broca's aphasia. Further research will have to clarify these alternative interpretations both theoretically and empirically.

ACKNOWLEDGEMENTS

This study was supported by a grant by the Deutsche Forschungsgemeinschaft to the first author. We would like to thank H. W. Schroiff and D. Sommer for their help in running the experiment, and G. Guillot for his help in the statistical evaluation of the data. We gratefully acknowledge the many helpful suggestions made on an earlier version of this paper by J. Bayer, R. De Bleser, K. Poeck, K.-J. Schlenck, and K. Willmes.

REFERENCES

Bates, E. & MacWhinney, B. (1981) Functionalist approaches to grammar. In L. Gleitman & E. Wanner (Eds.), *Language acquisition: The state of the art*. New York: Cambridge University Press.

Berndt, R. S. & Caramazza, A. (1980) A redefinition of the syndrome of Broca's aphasia: Implications for a neuropsychological model of language. *Applied Psycholinguistics*, *1*, 225–278.

Bever, T. G. (1974) The interaction of perception and linguistic structures: A preliminary investigation of neofunctionalism. In T. A. Sebeok (Ed.), *Current trends in linguistics. Linguistics and adjacent arts and sciences*. The Hague: Mouton.

Blumstein, S. E., Goodglass, H., Statlender, S., & Biber, C. (1983) Comprehension strategies determining references in aphasia: A study of reflexiviation. *Brain and Language*, *18*, 115–127.

Bradley, D. C., Garrett, M. F., & Zurif, E. B. (1980) Syntactic deficits in Broca's aphasia. In D. Caplan (Ed.), *Biological studies of mental processes*. Cambridge, Mass: MIT Press.

Caramazza, A. & Berndt, R. S. (1978) Semantic and syntactic processing in aphasia: A review of the literature. *Psychological Bulletin*, *85*, 898–918.

Caramazza, A. & Zurif, E. (1976) Dissociation of algorithmic and heuristic processes in comprehension: Evidence from aphasis. *Brain and Language*, *3*, 572–582.

Clark, H. H. (1965) Some structural properties of simple active and passive sentences. *J. Verb. Learn. Verb. Beh.*, *4*, 365–370.

Clark, H. (1978) Inferring what is meant. In W. J. M. Levelt & G. B. Flores d'Arcais (Eds.), *Studies in the perception of language*. New York: John Wiley & Sons.

Dixon, W. J. & Brown, M. B. (1977) *Biomedical computer programs*. P-series. Berkeley: University of California Press.

Ehrlichman, H. & Weinberger, A. (1978) Lateral eye movements and hemispheric asymmetry: A critical review. *Psychological Bulletin*, *85*, 1080–1101.

Forster, K. I. (1979) Levels of processing and the structure of the language processor. In W. E. Cooper & E. C. T. Walker (Eds.), *Sentence processing: Psycholinguistic studies presented to Merrill Garrett*. Hillsdale, N.J.: Lawrence Erlbaum Associates Inc.

Goodglass, H. (1968) Studies on the grammar of aphasics. In S. Rosenberg & J. H. Koplin (Eds.), *Developments in applied psycholinguistics research*. New York: Macmillan.

Goodglass, H. (1976) Agrammatism. In H. Whitaker & H. A. Whitaker (Eds.), *Studies in neurolinguistics*, vol. 2. New York: Academic Press.

Gordon, B. & Caramazza, A. (1982) Lexical decision for open- and closed-class words: Failure to replicate differential frequency sensitivity. *Brain and Language*, *15*, 143–160.

Heeschen, C. (1980) Strategies of decoding actor–object-relations by aphasic patients. *Cortex*, *16*, 5–19.

Holm, S. (1979) A simple sequentially rejective multiple test procedure. *Scandinavian Journal of Statistics*, *6*, 65–70.

Huber, W., Lüer, G., & Lass, U. (1983) Processing of sentences in conditions of aphasia as assessed by recording eye movements. In R. Groner, C. Menz, & R. Monty (Eds.), *Eye movements: An international perspective*. Hillsdale, N.J.: Lawrence Erlbaum Associates Inc.

Huber, W. Sprachliche Strukturen und Strategien bei Aphasie. Bern: Huber. (in press)

Huber, W., Poeck, K., & Willmes, K. (1984) The Aachen Aphasia Test (AAT). In F. C. Rose (Ed.), *Progress in aphasiology*. New York: Raven.

Jarvella, R. J. & Sinnott, J. (1972) Contextual constraints on noun distributions to some English verbs by children and adults. *J. Verb. Learn. Verb. Beh.*, *11*, 47–53.

Just, M. A. & Carpenter, P. A. (1976) Eye fixations and cognitive processes. *Cognitive Psychology*, *8*, 441–480.

Just, M. A. & Carpenter, P. A. (Eds.) (1977) *Cognitive processes in comprehension*. Hillsdale, N.J.: Lawrence Erlbaum Associates Inc.

Kean, M. L. (1977) The linguistic interpretation of aphasic syndromes. In E. Walker (Ed.), *Explorations in the biology of language*. Montgomery, VT: Bradford Books.

Kerschensteiner, M., Poeck, K., Huber, W., Stachowiak, F.-J., & Weniger, D. (1978) Die Broca-Aphasia. Klinisches Bild und Überlegungen zur neurolinguistischen Struktur. *J. Neurol.*, *217*, 223–242.

Kirk, R. E. (1968) *Experimental design: procedures for the behavioral sciences*. Belmont, Cal.: Brooks & Cole.

Kliegl, R., Olson, R. K., & Davidson, B. J. (1983) Perceptual and psycholinguistic factors in reading. In K. Rayner (Ed.), *Eye movements in reading: Perceptual and linguistic aspects*. New York: Academic Press.

Kudo, T., Tateishi, M., Kashiwagi, T., & Segawa, N. (1982) Sensitivity to functors in Japanese aphasics. *Neuropsychologia*, *20*, 641–651.

Lass, U., Huber, W., & Lüer, G. (1984) Eye movements and recognition of sequences of changing objects in the pictorial versus verbal modality. In A. G. Gale & F. Johnson (Eds.), *Theoretical and applied aspects of eye-movement research*. Amsterdam: North Holland.

Lesser, R. (1974) Verbal comprehension in aphasia: An English version of three Italian tests. *Cortex*, *10*, 278–284.

Linebarger, M. C., Schwartz, M. F., & Saffran, E. M. (1983) Sensitivity to grammatical structures in so-called agrammatic aphasics. *Cognition*, *13*, 361–392.

Lonzi, L. & Zanobio, E. (1983) Syntactic component in language responsible cognitive structure: Neurological evidence. *Brain and Language*, *18*, 177–191.

Parisi, D. & Pizzamiglio, L. (1970) Syntactic comprehension in aphasia. *Cortex*, *6*, 204–215.

Rayner, K. (1978) Eye movements in reading and information processing. *Psychol. Bulletin*, *85*, 618–660.

Reusser, M. & Groner, R. (1981) Informationsprozesse bei Globalisationsaufgaben. In K. Foppa & R. Groner (Eds.), *Kognitive Strukturen und ihre Entwicklung*. Bern: Huber.

Saffran, E. M., Schwartz, M. F., & Marin, O. S. M. (1980) The word order problem in agrammatism, II. Production. *Brain and Language*, *10*, 263–280.

Senders, J. W., Fisher, D. F., & Monty, R. A. (1978) *Eye movement and the higher psychological functions*. Hillsdale, N.J.: Lawrence Erlbaum Associates Inc.

Scholes, R. J. (1978) Syntactic and lexical components of sentence comprehension. In A. Caramazza & E. B. Zurif (Eds.), *Language acquisition and breakdown*. Baltimore, Md: Johns Hopkins University Press.

Schwartz, M. F., Saffran, E. M., & Marin, O. S. M. (1980) The word order problem in agrammatism, I. Comprehension. *Brain and Language*, *10*, 249–262.

Stockert, R. R. von (1972) Recognition of syntactic structure in aphasic patients. *Cortex*, *8*, 323–334.

Stockert, R. T. von & Bader, L. (1976) Some relations of grammar and lexicon in aphasia. *Cortex*, *12*, 49–60.

Vermeulen, J. (1982) Auditory language comprehension in aphasia: A factor-analytic study. *Cortex*, *18*, 287–300.

Willmes, K. (1982) A comparison between the Lehmacher & Wall rank tests and Pyhel's permutation test for the analysis of r-independent samples or response curves. *Biom. J.*, *24*, 717–772.

Willmes, K. & Pyhel, M. (1981) Permutationstests als Alternative zur Varianzanalyse. Der Split-Plot-Versuchsplan. *Zs. für Sozialpsychologie*, *12*, 186–198.

Willmes, K., Poeck, K., Weniger, D., & Huber, W. (1982) Facet theory applied to the construction and validation of the Aachen Aphasia Test. *Brain and Language*, *18*, 259–276.

Young, L. R. & Sheena, D. (1975) Survey of eye movement recording methods. *Behavior Research Methods and Instrumentation*, *7*, 397–429.

Zurif, E. B. (1980) Language mechanisms: A neuropsychological perspective. *American Scientist*, *68*, 305–311.

8 Localisation of Aphasia: Science or Fiction

R. De Bleser
Department of Neurology,
Pauwelsstrasse, Aachen, West Germany

PROBLEMS WITH THE DEFICIT THEORY OF LANGUAGE LOCALISATION

A basic idea behind the cognitive program is that there must be some form of compatibility between the brain and the psychological functions it carries. Cognitive psychologists and neuropsychologists agree on this tenet, though opinions differ on the validity of the deficit theory of psychological localisation. This theory contains the following assumptions:

1. There is a close-to-perfect correlation between lesioned brain areas and types of disturbed psychological functions.
2. Brain lesions do not create new functions; therefore, deficit localisation can be generalised to the localisation of normal functions.
3. There is a one-to-one mapping between brain areas and psychological functions.
4. Lesion localisation has reached a theoretical level of explanation. It has predictive power and can lead to the discovery of specific psychological mechanisms. If two different lesion sites are found for the same psychological deficits, then presumably the psychological function is underspecified and needs revision.

In the classical era of aphasiology, the deficit theory was defended by Wernicke (1874), Lichtheim (1885), and other diagram-makers. This "neurological" approach to localisation, as Pick (1913, pp. 20, 23) has called it, was criticised by "psychological" localisationists including Pick and Isserlin. They especially took offence at assumption 4, that the knowledge of brain and language relations would be sufficiently rich to explain psychological phenomena. They postulated that questions about anatomical localisation can only be asked after the disturbed function has been psychologically understood, and that they should take into account "the growing knowledge of the anatomical complexity of the cortex, which ridicules all 'straightforwardness'" (Pick, 1913, p. 29). As Isserlin put it (1922, p. 374), "the question of localisation should purposely be kept to the last. Its answer is the crowning of the work, but it can be detrimental if it comes too soon and with too little foundation." (Translation is mine.)

The issues have not significantly changed today after the introduction of computer imaging in brain-lesion localisation, the information-processing approach in cognitive psychology, and transformational grammar in the study of the "mental organ" that language is supposed to be.

Let us restate the modern version of "neurological" localisation with Geschwind (1980, p. 301):

> What we know about the brain in relation to language is not purely correlational ... A purely correlational theory is one that would simply indicate the particular symptoms and signs that occurred with damage to a particular region of the nervous system. Such a system would have no theoretical basis except of the crudest nature. By a non-correlational theory, I mean one that takes into account knowledge from other fields and explains existing facts as well as predicts new data.

This is taken one step further by Damasio and Damasio on conduction aphasia (1980, p. 349): "Anatomical data may help resolve the issue of behavioral interpretation. The variety of structures potentially involved makes it necessary to cast doubt on explanations based on a single disruptive factor (for example, mnestic defect)."

A modern version of "psychological" localisation can be found in Morton (1980, p. 29), among others, who states that "the essence of the information processing approach is to describe function without regard to the substrate ... What is important is the way in which the functions described in a psychological model are implemented in the brain. But note that without knowing what the psychological functions are, we cannot ask how they are implemented."

Few researchers in neuropsychology adhere to this position. They tentatively relate their psychological explanations of, for example, agrammatism to brain areas, so that the syntactic parser (Berndt & Caramazza, 1980, pp. 269–270) and the phonological component (Kean, 1977, p. 130) compete for Broca's area. It is worth noting that this is done without empirical evidence, and that the authors conservatively assume a one-to-one mapping of psychological mechanisms to the classical cortical areas. However, in contrast to the neurological approach, the validity of their explanation does not depend on the actual locus of the lesion but only on psycholinguistic arguments.

Problems for the theoretical claims of deficit localisation also arise from advances in neurophysiological research (Philips, Zeki, & Barlow, 1984). It is not sure whether and how the small neural modules, containing as little as 110 cells, combine and translate into cytoarchitectural differences between brain areas (Mountcastle, 1978). As in psychology, the relevant neuronal units will have to be established within an independent neurophysiological theory.

Given that neither the aphasic syndromes (Caramazza, 1984) nor the brain convolutions (Caplan, 1981) used by deficit theorists are plausible theoretical entities, it is surprising that predominantly strongly positive correlations have been reported in recent localisation literature (Kertesz, 1983).

Granted that new imaging techniques for lesion localisation and better psychometric procedures for syndrome classification allowed a fuller documentation of large numbers of patients, they surely did not affect the conceptual problems. Thus, compared to the frequently reported negative cases in classical literature, negative correlations should have become even more obvious in modern times.

Two explanations for their rare appearance are possible:

1. Current theoretical considerations are of minor importance. The classical psychoanatomical theory of language localisation somehow grasps the finer distinctions to be drawn in psychology and neurophysiology today. It could at least claim observational adequacy and provide an adequate taxonomy of correlations that would be of tremendous clinical value. This would support Ojemann's counter-intuitive opinion that "progress has been retarded more by empirical and methodological problems connected with the extent and quality of the data than by a lack of theoretical imagination" (1983, p. 189).
2. Modern localisational studies are often "playing tennis with the net down" (Marshall, 1980, p. 11). As in phrenology, they are looking only for confirming cases, paying little attention to examples "where a large bump was associated with limited talent, or a small bump with exceptional performance" (Marshall, 1980, p. 11).

Naeser et al. (1982), for example, explain away counter-examples in a rather unorthodox way. They describe three new aphasic syndromes:

anterior, posterior, and global capsular/putaminal aphasia. The posterior putaminal cases are said to differ from Wernicke's only in two *non-aphasic* symptoms: the presence of right hemiplegia and low non-verbal agility. Rather than treating their small putaminal lesions as negative cases for the lesion correlation of Wernicke's aphasia, the authors decide to treat hemiplegia and non-verbal agility as leading symptoms for a new *aphasic* syndrome, posterior putaminal aphasia, which would then be different from Wernicke's aphasia and would naturally have a lesion correlation of its own. If lesion size and site deviate from classical expectations, they become determinants of specific aphasic syndromes, and there are no longer counter-examples to one's theory of deficit–anatomical correlation.

Basso, Roch Lecours, Moraschini, and Vanier (1985, p. 226), in a rare study devoted to correlational exceptions, conclude that "any set of anatomoclinical rules valid for 86.5% to 90.3% of cases in any type of neuropsychological disorders should be adhered to as a basis for standard teaching. The results of this present study do not lead us to reject the main anatomoclinical principles of aphasiology, at least for those populations that have been extensively studied." However, the authors obtain their percentage of exceptions (9.7% to 13.5%) only by closing at least one eye. Taking their group of Wernicke patients, for example, which originally included 77 subjects, 12 subjects were disregarded because they had only deep lesions (i.e. they *were* exceptions). Of the 65 remaining patients, 13 were not included among the exceptions even though they had both anterior and posterior lesion components, because the anterior component was relatively limited (i.e. they *were* exceptions). Of the 52 remaining patients, 14 were treated as real exceptions. One patient had a lesion limited to the occipital lobe; eight patients had an extensive perisylvian lesion expected to produce global aphasia; and five had anterior lesions. This leaves 38 correct correlations of the original 77 in this group who had a lesion defined in gross anatomical terminology as cortical posterior, which is about 50% of cases rather than 90%.

We ourselves were too excited with the new CT technique for *in vivo* lesion detection to fully accept counter-examples (Blunk, De Bleser, Willmes, & Zeumer, 1981). We obtained relatively good results for *groups* of Broca's, Wernicke's, and global aphasics. However, there was considerable overlap between Broca and Wernicke patients. We argued that the anatomic correlate of the specific aphasic syndrome could best be determined by subtracting the overlapping lesions. We called the remaining the "typical" lesion, which was then in the "classical" Wernicke's area (but see Bogen & Bogen, 1976) for Wernicke's aphasia, and in the frontal white matter and the insula rather than in the classical Broca's area for Broca's aphasia. However, severe problems were encountered when we looked at the individual patients in the groups. Especially among patients with global aphasia, differences existed not only in size but also in locus of lesion. Lesions were large and small, anterior and posterior, cortical and subcortical. About 50% of the patients did not have the expected large perisylvian lesion (Poeck, De Bleser, & Keyserlingk, 1984a). In studies with Italian populations, considerable variability for patients with global aphasia (Mazzocchi & Vignolo, 1979) and other syndromes (Basso et al., 1985) had also been demonstrated. The authors appeal to traditional auxiliary explanations such as atypical lateralisation due to female sex, brain asymmetries, environmental effects, or other causes of individual variability.

The percentage of our negative examples was too high to be accounted for by such intangible variables. However, they could still be artefacts of our functional definitions of the deficit, and of differences in time-post-onset. The issue of syndrome-specific lesions would be confused if our functional definitions were somehow deviant or too little refined to avoid overlap among syndromes. Differences in time-post-onset can give rise to recovery syndromes that differ from the original and are not expected to match to the CT-lesion. In that case, a selection of functionally clear cases in the acute stage (between one and two months post-onset) should result in a near-perfect syndrome-lesion correlation.

DEFICIT–LESION CORRELATION

Selection of Subjects

Our pool of global aphasics certainly contained patients who were functionally on a transition from global to Broca. The boundaries between these two non-fluent syndromes are fuzzy. Clear cases of global aphasia have no functioning language system; clear cases of Broca's aphasia have considerable semantic and phonological abilities spared in the receptive and productive modalities. Syntax in those patients may still function relatively well at least at the level of simple sentences and especially in comprehension. Patients who have some language systematic functions left can accordingly be considered either global or Broca's aphasics, depending on the classification methods and criteria used. In the Aachen laboratory, a non-parametric discriminant analysis program (ALLOC) is used for the automatic classification of patients into one of the four standard syndromes (Global, Broca, Wernicke, Amnesic). Syndrome allocation is based on test results obtained with a psychometrically sound German aphasia battery (AAT or Aachen Aphasia Test, Huber, Weniger, Poeck, & Willmes, 1984; Willmes, Poeck, Weniger, & Huber, 1983) for which detailed normative data exist. Using a learning sample of 120 patients (30 per syndrome) in the discriminant analysis, some patients were classified as global, whereas they turned into Brocas when the sample was increased for standardisation to 314 patients, or the reverse.

Fuzziness also arose with respect to patients who were clinically classified as non-fluent transcortical (traditionally called mixed transcortical) aphasia. They performed as poorly as the fuzzy global aphasics in all tasks requiring central language processing, such as confrontation naming, matching spoken and written words to pictures, and the Token Test. However, their performance on repetition, which can bypass the cognitive language system and operate by auditory/phoneme conversion, was significantly better. Because patients with such unimodal preservations are relatively rare, they did not form a separate group in the learning sample. Their similarity to global aphasics was emphasised when ALLOC classified the majority of them as 100% global. In former correlational studies, we had treated them as a separate group on the basis of the clinical assignment of non-fluent transcortical aphasia, using an operational definition for AAT test results.

The functional definition of Wernicke's aphasia gave rise to similar problems as those encountered for global aphasia. Even though patients with jargon aphasia are definitely Wernicke's aphasics and are qualitatively very different from globals, their performance on the language systematic subtests of the AAT and in spontaneous speech is so disturbed that ALLOC cannot quantitatively distinguish them from global aphasics. For correlation purposes, the clinical assessment of Wernicke's aphasia had so far been used. However, lesions of Jargon Wernickes were treated together with those of Wernicke's aphasics without jargon. The latter included patients who were unambiguously classified as Wernickes with all criteria: different learning samples for ALLOC and clinical assessment. The sample of Wernicke's aphasics also contained patients who were on the borderline of amnesic aphasia according to at least one of the criteria. Treating these different types of patients together under the heading of Wernicke's aphasia might not be very useful as a strong test for deficit–CT-lesion correlation.

Another Wernicke-like subgroup of patients is that of fluent transcortical (traditionally called transcortical sensory) aphasia. They have spontaneous speech and AAT subtest characteristics of Wernicke patients without jargon. However, they show a dissociation between excellent repetition and poor performance on tasks requiring central language processing. Their similarity to Wernicke's aphasics without jargon was emphasised by the ALLOC classification, which assigned 100% Wernicke's aphasia to those patients. As with the non-fluent transcortical type, fluent transcortical aphasia is too rare to function as a separate syndrome in the learning sample used by ALLOC. Whereas the closest match for non-fluent cases was global aphasia, the test results of fluent transcorticals were most compatible with Wernicke's aphasia. For purposes of lesion correlation, the clinical assessment of fluent transcortical aphasia had been used so far, rather than the ALLOC classification of Wernicke's aphasia, and they were treated as a separate group. For the clinical assessment, an operational definition on the basis of the AAT test results was used.

The non-optimal correlation we had obtained in former studies between aphasic syndrome and CT-lesion could very well have been due to the heterogeneity of patients in a group, which is inherent to the syndrome approach. Groups included typical as well as borderline cases that overlapped with two pure groups in all modalities. Other patients were treated as separate groups because of differences in one single modality. There is no cogent a priori reason why differences in one single modality between two groups (e.g. good repetition in non-fluent transcorticals and poor repetition in fuzzy globals) should be more important for syndrome constitution and lesion correlation than differences in all modalities between two groups (e.g. fuzzy globals and real globals). This is a relic of the classical concept of language learning by way of repetition. During this process, a repetition route was supposed to be established in the brain. Cognitive language was assumed to be developed later and to occupy its own nervous system pathways. In aphasia acquired at a later age, this initial repetition route was thought to be selectively preserved in transcortical aphasia and selectively disturbed in conduction aphasia (Lichtheim, 1885). Since the concept of the function of repetition in language acquisition has changed in contemporary psycholinguistics, the postulated cerebral substrata has lost a good deal of its foundation.

Rather than relying on groups of unselected patients who were held together by a common syndrome name, the study to be reported here selected patients on the basis of their being extreme examples of a syndrome, or extreme examples of fuzziness.

Thus, from a pool of 72 non-fluent patients, four subgroups of seven patients each were chosen who were in the acute stage characteristically good, bad, and ugly globals and clear Broca's aphasics. (We do not intend to introduce this Spaghetti Western terminology into aphasiology. It is just a convenient shorthand for the patients selected in this study.)

Good globals were defined as being real globals, with no spontaneous speech and no performance to speak of in any of the AAT subtests investigating receptive and productive language modalities.

Bad globals were characterised by a unimodal preservation with above-average performance on repetition, non-fluent speech output restricted at best to simple sentences, and some performance on the different AAT subtests similar to ugly globals. They are an extreme selection from the syndrome of non-fluent or mixed transcortical aphasia.

Ugly globals were on the fuzzy boundary between Brocas and good globals, with agrammatic speech output and the appearance of some language processing in all modalities, even though they were 100% global according to the normative sample of the AAT.

Unlike the ugly globals, the real *Brocas* showed no overlap with the good globals on any of the AAT subtests. Like ugly globals, their spontaneous speech was non-fluent and agrammatic. They were 100% Broca according to the normative sample.

A better appreciation of the functional characteristics of the non-fluent patients can be gained by a comparison of the median percentile ranks on the AAT subtests for all four groups, which is given in Table 1.

From a pool of 47 patients with fluent aphasia, a similar selection was made of patients with prototypical characteristics in the acute stage of their illness. They constituted three subgroups of six patients each. *Good Wernickes* had severe disturbances in all modalities with the exception of somewhat better comprehension in two patients (four had phonological jargon aphasia, two had semantic jargon aphasia); *bad Wernickes* had unimodal preservation of repetition (fluent or transcortical sensory aphasia); and *ugly Wernickes* made up the fuzzy set, with some performance on all modalities (borderline between Wernicke's and amnesic aphasia).

The median percentile ranks on the AAT subtests are compared in Table 2.

Method of Deficit–Lesion Correlation

The digital-lesion information obtained by a computer tomograph (Siemens Siretom 2000) cannot be compared inter-individually without an intervening standardisation process because of the variability of scan incline and starting level. The method of lesion localisation on five standardised template grids used in the Aachen laboratory has been described in more detail elsewhere (Blunk et al., 1981; Poeck et al., 1984a).

The CT-lesions of the 46 patients in this study were drawn from a stored pool of 155 standardised lesions. They are stored as binary matrices for each of the five slices, with an entry of 1 signifying a grid point covered by a lesion, an entry of 0 standing for a grid point without a lesion. Anatomic areas are defined after Matsui and Hirano (1978) by the grid points they contain. Abbreviations of standardised anatomical areas for each of the five slices are given in Table 3, and the five slices are depicted in Fig. 1.

The complete matrix of lesion information can then be reduced by assigning 1 to an entire anatomic area if, e.g., a criterion is met of 30% or more grid points of 1 (lesioned points) contained by the area. Such reduced lesion information was used in this study.

In former correlation studies with large groups of unselected patients, we had performed frequency counts of lesioned areas per aphasic

TABLE 1

Median Percentile Ranks on AAT Subtests and Median Spontaneous Speech Ratings for Four Groups of Selected Non-fluent Aphasics

	AAT Subtests[a]					*Spontaneous Speech Ratings*[b]					
Patient Subgroup	*TT*	*REP*	*WRIT*	*NAME*	*COMP*	*COMM*	*ART*	*AUT*	*SEM*	*PHON*	*SYN*
Globals Good	7	9	5	6	16	0	0	0	0	0	0
($n = 7$)	(2–19)	(2–11)	(5–19)	(6–14)	(2–29)	(0)	(0)	(0)	(0)	(0)	(0)
Globals Bad	33	73	38	19	26	1	3	2	2	4	2
($n = 7$)	(7–50)	(64–83)	(20–49)	(6–32)	(20–38)	(1–2)	(2–5)	(1–3)	(1–3)	(2–4)	(1–2)
Globals Ugly	28	22	27	26	29	1	3	2	3	2	2
($n = 7$)	(13–31)	(16–31)	(5–50)	(15–49)	(16–43)	(1–2)	(1–5)	(1–3)	(2–3)	(2–4)	(1–2)
Brocas	44	39	40	49	45	1	2	3	3	2	2
($n = 7$)	(28–48)	(26–56)	(23–61)	(28–66)	(34–76)	(1–2)	(1–3)	(2–5)	(3–4)	(2–3)	(1–2)

[a] AAT subtests are abbreviated as follows: TT = token test; REP = repetition; WRIT = written language (reading and writing); NAME = confrontation naming; COMP = auditory and reading comprehension.

[b] Rating scales are abbreviated as follows: COMM = verbal communication; ART = articulation and prosody; AUT = automatic speech elements; SEM = semantics; PHON = phonology; SYN = syntax. A rating of 0 means severest disturbance, 5 is undisturbed.

TABLE 2

Median Percentile Ranks on AAT Subtests and Median Spontaneous Speech Ratings for Three Groups of Selected Fluent Aphasics

	AAT Subtests[a]					*Spontaneous Speech Ratings*[b]					
Patient Subgroup	*TT*	*REP*	*WRIT*	*NAME*	*COMP*	*COMM*	*ART*	*AUT*	*SEM*	*PHON*	*SYN*
Wernickes Good ($n = 6$)	16.0 (10–22)	16.5 (4–37)	18.5 (5–36)	16.5 (12–23)	15.0 (3–53)	1.0 (0–1)	4.0 (2–5)	2.0 (1–3)	1.0 (0–2)	1.0 (1–2)	0.0 (0–3)
Wernickes Bad ($n = 6$)	47.0 (39–60)	94.0 (84–99)	62.0 (49–72)	48.5 (34–52)	44.0 (21–53)	3.0 (2–3)	5.0 (4–5)	3.0 (2–4)	3.0 (2–3)	4.0 (3–4)	3.0 (3–4)
Wernickes Ugly ($n = 6$)	33.0 (28–53)	43.0 (16–56)	57.5 (41–77)	32.5 (22–62)	42.0 (17–64)	3.0 (1–3)	5.0 (5)	3.0 (2–5)	2.5 (2–3)	3.5 (2–4)	3.0 (3)

[a] AAT subtest abbreviations, see Table 1.

[b] Rating scale abbreviations, see Table 1.

TABLE 3
Area Information Stored per Slice

Abbr.	Anatomical Area	Slice 1	2	3	4	5
Fs	Superior Frontal Gyrus	+	+	+	+	+
Fm	Medial Frontal Gyrus	+	+	+	+	+
Fi	Inferior Frontal Gyrus	+	+	+	+	+
Mf	Frontal White Matter	+	+	+	+	+
Cr	Central Region				+	+
Sm	Supramarginalis Gyrus				+	+
Nc	Nucleus Caudatus		+	+		
Pp	Putamen & Pallidum		+	+		
Th	Thalamus		+	+		
Of	Frontal Operculum			+		
I	Insula		+	+		
We	Wernicke's Area			+		
Sy	Sylvian Fissure	+	+			
A	Angular Gyrus					+
Ts	Superior Temporal Gyrus	+	+	+	+	+
Tm	Medial Temporal Gyrus	+	+	+	+	+
Ti	Inferior Temporal Gyrus	+	+	+	+	
Oc	Occipital Gyrus	+	+	+	+	+
Mp	Posterior White Matter	+	+	+	+	+

syndrome (Blunk et al., 1981). This procedure tends to cover up the often widespread underlying individual variability, which is what interested us at this point. Rather than frequency counts for lesions of predefined syndromes, cluster analysis was performed on the lesions of the total population. Cluster analytic methods attempt to construct groups according to homogeneity, and their interpretation requires an interactive approach of the examiner with the individuals in the cluster (Hartigan, 1975; Morris, Blashfield, & Satz, 1981). If deficit–lesion correlation were to work, the presence or absence of lesion homogeneity as obtained by cluster analysis would correspond to the predefined functional homogeneity or fuzziness of the groups. Partitioning and hierarchical cluster analyses for binary data were performed on the standardised lesion data. Partitioning cluster analyses attempt to improve a given starting partition iteratively. Single objects are moved around among clusters until the best optimisation value is reached. In contrast, the assignment of an object to a certain cluster cannot be revised in hierarchical cluster analysis. The results of hierarchical cluster analysis were most unsatisfactory for interpretation. Therefore, only partitioning cluster analyses are reported. Though solutions up to seven clusters were obtained for all slices and for each slice separately, no substantial optimisation could technically be reached after

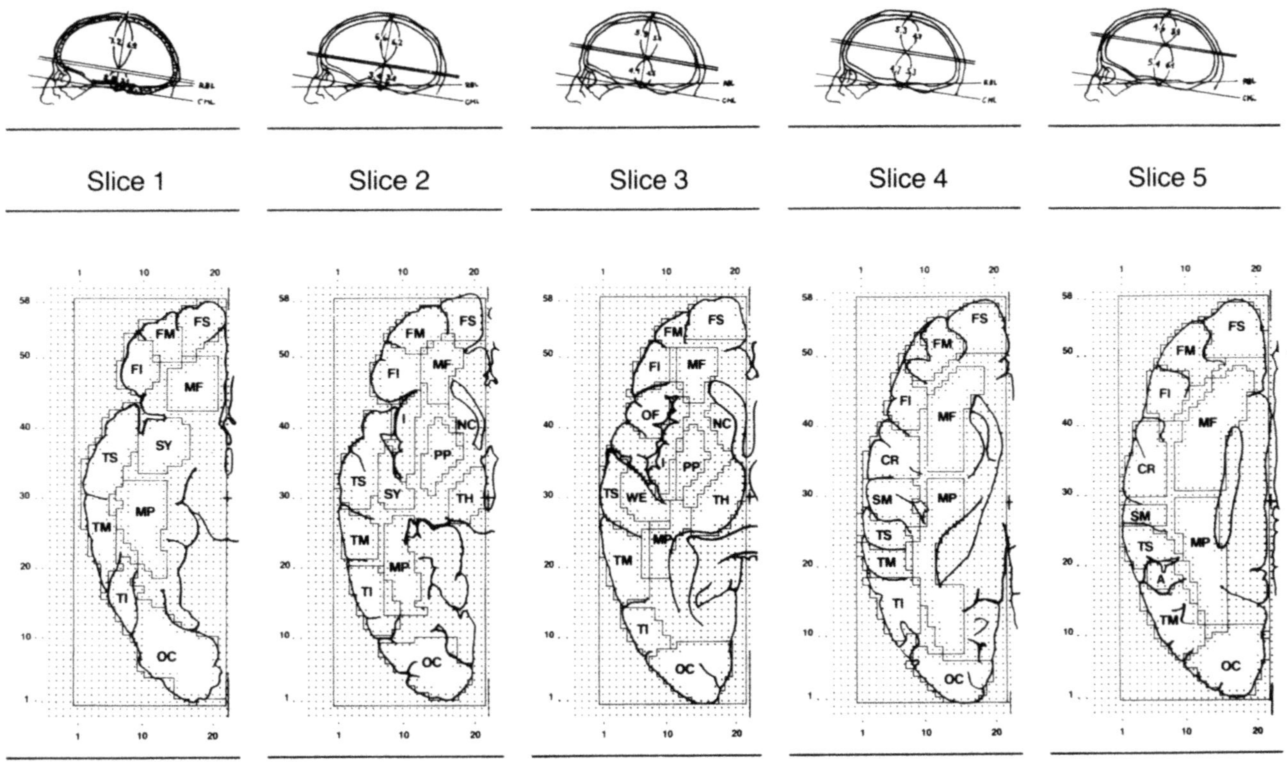

FIG 1. Standardised templates after Matsui and Hirano (1978) with anatomic landmarks. Lateral views of skull on top indicate level of slice. CML, canthomeatal line; RBL, Reid's baseline. See Table 3 for explanations of abbreviations of standardised morphologic areas.

the five-cluster solution. The six- and seven-cluster solutions were suboptimal for interpretation also.

Results

The solutions of partitioning cluster analyses for all five slices taken together yield similarities for the *total* lesion, its spatial seat as well as its anatomical location. The three-cluster solution yielded a cluster of lesions that could be interpreted as pre-rolandic, another as post-rolandic, and a third cluster as pre- and post-rolandic. For the sake of brevity, the clusters will be designated with such rough anatomic names indicating the lesioned areas they contain. The outer bounds of the lesion clusters are illustrated in Fig. 2. Lesions in the clusters could vary widely within those bounds. For the purpose of illustration, the lesion information over all five slices is condensed on slice 3, which contains the traditional speech area.

Table 4 shows how the functionally defined patients are assigned to the clusters. Four of six good Wernickes and five of six ugly Wernickes belong to the post-rolandic lesion cluster. The lesions of the remaining two good Wernickes have more similarity to those of six good globals. Brocas are distributed over the pre- and post-rolandic clusters, and ugly globals can be found in all three clusters. The majority of both bad types is in the pre-rolandic lesion cluster, with some exceptions in the post-rolandic one.

TABLE 4
Three-cluster Solution for Standardised Lesions of Aphasic Patients over All Five Slices

	Lesion Clusters[a]		
Patient Subgroup	*Pre- and Post-rolandic*	*Pre-rolandic*	*Post-rolandic*
Globals Good ($n = 7$)	6	1	
Globals Bad ($n = 7$)		6	1
Globals Ugly ($n = 7$)	2	3	2
Brocas ($n = 7$)		4	3
Wernickes Good ($n = 6$)	2		4
Wernickes Bad ($n = 6$)		4	2
Wernickes Ugly ($n = 6$)		1	5
Patients/Cluster	10	19	17

[a] For outer bounds of lesion areas in clusters, see Fig. 2.

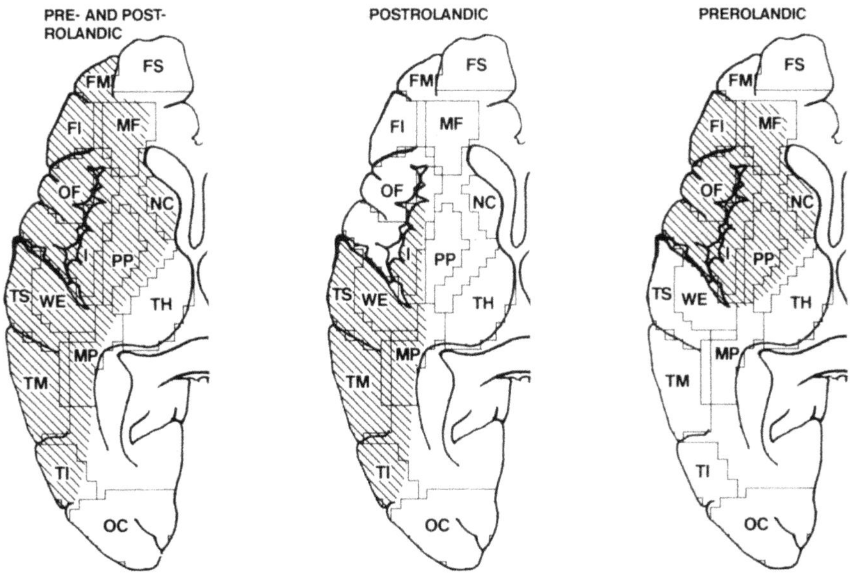

FIG. 2 Three-cluster solution for standardised lesion over all five slices, illustrated on slice 3. See Table 3 for explanations of abbreviations of anatomical areas.

The four-cluster solution did not bring any significant innovations: It created an additional "rest" cluster with patients who were the least homogeneous in the already established clusters. The five-cluster solution was technically the best. Figure 3 gives the outer bounds of the lesion clusters. Individual lesions within the clusters showed far less variability than in the three-cluster solution. For purposes of illustration, the lesion information over all five slices is condensed on slice 3.

There was one small pre-rolandic cluster, one small post-rolandic cluster, one large post-rolandic cluster, and one large post- and pre-rolandic cluster. The somewhat smaller apparently perisylvian cluster was actually a mixture of non-classifiable lesions of small size. Table 5 shows how the functionally defined patients are assigned to the clusters.

Six of seven good globals fall into the large lesion cluster, together with one good Wernicke with semantic jargon. The remaining five good Wernickes are in the large post-rolandic cluster, together with two ugly Wernickes and one bad Wernicke, one ugly global, and one Broca. In the small post-rolandic cluster, there are three ugly Wernickes, two Brocas, and one ugly global. The small pre-rolandic cluster has one bad global and one bad Wernicke and two ugly globals and two Brocas.

Fifteen patients were left unaccounted for in the unclassifiable lesion cluster. Their lesions involved one of five different anatomical regions that centred around the posterior putamen, the anterior putamen, the global putamen, the temporal lobe with sparing of the superior temporal gyrus,

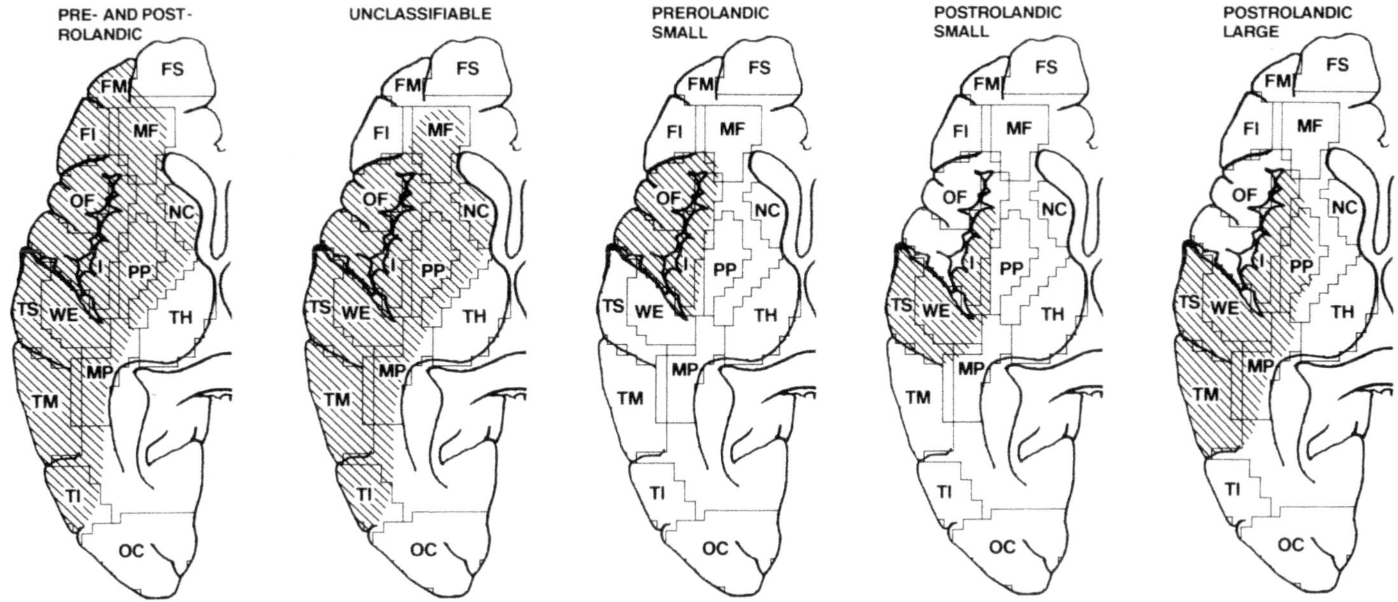

FIG 3. Five-cluster solution for standardised lesion over all five slices, illustrated on slice 3. See Table 3 for explanations of abbreviations of anatomical areas.

and pre-rolandic lesions that were too small to be homogeneously in the pre-rolandic cluster. The distribution of the patients over these subgroupings is given in Table 6.

By combining the large and small post-rolandic cluster of the five-cluster solution into a single post-rolandic group and not considering the unclassifiable cluster, it could be examined how consistently patients fell into the broad categories of post-rolandic, pre-rolandic, and global lesions with the three- and five-cluster solution. The results are listed in Table 7.

A comparison of the five-cluster solution is given in Table 8 for the major aphasia slices, slices 2 and 3. It shows the consistency of clustering participation over different slices. Adding slice 4, the parietal slice, only brought a change in the good Wernickes, which were consistently represented in two rather than four cases.

It is immediately clear from the results of this study that strong correlational claims cannot be upheld. A strong test of correlation would not accept any exceptions. Even in the very broad anatomical localisation of the three-cluster solution into post-rolandic, pre-rolandic, and pre- and post-rolandic (see Fig. 2 and Table 4), patients with very different functional deficits can be found together, jargon Wernickes with Globals, Brocas with Wernickes, and transcortical patients with Brocas. Weeding out the unclassifiable lesions in the five-cluster solution and making finer delineations in the rough anatomical areas did not solve the problem (see Fig. 3 and Table 5). No cluster of lesion could be ascribed to a single functional group without exceptions.

A weaker test of correlation would be satisfied with tendencies and explain counter-examples as problems of generalisation, which are inherent to an aphasic population.

The best results were obtained for the cluster of global pre- and post-rolandic lesions and the group of good globals: Although one patient had a small posterior putaminal lesion (Table 6), six of seven patients had their lesion consistently in the large lesion cluster using different cluster solutions (Table 7), and five of them over different slices (Table 8). However, these positive results are hard to interpret. Global aphasic patients who produce exclusively one and the same recurring CV-syllable have exactly the same AAT test profile as the good globals in this study, even though their lesions are as variable as those of ugly globals (Poeck, De Bleser, & Keyserlingk, 1984b). One would thus have to assume that it is the lack of spontaneous speech in the good globals that correlates with their lesion, and not the lack of more metalinguistic competence as tapped in the different AAT subtests, which they share with the poorly localisable CT-recurring utterance patients. But how could spontaneous speech be localised in the absence of a localisation of other more specific linguistic abilities.

In the category of Wernicke's aphasics, correlational tendencies may be observed for the good and ugly Wernicke's. Four of six good Wernickes

TABLE 5
Five-Cluster Solution for Standardised Lesions of Aphasic Patients over All Five Slices

	Lesion Clusters[a]				
Patient Subgroup	*Pre- and Post-rolandic*	*Unclassifiable*	*Small Pre-rolandic*	*Large Post-rolandic*	*Small Post-rolandic*
Globals Good ($n = 7$)	6	1			
Globals Bad ($n = 7$)		6	1		
Globals Ugly ($n = 7$)	2	1	2	1	1
Brocas ($n = 7$)		2	2	1	2
Wernickes Good ($n = 6$)	1			5	
Wernickes Bad ($n = 6$)		4	1	1	
Wernickes Ugly ($n = 6$)		1		2	3
Patients/cluster	9	15	6	10	6

[a] For outer bounds of lesion areas in clusters, see Fig. 3.

TABLE 6

Dissolution of the Unclassifiable Lesion Cluster in the Five-cluster Solution and Correlation of Subgroupings with Aphasic Patients

	Unclassifiable Lesion Cluster				
	Anterior Putamen	*Posterior Putamen*	*Global Putamen*	*Temporal Lobe Minus Superior Temporal Gyrus*	*Small Pre-rolandic*
Globals Good (1)		1			
Globals Bad (6)	2	1		1	1
Globals Ugly (1)			1		
Brocas (2)					2
Wernickes Bad (4)	2			2	
Wernickes Ugly (1)	1				
Patients/Subgroup	5	2	1	3	3

TABLE 7
Patients Correlating Consistently with the Same Lesion Cluster in the Three- and Five-cluster Solutions

	Lesion Clusters		
Patient Subgroup	*Pre- and Post-rolandic*	*Pre-rolandic*	*Post-rolandic*
Globals Good (7)	6		
Globals Bad (7)		1	
Globals Ugly (7)	2	2	2
Brocas (7)		2	3
Wernickes Good (6)	1		4
Wernickes Bad (6)		1	[illegible]
Wernickes Ugly (6)			5
Patients/Cluster	9	6	15

are consistently exclusively post-rolandic, and five of six ugly Wernickes (Table 7). Five good Wernickes shared a large post-rolandic lesion compared to only two ugly Wernickes in the five-cluster solution (Table 5). Moreover, only good Wernickes remain consistent over different slices, and none of the ugly Wernickes (Table 8). The biggest problems are posed by one good Wernicke patient with a global lesion (Tables 5, 7, 8) and one ugly Wernicke patient with a small anterior putaminal lesion (Table 6).

Lesion correlations for Broca's aphasia are more problematic. The four Broca patients with pre-rolandic lesions in the three-cluster solution (Table 4) are reduced to two in the five-cluster solution (Table 5). However, two of the unclassifiables turn out to have very small pre-rolandic lesions (Table 6), so that four of seven positive cases remain with gross anatomical approximations. Unfortunately, three patients have consistently the "wrong", post-rolandic lesion (Table 7), so that "Wernicke's area" might be held responsible for Broca's aphasia just as much as "Broca's area". This is not as surprising as it may sound. In the classical era, when brain lesions were determined by anatomical study (which is still the technique with higher precision than any of the contemporary, more easily available methods), Broca's area has not always been postulated for Broca's aphasia as we understand it today. Agrammatism, which is now the defining characteristic of Broca's aphasia, was held to correlate with temporal lobe lesions by many authors (e.g. Pick, 1913; see De Bleser, 1987, for a historical review). Broca's patients Tantan as well as Lelong, for whom

TABLE 8
Patients Correlating Consistently with the Same Lesion in Slices 2, 3, and 4 of the Five-cluster Solution

Patient Subgroup	*Pre- and Post-rolandic*	*Unclassifiable*	*Small Pre-rolandic*	*Large Post-rolandic*	*Small Post-rolandic*
Globals Good ($n = 7$)	5	1			
Globals Bad ($n = 7$)		3	1		
Globals Ugly ($n = 7$)	1	1	1	1	
Brocas ($n = 7$)		1	1		
Wernickes Good ($n = 6$)	1			4 (2)[a]	
Wernickes Bad ($n = 6$)		3	1		
Wernickes Ugly ($n = 6$)		1			
Patients/Cluster	7	10	4	5 (3)[a]	

[a] Change brought about by considering the parietal slice 4, in addition to the Wernicke slice 3 and the Broca/Wernicke slice 2.

Broca's area was immortalised, had an aphasia that by contemporary standards must be considered global aphasia (Poeck et al., 1984b). If anything, then, Broca's area should correlate well with global aphasia. However, the results for the ugly globals were as disparate as those for Broca's aphasia in this study.

Finally, there remain the patients with a unimodal preservation of repetition (bad globals and bad Wernickes). Good repetition in the absence of cognitive language processing is a very well-circumscribed function and could be expected to correlate better with a particular lesion. One could consider it a testing ground for postulating lesion correlations for selectively preserved or disturbed linguistic modalities or components. The three-cluster solution showed a strong trend towards pre-rolandic lesions (Table 4: six of seven bad globals, four of six bad Wernickes). However, the sharper delineation of the five-cluster solution moved most of them into the unclassifiable cluster (Table 5). The five unclassifiable bad globals were dispersed over four subgroups in this cluster, the four unclassifiable bad Wernickes over two of them (Table 5). Three unclassifiable bad globals had lesions involving the putamen, two had lesions sparing the putamen entirely. The strong correlation found in other studies between the anterior–posterior direction of putaminal lesions and Broca-like or Wernicke-like aphasia (Damasio & Damasio, 1982; Naeser et al., 1982) could not be established. Both bad Wernickes with a putaminal lesion had anterior, not posterior, putaminal lesions.

In summary, the strong correlational test that allows no exceptions to the localisation of functional disturbances was entirely negative. The weak correlational test could only be upheld with reservation for good globals, who had practically no language left, and for Wernicke's aphasics of both the good and the ugly type. For Broca's aphasics, there is no lesion correlation whatsoever, in which they are similar to ugly globals. Nor was there any specific lesion correlation for unimodal preservation of repetition. The only lesion characteristic that the functionally homogeneous patients with good repetition had in common was its rather small size. Thus, the only tendency towards correlation even for functionally selected patients could be found in gross anatomical terms for those globals who were most severely disturbed but did not produce recurring utterances, and for Wernickes with and without jargon. Most severe globals had large lesions extending widely into the pre- and post-rolandic cortical and subcortical areas, most Wernickes had lesions restricted to the post-rolandic region. The lesions for all other aphasia types were unspecific. Correlation tendencies were too weak for globals who were not totally without language, for Brocas, and for both types of transcortical aphasics, mixed transcortical, and transcortical sensory types.

DISCUSSION

The question was examined whether deficit–lesion correlations, which are the observational material for language localisation theories, have become better after the introduction of imaging techniques. Only Europeans have hitherto published negative correlations; therefore, we considered the possibility of artefacts in the data. Cluster analyses on selected material could show only weak correlational tendencies for the most severe global patients and for Wernicke's aphasics. No correlations, however, were exceptionless. In some cases, as for Broca's aphasia, the exceptions were as frequent as the expected rule. Thus, Basso et al.'s data (1985) for unselected patients (although not their interpretation) and our own (Poeck et al., 1984a) were confirmed by the "purified" data that entered this correlation study.

These negative results have a different impact on the questions that can be asked of lesion determination. Obviously, they can hardly question the immense progress that technical improvements such as CT, NMR, PET, and SPECT have brought for the neurological assessment of organicity, etiology, etc. There are, however, consequences for neuropsychological research, where a preselection of patients on the basis of gross similarity of lesion such as anterior and posterior, parietal, etc., is still very much in use. On the basis of our results, lesion information should not hold any special status in the psychological testing of patients: It can neither substitute functional testing nor is it necessary information.

It is surprising how uncritically cognitive neuropsychology has accepted the positive results of clinical correlation studies as hard facts about brain and language, even while rejecting the research paradigm in which such studies were conducted. Saffran (1982, p. 333) is just one of many examples when she writes:

> The syndrome-based approach reflects the origins of aphasia research, which lie in clinical medicine. The continued commitment to this approach is largely justified on the basis of secure links that the classical syndromes have to brain anatomy. *It is undeniable that Broca's aphasia is associated with a lesion in one part of the brain and Wernicke's aphasia with a lesion in another.* (My italics.) In describing the deficits of patients who fall within these classes, it is therefore possible to make claims about the functional commitment of brain areas.

After our initial attempts to rescue this position at all cost (Blunk et al., 1981), we are now ready to abandon it as insufficiently substantiated. It would seem to us that the only relatively hard fact about brain-and-language obtained in 100 years of aphasiology is that aphasia usually co-occurs with a lesion in the perisylvian region of the left hemisphere.

This is certainly not strong evidence for a fixed neuronal architecture of domain-specific modules such as language, a requirement of the modular program in cognitive psychology (Fodor, 1983; Marshall, 1984). However, one could in this program also follow Isserlin's suggestion and leave the question of localisation purposely to the last, after the function to be localised has been sufficiently understood. In the case of language, this is far from completed. There are at least three ways in which one can conceptualise the modularity of language (Tanenhaus, Carlson, & Seidenberg, 1984)!

1. The unimodular model: The entire linguistic system is one unified module. The general cognitive system has access only to the output.
2. The polymodular model: Each linguistic component (semantics, phonology, syntax) is a module. The general cognitive system has multiple access to the grammar. It can select the information coming out of one module that it wants to send along to the next module in the serial chain.
3. The rule-module model: Each of the rules, principles, and conditions of grammar is an independent module on its own. They are not co-extensive with components. The general cognitive system has multiple access, not to select the information but to select the module to which it will send the output.

Chomsky has expressed views that correspond to all three models (Chomsky, 1980, 1981; Huybregts & van Riemsdijk, 1982, pp. 114–117) but probably with this important difference that it is not the general cognitive system that intervenes in 2 and 3, but internal mechanisms of grammar. This conception of an autonomous language faculty conforming to 1, with autonomous subsystems as in 2, interacting in various ways as in 3 does not conform to Fodors's criterion for modularity, namely, that a faculty should not be assembled "in the sense of having been put together from some stock of more elementary subprocesses" (Fodor, 1983, p. 37).

Still, there is relatively strong consensus on the existence of an autonomous language faculty. The most feasible question one can thus ask at present within a deficit theory is whether lesions can provide knowledge about where and how this language faculty as a whole (the unimodular model 1) is localised. This may be assumed to be destroyed in patients with severe global aphasia. However, lesion correlations even for these patients have been far from perfect (Mazzochi & Vignolo, 1979; Poeck et al., 1984b). Rather than being extensively perisylvian, CT-lesions have been large and small, anterior and posterior, cortical and subcortical. Clearly, the possible intrusion of technical artefacts should further be diminished by complementing structural methods such as computer tomography (CT) with functional methods such as single positron emission tomography (SPECT). It will then be important that the negative cases that may still remain after this procedure are not eliminated by statistics or minimalised by ad hoc arguments but become objects of further study, because it might very well be the case that neither the information on blood flow nor that on brain metabolism provided by SPECT is rich enough to describe the lesion fully. Because the presumed language area is association cortex, its neuronal organisation is characterised by intricate wiring (Kornhuber, 1983) and localisations must ultimately be envisioned at this level rather than at that of gross anatomy. At any rate, one of the standard assumptions of deficit theory, that a simple one-to-one mapping obtains between brain areas and psychological functions, will have to be revised, and negative correlations should be allowed to become a source of knowledge. Clear localisation theories based only on positive cases might in the end be more fictitious than negative cases that do not immediately lead to a solid theory of brain and language, but which leave room for scientific search.

ACKNOWLEDGEMENTS

This work was supported by the DFG (Deutsche Forschungsgemeinschaft) grant no. Po41/16-1. The author wishes to acknowledge K. Willmes for performing cluster analyses, R. Hündgen and H. Zeumer for determining and standardising the CT-lesions, and K. Poeck for his support.

REFERENCES

Basso, A., Roch Lecours, A., Moraschini, S., & Vanier, M. (1985) Anatomoclinical correlations of the aphasias as defined through computerized tomography: exceptions. *Brain and Language*, *26*, 201–229.

Berndt, R. & Caramazza, A. (1980) A redefinition of the syndrome of Broca's aphasia: Implications for a neuropsychological model of language. *Applied Psycholinguistics*, *1*, 225–278.

Blunk, R., De Bleser, R., Willems, K., & Zeumer, H. (1981) A refined method to relate morphological and functional aspects of aphasia. *European Neurology*, *20*, 69–79.

Bogen, J. & Bogen, G. (1976) Wernicke's region—Where is it? In S. Harnad, H. Steklis, & J. Lancaster (Eds.), *Origins and evolution of language and speech*. Annals of the New York Academy of Science, *280*, 834–844.

Caplan, D. (1981) On the cerebral localization of linguistic functions: Logical and empirical issues surrounding deficit analysis and functional localization. *Brain and Language*, *14*, 120–137.

Caramazza, A. (1984) The logic of neuropsychological research and the problem of patient classification in aphasia. *Brain and Language*, *21*, 9–20.

Chomsky, N. (1980) Rules and representations. *The Behavioral and Brain Sciences*, *3*, 1–61.

Chomsky, N. (1981) *Lectures on government and binding. The Pisa lectures*. Dordrecht: Foris.

Damasio, H. & Damasio, A. (1980) The anatomical basis of conduction aphasia. *Brain*, *103*, 337–350.

Damasio, A. R., Damasio, H., Rizzo, M., Varney, N., & Gersh, F. (1982) Aphasia with nonhemorragic lesions in the basal ganglia and internal capsula. *Archives of Neurology*, *39*, 15–20.

De Bleser, R. (1987) From agrammatism to paragrammatism: German aphasiological traditions and grammatical disturbances. *Cognitive Neuropsychology*, *4*, 187–256.

Fodor, J. A. (1983) *The modularity of mind*. Cambridge, Mass: MIT Press.

Geschwind, N. (1980) Some comments on the neurology of language. In D. Caplan (Ed.), *Biological studies of mental processes*. Cambridge, Mass: MIT Press.

Hartigan, J. A. (1975) *Clustering algorithms*. New York: John Wiley & Sons.

Huber, W., Weniger, D., Poeck, K., & Willmes, K. (1984) The Aachen Aphasia Test (AAT). In F. C. Rose (Ed.), *Progress in aphasiology*. New York: Raven Press.

Huybregts, R. & van Riemsdijk, H. (1982) *Noam Chomsky on the generative enterprise*. Dordrecht: Foris.

Isserlin, M. (1922) Über Agrammatismus. *Zeitschrift für die gesamte Neurologie und Psychatrie*, *75*, 332–410.

Kean, M.-L. (1977) The linguistic interpretation of aphasic syndromes. In E. Walker (Ed.), *Explorations in the biology of language*. Montgomery, VT: Bradford Books.

Kertesz, A. (Ed.) (1983) *Localization in neuropsychology*. New York: Academic Press.

Kornhuber, H. H. (1983) Functional interpretation of the multimodal convergence in the central nervous system of vertebrates. *Fortschritte der Zoologie*, *28*, 99–111.

Lichtheim, L. (1885) On aphasia. *Brain*, *7*, 433–484.

Marshall, J. C. (1980) On the biology of language acquisition. In D. Caplan (Ed.), *Biological studies of mental processes*. Cambridge, Mass.: MIT Press.

Marshall, J. C. (1984) Multiple perspectives on modularity. *Cognition*, *17*, 209–242.

Matsui, T. & Hirano, A. (1978) *An atlas of the human brain for computerized tomography*. Tokyo: Igaku-Shoin.

Mazzochi, F. & Vignolo, L. (1979) Localization of lesions in aphasia: Clinical CT-scan correlations in stroke patients. *Cortex*, *15*, 627–654.

Morris, R., Blashfield, R., & Satz, P. (1981) Neuropsychology and cluster analysis: Potentials and problems. *Journal of Clinical Neuropsychology*, *3*, 79–99.

Morton, J. (1980) Language: Levels of characterization. Commentary to N. Chomsky: Rules and representation. *The Behavioral and Brain Sciences*, *3*, 29–30.

Mountcastle, V. B. (1978) An organizing principle for cerebral function: The unit module and the distributed system. In G. M. Edelman & V. B. Mountcastle (Eds.), *The mindful brain*. Cambridge, Mass. MIT Press.

Naeser, M., Alexander, M., Helm-Estabrooks, N., Levine, H., Laughlin, S., & Geschwind, N. (1982) Aphasia with predominantly subcortical lesion sites. *Arch. Neurol.*, *39*, 2–14.

Ojemann, G. (1983) Brain organization for language from the perspective of electrical stimulation mapping. *The Behavioral and Brain Sciences*, *6*, 189–230.

Philips, C. G., Zeki, S., & Barlow, H. B. (1984) Localization of function in the cerebral cortex: Past, present and future. *Brain*, *107*, 327–363.

Pick, A. (1913) *Die agrammatischen Sprachstörungen. Studien zur psychologischen Grundlegung der Aphasielehre. I. Teil.* Berlin: Springer-Verlag.

Poeck, K., De Bleser, R., & Keyserlingk (1984a) CT-Localization of standard aphasic syndromes. In F. C. Rose (Ed.), *Advances in neurology, vol. 42: Progress in aphasiology*. New York: Raven Press.

Poeck, K., De Bleser, R., & Keyserlingk (1984b) Neurolinguistic status and localization of lesion in aphasic patients with exclusively consonant–vowel recurring utterances. *Brain*, *107*, 199–217.

Saffran, E. (1982) Neuropsychological approaches to the study of language. *British Journal of Psychology*, *73*, 317–337.

Tanenhaus, M. K., Carlson, G. N., & Seidenberg, M. S. (1984) Do listeners compute linguistic representations? In D. R. Dowty, A. Zwicky, & L. Kartunnen (Eds.), *Natural language parsing: Psychological, computational, and theoretical perspectives*. Cambridge: Cambridge University Press.

Wernicke, C. (1874) *Der aphasische Symptomenkomplex*. Breslau: Max Cohn und Weigert.

Willmes, K., Poeck, K., Weniger, D., Huber, W. (1983) Facet theory applied to the construction and validation of the Aachen Aphasia Test. *Brain and Language*, *18*, 259–276.

PART III: READING AND WRITING

9 Modelling the Writing Process

A. W. Ellis
Department of Psychology, University of York, U.K.

INTRODUCTION

Of all the areas of cognition to come under the psychologist's microscope, spelling and writing are probably the ones in which cognitive neuropsychology has been most influential. In other domains, such as reading, speaking, or remembering, experimental cognitive psychology provided ready-made functional theories or models that cognitive neuropsychologists could use to shape their initial investigations. They could then support, contest, or develop those models using data gathered from brain-injured patients (see Coltheart, Sartori, & Job, 1987; Ellis, 1982a, 1984; Ellis & Young, 1988). In contrast, students of disorders of spelling and writing have largely been obliged to devise their models as they go along, with the only additional constraining data coming from a relatively small set of studies of adult spelling abilities, slips of the pen, and motor processes in writing (e.g. Ellis, 1982b; Frith, 1980a; Hotopf, 1983; Margolin, 1984).

In fact, the situation facing the modern cognitive neuropsychologist working on spelling and writing is reminiscent of that which faced the "diagram-makers" of the late nineteenth century (e.g. Charcot, 1889; Lichtheim, 1885; Wernicke, 1874). These scholars were forced to create functional models of normal cognitive processes whose disorders they studied. Theoretical development came almost entirely in response to data from new patients showing new patterns of disorder.

In this chapter I shall review theories of spelling and writing both old and new. Although I shall briefly consider some disorders of the more peripheral aspects of writing, extensive discussion of disorders of spelling will be left to Patterson (this volume). I shall begin, however, with some general considerations of the nature of writing itself that must constrain all efforts at theorising in this area.

WRITING SYSTEMS AND WRITING PROCESSES

When attempting to model the writing process there are two things that must constantly be borne in mind. The first is that writing as a system of communication is only some 5000 or so years old (Gelb, 1963) and has only become anything like widespread as an accomplishment in the present century. This means that there can be no genetically given cognitive modules for operations specific to the processing of written language (Ellis, 1987a). We cannot be predisposed to acquire phoneme–grapheme conversion rules in the same way that we might plausibly be thought to be predisposed to acquire, say, rules of syntax. If future research continues to support present beliefs that localised injury to the brain can destroy processes *specific* to producing or comprehending written language, it would seem to imply that in the course of development the brain devotes portions of itself to skills that are culturally transmitted and to a considerable degree artificial.

The second point to be borne in mind concerns the variations in the principles by which modern orthographic systems work. Whereas the earliest writing systems all appear to have been logographic, with one unanalysed symbol per word, different language–script combinations have subsequently evolved along very different lines (Sampson, 1985). Chinese has, with good reason, remained loyal to the logographic principle; Japanese is a subtle hybrid of logographic and syllabic scripts; whereas the ancient Greeks perfected the first true alphabet with one symbol (letter) for each phoneme (distinctive speech sound) in the language. Given the artificiality of writing discussed earlier, and the fact that any specialised modules that exist are formed as a result of education not evolution, we have no guarantee whatsoever that different language–script combinations will create the same cognitive modules in their users. A model for reading and writing Chinese might be utterly different from a model for reading and writing English. There may even be substantial differences between the processes used to handle languages like Italian or Finnish whose orthographies have retained their alphabetic transparency, and those used to handle languages like English and French whose orthographies abound with opaque, irregularly spelled words and complex correspondences between graphemes and phonemes (see Henderson, 1984; Luria, 1970; Marshall, 1976; Paradis, Hagiwara, & Hildebrandt, 1985, for discussion).

In sum, models should be generalised only with great caution from one language–script combination to another, and data from one combination should not be used to criticise a model created for a different combination (as Ellis (1982b) did when using data from English acquired dysgraphias to dispute a model proposed by Luria (1970) for the spelling of Russian).

HIGH-LEVEL PLANNING OF SPEECH AND WRITING

Of the four language modalities at the disposal of a literate adult (speaking, listening, writing, and reading) writing is undoubtedly the least used. Even the most prolific of one's acquaintances usually speak rather more than they write. In everyday parlance the term "writing" is used to denote everything from formulating ideas to moving the tip of one's pen across the paper, or pounding at the keys of a typewriter. It seems likely on a priori grounds that some language-formulation processes (generally speaking the "higher", more central ones) will be shared in common by speaking and writing, whereas others (generally speaking the "lower", more peripheral ones) will be specific to one or other modality. An important task for cognitive psychologists is to elucidate which processes are common to both modalities and which are modality-specific.

Starting as it were at the top, there is no doubt that there are marked textual, syntactic, and lexical differences between formal writing and casual speech (Akinasso, 1982), and it has been argued by some that we should regard them virtually as separate languages (e.g. Olson, 1977). It is conceivable that in mastering the stylistic demands of written prose the learner establishes high-level language-formulation processes that are separate and distinct from those employed in speaking. This, however, is unlikely. Although there are striking differences between formal writing and casual conversational speech, there are also circumstances under which writing can become very speech-like and speech very "literate". The written language of a quick note or letter to a friend lacks the formality of an essay, whereas the language of a speech, sermon, or lecture can bear all of the hallmarks of formal writing (Leech, Deuchar, & Hoogenraad, 1982).

Neuropsychological evidence (though admittedly none too strong) tends to argue against the separate languages position. When a patient has a high-level conceptual, semantic, or syntactic deficit, this seems to compromise both writing and speech. This type of argument from the association of deficits is, of course, the weakest form of neuropsychological argument. The case for separate (internal) languages would be greatly strengthened by just a few patients who show in speech but not in writing (or vice versa) the sort of conceptual–semantic jargon discussed by Kinsbourne and Warrington (1963) and Brown (1981), or the sentence construction deficit analysed by Saffran, Schwartz, and Marin (1980).

THREE THEORIES OF SPELLING

Most theorists are at least agreed that the primary divergence of speech and writing comes around the lexical level, for it is here that the ultimate requirement to produce phones in speech and strokes in writing must force a separation. That said, we can distinguish at least three broad classes of theory concerning how speech and writing interrelate at the word level.

Theory One asserts that the spellings of all words, even highly familiar ones, are assembled piecemeal from the sound of the word by the application of sublexical phoneme (sound) to grapheme (letter) conversion procedures. Thus, if you know how to say the word "street" and wish to spell it, according to this theory you first segment the word into its phonemes (/s/, /t/, /r/, /i/, /t/) then use your knowledge of alphabetic phoneme–grapheme correspondences to assemble the appropriate letter string. Such a theory was proposed by Luria (1970) as an account of spelling in Russian. The theory might indeed be valid as applied to languages like Russian or Italian that have highly, regular alphabets (though see the following). It cannot, however, suffice as an account of spelling in English. The reasons why it cannot work are by now well known (e.g., Ellis, 1982b, 1984; Hatfield & Patterson, 1983; Shallice, 1981) and need only be listed briefly here. First, English contains many irregular words whose spellings resist being assembled by sublexical rules. The list of irregular words contains many of the commonest in the language (e.g., *WAS*, *KNOW*, *SURE*, *HAVE*, *TWO*, *WOULD* as well as such well-known oddities as *YACHT*, *SWORD*, and *COLONEL*). Second, a surprisingly large number of words—again including many of the commonest ones—have homophones that are spelt differently (e.g., *WHICH–WITCH*, *TWO–TOO*, *THEIR–THERE*, *WOULD–WOOD*, *KNOW–NO*). The correct spellings for such words cannot be deduced purely from their sounds: The spelling system must also know which meaning is required. The third objection concerns the fact that there are far fewer reliably predictable correspondences in the sound to spelling direction than in the spelling to sound direction. *STREET*, *MEAT*, and *BRIEF* are all classed as "regular" words because they are all pronounced in the manner one would predict from their spelling, but if you knew only how to pronounce "street" you would have no way of reliably choosing between *STREET* and *STREAT* (or even *STRIET* or *STRETE*) as candidate spellings. Finally, we have good cognitive neuropsychological evidence for the inadequacy of Theory One as an account of English spelling (see Patterson, this volume, for details).

Theory Two, advocated by Weigl (1975), Dodd (1980), Frith (1980b), and Nolan and Caramazza (1983) attempts to retain some role for sublexical phoneme–grapheme conversion in the spelling of familiar words while avoiding some of the criticisms levelled at Theory One. This theory proposes that only those portions of familiar words that cannot be predicted from regular phoneme–grapheme correspondences are retrieved from memory. These unpredictable elements then provide a framework that is completed by phoneme–grapheme correspondences filling in the predictable parts. The first objection to Theory Two is the point also levelled against Theory One that surprisingly few elements *are* entirely predictable sublexically. The second objection is neuropsychological. Several patients discussed in detail by Patterson (this volume) can correctly spell words of whose spoken form they have little or no knowledge. Also, patients labelled as "phonological dysgraphics" can no longer use phoneme–grapheme conversion procedures but can still correctly spell many familiar words, both regular and irregular, and can correctly reproduce even the "regular" portions of "irregular" words.

Theory Three—the one that has found greatest favour among cognitive neuropsychologists—asserts that the spellings of all familiar words, both regular and irregular, are normally retrieved in their entirety from memory or, more specifically, from an internal word-store or lexicon that forms part of one's long-term memory. Only words whose spellings have not yet been stored in memory are assembled by sublexical procedures. The vagaries of English spelling mean that the sublexical strategy is less effective for English than it would be for, say, Russian or Italian, and is certainly less successful than looking the word up in a dictionary! Variants of Theory Three have been proposed by Seymour (1979), Morton (1980), Newcombe and Marshall (1980), Allport and Funnell (1981), and Ellis (1982b, 1984) among others.

An important source of disagreement among advocates of Theory Three concerns the question of whether the word-store or lexicon from which spellings is retrieved is *specific* to writing or also plays a part in other language modalities, particularly reading. In the original formulation of Morton's influential "logogen model" a single, central "logogen system" was responsible for recognising and producing words in both speech and writing (e.g., Morton, 1970, 1979a). In response to certain experimental findings, which need not be gone into here, Morton divided the original unitary logogen system into four—an auditory input logogen system for recognising spoken words, a visual input logogen system for recognising written words, a speech output logogen system for producing spoken words, and a graphic output logogen system for producing written words (Morton, 1979b, 1980). Figure 1 shows a (reduced) version of the Mk II logogen model.

Other proponents of four lexicons include Seymour (1979), Newcombe and Marshall (1980), Ellis (1982b, 1984) and, apparently, Charcot (1889). In Fig. 2 I have redrawn Charcot's diagram to make it more easily

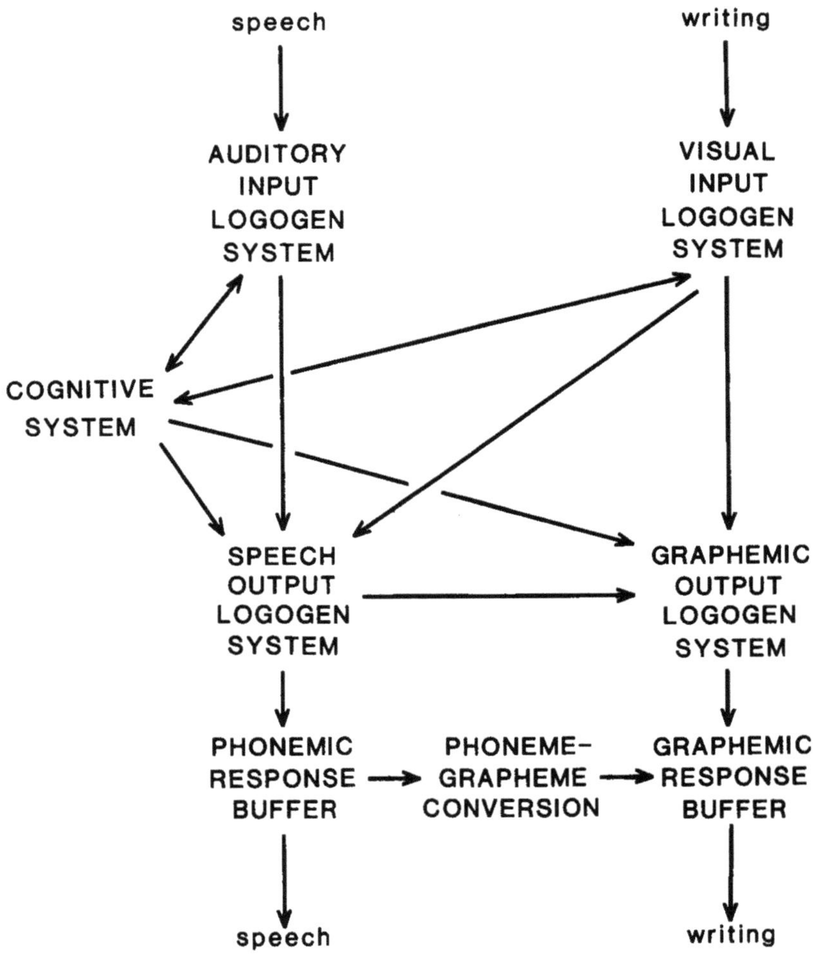

FIG 1. Version of Morton's logogen model emphasising the components involved in writing.

assimilable to the schemata of the modern cognitive neuropsychologist and to highlight the similarities between it and more recent formulations. Although there is undoubtedly a danger that diagrams, particularly old ones, can act rather like ink-blots upon which to project one's current theoretical fancies, nevertheless the similarity between Charcot's diagram and other, more recent ones is striking.

In (partial) opposition to the four lexicon theorists stand Allport and Funnell (1981) and Allport (1983). They argue that Morton went further than was necessary in dividing the original logogen system into four, and

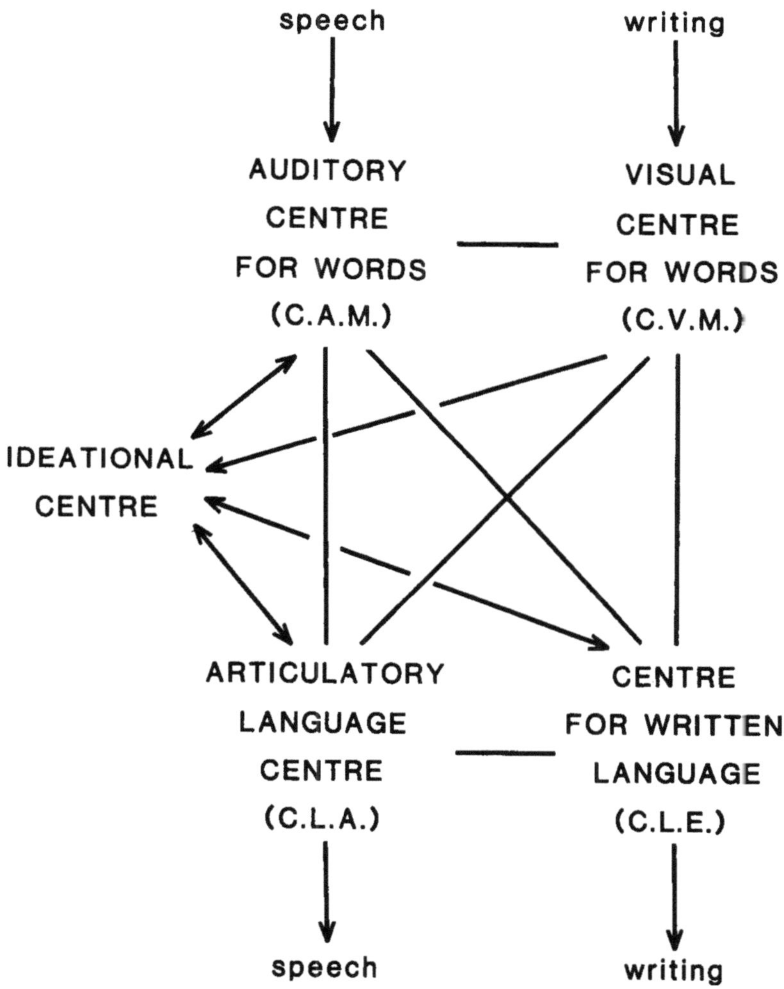

FIG 2. Redrawn representation of Charcot's (1889) diagram for word recognition and production. (Note that arrow heads have only been drawn in when the directions of connections are shown in Charcot's original diagram.)

that a division into two is sufficient. In Allport and Funnell's formulation (shown in Fig. 3) there is a set of "phonological word-forms" (i.e. a phonological lexicon) responsible for both recognising and producing spoken words, and a separate set of "orthographic word-forms" (i.e. an orthographic lexicon) responsible both for recognising and producing written words. The two- v. four-lexicon debate has not yet come to a conclusion, though parsimony should perhaps lead us to favour the former. Monsell (1985) discusses some of the relevant evidence from normal

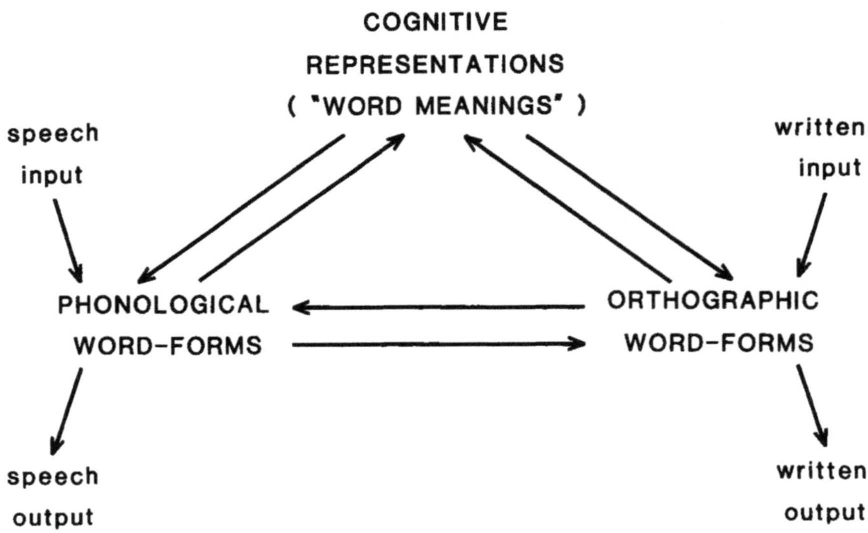

FIG 3. Allport and Funnell's two-lexicon model for word recognition and production.

experiments, whereas Coltheart and Funnell (1987) and Patterson (this volume) consider the neuropsychological evidence.

A COMPROMISE MODEL

In this section I should like to sketch briefly a model that, by hedging on the controversial issues, is designed to emphasise what I take to be the main areas of agreement among current modellers of spelling. I shall once again express the theory through a diagram, but would add that a diagram is only a device for imaging a theory. It happens to be a very convenient device where modular systems like the mind and brain are concerned (Ellis, 1987b), but the theory it encapsulates could perfectly well be conveyed in words. Indeed, a diagram alone is always insufficient: It must always be accompanied by a verbal exposition of the internal workings of each part and the nature of the intercommunications between them.

The compromise model is shown in Fig. 4. It assumes that speaking or writing a word under normal conditions (i.e. not writing to dictation or copying) begins by activating the internal representation of the word in a semantic system that is common to all language modalities. Two word-stores or lexicons are shown. The speech (output) lexicon contains units (alias nodes, or logogens) for each word in one's expressive spoken vocabulary. When a particular word's meaning is activated in the semantic system this activates the representation of the word in the speech (output) lexicon, which in turn makes available to the phoneme level the represen-

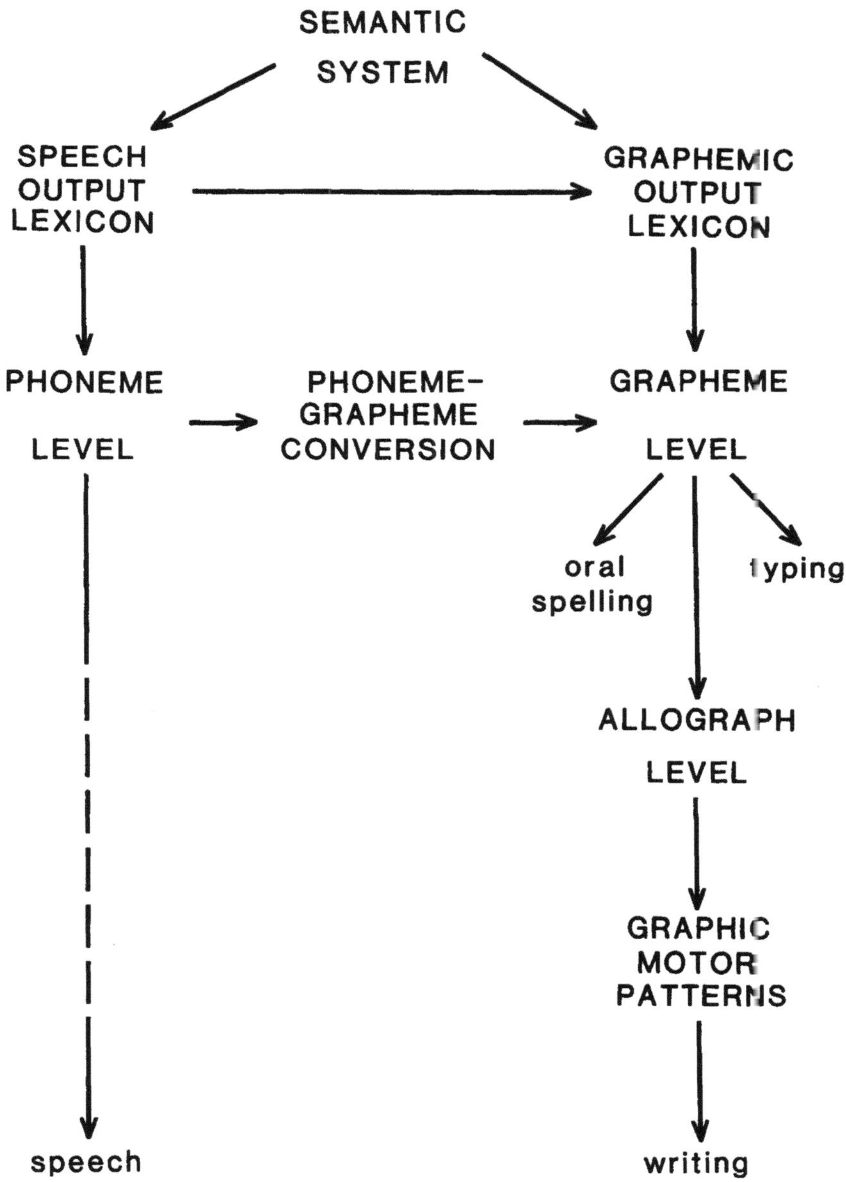

FIG 4. A compromise model for writing.

tation of the word in terms of a sequence of phonemes (speech sounds) ready for articulation if so desired. In some models, such as the logogen model, this sequence of events involves the actual transmission of semantic and phonemic "codes" between the components involved, whereas in an "interactive activation" theory such as that of Stemberger (1985) the codes stay within the boxes (or "levels") and only activation and inhibition pass along the arrows. The latter class of model has been in the ascendant in recent years.

If a word whose meaning has become activated is one whose spelling is known to the writer, then the unit or node for the word in the graphemic (output) lexicon will also become activated. There is good neuropsychological evidence (Patterson, this volume) for postulating a direct link between the semantic system and the graphemic lexicon, but there are also good reasons for supposing that a second source of activation may come from the speech (output) lexicon. Normal, skilled writers of English occasionally make an involuntary and unintended slip of the pen that takes the form of writing in the place of an intended word a real-word homophone of it. Thus a writer may produce *SCENE* where *SEEN* was intended, or *SOUGHT* for *SORT*. Occasionally a word similar but not identical in sound is written, for example *SURGE* for *SEARCH* (see Hotopf, 1983).

Now there are two important points to be made about these sound-based slips of the pen. First, non-words are rarely produced as slips: *SEEN* may be inadvertently written as *SCENE*, but *SENE*, *SIEN*, and *SEAN* are highly unlikely. Second, the words produced as errors often belong to that large class of words in English that are either grossly irregular or unpredictable due to the presence of phonemes with more than one common written equivalent. These two facts mean that, although it would be unwise to assert that sublexical phoneme–grapheme conversion never plays a part in generating English slips of the pen, nevertheless these sort of sound-based lexical substitution errors in writing almost certainly emanate from the graphemic (output) lexicon. As Morton (1980) observed, this implies an involvement of phonology in the selection of words from the graphemic (output) lexicon. In his model this involvement takes the form of the transmission of a phonemic code from the speech output logogen system to the graphic output logogen system where that code combines with the semantic code to trigger the desired logogen and release the appropriate graphemic code.

In an interactive activation framework, activation could be seen as coming from nodes in both the semantic system and the speech (output) lexicon. The locus of homophone and similar-sound slips of the pen would be the same as the locus of those slips of the tongue commonly referred to as "malapropisms" (e.g. Fay & Cutler, 1977) that result in the substitution in speech of a word similar in sound to the one intended. According to Stemberger (1985) these occur when interactive feedback from the phoneme level activates the node in the speech (output) lexicon for a word that shares many phonemes in common with the target. Of course, the node that is maximally similar to an intended word in terms of shared phonemes is a homophone, but homophones would never be detected as slips of the tongue (i.e. you would presumably never know if you had said "WOULD" instead of "WOOD"). They can, however, be detected as slips of the pen, as can similar-sound errors that would from this perspective be regarded as malapropism errors translated into writing. An outstanding problem for both the interactive activation and code transmission approaches remains the question of why, if semantic and phonological inputs combine at the graphemic (output) lexicon, homophone and similar-sound errors are so much more common as slips of the pen than are purely semantic errors (cf. Hotopf, 1983).

As noted earlier, neuropsychological evidence shows clearly that phonological information is not *essential* in order to sustain fluent writing of familiar words by skilled writers. Nevertheless, writing does seem to be naturally accompanied by inner speech, which, because speech is faster than writing, can be used to "try out" a phrase before it is committed to the page. Following Morton (1970, 1979a), Ellis (1984) envisages this inner speech as a recycling back from the phoneme level to the auditory processes activated in speech perception, thereby allowing the writer to "hear", monitor, evaluate, and possibly amend his or her language output before ever a word is written. Evaluation and reformulation are important functions in much writing and can certainly be done by re-reading a drafted piece (Flower & Hayes, 1980), but inner speech can also perform these functions more immediately if covertly.

Another role for phonology in writing comes when a writer wishes to create a plausible spelling for a word whose conventional spelling the writer does not know. We have already noted that this is a hazardous strategy for a writer of English given that language's frequent departures from perfect alphabetic transparency. Nevertheless, writers of English do learn low-level phoneme–grapheme correspondences and can when required employ them to assemble candidate spellings for unfamiliar words or a psychologist's invented non-words. In the compromise model this capacity is assigned to the component labelled "phoneme–grapheme conversion", though this must certainly be a gross oversimplification. Assembling a novel spelling must require at least three operations (Ellis, 1984). First, the spoken word must be segmented into its component phonemes; second, the common graphemic correspondences of those phonemes must be retrieved or activated; and third, the letters must be assembled into an ordered string. Impairment to any of these three processes would affect a writer's ability to employ the strategy of sublexical spelling. Finally, some form of interaction between the two spelling "routes"—lexical and sublexical—is implied by Campbell's (1983) finding, discussed at greater length by Patterson (this volume), that the particular phoneme–grapheme correspondences employed to spell non-words can be affected by recent experience with familiar words whose conventional spelling *is* known.

SPELLING ERRORS

Spelling errors must be clearly distinguished from slips of the pen. A slip of the pen is an involuntary performance error occurring when a writer knows perfectly well how a word should be written. A spelling error, in contrast, is an error of knowledge occurring when a writer has not successfully internalised in his or her graphemic (output) lexicon the conventional spelling of a word.

Studies that have examined the spelling errors of individuals or groups often divide the errors into "phonetic errors" that when pronounced sound like the target word, and "non-phonetic errors" (the rest). Of the two classes of error the former has tended to be more highly regarded than the latter. This may not seem entirely unreasonable given the results of those studies that reported a higher proportion of "phonetic" errors among the spelling errors of good spellers than among those of poor spellers (e.g. Spache, 1940; Williams, 1974). These early studies did not, however, distinguish between errors to targets whose spellings are regular and errors to targets whose spellings are irregular. Which are we to rate more highly as an attempt to spell *colonel*, *KERNUL* (phonetic) or *COLNEL* (non-phonetic)? *KERNUL* displays a grasp of some English phoneme–grapheme correspondences but no word-specific information about the spelling of the target word. The speller who produces *COLNEL*, in contrast, knows that the target is irregular and has, indeed, internalised much though not all of the spelling of that particular word.

Ellis (1982b) used the term "partial lexical knowledge" to refer to errors that, though they may be non-phonetic, display evidence that the speller possesses word-specific information about how a word is spelt. Partial lexical knowledge is most clearly seen when an error incorporates letters whose presence in the target word cannot be predicted from the word's spoken form by the application of phoneme–grapheme conversion procedures, for example the *–olo–* sequence in *colonel*, the *–hy–* in *rhythm*, or the *p–* in *pneumonia*. Errors such as *COLORNEL*, *COLNEL*, *RHYTHMN*, *RHYTHUM*, *PNEMONIA*, and *PNEWMONIA* from Baron, Treiman, Wilf, and Kellman's (1980) student spellers clearly show partial lexical knowledge. Barron (1980) found that whereas both good and poor readers aged 9–12 years were better at spelling regular than irregular words this difference was greater for the poor readers. Of special interest here is Barron's finding that whereas 27.5% of the errors made by poor readers to irregular targets were "phonetic", only 11.9% of the errors of good readers to the same targets fell into that category. The good readers seemed to know more often when a target was irregular; that is, when a wholly phonetic assembled spelling would be inappropriate. In a *post hoc* analysis Barron (1980) found that the errors of good readers were more likely to incorporate unpredictable "silent letters" from their targets (i.e. more likely to show partial lexical knowledge) than were the errors of poor readers.

The occurrence of spelling errors that show word-specific partial lexical knowledge indicates that the registration of a spelling in the graphemic (output) lexicon is not an all-or-nothing thing (just as retrieval is not all-or-nothing; see Ellis, 1984; Miller & Ellis, 1987; and Patterson, this volume). It appears that writers may sometimes have internalised part, but not all, of a word's spelling and may therefore be obliged to construct a candidate spelling using such graphemic information as they can retrieve from the graphemic (output) lexicon, supplemented perhaps by phoneme–grapheme conversion. It should be noted that so-called phonetic errors may nevertheless display partial lexical knowledge: The errors *RHYTHUM* and *PNEWMONIA* cited above could both be regarded as "phonetic" by some standards at least, yet both contain unpredictable letters.

So the phonetic/non-phonetic distinction does not map in any straightforward way onto the distinction between the two acknowledged spelling routes, sublexical (phoneme–grapheme) and lexical (via the graphemic [output] lexicon). It is, nevertheless, possible to use error analysis alongside other indicators to assay the relative strengths of the two spelling routes in individuals or groups. Correct spelling of irregular words (and consistently correct spelling of regular words) indicate use of the lexical (graphemic [output] lexicon) route, as do errors showing partial lexical knowledge. Successful production of plausible spellings for non-words is the clearest indicator of an efficient phoneme–grapheme route (though, as we have seen, Campbell's (1983) results suggest that this route is not necessarily insulated from knowledge embodied in the lexical route).

It is, of course, possible for both routes to work well in an individual, or for both to work poorly, but we know that the two can be dissociated. An individual with an efficient lexical route but an inefficient sublexical route will spell regular and irregular words equally well, will produce a low proportion of "phonetic" errors but a high proportion of errors showing partial lexical knowledge, and will be poor at devising plausible spellings for non-words. In contrast, an individual with an inefficient lexical route but an efficient sublexical route will spell regular words better than irregular ones, will produce a high proportion of phonetic errors not displaying partial lexical knowledge, and will be good at devising plausible spellings for non-words. Each form of unequal efficiency has been found, both with respect to individual differences within the normal population and among patients with acquired dysgraphia (Ellis, 1982b, 1984; Patterson, Chapter 10).

Having outlined a compromise model of spelling at the word level we are now in a position to move to the letter level and consider how a letter sequence derived either lexically or sublexically is ultimately converted into pen movements. First, however, we shall devote a little space to considering what is meant by the term "letter".

WHAT IS A LETTER?

The title of this section is borrowed from a paper by Abercrombie (1949/1965) in which he discusses the use of the word *letter* down the ages. According to Abercrombie the Latin word *litera* was ambiguous, being applied both to the appearance of a letter and to its sound. Abercrombie provides several illustrations of this ambiguity in the works of English writers from the seventeenth to the nineteenth century, and the ambiguity is still frequently seen in everyday contexts. The Greeks, in contrast, appear to have been rather clearer in their usage. For them *litera* had three aspects: *Nomen*, the name of the letter; *figura*, its written form; and *potestas*, its pronunciation.

Nowadays we would generally use *phoneme* or *phone* when referring to *potestas* and reserve *letter* for the written symbol (*figura*). Even when its usage is restricted in this way, however, we still have problems with *letter* as a theoretical term. If, *F*, and f are the same letter, what term shall we use to distinguish between them? Very few linguists have looked in detail at written language, but those who have (e.g. Gleason, 1955; Hamp, 1959; McIntosh, 1956; Pulgram, 1951) have provided a useful three-tier set of terms. A *grapheme* is a letter of the alphabet[1]: English has 26 of them, and there is no longer a one-to-one correspondence between graphemes and phonemes. Each grapheme has multiple variants that are its allographs: *F*, ℱ, *f*, and ƒ are allographs of the grapheme <*f*> as *Z*, *z*, and ʒ are allographs of the grapheme <*z*>. Finally, the same allograph will take perceptually different forms in different peoples' handwritings, and in the same person's handwriting from one occasion to another. That is, an allograph can be realised as many perceptually different graphs.

1 This usage of the term "grapheme" is in fact one of two usages at large in linguistics (Henderson, 1986). In the alternative usage, a grapheme is a letter or group of letters that corresponds to a single phoneme in the spoken form of the word. I prefer the sense used here, but no confusion should arise as long as one is clear which sense is meant.

Now, scholastic nitpicking of this sort is only of value to the psychologist if it ultimately leads us to a better understanding of the psychology—and neuropsychology—of writing. Ellis (1979, 1982b) proposed that it might, and that the linguistic terms grapheme, allograph, and graph might have psychological reality as three successive planning stages in the production of writing.

The systems that retrieve the spellings of familiar words as wholes or assemble candidate spellings for unfamiliar words do not want to concern themselves with whether the word is going to be written in upper or lower case, typed, or spelled aloud. These systems arguably specify the spelling of a word as a set of abstract graphemes capable of being realised in any of these ways. That is, the graphemic output lexicon and phoneme–grapheme conversion processes create or activate abstract graphemic representations, and it is the responsibility of later processes to shape those representations into appropriate graphic output.

If handwriting is the chosen mode, then according to Ellis's (1982b) model the stage after the grapheme level involves the selection of an appropriate allograph as a spatial description of the shape to be produced. Each allograph must then be executed as a sequence of strokes. Van Galen (1980) argued that these are not created *de novo* each time a letter is written but are themselves stored in memory as a set of *graphic motor patterns.* The final stage in the model, then, involves the selection and execution of the appropriate graphic motor pattern for a particular allograph to create the desired written graph on the page.

LETTER-LEVEL SLIPS OF THE PEN

In addition to the word-level slips of the pen discussed earlier, normal fluent writers also make letter-level errors. These take various forms. One variety involves anticipating a letter before its due place in a sequence; for example, intending to write *pencil* and instead writing *cen* with the *c* transposed unintentionally to the front of the word. The interesting feature about these errors is what happens when a letter moves from a position where it would have been realised in lower case to one in which the intended (misplaced) letter would have been in upper case, or vice versa. The answer, attested by Wells (1906), Ellis (1979), and Hotopf (1983) is that the transposing letter changes its form and becomes capitalised or de-capitalised to match the case that the intended letter in that position would have taken. This sort of "accommodation" of a transposed element to suit its new context is well known in the speech-error literature (e.g., Garrett, 1975; Meara & Ellis, 1981) and provides insights into the ordering of pre-motoric cognitive processes. In the present instance it shows that letter anticipations occurs *before* the choice between upper and lower case allographic variants occurs; that is, they occur at the grapheme level.

The grapheme level knows nothing of letter case or letter shape. If a type of error shows sensitivity to either of these factors then it must, *ex hypothesi*, be occurring at or below the allographic level. "Letter masking" is the term given by Ellis (1979) to a type of error involving the omission of a letter that is repeated earlier or later in the word, for example writing *satifa* for *satisfactory* with the second *s* omitted, or *adpt* for *adapt* with the second *a* missing. Now, the point here is that all the recorded instances of such errors involve pairs of letters that are both upper case or both lower case. Logically possible masking errors such as *Adpt* for *Adapt* or *Garae* for *Garage* have not been reported. Admittedly one is on shaky ground when arguing from the *non*-occurrence of a particular error type, but Ellis (1982b) tentatively proposed on the basis of this same-case effect that letter-masking errors occur at or around the allographic level.

Figure 5 shows some examples of yet another type of letter-level slip called "switches" by Ellis (1979). A switch occurs when two letters, usually adjacent ones, contain strokes that share a common direction of movement. What happens is that the writer begins to write one letter but then switches into writing the other at the point where they share a common direction of movement. If one switches from, say, an *n* to an *m*, the result may still be a real letter (the *m*), but the more dramatic switches are those like the examples in Fig. 5 that result in the production of a non-letter. These slips are clearly low-level motoric errors that in terms of the framework outlined earlier seem attributable to lapses in the execution of graphic motor patterns.

Having sought some justification for the grapheme/allograph/graph framework by reference to slips of the pen we shall now look at the extent to which it can explain different forms of peripheral dysgraphia.

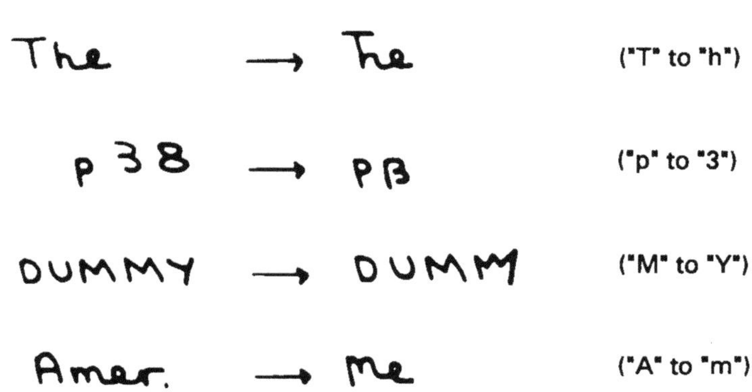

FIG 5. "Irregular switches"—slips of the pen from the author's own corpus.

PURE DYSGRAPHIAS

The term "dysgraphia" can refer to a difficulty with spelling (knowing the correct sequence of letters that constitutes the socially accepted correct form of a word), or it can refer to a difficulty with executing a spelling as handwriting. Patterson (this volume) reviews acquired spelling disorders; in this section I shall briefly review three cases of the latter type of dysgraphia, emphasising the differences between them and considering their interpretation within the framework just outlined.

The first case for consideration is an Italian patient, FV, reported by Miceli, Silveri, and Caramazza (1987). FV had no detectable problems with spoken language or with reading; his acquired deficit was exclusive to writing. His errors took the form of substitutions, deletions, insertions, and a few transpositions of letters. Examples include *FINESTRA* written as *FIRESTRA* (substitution), *DIETA* as *DETA* (deletion), *PIEDE* as *PIEDRE* (insertion), and *FANALE* as *FALANE* (transposition). Bearing in mind the previously mentioned strictures against incautious generalisation across language–script combinations, can FV's deficit still be accounted for by the compromise model?

FV was as likely to misspell a common word as an uncommon one, showed no effect of word imageability or grammatical class, and made the same sort of errors in the same proportions whether writing words or non-words. Longer words were more likely to be misspelled than shorter ones. All of these findings argue for a peripheral (letter-level) rather than central (word-level) deficit. FV's letter formation was good, and he made the same errors at a slightly higher frequency when typing. We would therefore seem justified in excluding an impairment in the activation or execution of graphic motor patterns.

Italian is a language with highly regular phoneme–grapheme correspondences. Logically the need for a graphemic (output) lexicon is not as pressing as it is for English. We have already noted that FV made errors in writing both words and non-words: One might be tempted on the basis of this to locate the deficit in the phoneme–grapheme conversion system and argue that this is the only spelling route used when writing Italian. Miceli et al., however, present evidence that creates problems for such a proposal. In simple writing to dictation, FV made around 30% errors to both words and non-words. In one task he was asked again to write words and non-words to dictation, but this time to write them while simultaneously articulating over and over again a meaningless CVCV non-word. The error rate for real words remained at around 30%, but the error rate for non-words increased dramatically to 75%.

In terms of the compromise model, repeatedly articulating a meaningless non-word will cause interference at the phoneme level thereby affecting input to phoneme–grapheme conversion. One would therefore expect non-word spelling to suffer as it did. The fact that FV's spelling of familiar Italian words did not also deteriorate implies that these latter spellings are not assembled by phoneme–grapheme conversion but are instead retrieved from the graphemic (output) lexicon. Thus even where it is not strictly necessary, as in the case of Italian, spelling from a lexicon seems to be preferred over assembled spelling for writing familiar words. That is to say, Theory Three may well apply to languages written with transparent alphabets even though Theory One would in principle suffice.

The fact that under normal circumstances (i.e. without concurrent articulation) FV made errors to words and non-words alike points to a locus for the deficit at or beyond the point of convergence of the lexical and sublexical routes. One candidate locus is the graphemic level. To venture a hypothesis, FV's deficit may be a problem activating grapheme units via the graphemic (output) lexicon or phoneme–grapheme conversion. Occasional activation of the wrong grapheme unit would result in a substitution or addition; insufficient activation would result in a letter omission. FV was able to copy both words and non-words from upper case (capital) letters to lower case print. Such copying, involving as it does a transcoding from *A* to *a*, or *R* to *r*, cannot be simply pictorial and must be graphemically mediated. Morton (1980) proposes an input to the grapheme level (his graphemic buffer) from the visual analysis system responsible for identifying letters. If FV's intact cross-case copying is interpreted along these lines then we must propose that for FV visual input to the grapheme level was intact though the transmission of information or activation from the lexicon and phoneme–grapheme conversion are both impaired. The fact that FV could still copy well even when a 10-second delay was interposed between presentation and reproduction suggests that the maintenance of information at the grapheme level is normal in FV. His accurate reproduction of letter shapes, even when the letters are incorrect, implies that processes below the grapheme level are also intact.

The second patient to be discussed was reported by Rosati and de Bastiani (1979). Again this patient was not aphasic or dyslexic. He could spell aloud correctly (de Bastiani, pers. comm.) and could also spell words using letter blocks. Written letter formation was reasonably good, but his attempts to write words were replete with omissions, transpositions, and incorrect repetitions of letters. Intact oral spelling and spelling with letter blocks implies intact processing up to and including the grapheme level. Good letter formation implies a preserved ability to execute stored graphic motor patterns. The deficit in this patient must therefore lie somewhere between the graphemic and graphic levels, namely (as far as the framework presented here is concerned) at the allographic level. Having formulated a graphemic sequence, the patient apparently had difficulty activating the appropriate sequence of particular letter shapes in the correct sequence. If this interpretation is along the right lines there should be a similarity between the errors made by patients like this and those slips of the pen attributable to the allographic level. Goodman and Caramazza (1986) also report a patient with pure dysgraphia whose writing problems are explained by arguing that "the allographic process for assigning the visual shape to a graphemic unit is impaired".

The final patient to be considered was reported by Margolin and Binder (1984). Again no aphasia or dyslexia was present, and, like the previous case, this (English-writing) patient could spell correctly either orally or with letter blocks. Where this patient differed from the previous one is that his letters were very poorly executed. Specifically, letters were distorted by the repetition, addition, and mislocation of strokes. Margolin and Binder (1984) themselves interpret the deficit here as being a problem with retrieving and executing graphic motor patterns (see also Baxter & Warrington, 1986).

Though I have dealt with each patient only briefly, I have tried to demonstrate the potential relevance of a model of peripheral writing processes to the interpretation of those dysgraphias that compromise handwriting rather than higher-level spelling processes. The most important point to note is that there is heterogeneity even within the highly selected population of "pure dysgraphics". The patients of Miceli et al. (1987), Rosati and de Bastiani (1979), and Margolin and Binder (1984) were all unimpaired as far as speech production, speech comprehension, and reading were concerned. They thus belonged to a small group of pure, peripheral dysgraphics (along with other patients whose difficulties are less fully documented, such as the patients of Valenstein & Heilman, 1979, Gersch & Damasio, 1981, and Roeltgen & Heilman, 1983). Yet when one looks closely at the precise nature of the difficulty in these patients, numerous individual differences are apparent. The precise patterns of difficulty and error differ from patient to patient and demand different explanations from the cognitive neuropsychologist.

The framework I have outlined here will hopefully be superseded in the near future by better, more explicit ones. The cognitive neuropsychological analysis of patients such as those described earlier, and also phenomena such as "spatial dysgraphia" (Ellis, Young, & Flude, 1987; Hécaen & Marcie, 1974; Lebrun & Rubio, 1972) and mirror writing (Critchley, 1928; Fuller, 1916) should play an important part in developing those better models—provided, that is, that we concentrate our efforts on explaining the precise difficulties of individual, closely studied patients and do not fall into the trap of seeking unitary explanations for heterogeneous "syndrome" categories (cf. Caramazza, 1984; Ellis, 1987b; Schwartz, 1984).

ACKNOWLEDGEMENTS

This paper is based on a talk given at the January 1984 conference on Perspectives in Cognitive Neuropsychology. The preparation of this paper was assisted by grant number G8305511N from the Medical Research Council, and by a grant from the University of Lancaster Research Fund.

REFERENCES

Abercrombie, D. (1949) What is a "letter"? *Lingua*, 1949, 2. Reprinted, 1965 in D. Abercrombie, *Studies in phonetics and linguistics*. London: Oxford University Press.

Akinasso, F. N. (1982) On the differences between spoken and written language. *Language and Speech*, *25*, 97–125.

Allport, D. A. (1983) Language and cognition. In R. Harris (Ed.), *Approaches to language*. Oxford: Pergamon Press.

Allport, D. A. & Funnell, E. (1981) Components of the mental lexicon. *Philosophical Transactions of the Royal Society of London Series B*, *295*, 397–410.

Baron, J., Treiman, R., Wilf, J. F., & Kellman, P. (1980) Spelling and reading by rules. In U. Frith (Ed.), *Cognitive processes in spelling*. London: Academic Press.

Barron, R. W. (1980) Visual-orthographic and phonological strategies in reading and spelling. In U. Frith (Ed.), *Cognitive processes in spelling*. London: Academic Press.

Baxter, D. M. & Warrington, E. K. (1986) Ideational agraphia: A single case study. *Journal of Neurology, Neurosurgery and Psychology*, *49*, 369–374.

Brown, J. (1981) Semantic jargon. In J. Brown (Ed.), *Jargonaphasia*. New York: Academic Press.

Campbell, R. (1983) Writing nonwords to dictation. *Brain and Language*, *19*, 153–178.

Caramazza, A. (1984) The logic of neuropsychological research and the problem of patient classification in aphasia. *Brain and Language*, *21*, 9–20.

Charcot, J. M. (1889) *Clinical lectures on diseases of the nervous system, Vol. 3*. London: New Sydenham Society.

Coltheart, M. & Funnell, E. (1987) Reading and writing: One lexicon or two? In D. A. Allport, D. G. Mackay, W. Prinz, & E. Scheerer (Eds.), *Language perception and production: Shared mechanisms in listening, reading and writing*. London: Academic Press.

Coltheart, M., Sartori, G., & Job, R. (1987) *The cognitive neuropsychology of language*. London: Lawrence Erlbaum Associates Ltd.

Critchley, M. (1928) *Mirror writing*. London: Kegan Paul, Trench, Trubner & Co.

Dodd, B. (1980) The spelling abilities of profoundly pre-lingually deaf children. In U. Frith (Ed.), *Cognitive processes in spelling*. London: Academic Press.

Ellis, A. W. (1979) Slips of the pen. *Visible Language*, *13*, 265–282.

Ellis, A. W. (1982a) *Normality and pathology in cognitive functions*. London: Academic Press.

Ellis, A. W. (1982b) Spelling and writing (and reading and speaking). In A. W. Ellis (Ed.), *Normality and pathology in cognitive functions*. London: Academic Press.

Ellis, A. W. (1984) *Reading, writing and dyslexia: A cognitive analysis*. London: Lawrence Erlbaum Associates Ltd.

Ellis, A. W. (1985) The production of spoken words. In A. W. Ellis (Ed.), *Progress in the psychology of language, Vol. 2*. London: Lawrence Erlbaum Associates Ltd.

Ellis, A. W. (1987a) On problems in developing culturally-transmitted modules: Review of P. H. K. Seymour, "Cognitive analysis of dyslexia". *Mind and Language*, *2*, 241–252.

Ellis, A. W. (1987b) Intimations of modularity, or, the modelarity of mind: Some problems and prospects of cognitive neuropsychology. In M. Coltheart, G. Sartori, & R. Job (Eds.), *The cognitive neuropsychology of language.* London: Lawrence Erlbaum Associates Ltd.

Ellis, A. W. & Young, A. W. (1988) *Human cognitive neuropsychology.* London: Lawrence Erlbaum Associates Ltd.

Ellis, A. W., Young, A. W., & Flude, B. M. (1987) "Afferent dysgraphia" in a patient and in normal subjects. *Cognitive Neuropsychology, 4*, 465–486.

Fay, D. & Cutler, A. (1977) Malapropisms and the structure of the mental lexicon. *Linguistic Inquiry, 8*, 505–520.

Flower, L. S. & Hayes, J. R. (1980) The dynamics of composing: Making plans and juggling constraints. In L. W. Gregg & E. R. Steinberg (Eds.), *Cognitive processes in writing.* Hillsdale, N.J.: Lawrence Erlbaum Associates Inc.

Frith, U. (1980a) *Cognitive processes in spelling.* London: Academic Press.

Frith, U. (1980b) Unexpected spelling problems. In U. Frith (Ed.), *Cognitive processes in spelling.* London: Academic Press.

Fuller, J. K. (1916) The psychology and physiology of mirror writing. *University of California Publications in Psychology, 2*, 199–265.

Garrett, M. F. (1975) The analysis of sentence production. In G. H. Bower (Ed.), *The psychology of learning and motivation, Vol. 9.* New York: Academic Press.

Gelb, I. J. (1963) *A study of writing* (2nd ed.). Chicago: Chicago University Press.

Gersh, F. & Damasio, A. R. (1981) Praxis and writing of the left hand may be served by different callosal pathways. *Archives of Neurology, 38*, 634–636.

Gleason, H. A. (1955) *An introduction to descriptive linguistics.* New York: Holt Rinehart & Winston.

Goodman, R. A. & Caramazza, A. (1986) Dissociation of spelling errors in written and oral spelling: The role of allographic conversion in writing. *Cognitive Neuropsychology, 3*, 179–206.

Hamp, E. (1959) Graphemics and paragraphemics. University of Buffalo, Department of Anthropology and Linguistics. *Studies in Linguistics, 14*, 1–6.

Hatfield, F. M. & Patterson, K. E. (1983) Phonological spelling. *Quarterly Journal of Experimental Psychology, 35A*, 451–468.

Hécaen, H. & Marcie, P. (1974) Disorders of written language following right hemisphere lesions. In S. J. Dimond & J. G. Beaumont (Eds.), *Hemisphere function in the human brain.* London: Elek.

Henderson, L. (1984) (Ed.). *Orthographies and reading.* London: Lawrence Erlbaum Associates Ltd.

Henderson, L. (1986) On the uses of the term "grapheme". *Language and Cognitive Processes, 1*, 135–148.

Hotopf, W. H. N. (1983) Lexical slips of the pen and tongue: What they tell us about language production. In B. Butterworth (Ed.), *Language production, Vol. 2.* London: Academic Press.

Kinsbourne, M. & Warrington, E. K. (1963) Jargon aphasia. *Neuropsychologia, 1*, 27–37.

Lebrun, Y. & Rubio, S. (1972) Réduplications et omissions graphiques chez des patients attients d'une lésion hémisphérique droite. *Neuropsychologia, 10*, 249–251.

Leech, G., Deuchar, M., & Hoogenraad, R. (1982) *English grammar for today.* London: The Macmillan Press.

Lichtheim, L. (1885) On aphasia. *Brain, 7*, 433–484.

Luria, A. R. (1970) *Traumatic aphasia.* The Hague: Mouton.

Margolin, D. I. (1984) The neuropsychology of writing and spelling: Semantic, phonological, motor and perceptual processes. *Quarterly Journal of Experimental Psychology, 36A*, 459–489.

Margolin, D. I. & Binder, L. (1984) Multiple component agraphia in a patient with atypical cerebral dominance: An error analysis. *Brain and Language*, *22*, 26–40.

Marshall, J. C. (1976) Neuropsychological aspects of orthographic representation. In E. C. T. Walker & R. J. Wales (Eds.), *New approaches to language mechanisms*. Amsterdam: North Holland.

McIntosh, A. (1956) The analysis of written Middle English. *Transactions of the Philological Society*, *1956*, 22–55.

Meara, P. & Ellis, A. W. (1981) The psychological reality of deep and surface phonological representations: Evidence from speech errors in Welsh. *Linguistics*, *19*, 797–804.

Miceli, G., Silveri, M. C., & Caramazza, A. (1987) The role of the phoneme-to-grapheme conversion system and of the graphemic output buffer in writing. In M. Coltheart, G. Sartori, & R. Job (Eds.), *The cognitive neuropsychology of language*. London: Lawrence Erlbaum Associates Ltd.

Miller, D. & Ellis, A. W. (1987) Speech and writing errors in "neologistic jargonaphasia": A lexical activation hypothesis. In M. Coltheart, G. Sartori, & R. Job (Eds.), *The cognitive neuropsychology of language*. London: Lawrence Erlbaum Associates Ltd.

Monsell, S. (1985) Repetition and the lexicon. In A. W. Ellis (Ed.), *Progress in the psychology of language*, *Vol. 2*. London: Lawrence Erlbaum Associates Ltd.

Morton, J. (1970) A functional model for memory. In D. A. Norman (Ed.), *Models of human memory*. New York: Academic Press.

Morton, J. (1979a) Word recognition. In J. Morton & J. C. Marshall (Eds.), *Psycholinguistics series*, *Vol. 2*. London: Elek Science and Cambridge, Mass.: MIT Press.

Morton, J. (1979b) Facilitation in word recognition: Experiments causing change in the logogen model. In P. A. Kolers, M. Wrolstad, & H. Bouma (Eds.), *Processing of visible language*, *Vol. 1*. New York: Plenum.

Morton, J. (1980) The logogen model and orthographic structure. In U. Frith (Ed.), *Cognitive processes in spelling*. London: Academic Press.

Newcombe, F. & Marshall, J. C. (1980) Transcoding and lexical stabilization in deep dyslexia. In M. Coltheart, K. E. Patterson, & J. E. Marshall (Eds.), *Deep dyslexia*. London: Routledge & Kegan Paul.

Nolan, K. A. & Caramazza, A. (1983) An analysis of writing in a case of deep dyslexia. *Brain and Language*, *20*, 305–328.

Olson, D. R. (1977) From utterance to text: The bias of language in speech and writing. *Harvard Educational Review*, *47*, 257–281.

Paradis, M., Hagiwara, H., & Hildebrandt, N. (1985) *Neurolinguistic aspects of the Japanese writing system*. Orlando, Fla: Academic Press.

Pulgram, E. (1951) Phoneme and grapheme: A parallel. *Word*, *7*, 15–20.

Roeltgen, D. P. & Heilman, K. M. (1983) Apractic agraphia in a patient with normal praxis. *Brain and Language*, *18*, 35–46.

Rosati, G. & Bastiani, P. de (1979) Pure agraphia: A discrete form of aphasia. *Journal of Neurology, Neurosurgery and Psychiatry*, *42*, 266–269.

Saffran, E. M., Schwartz, M. F., & Marin, O. S. M. (1980) The word order problem in agrammatism II. Production. *Brain and Language*, *10*, 249–262.

Sampson, G. (1985) *Writing systems*. London: Hutchinson.

Schwartz, M. F. (1984) What the classical aphasia categories can't do for us, and why. *Brain and Language*, *21*, 3–8.

Seymour, P. H. K. (1979) *Human visual cognition*. West Drayton: Collier Macmillan.

Shallice, T. (1981) Phonological agraphia and the lexical route in writing. *Brain*, *104*, 413–429.

Spache, G. (1940) Characteristic errors of good and poor spellers. *Journal of Educational Research*, *40*, 182–189.

Stemberger, J. P. (1985) An interactive activation model of language production In A. W. Ellis (Ed.), *Progress in the psychology of language, Vol. 1*. London: Lawrence Erlbaum Associates Ltd.

Valenstein, E. & Heilman, K. M. (1979) Apraxic agraphia with neglect-induced paragraphia. *Archives of Neurology, 36*, 506–508.

van Galen, G. P. (1980) Handwriting and drawing: A two-stage model of complex motor behaviour. In G. Stelmach & J. Requin (Eds.), *Tutorials in motor behaviour*. Amsterdam: North Holland.

Weigl, E. (1975) On written language: Its acquisition and its alexic–agraphic disturbances. *Linguistics, 154/5*, 137–160 (in German). Translation in E. Weigl (1981), *Neuropsychology and neurolinguistics*. The Hague: Mouton.

Wells, F. L. (1906) Linguistic lapses. In J. McK. Cattell & F. J. E. Woodbridge (Eds.), *Archives of philosophy, psychology and scientific methods no. 6*. New York: Science Press.

Wernicke, C. (1874) *Der Aphasische Symptomencomplex*. Breslau: Cohn & Weigart. (Translated in G. H. Eggert (1977), *Wernicke's works on aphasia*. The Hague: Mouton.)

Williams, A. (1974) A study of spelling errors. In B. Wade & K. Wedell (Eds.), *Spelling: Task and learner*. Birmingham, UK: University of Birmingham, Educational Review, Occasional Papers No. 5, 45–50.

10 Acquired Disorders of Spelling[1]

K. Patterson
MRC Applied Psychology Unit, Cambridge, U.K.

SPELLING WITH PHONOLOGY

Current views of the procedures involved in spelling perhaps diverge most from the views of previous generations with respect to the necessity of a phonological component. Few people in 1988 are surprised by the claim that at least some degree of spelling competence can be demonstrated in a subject or patient with virtually no phonological skills; but this would have been an arresting statement to some previous generations whose models often viewed spelling as parasitic upon speech or at least upon some kind of phonological processing. Before one dismisses such a conception as nonsense, it is perhaps worth looking briefly at the factors that motivated it. Irrespective of which population of subjects one interrogates—normal adult spellers, normal children learning to spell, or individuals with impaired spelling—much of the evidence seems to suggest the involvement of phonology. For example, of normal adults' spelling errors in English, whether these are apparent slips of the pen such as homophone substitutions (e.g. *THERE* ⇄ *THEIR*) or perhaps genuine misspellings (e.g. *COMMITTAL* → *COMMITAL*), the vast majority are phonologically plausible spellings (see, for example, Campbell & Butterworth, 1985; Wing & Baddeley, 1980). As emphasised by Ellis (Chapter 9), errors of

[1] This chapter, based on a paper presented to the second Bressanone meeting in January 1984, was written in 1984, with minor revisions in 1987 to incorporate just a few of the many neuropsychological studies of spelling published in the intervening three years.

these types constitute part of the empirical basis for the design of process models of spelling like the one in Fig. 1 (see also Figs. 1 and 4 in Ellis's Chapter 9). That is, homophone substitutions support the notion that the

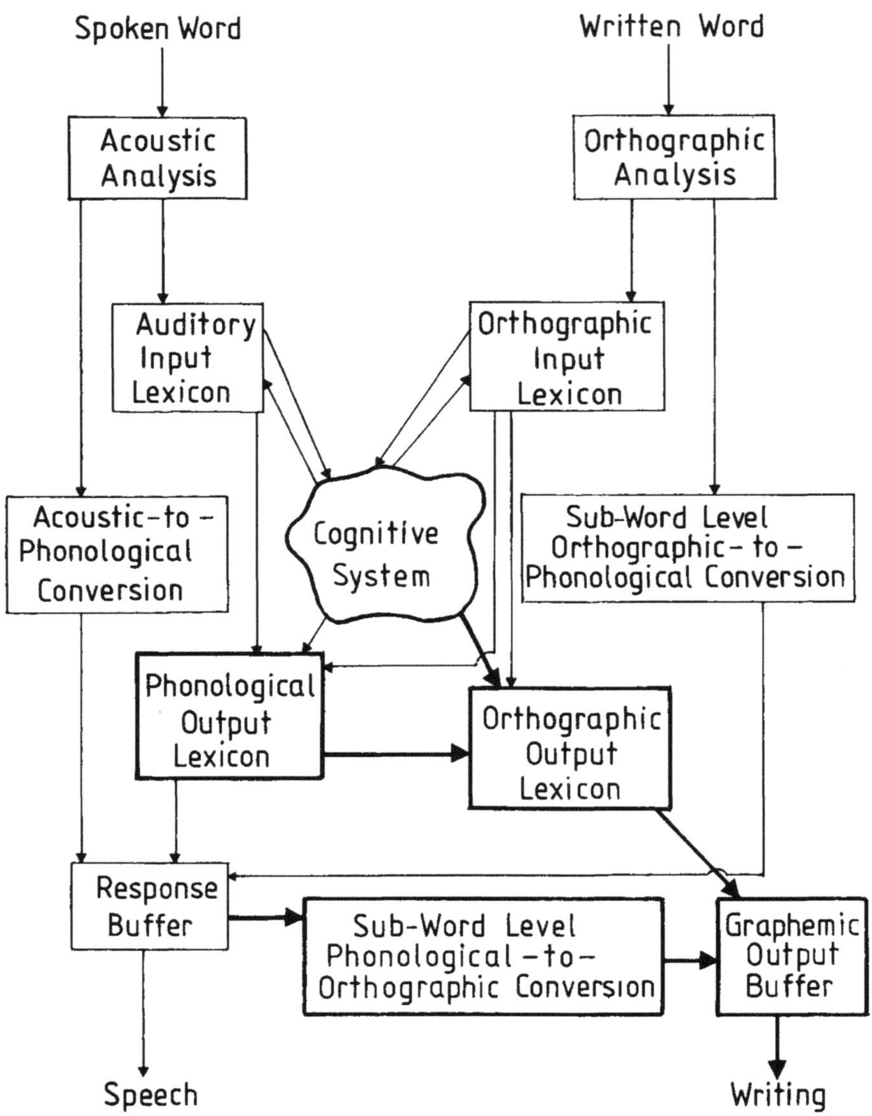

FIG 1. A model of the main procedures involved in recognising, comprehending, and producing single spoken and written words, based primarily on Morton's logogen model (e.g. Morton, 1979; Morton & Patterson, 1980).

orthographic output lexicon accepts codes or activation from the phonological output lexicon; and the high proportion of phonologically plausible misspellings suggests a contribution of general knowledge about sub-word level phonological-to-orthographic translation in everyday spelling.

Even among adult neurological patients, some of whom offer the most persuasive evidence (to be reviewed shortly) that it is possible to spell without phonology, there are plenty of cases that might lead one to just the opposite conclusion. In other words, for many patients, written spelling does seem to mirror speech. Two examples where this is so, but involving very different patterns of speech, will now be described.

Patient P.Wh. presented as an interesting neuropsychological case not because of her spelling performance (which was in fact unremarkable) but because of a dramatic dissociation between her spontaneous speech and her performance in other tasks requiring verbal output, namely oral reading and repetition. Her spontaneous speech was severely dysfluent, agrammatic, and telegrammatic. Her verbal output in other tasks was fluent, not in articulation and prosody, which were always somewhat slow and stiff, but in content: She read everything (word lists, sentences, paragraphs) correctly without a hint of grammatical difficulties, and she repeated sentences (unless they were very long and complicated) without error. (Because this case is unpublished, a brief case report is presented in the Appendix.) Now, what about her writing? As displayed by her written description (Table 1) of the "Cookie Theft" picture from Goodglass and Kaplan (1972), her written output was just like her spontaneous speech: dysfluent and agrammatic. She was not incapable of writing grammatically, because she competently wrote sentences to dictation (though once again, as with oral repetition, this good performance would begin to suffer if the sentences were long and complex, when she might paraphrase or omit a few words). It appears, therefore, that either her spontaneous writing was actually based upon speech output, a conclusion suggested by the fact that

TABLE 1
P.Wh.'s Written Description of the "Cookie Theft" Picture (from the Boston Diagnostic Aphasia Test)

Cookie jar falling over
The boy falling of stool
Left hand the girl
Lady falls them onto the floor (washing up water)
Drying a plate
Lady apron
Washing up cloth
Away from garden
Garage

she spoke aloud each bit of the Cookie Theft story as or just before she wrote it or both spontaneous speech and spontaneous writing were driven by a common process. In any case, observation of a patient like P.Wh. would certainly incline one to believe that written spelling is, or can be, closely related to speech.

Patient T.P. has been presented in a number of papers (e.g. Hatfield & Patterson, 1983, 1984; Patterson & Kay, 1982) due to a collection of interesting reading and spelling impairments. A posterior left-hemisphere CVA at age 50 left her with fluent, grammatical, and very anomic spontaneous speech. Unfortunately, no written version of the "Cookie Theft" description is available for T.P., but Fig. 2 displays her written description of a picture (actually a picture sequence) where two children are building a snowman, which by the final picture is melting in the sun. Once again, the striking characteristic of T.P.'s writing is how closely it mirrors the pattern of her speech. Her written sentences were correctly constructed and appropriately supplied with function words and rather general content words but lacked many specific content words. For both T.P. and P.Wh., then, it appears that writing was dependent on or closely related to speech.

Of course, even someone wanting to use patients such as these two as evidence for the role of speech in writing would have to acknowledge that two rather different descriptions are needed for the two cases. For P.Wh., her speech determined what she wrote (i.e. what words); but her spelling otherwise showed no particular influence of phonology. Her only spelling error in Table 1 (*OFF*→ *OF*) was either a slip of the pen or a visual error; and while there are no very complicated words here (either in terms of orthographic complexity or sound-to-spelling regularity), plenty of other data on P.Wh. establish that she had no real spelling problem. T.P.'s speech also determined what she wrote; thus the words that she could not say (specific content words), she also could not begin to write and was forced either to leave blank (as with the word *SNOW*) or to substitute a drawing (as with the words *BUTTONS* and *PIPE*). In addition, however, T.P. had a genuine spelling deficit displaying a clear influence of phonology. As catalogued by Hatfield and Patterson (1983), she made the sort of phonologically plausible spelling errors (like *ON*→ *ONN*, *WAY*-→ *WHAY*, and *THOUGH*→ *THOW* in Fig. 2) that are characteristic of "surface" or "lexical" dysgraphia (see, for example, Beauvois & Derouesné, 1981). In fact, T.P.'s spontaneous writing is not especially revealing about such errors because of all the omissions; her spelling to dictation, on the other hand, is replete with both phonologically plausible errors (e.g. "loosen"→ *LUCEN*, "nephew"→ *NEFFUE*) and so-called phoneme–grapheme errors (e.g. "better"→ *BETER*, "biscuit"→ *BISCIT*). Such errors are usually interpreted as indicating impairment of the routine in which spellings of whole specific words are retrieved from the

The boy and the girl have both but there morme hats and coats onn.

They have put a lot of the ··· up and have made the ··· very nice.

It looks nice the whay they have made it.

It has some ! at the front and also the .

It looks as thow the ... has fallen because it brobably isn't so cold now.

FIG 2. Patient T.P.'s written description of the following picture sequence: In picture 1 two children appear warmly dressed for winter; in 2 they begin building a snowman; in 3 they finish the snowman, complete with buttons and pipe; in 4 the snowman is dissolving under a sunny sky.

orthographic output lexicon. Failing this routine, the patient is forced to rely on an alternative procedure involving translation of sub-word-sized phonological segments into orthographic representations. Figure 2, by the way, also contains examples of another type of error commonly made by T.P. that need not concern us further here, namely errors arising from confusion between visually similar letters such as *W* and *M* (thus *WARM→MORME*) or *P* and *B* (thus *PUT→BUT* and *PROBABLY→BROBABLY*).

The written spelling patterns of these patients provide or support two conclusions germane to an understanding of spelling. First, written spelling can be closely tied to phonological processes. Second, these phonological processes are of two very different kinds, as captured in many models of spelling by postulating two different routines for spelling: (1) a word-level routine in which the spellings of known words in an orthographic output lexicon may be activated wholly or partly by lexical phonological codes; and (2) a sub-word-level routine involving phonological decomposition and assignment of graphemic segments to the phonological segments.

TABLE 2
G.A.'s Spoken and Written Descriptions of the "Cookie Theft" Picture

Spoken
"Oh, is this sad! And you see what they're doing ... this one, she, but she couldn't do, and the little one was ... /wɔ:d/ on the ... one. That little one, she's with ... /wɔ:/, the big ones ... and the tin is out the ... that's the one.
Written
Mummy tap sick tap under cups under tap. Boys cookie under claper girls.

SPELLING WITHOUT PHONOLOGY

We begin this more interesting section with a reminder of just how different speech and writing can be in the same patient. G.A., who suffered a major left-hemisphere CVA in her early seventies (Patterson & Shewell, 1987), provided the spoken and written versions of the "Cookie Theft" picture that are displayed in Table 2. There is no similarity between the two, either in terms of the specific words available to her or in the "structure" (if such a word can be applied to her written output) of the two descriptions. There are various lines of evidence for the claim that spelling performance can proceed essentially without involvement of one or both levels of phonological input to the spelling process.

Patients Who Can Write Words But Not Non-words

There is no shortage of patients with impaired spelling of familiar words who fail utterly to spell novel words or non-words (G.A. is one of these); but of much more compelling interest, of course, are those patients who spell words competently yet fail on non-words. Two well-documented cases of this phenomenon are patients P.R. (Shallice, 1981) and M.H. (Bub & Kertesz, 1982); both were 90–100% correct in written spelling of individual real words but managed only around 10% correct when asked to generate written spellings of simple nonsense words. Further cases are described by Roeltgen, Sevush, and Heilman (1983). Such performance does not, of course, rule out participation of the speech output system in addressing spellings of known words in the orthographic output lexicon; it does, however, suggest that adequate spelling of words within the language demands only a functioning orthographic output lexicon receiving adequate activation from semantic and/or (lexical) phonological codes. That is, while sub-word-level translation from phonology to orthography may contribute to spelling performance in the neurologically intact individual, patients who lack this routine but can still competently spell words demonstrate that it is not required. It is partly on this basis that we can reject any theory postulating obligatory mediation of the spelling process by phoneme–grapheme translation (Theories One and Two discussed by Ellis, this volume).

Patients with Better Written Than Oral Naming

Table 3 shows five different recently studied cases where, the same pictures having been presented for both oral and written naming, the patients were significantly more successful at written naming. This pattern of performance suggests that the spelling routine based on semantic activation of the orthographic output lexicon is sufficient to support adequate performance, at least of written naming. Of course, only two of the cases listed in Table 3 (those studied by Bub & Kertesz, 1982 and by Marshall, Rappaport, & Garcia-Bunuel, 1985) really showed such adequate performance; the other patients presumably had additional deficits either of the orthographic output lexicon itself or of the process whereby the representations in this lexicon are activated from the semantic system. All five patients demonstrate, however, that correct production of a written word need not entail availability of an intact speech code for that word.

Semantic Paragraphic Errors

As emphasised by Ellis (Chapter 9) and many others, error analysis by itself is an insufficient basis for conclusions about the impairment or intactness of various cognitive routines. In conjunction with other indicators, however, the predominance of a particular type of error can be revealing. One such error type, which in oral reading has enjoyed considerable attention in the reading disorder known as deep dyslexia (Coltheart, Patterson, & Marshall, 1980), involves the substitution of a word similar in meaning to the target but sharing essentially no orthographic or phonological features. Examples of semantic paragraphic errors in writing single words (i.e. with no context) to dictation from a French-speaking patient are "tigre"→ *LION* and "toit"→ *MUR* (Assal, Buttet, & Jolivet, 1981). Examples of such errors from patient G.A. (Patterson & Shewell, 1987) are "room"→ *LOUNGE*, "cigarette"→ *SMOKER*, "duck"→ *SWAN*, and "worry"→ *TROUBLE*.

TABLE 3
Per Cent Correct Picture Naming

		Oral	*Written*
A.F.	(Hier & Mohr, 1977)	4	52
M.H.	(Bub & Kertesz, 1982)	10	95
R.D.	(Ellis, Miller, & Sin, 1983)	17	57
Patient	(Marshall, Rappaport, & Garcia-Bunuel, 1985)	33	100
G.A.	(Patterson & Shewell, 1987)	4	37

Semantic paragraphic errors in writing to dictation suggest the production of a response without any reference whatsoever to a phonological representation. However, in line with the comment earlier about the perils of conclusions based on error analysis alone, it should be noted that semantic errors do not prove that the patient is totally lacking in phonological ability. While there is no report of a patient with intact sub-word-level orthographic-to-phonological skills who made semantic errors in oral reading or a patient with intact sub-word-level phonological-to-orthographic skills who made semantic paragraphic errors, none the less G.A. (and doubtless other patients) combined semantic errors in writing with at least partial knowledge of correspondences between individual phonemes and graphemes. Thus, dictated the sound "/də/" she could write the letter *D*; yet dictated the word "duck", she wrote *SWAN*. The point here is not to emphasise G.A.'s phonological abilities, which were very slim indeed, but rather to note that different routines or strategies may be recruited by different tasks. Just because a person has available some information does not necessarily mean that he or she will use it in a task that is more "naturally" performed with a different strategy. Discussions of this issue with respect to oral reading strategies can be found in Goldblum (1985) and Margolin, Marcel, and Carlson (1985).

Equivalent Performance in Written Naming and Writing to Dictation

Several of the documented cases of spelling without phonology, namely A.F. (Hier & Mohr, 1977) and R.D. (Ellis et al., 1983), could not write to dictation at all due to deficits of the auditory input lexicon or even (in the case of R.D.) in the process of acoustic analysis that permits access to this lexicon. Such deficits were confirmed by the patients' performance in oral repetition, auditory word-to-picture matching, etc. G.A., on the other hand, had at least no major deficit at these "earlier" stages (for example she was 90% correct on the auditory version of Bishop's word-to-picture matching test; see Bishop & Byng, 1984); therefore, one can compare her success in written naming and in spelling to dictation. If she could make any use at all of the phonology of a word in retrieving its spelling, then she should have been more successful at writing words to dictation (where she was given a phonological model) than in writing those same words in a written picture-naming task (where, as evidenced by her almost complete failure in oral naming of pictures—see Table 3—she had no phonological information). Patterson and Shewell (1987) have demonstrated that this was not the case. On a set of 85 words written twice, once to dictation and once in written picture naming, G.A. produced very similar proportions of correct responses in the two tasks and also very similar error patterns across the two tasks. This result suggests that G.A. could not or at least did not make any use of phonological information in spelling.

Differential Word-class Effects in Speaking and Writing

Another demonstration that phonology is largely irrelevant to the spelling procedures utilised by patients like G.A. is the fact that the words she was most likely to succeed in producing orally are those she was least likely to be able to write, and vice versa (Patterson & Shewell, 1987). If the modality of output was oral (either oral reading or repetition) then G.A.'s performance was better with function words than with content words; when the modality of output was written, this pattern was reversed. One must remember the valid and important point made by Ellis, Miller, & Sin (1983) that the function-word advantage in oral output may not represent a genuine word-class effect. On average, function words are both more frequent and shorter than content words, and one or both of these differences may account for or at least contribute to a patient's success with function words. This alternative interpretation is, however, beside the point of relevance here. Whatever the reason for the function-word advantage in oral tasks, if phonology could assist G.A.'s spelling, then one would expect an association rather than a dissociation between her oral and her written output—the sort of association shown by patients P.Wh. and T.P. discussed in the first section.

"Language in the Absence of Inner Speech"

As a final source of evidence about spelling without phonology, we have the patient E.B. (Levine, Calvanio, & Popovics, 1982). This is a fish from a very different kettle. The other patients reported with essentially no demonstrable use of any variety of phonology in spelling have all had spelling deficits. Even the patients reported by Michel (1979) and Marshall et al. (1985), for whom written language was very dramatically better than speech, were somewhat dyssyntactic in writing. As Beauvois and Derouesné (1979) noted when they published the first case of phonological dyslexia, if one wants to argue that reading (or spelling) can proceed competently in the absence of any phonological skills, then the ideal source of evidence is not a patient with phonological deficits and *poor* reading (or spelling) but rather one with phonological deficits and *unimpaired* reading (or spelling). For spelling, this hope seems to be realised by patient E.B. He was mute, and furthermore displayed no evidence of any kind of phonological ability whatsoever: (1) his rhyme judgements of pairs of printed words were based entirely on visual similarity (or its absence) of the word endings; (2) in auditory rhyme judgements, he performed the task by writing down the two words—with the same result as in (1); (3) his performance was at chance level in auditory–visual matching of letter sounds or non-words; and (4) even his auditory–auditory matching of non-words was no better than chance. Thus E.B. displayed no evidence of phonological ability (or "inner speech", as the authors term it); yet his comprehension of speech and printed text were both excellent (though slow) and his spontaneous writing was error-free. To my knowledge, such a pattern is, thus far, unique in the neuropsychological literature, and so one might choose to stop short of absolute confidence in stating its implications. At least tentatively, however, it appears that fully accurate and fluent written spelling may be achievable without any phonological assistance. In other words, the spelling routine whereby representations in an orthographic output lexicon are activated by codes from the semantic/cognitive system (a) is probably a separate or at least separable routine, and (b) may on its own support adequate written language.

To summarise the first two sections, it appears that the various patterns of spelling abilities and impairments that have been observed provide reasonably convincing evidence for several different separable routines in written spelling. With reference to Fig. 1, the first basic distinction is whether the spelling of a particular word is retrieved as a whole from the orthographic output lexicon or is constructed from sub-word-level segments achieved by phonological segmentation plus phonological-to-orthographic translation. Second, the model suggests that representations in the orthographic output lexicon can be addressed both by semantic codes from the cognitive system and by phonological codes from the speech output lexicon. Do these two sources of input to the spelling lexicon constitute separable routines? Certainly patients like E.B. (Levine et al., 1982), R.D. (Ellis et al., 1983), and G.A. (Patterson & Shewell, 1987) suggest evidence for the former, i.e. a purely cognitive/semantic routine for spelling. It is also possible that cases of word-meaning deafness (e.g. Bramwell, 1897; Ellis, 1984; Kohn & Friedman, 1986) and/or of lexical but non-semantic spelling (Patterson, 1986; Roeltgen, Rothi, & Heilman, 1986) represent spelling performance in which lexical orthographic entries are (at least in spelling to dictation) addressed primarily by the phonological output lexicon.

THE NATURE OF THE SUB-COMPONENTS OF SPELLING: WHAT CAN WE LEARN FROM PATIENTS?

The Orthographic Output Lexicon

Errors of Partial Lexical Knowledge. Ellis (Chapter 9) discusses spelling errors by normal subjects (like *COLONEL→COLNEL*) that display word-specific partial lexical knowledge. Such errors demonstrate that the representation of a word's spelling in the orthographic output lexicon need not be wholly correct and/or that retrieval of that representation need not be all-or-none. Errors of partial lexical knowledge are a prominent feature of certain patients' spelling disorders. This was, for example, the most common type of error made by G.A. (Patterson & Shewell, 1987) both in writing to dictation (e.g. "daughter" → *DAUGHER*, "necklace" → *NELECAFE*) and in written naming of pictures (snail → *SNIALS*, binoculars → *BINCOLUAN*). Furthermore, such errors can, not surprisingly, be found in combination with other error types like semantic paragraphias, as in G.A.'s "knee" → *ENSLOW* (presumably ELBOW) and "razor" → *SHAIRE* (presumably SHAVER).

The explanation of errors of partial lexical knowledge is unlikely to be an inaccurate representation in the orthographic output lexicon *per se*. This is because, according to the widely accepted logic introduced by Warrington and Shallice (1979), an impaired representation should yield consistent errors whereas errors of partial lexical knowledge are generally characterised by inconsistency. (This inconsistency has two dimensions: A given word may be spelt correctly on one occasion and incorrectly on another and/or its spelling may be wrong on both occasions but in different ways; e.g., G.A. has, on different occasions, spelt ELBOW → *ELBOW*, *EBLOW*, and *ENSLOW*.) A more likely interpretation, therefore, is either (a) that only a portion of the correct representation is activated or retrieved on some occasions, or (b) that the representation retrieved from the orthographic output lexicon is subject to decay or degradation in the process of transfer to or output from the graphemic output buffer. (See Ellis et al., 1983, for a discussion of such errors that compares them to neologisms in jargon aphasia.)

Neglect Dysgraphia. Baxter and Warrington (1983) have described a patient who could spell forwards and backwards with equal facility and with a clear gradient of errors in which the letters at the left (i.e. the beginning) of the word were much more error-prone than those at the right (i.e. the end) of the word, irrespective of word length. (Note that this was a left-handed patient with a right-hemisphere lesion and that the data refer to oral spelling because the patient suffered from a severe motor impairment.) Such a pattern suggests that the representation in the orthographic output lexicon is or can be translated into something very like a visual image.

The Graphemic Output Buffer

Miceli, Silveri, and Caramazza (1987) have described the patient F.V. with a very pure spelling disorder. His pattern of spelling performance (also discussed by Ellis, Chapter 9) might at first glance seem to suggest a deficit of the graphemic output buffer, except that the patient was essentially perfect at copying printed words even with a 10-second delay interposed between presentation and response. This case, together with interpretation of other dysgraphias, has implications for the ways in which an ephemeral representation in the graphemic output buffer may get refreshed by one or both of the sub-components that send information to it (see Fig. 1).

Sub-word Phonological-to-Orthographic Conversion

As usual, research on spelling lags a little behind that on reading; thus, while the nature of sub-word-level translation between spelling and sound in oral reading has been an intense focus of debate in the last decade, interest in spelling's counterpart is just beginning to quicken. In parallel with the issues for reading, some of the interesting questions for spelling include:

1. Are the mappings one-to-one or one-to-many? The vagaries of correspondence between phonology and orthography in languages like English and French might dispose one to argue that the answer to this question, for these languages at least, must surely be one-to-many. And indeed performance from Beauvois and Derouesné's French patient R.G., whose spelling was primarily based on sub-word phonological-to-orthographic translation, seems to support this conclusion. For example, he represented the sound /o/ at the end of a word (sometimes correctly but often incorrectly for the specific word in question) in at least four different ways: *–O*, *–OT*, *–AU*, and *–EAU*. The same conclusion applies to the English-speaking (and spelling) patient J.G., studied by Goodman and Caramazza (1986).

2. The size of the units involved: is translation based on individual phonemes and graphemes or are larger chunks involved as well? In oral reading, there are now innumerable proposals that the smallest level will not suffice (Glushko, 1979; Henderson, 1982; Kay & Marcel, 1981; Parkin, 1984; Patterson & Morton, 1985; Shallice & McCarthy, 1985). As yet there is rather little evidence germane to this issue in the domain of spelling. Goodman and Caramazza (1986) have, however, demonstrated that patient J.G., with considerable reliance on this sub-word level for spelling, was very sensitive to contextual constraint. Thus, for example, when the sound /s/ can be legally represented by either *C* or *S* (that is, prior to *E*, *I*, or *Y*) she divided her spellings in roughly equal proportions between *C* and *S*; but when only *S* is legal (before vowels *A*, *O*, *U*, where use of *C* would yield /k/ rather than /s/) 96% of her spellings employed *S* and only 4% *C*.

3. Are the procedures for phonological-to-orthographic conversion separate and non-lexical or merely segmental and based on representations in the lexicon? Although Fig. 1 appears to have decided its answer to this question, in fact there is no really conclusive evidence to settle this issue,

for either reading or spelling. Part of the issue's resistance to resolution no doubt resides in the fact that some of the differences between the theories are more apparent than real (see Norris & Brown, 1985, and Patterson & Coltheart, 1987, for a discussion of this point with reference to pronunciation of print). Therefore, it is often difficult to specify clearly different and testable predictions. It is certainly the case that the same result can sometimes be claimed as support by both sides. Take, for example, Campbell's (1983) paper on spelling non-words to dictation, demonstrating that normal spellers in English show a significant biasing effect, in their spelling of non-words, from a previously heard real word. Thus the spoken non-word /prein/ tends to be spelt *PRANE* if "crane" has just been heard but *PRAIN* if the preceding word was "brain". Campbell also reported that a surface dysgraphic patient E.E. showed no such priming effect. E.E.'s ability to spell non-words was fair but not perfect. Focusing on its relative success, Patterson and Morton (1985) interpreted the lack of a priming effect as evidence for the separability of a non-lexical routine from the lexical one. Focusing instead on the fact that E.E.'s spelling of non-words was not at a normal level, Campbell concluded that, without adequate lexical ability (which E.E. clearly did not have), one also cannot deal with non-lexical stimuli—i.e. that non-words are spelt by analogy with real words.

Separate Input and Output Lexicons?

This issue is also discussed by Ellis (Chapter 9). Both his process model (his Fig. 4) and Fig. 1 in the current chapter follow the view of separate input and output orthographic lexicons (Morton, 1979; Morton & Patterson, 1980) rather than a single orthographic lexicon (Allport & Funnell, 1981); however, this issue, like the previous one, remains to be resolved. Relevant data and discussions favouring the single lexicon view can be found in Bub, Black, and Hampson (1986) and Coltheart and Funnell (1987), whereas results and theorising in support of separate input and output representations are available in Monsell (1987) and Campbell (1987). One pertinent observation on the phonological side of this issue involves patients who make semantic errors in immediate single-word repetition (see, for example, Michel, 1979, and Morton, 1980). This phenomenon seems difficult to explain with a single-lexical system, unless one postulates the sort of differential threshold levels for recognition and production that may make the single system functionally equivalent to a separate-systems model (see Howard & Franklin, 1988, for discussion). Following the same logic on the orthographic side of the process model (which is by convention drawn to have a parallel structure to the phonological side but, of course, logically need not), it would be of interest to observe a patient who, shown a printed word and then asked to write it immediately after the word had been removed, made semantic paragraphic errors.

Whether or not this particular phenomenon turns up, there is no doubt that conceptions about spelling procedures will be rapidly changing in the near future, partly as a result of neuropsychological data.

REFERENCES

Allport, D. A. & Funnell, E. (1981) Components of the mental lexicon. In H. C. Longuet-Higgins, J. Lyons, & D. E. Broadbent (Eds.), *The psychological mechanisms of language.* London: The Royal Society.

Assal, G., Buttet, J., & Jolivet, R. (1981) Dissociations in aphasia: A case report. *Brain and Language, 13*, 223–240.

Baxter, D. M. & Warrington, E. K. (1983) Neglect dysgraphia. *Journal of Neurology, Neurosurgery and Psychiatry, 46*, 1073–1078.

Beauvois, M. F. & Derouesné, J. (1979) Phonological alexia: Three dissociations. *Journal of Neurology, Neurosurgery and Psychiatry, 42*, 1115–1124.

Beauvois, M. F. & Derouesné, J. (1981) Lexical or orthographic agraphia. *Brain, 104*, 21–49.

Bishop, D. (1982) *TROG: Test for reception of grammar.* Abingdon, Oxon: Thomas Leach (for the Medical Research Council).

Bishop, D. & Byng, S. (1984) Assessing semantic comprehension: Methodological considerations, and a new clinical test. *Cognitive Neuropsychology, 1*, 233–244.

Bramwell, B. (1897) Illustrative cases of aphasia. *The Lancet, 1*, 1256–1259.

Bub, D., Black, S., & Hampson, E. (1986) *Are there separate input and output lexicons?: Evidence from a patient with surface dyslexia and surface dysgraphia.* Paper presented to the Academy of Aphasia.

Bub, D. & Kertesz, A. (1982) Evidence for lexicographic processing in a patient with preserved written over oral single word naming. *Brain, 105*, 697–717.

Campbell, R. (1983) Writing nonwords to dictation. *Brain and Language, 19*, 153–178.

Campbell, R. (1987) One or two lexicons for reading and writing words: Can misspellings shed any light? *Cognitive Neuropsychology, 4*, 487–499.

Campbell, R. & Butterworth, B. (1985) Phonological dyslexia and dysgraphia in a highly literate subject. *Quarterly Journal of Experimental Psychology, 37A*, 435–475.

Coltheart, M. & Funnell, E. (1987) Reading and writing: One lexicon or two? In D. A. Allport, D. G. MacKay, W. Prinz, & E. Scheerer (Eds.), *Language perception and production: Relationships among listening, speaking, reading and writing.* London: Academic Press.

Coltheart, M., Patterson, K., & Marshall, J. C. (1980) *Deep dyslexia.* London: Routledge & Kegan Paul.

Coughlan, A. K. & Warrington, E. K. (1978) Word-comprehension and word retrieval in patients with localised cerebral lesions. *Brain, 101*, 163–185.

Ellis, A. W. (1984) Introduction to Byrom Bramwell's (1897) case of word meaning deafness. *Cognitive Neuropsychology, 1*, 245–258.

Ellis, A. W., Miller, D., & Sin, G. (1983) Wernicke's aphasia and normal language processing: A case study in cognitive neuropsychology. *Cognition, 15*, 111–144.

Glushko, R. J. (1979) The organization and activation of orthographic knowledge in reading aloud. *Journal of Experimental Psychology: Human Perception and Performance, 5*, 674–691.

Goldblum, M.C. (1985) Word comprehension in surface dyslexia. In K. Patterson, J.C. Marshall, & M. Coltheart (Eds.), *Surface dyslexia: Neuropsychological and cognitive studies of phonological reading*. London: Lawrence Erlbaum Associates Ltd.

Goodglass, H. & Kaplan, E. (1972) *The assessment of aphasia and related disorders*. Philadelphia: Lea & Febiger.

Goodman, R. A. & Caramazza, A. (1986) Aspects of the spelling process: Evidence from a case of acquired dysgraphia. *Language and Cognitive Processes*, *1*, 263–296.

Hatfield, F.M. & Patterson, K.E. (1983) Phonological spelling. *Quarterly Journal of Experimental Psychology*, *35A*, 451–468.

Hatfield, F.M. & Patterson, K.E. (1984) Interpretation of spelling in aphasia: The impact of recent developments in cognitive psychology. In F.C. Rose (Ed.), *Progress in aphasiology*. New York: Raven Press.

Henderson, L. (1982) *Orthography and word recognition in reading*. London: Academic Press.

Hier, D.B. & Mohr, J.P. (1977) Incongruous oral and written naming: Evidence for a subdivision of the syndrome of Wernicke's aphasia. *Brain and Language*, *4*, 115–126.

Howard, D. & Franklin, S. (1988) *Missing the meaning?* Cambridge, Mass.: MIT Press.

Kay, J. & Marcel, T. (1981) One process, not two, in reading aloud: Lexical analogies do the work of non-lexical rules. *Quarterly Journal of Experimental Psychology*, *33A*, 397–413.

Kohn, S.E. & Friedman, R.B. (1986) Word-meaning deafness: A phonological-semantic dissociation. *Cognitive Neuropsychology*, *3*, 291–308.

Levine, D.N., Calvanio, R., & Popovics, A. (1982) Language in the absence of inner speech. *Neuropsychologia*, *20*, 391–409.

Margolin, D.I., Marcel, A.J., & Carlson, N. (1985) A comparison of processing deficits in dysnomia and post-semantic surface dyslexia. In K. Patterson, J.C. Marshall, & M. Coltheart (Eds.), *Surface dyslexia: Neuropsychological and cognitive studies of phonological reading*. London: Lawrence Erlbaum Associates Ltd.

Marshall, R.C., Rappaport, B.Z., & Garcia-Bunuel, L. (1985) Self-monitoring behavior in a case of severe auditory agnosia with aphasia. *Brain and Language*, *24*, 297–313.

Miceli, G., Silveri, M.C., & Caramazza, A. (1987) The role of the phoneme-to-grapheme conversion system and of the graphemic output buffer in writing: Evidence from an Italian case of pure dysgraphia. In M. Coltheart, R. Job, & G. Sartori (Eds.), *Cognitive neuropsychology of language*. London: Lawrence Erlbaum Associates Ltd.

Michel, F. (1979) Préservation du langage écrit malgré un déficit majeur du langage oral. *Lyon Medical*, *241*, 141–149.

Monsell, S. (1987) Nonvisual orthographic processing and the orthographic input lexicon. In M. Coltheart (Ed.), *Attention and performance XII*. London: Lawrence Erlbaum Associates Ltd.

Morton, J. (1979) Facilitation in word recognition: Experiments causing change in the logogen model. In P.A. Kolers, M.E. Wrolstad, & H. Bouma (Eds.), *Processing of visible language, Vol. 1*. New York: Plenum.

Morton, J. (1980) Two auditory parallels to deep dyslexia. In M. Coltheart, K. Patterson, & J.C. Marshall (Eds.), *Deep dyslexia*. London: Routledge & Kegan Paul.

Morton, J. & Patterson, K. (1980) A new attempt at an interpretation, or, an attempt at a new interpretation. In M. Coltheart, K. Patterson, & J. C. Marshall (Eds.), *Deep dyslexia*. London: Routledge & Kegan Paul.

Nelson, H.E. & O'Connell, A. (1978) Dementia: The estimation of premorbid intelligence levels using the new Adult Reading Test. *Cortex*, *14*, 234–244.

Norris, D. & Brown, G. (1985) Race models and analogy theories: A dead heat? A reply to Seidenberg. *Cognition*, *20*, 155–168.

Parkin, A.J. (1984) Redefining the regularity effect. *Memory and Cognition*, *12*, 287–292.

Patterson, K. (1986) Lexical but nonsemantic spelling? *Cognitive Neuropsychology*, *3*, 341–367.

Patterson, K. & Coltheart, V. (1987) Phonological processes in reading: A tutorial review. In M. Coltheart (Ed.), *Attention and performance XII*. London: Lawrence Erlbaum Associates Ltd.

Patterson, K. & Kay, J. (1982) Letter-by-letter reading: Psychological descriptions of a neurological syndrome. *Quarterly Journal of Experimental Psychology*, *34A*, 411–441.

Patterson, K. & Morton, J. (1985) From orthography to phonology: An attempt at an old interpretation. In K. Patterson, J. C. Marshall, & M. Coltheart (Eds.), *Surface dyslexia: Neuropsychological and cognitive studies of phonological reading*. London: Lawrence Erlbaum Associates Ltd.

Patterson, K. & Shewell, C. (1987) Speak and Spell: Dissociations and word-class effects. In M. Coltheart, R. Job, & G. Sartori (Eds.), *Cognitive neuropsychology of language*. London: Lawrence Erlbaum Associates Ltd.

Roeltgen, D. P., Rothi, L. G., & Heilman, K. M. (1986) Linguistic semantic agraphia: A dissociation of the lexical spelling system from semantics. *Brain and Language*, *27*, 257–280.

Roeltgen, D. P., Sevush, S., & Heilman, K. M. (1983) Phonological agraphia—writing by the lexical–semantic route. *Neurology*, *33*, 755–765.

Shallice, T. (1981) Phonological agraphia and the lexical route in writing. *Brain*, *104*, 413–429.

Shallice, T. & McCarthy, R. (1985) Phonological reading: From patterns of impairment to possible procedures. In K. Patterson, J. C. Marshall, & M. Coltheart (Eds.), *Surface dyslexia: Neuropsychological and cognitive studies of phonological reading*. London: Lawrence Erlbaum Associates Ltd.

Warrington, E. K. (1974) Deficient recognition memory in organic amnesia. *Cortex*, *10*, 289–291.

Warrington, E. K. & Shallice, T. (1979) Semantic access dyslexia. *Brain*, *103*, 43–63.

Wing, A. M. & Baddeley, A. D. (1980) Spelling errors in handwriting: A corpus and a distributional analysis. In U. Frith (Eds.), *Cognitive processes in spelling*. London: Academic Press.

APPENDIX: CASE REPORT[2]

P.Wh., a right-handed chief airline stewardess, suffered a CVA in October 1983 at the age of 38, producing right-sided hemiparesis and aphasia. A CT-scan showed multiple ill-defined low-density areas in the left hemisphere and a single similar area in the right (posterior superior) frontal region. Her speech output was dysfluent and agrammatic. Asked (at 5 weeks post-CVA) to describe what had happened to her, she replied:

> "Feeling unwell. Kitchen, quarter-past ten ... Orange juice, and ... the kitchen ... um, sways and ... unconscious, standing but unconscious. J. was coming home ... maybe one hour away. Still /kʌn/ unconscious. Five to twelve, Addenbrooke's Hospital, five weeks today. Completely paralysed." (Examiner: "And you couldn't say anything?") P.Wh.: "A week, 'yes' and 'no'; eight days, 'yes' and 'no' and 'chocolate'!"

---

[2] I am grateful to Dr I. M. S. Wilkinson, Addenbrooke's Hospital, Cambridge, for permission to publish details of this case.

Her naming ability was adequate to confrontation, less good to description (14/15 and 11/15, respectively, on the naming tests from Coughlan & Warrington, 1978).

Her short-term auditory verbal memory was relatively good (digit span = 6 forwards, 4 backwards), but her longer-term verbal memory was severely impaired. For example, on Warrington's (1974) two-alternative forced choice recognition memory test for words, she scored only 62%, scarcely better than chance.

P.Wh.'s comprehension (in both speech and reading) was good for single words. On a test of judging whether printed pairs of words are synonyms (test designed by Coltheart, personal communication), she was 100% correct on pairs of imageable words (an example of an imageable synonym pair is *PROFILE–SILHOUETTE*) but did less well (86%) with abstract words (e.g. *CLEMENCY–MERCY*).

Her comprehension of sentences, again both spoken and written, was good though not error-free. Bishops's (1982) TROG requires matching of a spoken or written sentence to one of four pictures, and tests various grammatical constructions including negation, plurals, reversible sentences, embedded clauses, etc. On the first 52 sentences of this test (chance = 25% correct), P.Wh. scored 77% (auditory presentation, three weeks post-CVA), 83% (visual presentation at three weeks), and 92% (auditory presentation again, four weeks post-onset).

P.Wh.'s oral reading, apart from rather stiff articulation, was excellent. In fact, she had no difficulties on any material: words, non-words, or sentences. Her score on the Adult Reading Test of low-frequency irregular words (Nelson & O'Connell, 1978) was 30/50, yielding a pre-morbid IQ estimate of 111.

In standard aphasia classifications, P.Wh.'s non-fluent spontaneous speech coupled with good repetition is perhaps best captured by the description of transcortical motor aphasia.

11 Independence of Access to Meaning and Phonology: Arguments for Direct Non-semantic Pathways for the Naming of Written Words and Pictures

H. Kremin
CRNS, Paris, France

INTRODUCTION TO FRAME OF REFERENCE

Over the past 15 years there has been a renewal of approaches to explain how we proceed from print to meaning and/or from print to oral output. They share the common perspective that the activity of reading can be viewed in terms of information processing. After Marshall and Newcombe's (1973) inspiring observations, research on acquired reading disorders indeed became a question of theoretical concern. Deep dyslexia and surface dyslexia—both originally described as patterns of reading errors—then played an important role in the description of processes of reading, because it is largely agreed that the performance of neurological patients can reveal separable subsystems of normal function rather than document the substitution of one subsystem for another (cf. Shallice, 1979).

In spite of different approaches and interpretations, two different models have been proposed to account for the processes implicated in the reading of isolated words: a two-route model (favoured by numerous authors) and a three-way account (Morton's logogen model). Both theories assume that there is a visuo-semantic pathway of word production (bypassing pre-lexical phonology that is retrieved post-lexically as a whole) and a non-lexical pathway in which letter strings are processed by means of grapheme-to-phoneme conversion. The logogen model (Morton & Patterson, 1980) is specific in that it proposes yet another way of reading aloud a written word, i.e. by means of direct print-to-sound associations between visual input logogens and output logogens. The relevance of this approach comes from outside neuropsychology as it is basically derived from experimental studies of normal subjects (Morton, 1979).

The proposal concerning direct links from categorisation processes to the output lexicon that are lexical but contain no semantic information has received some support from studies of brain-damaged patients. Thus Schwartz, Saffran, and Marin (1980) presented a patient who could read aloud words that he could not understand. Heilman and Rothi (1982) reported similar findings with patients suffering from mixed or sensory transcortical aphasia. Note that these patients could also use grapheme-to-phoneme translation. But the use of this conversion set should guarantee only the pronunciation of regular words. The empirical finding, however, that these patients correctly read many words with irregular spelling patterns cannot be accounted for by use of the peripheral reading strategy. It rather suggests the use of a direct (non-semantic) pathway from print to sound, the existence of which has been postulated by the logogen model. Warren and Morton (1982, pp. 127–128) argue that, normally, "words are read aloud via a direct connection between input and output lexicon. At the same time they are automatically subject to semantic analysis, but such cognitive processing would not affect naming times." They explicitly state (p. 128): "If there existed direct input–output connections for pictures, one would expect to find brain-damaged patients who could name pictures without understanding them"—a dissociation that has not been reported in the literature. The authors admit that such negative evidence is weak and presents a clear challenge for other researchers. We therefore experimentally investigated (Kremin, 1986) whether patients can be found with a disorder of object recognition that consists of the preservation of the ability to name objects, without, however, any evidence of semantic comprehension. It is possible that such cases have remained unnoticed because the patients' knowledge about objects is probably rarely investigated if they have named them correctly.

The purpose of this chapter is thus twofold: On the one hand, I will discuss data from recent investigations that suggest that the interpretation of patients' reading performances cannot any more be dealt with in the frame of a dual processing approach; on the other hand, I will argue—in analogy to reading—for the possible existence of a direct non-semantic pathway for picture naming on the basis of experimental data from pathology.

READING THROUGH SEMANTICS

Numerous cases of deep dyslexic patients (see Coltheart, Patterson & Marshall, 1980) have indeed demonstrated that a phonological output can be assessed post-lexically through semantics even in the absence of any phonological reading ability, that is in spite of the patients' failure to read nonsense syllables. It remains questionable, however, if the deep dyslexic reading behaviour plays any role in normal reading. It has also early been pointed out that the pattern of deep dyslexia (with nouns better read than functors, an influence of the concrete/abstract dimension, the inability to read meaningless items, and the production of semantic paralexias) may reflect a "multi-component syndrome" (Shallice & Warrington, 1980). The production of semantic paralexias—sometimes considered to be the crucial variable to define deep dyslexia and supposed to "guarantee" the occurrence of the other symptoms (Coltheart, 1980)—is in fact not necessarily associated with the influence of the other three variables on the patient's reading performance (see Kremin, 1982; Sartori, Barry, & Job, 1984 for reviews). Funnell's (1983) recent case description clearly demonstrates that the inability to read nonsense syllables can be an independent deficit that does not interfere with any of the lexical dimensions reported for deep and/or phonological dyslexia (Beauvois & Derouesné, 1979; Patterson, 1982). Consequently, formerly described cases of phonological dyslexia (characterised by various degrees of agrammatic reading, the inability to read nonsense syllables, and the absence(!) of semantic paralexias) may be considered a milder form of the deep dyslexic syndrome, perhaps in the course of regression of the deficit (Sartori et al., 1984). Funnell's case study has important implications for theoretical models of reading. Her experimental data along with others that we will mention later on in this chapter convincingly demonstrate the existence of a direct lexical non-semantic route to phonology. This reading by direct print-to-sound associations for all words ought to be distinguished from the deep dyslexics' reading through semantics. It can only be accounted for by a three-route approach to oral reading.

But let us go back to deep dyslexia and the pathway through semantics. Another argument against too simple an analogy between deep dyslexic reading behaviour and normal functioning comes from the clinically often described bi- or multi-directionality of the deficit with the consequence of similar (semantic) errors in object naming, and/or in repetition, or in writing to dictation (see Kremin, 1982, for a review). This pattern of associated deficits is usually taken to reflect a central modality independent disturbance of "lexical knowledge" (Nolan & Caramazza, 1982). In this view the frequent (but not necessary!) association of semantic paralexias with an effect of word class and of the concrete/abstract dimension is taken to "prove" a disturbance at the level of the lexical system. Because some cases have been described that showed the reverse pattern of deep dyslexia—(homophonic) functors were better read than nouns (Marin, Saffran, & Schwartz, 1976) and abstract words better than concrete ones (Warrington, 1981)—these dissociation data may be taken to suggest that semantic organisation is based upon linguistic parameters. Some authors (Marin et al., 1976), however, pointed to an alternative possibility: "That the lexicon is organised with regard to representational derivation of its entries: that is the degree to which their meaning can be specified by sensori-motor images and contextual memories and associations" (p. 881). This organising principle would thus polarise concrete words (independent of grammatical category), on the one hand, and abstract items (including many functors, but not all) on the other hand. Because imageability is a strong predictor of whether a word will be read successfully by deep dyslexic patients (Richardson, 1975; Shallice & Warrington, 1975), it can also be questioned whether the reading pattern is not a consequence of semantically based difference in imageability. In this context it should be noted that the distinction between meaningfulness and non-meaningfulness with regard to functors was indeed discriminating not only for oral reading (Beauvois & Derouesné, 1979) but also for comprehension (Goodenough, Zurif, & Weintraub, 1977). It should, furthermore, be noted that the patient with "concrete word dyslexia" (Warrington, 1981) suffered also from visual object agnosia. It has also been pointed out that the deep dyslexics' reading errors on function words (which are usually substitutions within the same category, see Coltheart, 1980) may arise from the same underlying deficit as (some) semantic paralexias, that is a "naming" deficit (Kremin, 1982). Finally, the Wernicke's aphasics' superior reading of functors as compared to nouns (Marin et al., 1976) may, according to Ellis, Miller, & Sin's (1983) experimental data, not necessarily reflect the word-class effect but the word-frequency effect. Recent investigations, furthermore, suggest that the apparent effect of grammatical class could in fact be an imageability effect (Allport & Funnell, 1981; Johnston, 1983). When oral reading of five deep dyslexic patients was investigated (on words matched in imageability and in frequency) no consistent advantage of nouns over verbs remained (Allport & Funnell, 1981). Moreover, the imageability effect that was found in deep dyslexics' oral reading (Patterson & Marcel, 1977; Richardson, 1975; Shallice & Warrington, 1975) had no influence at all on W.B.'s oral reading (Funnell, 1983). W.B.'s "pure" phonological dyslexia, which is characterised by only one symptom of oral reading impairment (the inability to read nonsense syllables), can thus be discriminated from the multi-component syndrome of deep dyslexia by the semantically based variable of imageability: Deep dyslexic reading takes place through semantics whereas direct print-to-sound reading of words relies on a lexical but non-semantic pathway.

If semantic paralexias do not necessarily co-occur with the other lexical features of deep dyslexic reading, why, then, do they occur? Newcombe and Marshall's (1980) early suggestion "that very minimal phonological recoding can block the overt expression of semantic errors in reading" (p. 185) appears now less convincing because in many cases of so-called phonological dyslexia that have meanwhile been described no semantic paralexias have been observed in spite of the patients' (sometimes total) inability to read nonsense syllables (see Sartori et al., 1984).

It has, furthermore, been pointed out that semantic paralexias may be due to different loci of disruption in the course of the information processing (Morton & Patterson, 1980; Shallice & Warrington, 1980). All the considered causes of semantic paralexias are, however, specific to pathology and ought not to intervene during normal functioning of the system.

According to Shallice and Warrington (1980) semantically related responses to the written target word can be due to a problem with the access of meaning, limited to the visual input modality. This seems to be the case for A.R. (Shallice & Warrington, 1980) and Jeanne (Lebrun & Devreux, 1984), patients who also suffered from optic aphasia.

Semantic paralexias may also (and more often) occur because of an output problem at the level of "naming" (Hecaen & Kremin, 1976; Shallice & Warrington, 1980). In terms of the logogen model this naming deficit would be due to response blocking after attainment of the correct and full semantic code (Morton & Patterson, 1980). This account of semantic paralexias predicts similar errors in oral tasks other than reading because the same output logogens are required. This occurrence of semantic errors not only in reading but also across different language tasks has indeed been documented (Friedman & Perlman, 1982; Nolan & Caramazza, 1982).

Central damage to the semantic system itself may be another source for the production of semantic paralexias. In this constellation, semantic errors in oral production should be paralleled by errors in word comprehension. Some deep dyslexic patients are indeed reported to be far from perfect in comprehension tasks concerning written words (Newcombe & Marshall, 1980; Patterson, 1981), and for some patients parallel deficits have been reported in tasks that did not involve the written word (Friedman & Perlman, 1982).

Friedman and Perlman's (1982) experiments offered evidence for two causes of semantic paralexias: word retrieval and impaired concept arousal. Central damage can indeed not be the only source of semantic paralexias because patients often (although not always) know that they have made a semantic error (Patterson, 1978).

The observation that patients sometimes do accept their own semantic misreading (especially when the target words are close synonyms or highly abstract words, see Patterson, 1978) raised the possibility of yet another source of semantic paralexias and paraphasis: the "normal limitations of a semantic specification". Morton and Patterson (1980, pp. 98–99) thus suggest that "some semantic paralexias may arise because the deep dyslexics' only reading route to the output logogen system is through the semantic system". This view, however, "will not account for the many paralexias which are neither synonymous nor abstract and where the patients know that their responses are wrong" (p. 99).

If reading through semantics without phonology relies on the direct transfer of orthographic codes to cognitive codes (Saffran, 1980) without any use of word-specific lexical codes then the reading and comprehension performance of "pure" semantic readers (i.e. those not yet described without any central disturbance at all) should reflect the organisation of the cognitive system itself. A recent investigation by Allport and Funnell (1981) followed this line of reasoning and furnished data on the word comprehension of a severe aphasic subject. Unfortunately, we do not get a detailed case description. The authors underline, however, that A.L. could not read (nor match) nonsense syllables. In spite of this phonological reading impairment, the patient was perfectly capable of matching written words to a spoken target when the written words were semantically close but distinct (e.g. *glove/sock*—"glove"). However, when the written word pairs were almost identical in meaning (e.g. *dress/frock*—"dress") the patient's performance dropped to chance. Allport and Funnell (1981, p. 402) point out that "if the cognitive codes ... had a one–one correspondence with words in the language—i.e. if they presented lexemes—there should still be no difficulty in discriminating dress and frock ... On the other hand, if the cognitive codes represent only non-linguistic, sensory, functional and other attributes, the task should be impossible for anyone ... who cannot translate from print to sound."

With regard to Morton and Patterson's (1980) initial suggestions about the normal limitations of a semantic specification, it should be underlined, however, that translation "from print to sound" in this context ought to relate to both routes, the direct lexical pathway from orthography to phonology and the peripheral non-lexical route by grapheme-to-phoneme correspondence (GPC) rules. If direct translation of orthographic to phonological codes is preserved, word matching (with synonymic distractors) is indeed easily accomplished even by patients without any oral output at all and in spite of a severe phonological reading impairment. Take, for example, our patient BER (unpublished data). He did not read success) on a difficult test of written homophonic word association, e.g. *PORC* (*porc*) = *PORT* (*harbour*) ≠ *PORTE* (*door*). The patient had indeed no problem at all with a French version of the Allport and Funnell word-matching task with synonymic distractors. This performance was due, I think, to the patient's ability to attain the representational level of the output logogens (in spite of a severe disturbance to access phonology through GPC rules). In the light of the scarcity of the published data on A.L., the underlying hypotheses—"cognitive codes represent only non-linguistic, sensory, functional and other attributes" (Allport & Funnell, 1981, p. 402), eventually documenting the "normal limitations of a semantic specification" (Morton & Patterson, 1980, p. 98)—seem thus neither confirmed nor invalidated. The discussion of the existence of several semantic systems (verbal and others) has indeed just begun. Beauvois (1982) recently outlined possible interactions between visual and verbal semantic processes, interactions that may be impaired "without any visual or verbal impairment at all" (p. 43).

THE PERIPHERAL READING STRATEGY

Another type of acquired reading disorder—surface dyslexia—can be quoted when the possibility of a separate phonological route (or even its mode of operation) are being considered. Standard interpretation of this syndrome supposes that it reflects the operation of the phonological route in a more or less intact fashion—with the other route(s) being relatively inoperative. The phonological route operating in isolation should thus show the following main characteristics: (1) a strong effect of the regularity of the words' grapheme-to-phoneme correspondences, with regular words being read more easily than irregular ones; (2) nonsense syllables should be read as well as regular words; and (3) reading errors should be typically non-lexical regularisations. According to Marcel (1980), this error pattern should arise because surface dyslexics have lost the orthographic specifications for some words. That is, they read words without orthographic lexical knowledge and without prior or simultaneous understanding of the written stimuli as if they were nonsense syllables. According to overwhelmingly confirmed findings, surface dyslexics read regular words better than irregular ones. But it should also be stressed that they do read a great proportion of irregular words successfully (eventually showing no statistically significant difference between the oral reading of both types of words, see Kay & Patterson, 1985). And recently some patients have been presented who read nonsense syllables fairly well (Kremin, 1980, 1985; Shallice, Warrington, & McCarthy, 1983). The third theoretical claim, however (that errors should be non-lexical regularisations), is often not met by the published experimental data. Table 1 clearly shows that surface dyslexics' errors are not satisfactorily explained by use of otherwise valid grapheme-to-phoneme correspondence rules. In fact, the cited cases present about as many errors in the application of these rules. Still, errors ascribed to the correct or incorrect functioning of GPC rules are, of course, the kinds of errors most frequently associated with surface dyslexia.

However, as common as either of these types of errors is a visual misreading of the stimulus word. Temple (1985) pointed out that visual errors may occur at different stages during the processing of the written stimulus, even within the phonological route itself. Visual errors that result from malfunctioning of the phonological pathway should yield visually similar non-word responses. This has indeed been observed by Kremin (1980, 1982b). For some other cases with surface dyslexia, however, a strong tendency for lexicalisation has been reported. Thus Coltheart, Mastersen, and Byng (1982) observed that visual errors usually resulted in real-word responses. Visual whole-word errors, however, would have some other locus than errors based on faulty application of GPC rules. (In this context it should be underlined that visual whole-word errors are also produced by so-called phonological dyslexics and by deep dyslexics who are both supposed to use the visual input logogen system.)

Moreover, the foregoing observations have to be completed by the findings that some cases with surface dyslexic reading presented many successful self-corrections (Deloche, Andreewsky, & Desi, 1982; Kremin, 1980, 1985b): Patients were capable of correctly reproducing the target in spite of initial reading errors, even when they were phonological in nature. This pattern is at variance with the classically described reading comprehension of surface dyslexics such as J.C. and S.T. (Marshall & Newcombe, 1973) whose reading comprehension did not refer to the visual input but to their own verbal output, through "attempts after meaning". Recent research thus suggests that in some surface dyslexic readers the comprehension of the written stimuli is achieved by the same pathway of orthographic whole-word recognition as in deep dyslexia. We therefore proposed to distinguish two different types of surface dyslexic readers (Kremin, 1982) on the basis of different loci of access to the semantic system:

1. In accordance with the classical description of the syndrome, the disturbance can be due to a failure of "recognition" at the level of the visual input logogens. The patient therefore adopts a sounding-out strategy by grapheme-to-phoneme mapping. In this variety, words are not understood simultaneously, even when they are read correctly, because the access to the cognitive system takes place only after grapheme-to-phoneme translation, usually by auditory checking procedures. Such patients seem to have an additional deficit to reading (and writing). They seem indeed to have lost the orthographic specifications for words (cf. Marcel, 1980): J.C.'s and M.S.'s semantic comprehension of homophonic words (*BE* v. *BEE* went one way or the other (Newcombe & Marshall, 1981, 1985).

2. The disturbance can be due to a disruption at the level of the output logogens. Again, the patients opt for phonological reading. But in this

TABLE 1
Types of Errors in the Reading of Isolated Words by Surface Dyslexics

Error Types (% of Total Errors)	Subjects									
	A.B.[a]	*H.T.R.*[a]	*P.M.*[a]	*C.H.*[a]	*E.E.*[a]	*K.M.*[a]	*F.R.A.*[b]	*H.A.M.*[c]	*J.C. & S.T.*[d]	*A.D.*[e]
Regularisations (and Stress Errors)	21	46	12	17	22	22				
Errors in GPC Rules	21	14	49	40	42	15				
Mean Percentage of Phonological Errors	21	30	30.5	28.5	33	18.5	68	51	?	≈36
Visual Errors	50	29	23	27	21	59		30	?	≈28
Lexicalisations	67	25	40	33	19	65			≈25	≈10
Autocorrections	?	?	?	?	?	?	51	70	?	59

[a] Coltheart, Masterson, and Byng (1982)
[b] Kremin (1980)
[c] Kremin (1985)
[d] Marcel (1980)
[e] Deloche, Andreewsky, and Desi (1982)

type, the written target word is correctly understood in spite of reading errors on (at least) irregular words. For such patients, surface dyslexic reading seems to be a freely chosen compensatory strategy for the pronunciation of written words. Patients who are aware of their general output problems (in naming, spontaneous speech, etc.) may adopt the left-to-right mapping of grapheme-to-phoneme conversion for reading aloud to overcome the aphasic deficit at the level of the output logogens. This seems to be true for cases recently presented by Goldblum (1985), Kremin (1985), Margolin, Marcel, and Carlson (1985). This second variety of surface dyslexic oral readers is best characterised by a post-lexical disturbance of accessing phonology (which is compensated for by assembled phonology).

DIRECT PRINT-TO-SOUND ASSOCIATIONS

Further evidence for some lexical representation in acquired surface dyslexia has been put forward by Bub, Cancelliere, and Kertesz' (1982) case study. Examining the naming latency to words of different frequency, they found that the frequency effect occurred in a similar fashion on regular and on irregular words (with high-frequency items being approximately 50 msec faster than low-frequency items). According to Patterson and Morton (1985), however, reaction times as a function of word frequency should be a characteristic of the direct (non-semantic) pathway. Yet the patient (who read a high proportion of irregular words) made the typical reading errors of surface dyslexics, especially for irregular words of low frequency: The incorrect pronunciations all involved misapplication of stereotyped rules. This implies that some of the patient's reading took place by means of phonological rather than lexical coding, and suggests the presence of both a rule-based and a whole-word system underlying the oral reading performance of this surface dyslexic with disturbed semantic access.

More evidence that surface dyslexia does not arise solely from the inaccessibility of visual input logogens comes from homophone confusion with irregularly spelt homophones. A.B., a patient with acquired surface dyslexia (Coltheart et al., 1983), comprehended for example the irregular word *BURY* as "a fruit on the tree". Because the patient's definition indicated that the target word was confused with its homophone (*BERRY*), the correct phonological representation of the target word must have been obtained. But the phonological form cannot have been obtained via GPC rules because this system yields incorrect pronunciations for irregular words. The correct phonological code for *BURY* can only be provided by the output logogen system. Why, then, was this word misunderstood in spite of apparently correct access to the input/output logogen system? Coltheart and co-workers (1983) propose the following explanation: "There is correct access within the visual input logogen system, but a failure between this system and the cognitive system, whilst at the same time communication from the visual input logogen system to the output system is achieved; and a phonological code can thus be obtained this way. If comprehension is required, this phonological code can access the semantic system, perhaps via the auditory input logogens" (p. 492). As the authors pointed out themselves, one reason for the theoretical importance of these irregular-homophone confusions is that they would require for their explanation the existence of a direct (and non-semantic) pathway from visual input logogens to phonological output logogens.

The existence of a direct non-semantic reading route to phonology has now been convincingly demonstrated. On the one hand, patients have been described who were able to read words correctly in spite of grossly impaired reading comprehension and other cognitive skills (Bub, Cancelliere & Kertesz, 1985, Heilman & Rothi, 1982; Schwartz et al., 1980; Symonds, 1953). On the other hand, some patients' reading of isolated words contrasts with their oral reading of words in the frame of a sentence (Bub & Kertesz, 1982; Newcombe & Marshall, 1981). The latter dissociation can, again, only be accounted for by a three-route approach. One of our patients—unable to read nonsense syllables and with telegrammatic spontaneous speech—reads words, when they are in isolation, quite well and without any influence of the part of speech dimension. This variable, however, becomes crucial when the same words are to be decoded in the frame of a sentence because the patient's reading performance turns into "deep dyslexia at the level of sentences" (Kremin, 1984). This dissociation in the reading of the same words individually and in sentences would apparently suggest different treatment of the stimuli: Words in a sentence were reproduced via the semantic pathway (and thus reflected the patient's general agrammatic disturbance), whereas the reading of isolated words seems to have been achieved by direct point-to-sound associations of the lexical (non-semantic) pathway.

Furthermore, let me note that even the consideration of deep and surface dyslexia (which have been quoted mainly to demonstrate the psychological reality of a semantic v. a rule-governed pathway to phonology) offers suggestive arguments supporting the existence of a direct route. We already mentioned that surface dyslexic patients often read (some) words with irregular spellings. This should be accomplished by use of the direct route. And F.D., who satisfies the criteria of deep dyslexia, "sometimes uses a direct route to a word's name" (Friedman & Perlman,

1982, p. 565) because written words were less likely to be misnamed than pictures (13% v. 46% errors).

On the basis of the foregoing results and arguments I think that "routine" reading of isolated words entails direct whole-word print-to-sound associations. A partial or a total disturbance of this direct route, however, will leave operative two different strategies to assign pronunciation to a written word: If grapheme-to-phoneme conversion is available (as shown by the possibility to read nonsense syllables), the patient's oral production will show the surface pattern; if phonological reading is not available at all, a phonological output may still be derived from the recognition/comprehension of the written stimulus via semantics, thus resulting in phonological or in deep dyslexia.

We know little with regard to the functioning of the direct pathway itself. Funnell's (1983) case study suggests that not only root morphemes but also affixes/suffixes may be read aloud via the direct pathway; the latter, however, "do not appear to be represented in the lexical phonological store as independent items" (p. 8). Friedman and Perlman (1982) think "that this direct route does not depend upon grapheme-to-phoneme conversion" (p. 564) because (according to unpublished data they mention) even in Chinese, where grapheme-to-phoneme correspondences do not exist, written words require less time to be named than pictures.

INDEPENDENCE OF ACCESS TO MEANING AND PHONOLOGY FOR WRITTEN WORDS AND PICTURES: AN EXPERIMENTAL STUDY

If we have no idea yet of how written stimuli are converted to sound by direct "mapping", there is growing experimental evidence, however, that access to meaning and lexical phonology are independent. Some studies with normal subjects seem to support such a view. Discussing the results of an experiment by Durso and Johnson (1979), Warren and Morton (1982, p. 127) pointed out:

> One of their conditions involved subjects naming a sequence of pictures and (written) words. Items were repeated on occasions and the facilitative effect of this could be calculated. Among other things they found that there was considerable facilitation on picture naming given prior presentation and naming of the equivalent word. However, there was virtually no advantage to word naming following presentation of the picture. We see this as supporting the idea that words are read aloud via a direct connection between input and output lexicon.

None the less, the main argument for the operation of a direct pathway stems from pathology, that is from dissociation data with regard to (good) oral reading and (impaired) comprehension of the same words. This pattern of performance most often seems to indicate a damage to a central system responsible for semantic and conceptual representation (see Funnell, 1983; Schwartz et al., 1980). However, in the framework of the "semantic attainment theory", Shallice and Coughlan (1980) argued for the possible existence of a modality-specific word-comprehension deficit: their patient P.S. indeed performed significantly better on several word-comprehension tasks given auditory as compared to visual input.

We therefore investigated our patients' comprehension of pictures and corresponding written words in a pairwise-association task together with their performances in confrontation naming, oral reading of words, and two word-matching tasks.[1]

EXPERIMENT

Subjects

Forty right-handed subjects with aphasia due to left-sided lesions of the brain and two subjects with multiple lesions and aphasia. The latter ones, cases AND and ORL, were excluded from the statistical analysis.

Method and Material

1. Patients had to name visually presented common objects (fork, glass, etc.) (n = 20).
2. Patients had to match a given picture of those objects with the only semantically related candidate among a multiple choice of five pictures (e.g. fork/knife) (n = 25).
3. Patients had to read aloud the corresponding written words of the objects' names (n = 25).
4. Patients had to match a given written word with the only semantically related candidate among a multiple choice of five written words (n = 25).
5. Patients had to match a given object with the corresponding written word in a multiple choice of four words (target, semantic distractor, phonological distractor, item without any relation) (n = 20).
6. Patients had to match a spoken word and the corresponding picture in a multiple choice of four pictures (the names of which were all phonologically similar to the target) (n = 18).
7. We furthermore tested for general verbal comprehension in terms of execution of orally given commands (n = 12).

[1] Preliminary version presented to the INS 7th European Conference, Aachen, West Germany, June 13–15, 1984.

Results and Comments

We did not find a statistically significant difference in our aphasics' comprehension performances of written words as compared to pictures in the word-association test (see Table 2). (In both tasks the subjects had to match a target item [e.g. œuf/egg] with the only semantically related candidate [e.g. poule/chicken] among five items.) With regard to the problem of access of semantic knowledge, the general pattern of performance of a large series of aphasic patients thus lends support to the notion of a central supra-modal semantic system.

The descriptive statistics of the performances of the 40 non-selected aphasic subjects on the test battery are represented in Table 3.

These statistical results, however, conceal dissociations that occur in the individual performances of some patients only. Table 4 clearly shows that the comprehension of written words as compared to pictures can be selectively disturbed. This pattern may even occur in spite of correct oral reading, and thus documents problems of semantic access specific to written words (see patients DUM, PIG, BUS). The performances of our patients DUM, PIG, and BUS thus seem to support Shallice and Coughlan's (1980) hypothesis concerning the possible existence of a modality-specific comprehension deficit. But they also lend support to the notion that separate modes of accessing semantic knowledge are furthermore distinguishable within the visual modality: one for written words and another one for pictures. This state of affairs is in agreement with current models of word recognition (cf. Warren & Morton, 1982). Another difference between Shallice and Coughlan's case and our patients should also be stressed: P.S.'s visual word comprehension was indeed near chance "unless she could read the word" (p. 870). Our three patients, however, read the target words almost perfectly (92% to 100% correct). Notwithstanding the success in reading aloud, their comprehension of the same written words was severely impaired as shown by the patients' problems in matching the written word pairs which resulted only in 10% to 48% correct responses. These dissociations would be plausibly explained by P.S.'s use of the visual/semantic pathway for oral reading (resulting in a deep

TABLE 2
The Understanding of Words: Comparison of Images and Written Words in a Pairwise-association Task (% Correct)

$n = 40$	*Images* ($n = 25$)	*Written Words* ($n = 25$)	*Wilcoxon*
$\bar{x}$	85.50	82.70	$n^* = 21$
s	18.39	26.08	$W = 104$
Range	40–100	20–100	$P = 6894$ n.s.

TABLE 3
Descriptive Statistics of the Performances of 40 Non-selected Aphasic Subjects on the Test Battery (% Correct)

	$\bar{x}$	*s*	*Range*
1. Oral Naming of Objects	52.12	34.65	0–100
2. Comprehension of Pictures (Pairwise-association Task)	85.50	18.39	40–100
3. Oral Reading of Written Words	81.00	35.50	0–100
4. Comprehension of Written Words (Pairwise-association Task)	82.70	26.08	20–100
5. Matching of Object with Written Word	90.74	21.67	10–100
6. Matching of Spoken Word with Picture	93.25	11.35	60–100
7. Execution of Oral Commands	66.87	25.52	18–100

TABLE 4
Individual Performances of Five Aphasic Subjects on the Test Battery (% Correct)

	Subjects				
	DUM	*PIG*	*BUS*	*AND*	*ORL*
1. Oral Naming	100	50	65	95	100
2. Comprehension of Pictures	100	100	80	52	48
3. Oral Reading	92	100	100	100	100
4. Comprehension of Written Words	48	44	10	72	12
5. Matching Object/Written Word	100	30	25	90	75
6. Matching Spoken Word/Picture	100	100	?	?	66
7. Execution of Commands	40	40	48	100	52

dyslexic pattern) whereas our three patients' oral reading relies on the use of the direct lexical (non-semantic) pathway to phonology.

Table 4 also shows that two patients, AND and ORL, were able to name pictures correctly although their "semantic comprehension" of the same items (pairwise association of pictures and of written words) was severely impaired. Indeed, AND and ORL correctly named 95% and 100% of the presented pictures, but they correctly matched only 52% and 48% respectively of the same pictures when presented for pairwise association with the only semantically related candidate among a multiple choice of five pictures. Both AND and ORL show the unusual pattern of preserved confrontation naming in spite of impaired picture association. (For more details on AND and ORL see Kremin, 1986.)

Scrutinising the literature for similar findings we found that Heilman, Tucker, and Valenstein (1976) presented a case whose oral naming was close to perfect (92%) but who in a "semantic categorisation test" (which highly resembles our pairwise-association task) got only 37/38 trials correct. This suggests that the patient did have a semantic categorisation deficit for pictures in spite of relatively preserved oral naming.

On the basis of this case study as well as on the basis of theoretical considerations Heilman and co-workers (1976, 1981) distinguished a special type of aphasic impairment—"transcortical aphasia with intact naming". Such patients should be characterised by poor comprehension (of spoken and written language) with preserved repetition, reading aloud, spontaneous speech, and naming.

Our patients indeed exhibit some characteristic features of transcortical aphasia: Both of them repeat meaningful and meaningless material flawlessly. In spontaneous language and in verbal tasks, echolalia is a prominent feature. The patients' memory span is six and seven digits respectively. Their spontaneous language is "normal" in the sense that there are neither phonemic and/or semantic paraphasias nor agrammatism.

However, whereas AND's spontaneous output is structurally normal (although full of fabulousness), ORL's spontaneous output is extremely empty (through lack of content words). Moreover, ORL's comprehension deficit is severe and general (pictures, spoken words, written words, execution of commands), whereas AND's less severe comprehension deficit seems to be limited to pictures and isolated words: It co-exists with preserved and flawless comprehension of oral (and of written) commands.

On the basis of the foregoing observations, we would argue that ORL suffers from a general central (representational) disturbance. Damage to the central system thus hinders comprehension in all tasks independently of the mode of input. The total emptiness of her spontaneous speech would also be accounted for by a central disturbance. (In fact, the patient was totally disoriented in time and space, and we had to ask her husband about her history.)

There is, of course, an alternative explanation of ORL's verbal behaviour that would, however, require a multitude of functional lesions: problems of access to the (preserved but totally isolated) semantic system given auditory input, given pictorial input, given graphic input ... combined with a severe "anomia" specific for spontaneous speech, etc. We did not conceive of the task to cope experimentally with these alternatives.

AND's perturbation, in contrast, seems to support the notion of problems of semantic attainment specific for pictures and (at least) written words. (Unfortunately we do not have data concerning the patient's comprehension of isolated spoken words.) The patient's flawless execution of even more complex oral and written commands suggests "normal" comprehension.

Now, how may good comprehension of commands and deficient

comprehension of words be reconciled? A short reflection about the task demands may help: For the execution of "Put the pencil into the ashtray" mere comprehension of "put into" plus simple matching of the words with the corresponding objects may be sufficient. Note the absence of "semantic distractors and/or decisions" in such a task.

It seems that the presence of only one semantic distractor (in the task of matching an object with the corresponding written word) constitutes enough "processing charge" to worsen the patient's performance. When, moreover, a precise semantic relationship has to be activated (as in the pairwise-association task), the patient's performance drops even more.

Note that the loss of the faculty to achieve semantic categorisation for precise word pairs is a problem specific to AND and ORL, because aphasics, on an average, are much more successful in doing so (in spite of their rather impaired execution of commands).

CONCLUDING REMARKS

Notwithstanding individual differences, both ORL and AND show the unusual pattern of preserved naming in spite of impaired word comprehension. This rare dissociation should be best accounted for by postulating the existence of a non-semantic pathway for oral naming. As pointed out earlier, the existence of a direct non-semantic pathway for reading has meanwhile been experimentally established. In analogy to reading, one may thus conceive of a non-semantic direct pathway for oral naming, too. As a consequence, such a view admits a disorder of object recognition consisting of the preservation of the ability to name objects without, however, any evidence of semantic comprehension (because of an impairment in the semantic system and/or loss of access to it). A direct pathway for naming—i.e. a direct connection between the "pictogen"[2] and the output logogen system that bypasses the semantic system—has indeed been considered a theoretical possibility in models of object recognition (Warren & Morton, 1982). (See also Ratcliff & Newcombe, 1982, who postulated such direct connections on the grounds of totally different assumptions and pathological data, i.e. optic aphasia.) In the current version of the logogen model, however, such direct pictogen→output logogen connection is refuted on the basis of experimental data from normal subjects (Morton, 1984).

[2] Warren and Morton (1982) showed that there is facilitation between pictures that are different but have the same name. They assume that there is a means of categorising pictures in which all pictures with the same name share a common fate. "This process, called the Pictogen System, has properties which lead to the facilitation and, since there were no effects from words to pictures, it must be completely independent of the processes responsible for verbal processing" (Morton, 1984, p. 220).

Notwithstanding the possible issue of the theoretical controversy, one could mention some data that seem to be in conflict with the notion of just one pathway for picture naming by means of mobilising semantic knowledge. Indeed, there are suggestions from clinical data that some groups of aphasics remain unable to name objects if the name does not come to mind at once. Goodglass, Kaplan, Weintraub, and Ackerman (1976) studied the "tip-of-the-tongue" phenomenon in aphasia by asking for syllable length and first-letter report in response to each picture the patients failed to name. Because in the cited experiment all patient groups had equal success in confrontation naming, group differences in partial retrieval of word structure may be taken to indicate the use of different strategies for lexical access. On the basis of such observations, Goodglass (1980, p. 653) conjectured "that there are two major paths to the emission of a word—one proceeding automatically from stimulus to oral response and based on a one-to-one associative link between concept and output. The other occurring when immediate association fails, involving a search process and the mobilization of peripheral semantic and phonological associations." Goodglass, furthermore, suggests that the first mode of retrieval characterises immediate responses of all subjects; the second mode "would appear to be available to conduction aphasics and to Broca's aphasics as well as to normal speakers, but less available to those with marked anomia—i.e. patients with anomic and Wernicke's aphasia" (p. 653). Goodglass also conjectured that word search by means of mobilising knowledge results in slower response latencies than the "automatic" mapping via direct picture–word associations.

The notion that naming may involve two different processes has testable implications for response latencies for normal subjects. Goodglass, Theurkauf, and Wingfield (1984) followed this line of reasoning; specifically, they proposed that "if a rapid associative naming phase is succeeded by a 'voluntary' search phase, there may be a corresponding drop in the influence of word frequency or item difficulty on naming latency due to the intervention of other factors less determined by stimulus difficulty *per se*" (p. 136). Goodglass and co-workers tested 24 normal adults presented with a total of 83 pictures. Analysis of naming performances by word frequency/item difficulty showed on the one hand that very long latencies occur most often for the difficult, low-frequency items, whereas the shortest latencies show little effect of item difficulty or frequency. On the other hand, analysis by response–latency ranges showed that the relationship between item difficulty and latency for responses is highly correlated with "short" responses (500–1500 msec), whereas in the longer reaction-time ranges, this clear relationship disappears. Goodglass et al. (1984, pp. 143–144) conclude: "At least on a descriptive level, we do seem to be dealing with what may well be more than one word-finding process. One of these is represented by a population of shorter latencies which are directly dependent on item difficulty, and a longer population which is less so. We could describe these processes as indicating 'automatic' versus 'voluntary' search, so long as we are careful to limit our definitions of these processes." With regard to Goodglass's (1980) early suggestions concerning the naming behaviour of patients with different aphasic syndromes, the authors suggest that "an apparent word-finding difficulty might be due to problems in one of the retrieval processes, forcing the patient to attempt to rely solely upon the other" (p. 144).

It is evident that only future research with normal as well as brain-damaged subjects will enable us to cope more precisely with the process(es) of naming. It does not seem to be impossible, however, that, in analogy to the two lexical pathways of retrieving phonology for the reading of words, "normal", i.e. rapid automatic naming, is achieved via direct pictogen–logogen connections and thus contrasts with another strategy for naming that is based upon more conscious word search in the frame of representational knowledge.

REFERENCES

Allport, A. & Funnell, E. (1981) Components of the mental lexicon. *Philosophical Transactions of the Royal Society of London*, *B295*, 397–410.

Beauvois, M. F. (1982) Optic aphasia: A process of interaction between vision and language. *Philosophical Transactions of the Royal Society of London*, *B298*, 35–47.

Beauvois, M. F. & Derouesné, J. (1979) Phonological alexia: Three dissociations. *Journal of Neurology, Neurosurgery and Psychiatry*, *42*, 1115–1124.

Bub, D. N. & Kertesz, A. (1982) Deep agraphia. *Brain and Language*, *17*, 146–165.

Bub, D. N., Cancelliere, A., & Kertesz, A. (1985) Whole-word and analytic translation of spelling to sound in a non-semantic reader. In K. E. Patterson, J. C. Marshall, & M. Coltheart (Eds.), *Surface dyslexia*. London: Lawrence Erlbaum Associates Ltd.

Coltheart, M. (1980) Deep dyslexia: A review of the syndrome. In M. Coltheart, K. E. Patterson, & J. C. Marshall (Eds.), *Deep dyslexia*. London: Routledge & Kegan Paul.

Coltheart, M., Masterson, J., Byng, S., Prior, M., & Riddoch, J. (1983) Surface dyslexia. *Quarterly Journal of Experimental Psychology*, *35A*, 469–495.

Coltheart, M., Masterson, J., & Byng, S. (1982) *Types of error in surface dyslexic reading*. Paper presented at the Surface Dyslexia Conference, Oxford.

Coltheart, M., Patterson, K. E., & Marshall, J. C. (1980) *Deep dyslexia*. London: Routledge & Kegan Paul.

Deloche, G., Andreewsky, E., & Desi, M. (1982) Surface Dyslexia: A case report and some theoretical implications to reading models. *Brain and Language*, *15*, 11–32.

Durso, F. T. & Johnson, M. K. (1979) Facilitation in naming and categorizing repeated pictures and words. *Journal of Experimental Psychology: Human Learning and Memory*, *5*, 449–459.

Ellis, A. W., Miller, D., & Sin, G. (1983) Wernicke's aphasia and normal language processing: A case study in cognitive neuropsychology. *Cognition*, *15*, 111–144.

Friedman, R. B. & Perlman, M. B. (1982) On the underlying causes of semantic paralexias in a patient with deep dyslexia. *Neuropsychologia*, *20*, 559–568.

Funnell, E. (1983) Phonological processes in reading: New evidence from acquired dyslexia. *British Journal of Psychology*, *74*, 159–180.

Goldblum, M. C. (1985) Word comprehension in surface dyslexia. In K. E. Patterson, J. C. Marshall, & M. Coltheart (Eds.), *Surface Dyslexia*. London: Lawrence Erlbaum Associates Ltd.

Goodenough, C., Zurif, E. B., & Weintraub, S. (1977) Aphasics' attention to grammatical morphemes. *Language and Speech*, *20*, 11–19.

Goodglass, H. (1980) Disorders of naming following brain injury. *American Scientist*, *68*, 647–655.

Goodglass, H., Kaplan, E., Weintraub, S., & Ackerman, N. (1976) The "tip-of-the-tongue" phenomenon in aphasia. *Cortex*, *12*, 145–153.

Goodglass, H., Theurkauf, J. C., & Wingfield, A. (1984) Naming latencies as evidence for two modes of lexical retrieval. *Applied Psycholinguistics*, *5*, 135–146.

Hecaen, K. & Kremin, H. (1976) Neurolinguistic research on reading disorders resulting from left hemisphere lesions. Aphasic and "pure" alexias. In H. Whitaker and H. A. Whitaker (Eds.), *Studies in neurolinguistics*, *Vol. 2*. New York: Academic Press.

Heilman, K. M. & Rothi, L. J. (1982) Acquired reading disorders: A diagrammatic model. In R. N. Malatesha & P. G. Aaron (Eds.), *Reading disorders—varieties and treatment*. New York: Academic Press.

Hecaen, K. & Kremin, H. (1976) Neurolinguistic research on reading disorders resulting from left hemisphere lesions. Aphasic and "pure" alexias. In H. Whitaker & H. A. Whitaker (Eds.), *Studies in neurolinguistics*, *Vol. 2*. New York: Academic Press.

Heilman, K. M. & Rothi, L. J. (1982) Acquired reading disorders: A diagrammatic model. In R. N. Malatesha & P. G. Aaron (Eds.), *Reading disorders—varieties and treatment*. New York: Academic Press.

Heilman, K. M., Rothi, L., McFarling, D., & Rottmann, A. L. (1981) Transcortical sensory aphasia with relatively spared spontaneous speech and naming. *Archives of Neurology*, *38*, 236–239.

Heilman, K. M., Trucker, D. M., & Valenstein, E. (1976) A case of mixed transcortical aphasia with intact naming. *Brain*, *99*, 415–426.

Johnston, R. S. (1983) Developmental deep dyslexia. *Cortex*, *19*, 133–139.

Kay, J. & Patterson, K. E. (1985) Routes to meaning in surface dyslexia and dyographia. In K. E. Patterson, J. C. Marshall, & M. Coltheart (Eds.), *Surface dyslexia*. London: Lawrence Erlbaum Associates Ltd.

Kremin, H. (1980) Deux stratégies de lecture dissociables par la pathologie: Description d'un cas de dyslexie profonde et d'un cas de dyslexie de surface. In Etudes Neurolinguistiques. Université de Toulouse, Le mirail, *Grammatica*, *7*, 131–156.

Kremin, H. (1982) Alexia: Theory and research. In R. N. Malatesha & P. G. Aaron (Eds.), *Reading disorders—varieties and treatments*. New York: Academic Press.

Kremin, H. (1985) Routes and strategies in surface dyslexia. In K. E. Patterson, J. C. Marshall & M. Coltheart (Eds.), *Surface dyslexia*. London: Lawrence Erlbaum Associates Ltd.

Kremin, H. (1984) Comments on pathological reading behavior due to lesions of the left hemisphere. In R. N. Malatesha & H. A. Whitaker (Eds.), *Dyslexia: A global issue*. The Hague: Martinus Nijhoff.

Kremin, H. (1985) Routes and strategies in surface dyslexia. In K. E. Patterson, J. C. Marshall & M. Coltheart (Eds.), *Surface dyslexia*. London: Lawrence Erlbaum Associates Ltd.

Kremin, H. (1986) Spared naming without comprehension. *Journal of Neurolinguistics*, *2*, 131–150.

Lebrun, Y. & Devreux, F. (1984) Alexia in relation to aphasia and agnosia. In R. N. Malatesha & H. A. Whitaker (Eds.), *Dyslexia: A global issue*. The Hague: Martinus Nijhoff.

Marcel, T. (1980) Surface dyslexia and beginning reading: A revised hypothesis of the pronunciation of print and its impairments. In M. Coltheart, K. E. Patterson, & J. C. C. Marshall (Eds.), *Deep dyslexia*. London: Routledge & Kegan Paul.

Margolin, D., Marcel, T., & Carlson, N. (1985) Common mechanisms in dysnomia and post-semantic surface dyslexia. In K. E. Patterson, J. C. Marshall, & M. Coltheart (Eds.), *Surface dyslexia*. London: Lawrence Erlbaum Associates Ltd.

Marin, O. S. M., Saffran, E. M., & Schwartz, M. T. (1976) Dissociations of language in aphasia: Implications for normal function. *Annals of the New York Academy of Sciences*, *280*, 868–884.

Marshall, J. C. & Newcombe, F. (1973) Pattern of paralexia: A psycholinguistic approach. *Journal of Psycholinguistic Research*, *2*, 175–199.

Morton, J. (1979) Facilitation in word recognition: Experiments causing change in the logogen model. In P. A. Kolers, M. E. Wrolstad, & H. Bouma (Eds.), *Processing of visible language*. New York: Plenum Publishing Company.

Morton, J. (1984) Naming. In S. Newman & R. Epstein (Eds.), *Dysphasia*. Edinburgh: Churchill Livingston.

Morton, J. & Patterson, K. E. (1980) A new attempt at an interpretation or an attempt at a new interpretation. In M. Coltheart, K. E. Patterson, & J. C. Marshall (Eds.), *Deep dyslexia*. London: Routledge & Kegan Paul.

Newcombe, F. & Marshall, J. C. (1980) Transcoding and lexical stabilization in deep dyslexia. In M. Coltheart, K. E. Patterson, & J. C. Marshall (Eds.), *Deep dyslexia*. London: Routledge & Kegan Paul.

Newcombe, F. & Marshall, J. C. (1981) On psycholinguistic classifications of the acquired dyslexias. *Bulletin of the Orton Society*, *31*, 29–46.

Newcombe, F. & Marshall, J. C. (1985) Reading and writing by letter sounds. In K. E. Patterson, J. C. Marshall, & M. Coltheart (Eds.), *Surface dyslexia*. London: Lawrence Erlbaum Associates Ltd.

Nolan, K. A. & Caramazza, A. (1982) Modality: Independent impairments in word processing in a deep dyslexic patient. *Brain and Language*, *16*, 237–264.

Patterson, K. E. (1978) Phonemic dyslexia: Errors of meaning and the meaning of errors. *Quarterly Journal of Experimental Psychology*, *30*, 587–601.

Patterson, K. E. (1981) Neuropsychological approaches to the study of reading. *British Journal of Psychology*, *72*, 151–174.

Patterson, K. E. (1982) The relation between reading and phonological coding: Further neuropsychological observations. In A. W. Ellis (Ed.), *Normality and pathology in cognitive functioning*. London: Academic Press.

Patterson, K. E. & Marcel, A. J. (1977) Aphasia, dyslexia and the phonological coding of written words. *Quarterly Journal of Experimental Psychology*, *29*, 307–318.

Patterson, K. E. & Morton, J. C. (1985) From orthography to phonology: An attempt at an old interpretation. In K. E. Patterson, J. C. Marshall, & M. Coltheart (Eds), *Surface Dyslexia*. London: Lawrence Erlbaum Associates Ltd.

Ratcliff, G. & Newcombe, F. (1982) Object recognition: Some deductions from clinical evidence. In A. W. Ellis (Ed.), *Normality and pathology in cognitive functions*. London: Academic Press.

Richardson, J. T. E. (1975) Further evidence on the effect of word imageability in dyslexia. *Quarterly Journal of Experimental Psychology*, *27*, 445–449.

Saffran, E. M. (1980) Reading in deep dyslexia is not ideographic. *Neuropsychologia*, *18*, 219–244.

Sartori, G., Barry, C., & Job, R. (1984) Phonological dyslexia: A review. In R. N. Malatesha & H. A. Whitaker (Eds.), *Dyslexia: A global issue*. The Hague Martinus Nijhoff.

Shallice, T. (1979) Case study approach in neuropsychological research. *Journal of Clinical Neuropsychology*, *1*, 183–211.

Shallice, T. & Coughlan, A. K. (1980) Modality specific word comprehension deficits in deep dyslexia. *Journal of Neurology, Neurosurgery and Psychiatry*, *43*, 866–872.

Shallice, T. & Warrington, E. K. (1975) Word recognition in a phonemic dyslexic patient. *Quarterly Journal of Experimental Psychology*, *27*, 187–199.

Shallice, T. & Warrington, E. K. (1980) Single and multiple component central dyslexia syndromes. In M. Coltheart, K. E. Patterson, & J. C. Marshall (Eds.), *Deep dyslexia*. London: Routledge & Kegan Paul.

Shallice, T., Warrington, E. K., & McCarthy, R. (1983) Reading without semantics. *Quarterly Journal of Experimental Psychology*, *35A*, 111–138.

Schwartz, M. F., Saffran, E. M., & Marin, O. S. M. (1980) Fractioning the reading process in dementia: Evidence for word specific print-to-sound associations. In M. Coltheart, K. Patterson, & J. C. Marshall (Eds.), *Deep dyslexia*. London: Routledge & Kegan Paul.

Symonds, C. Sir (1953) Aphasia. *Journal of Neurology, Neurosurgery and Psychiatry*, *16*, 1–6.

Temple, C. (1985) Surface dyslexia and the development of reading. In K. E. Patterson, J. C. Marshall, & M. Coltheart (Eds.), *Surface dyslexia*. London: Lawrence Erlbaum Associates Ltd.

Warrington, E. K. (1981) Concrete word dyslexia. *British Journal of Psychology*, *72*, 175–196.

Warren, C. & Morton, J. (1982) The effects of priming on picture recognition. *British Journal of Psychology*, *73*, 117–129.

Warrington, E. K. (1981) Concrete word dyslexia. *British Journal of Psychology*, *72*, 175–196.

12 Mechanisms for Reading Non-words: Evidence from a Case of Phonological Dyslexia in an Italian Reader

P. De Bastiani
Istituto di Clinica Neurologica, Università di Ferrara, Ferrara, Italy

C. Barry[1]
School of Psychology, University of Wales, College of Cardiff, U.K.

M. Carreras
Istituto di Clinica Neurologica, Università di Ferrara, Ferrara, Italy

INTRODUCTION

Normal adult readers experience relatively little difficulty reading aloud orthographically legal, pronounceable, but quite meaningless non-words (such as *POG*, *KEAB*, or even the "Italian" *MIZIO*). That is, they are able to construct an acceptable phonological code, and articulate it, for items that a priori cannot be fully represented in their store of word knowledge, the internal lexicon. Patterson (1982) refers to this ability as *assembled* phonological recoding, and distinguishes it from the means by which all words may be pronounced: *Addressed* phonology becomes available only after words have been recognised and their pronunciations retrieved from an internal phonological lexicon. Although assembled phonological recoding may be involved in the pronunciation of words (at least, that is, some words, some of the time), it is logically necessary for reading aloud non-words. Two main classes of psychological theory have been proposed to account for the mechanism by which assembled phonological recoding occurs: those that impute the use of purely *non-lexical* spelling-to-sound correspondences, and those that imply that the

[1] Dr Barry was supported by a fellowship from the European Training Programme in Brain and Behaviour Research (from the European Science Foundation).

oral reading of non-words involves a process of analogy operating upon stored lexical knowledge. We shall now consider each of these two classes of models (rule-based correspondences and lexical analogy) in turn.

Dual Route Models

A popular version of a "dual-route" model of oral reading is shown in Fig. 1. Within this model (advocated most persuasively by Coltheart, 1981, 1984), non-words are pronounced by a non-lexical phonological recoding system that is separate from (and operates independently of) the lexical-processing system. Coltheart (1978, 1980) argues that the non-lexical system uses a set of lexically abstracted grapheme-to-phoneme correspondence (GPC) rules. A letter-string would be orthographically parsed into graphemes to which GPC rules would assign phonemes, which are then blended into a single, coherent pronunciation. The GPC rules are assumed to operate on the basis of how graphemes, or what Venezky (1970) calls "functional spelling units", are most commonly pronounced in words. For example, Venezky identifies the *major correspondence* of the grapheme EA as /i:/ (as in *EACH* and *CLEAN*). and so this vowel phoneme would be assigned to this grapheme by the GPC rules. In this model, the non-word *KEAB*, for example, should be parsed into the graphemes K + EA + B, to which GPC rules would assign the major phonological correspondences /k/ + /i:/ + /b/, which would then be blended into the pronunciation "keeb". Note that such GPC rules would produce incorrect pronunciations for a substantial minority of English words, as in the following examples of words that contain *minor* correspondences: *GREAT* and *STEAK* (where EA is pronounced /ei/), and *HEAD* and *SWEAT* (where EA is pronounced /e/). Such words are often called "irregular" or "exception" words, as are others with unique and/or more exotic spelling-to-sound correspondences (such as *SEW*, *COLONEL*, and *YACHT*). Dual-route models assume that all known words may be read using the lexical "route" (i.e. commencing with the word-recognition system shown in Fig. 1), and that regular (but not exception) words may also be correctly pronounced by the non-lexical "route". Non-words can be pronounced only by the non-lexical route. Dual-route models have been generally reticent as to how spelling-to-sound conversion rules come to be acquired; they may be explicitly taught, or they may come to be abstracted from developing lexical knowledge. However, a major feature of dual-route models is that such rules are implemented essentially independently of lexical processing.

Patterson and Morton (1985) have proposed a model in which the non-lexical route implements spelling-to-sound recoding at two levels simultaneously: The phonological correspondences of both graphemes and what

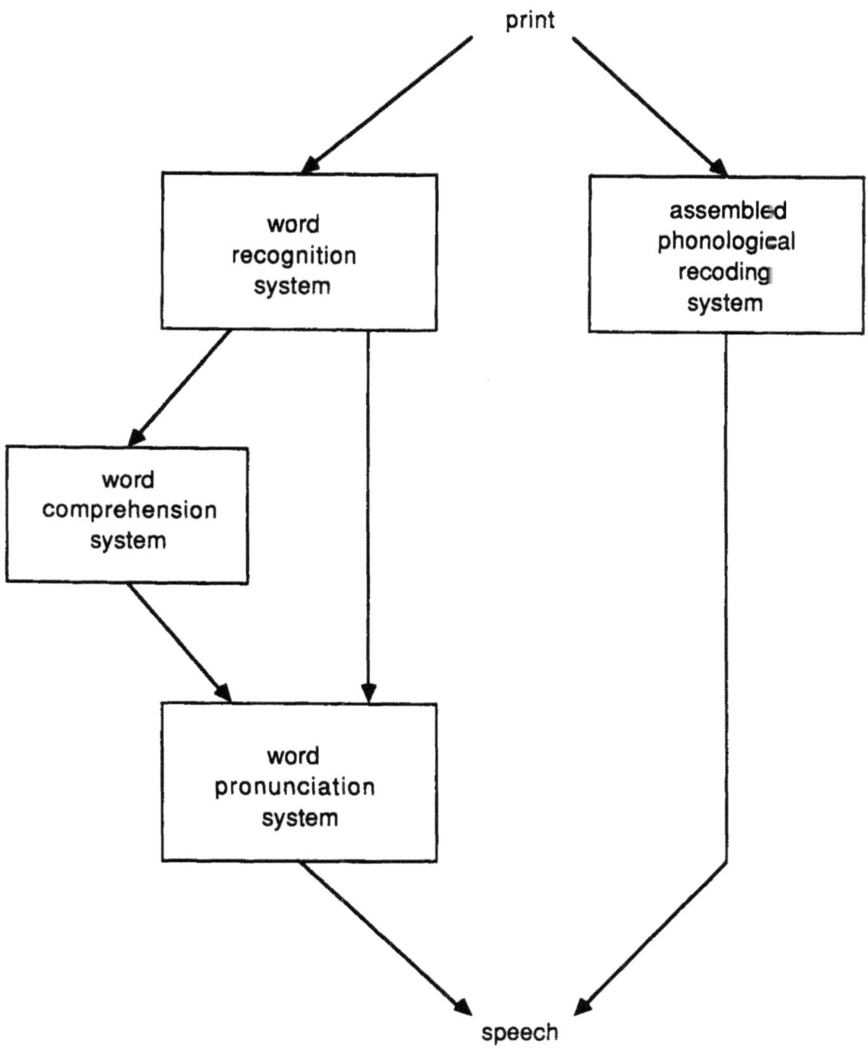

FIG 1. A dual-route model of oral reading (adapted from Coltheart, 1981).

they call orthographic "bodies" (which are terminal vowel plus consonant units, such as -EAD) are assumed to be activated. For example, the nonword *VEAD* would be given the pronunciation /vi:d/ by the GPC system, but the pronunciation /ved/ by the body system, because the majority of words ending in -EAD are pronounced -/ed/ (i.e. this system uses the major correspondences of the orthographic bodies). Patterson and Morton propose that the GPC system is the one that usually determines which pronunciation is given, although conflicting outputs from the two may produce interference (and so slow processing). Shallice, Warrington, and McCarthy (1983) have also proposed a model in which the assembled phonological recoding system is assumed to operate simultaneously on the phonological correspondences of orthographic units of a variety of different sizes, although they suggest that these range from graphemes and consonant clusters, to sub-syllables ("bodies" such as -EAD) and syllables, to morphemes. The non-word *POG*, for example, might be parsed (by Shallice et al.'s postulated "visual word-form system"), and appropriate phonological forms accessed for, P + OG and PO + G, as well as P + O + G.

However, both Patterson and Morton's and Shallice et al.'s models are still essential "dual-route" models, in that they preserve the distinction between assembled and addressed phonological recoding as being systems that operate using different kinds of stored knowledge: word reading generally uses lexically-specific pronunciation knowledge, whereas non-word reading utilises separately represented knowledge of the phonological correspondences of orthographic units smaller than words.

Lexical Analogy Models

In contrast to dual-route models, which posit separate representational systems for lexical and non-lexical (or, perhaps more appropriately, *sub*lexical) processing, the lexical-analogy family of models propose that assembled phonological recoding is a processing system that operates upon a single representational system of print-to-sound correspondences common to all reading processes, namely the stored knowledge of how words are pronounced (i.e. addressed phonology). The phonological forms of new words and non-words can be assembled from this lexical knowledge by processes of segmentation and analogy.

Glushko (1979) found that non-words with orthographic segments that are pronounced inconsistently in real English words (such as AVE, as in *CAVE* and *HAVE*), took longer to read aloud than control non-words (with consistently pronounced segments, such as -AZE, which is always pronounced as in *GAZE*, *HAZE*, etc.), and that they were also occasionally pronounced with the minor correspondence of the vowel grapheme (i.e. "irregularly"), such as *TAVE* = /tæv/. At the very least, this result suggests that simple, deterministic GPC rules are not the only source of information utilised in non-word reading. Subsequent research by Kay and Marcel (1981) has further shown that the actual pronunciations given to non-words with inconsistently pronounced segments may be biased by the prior presentation of orthographically similar words. For example, *HEAF* was pronounced with the minor correspondence of the vowel EA (as /hef/), and not "regularly" as /hi:f/, more often if the irregular word *DEAF* had preceded the non-word. This suggests that assembled phonological recoding does not take place independently of lexical influence.

As an alternative to how non-words are assumed to be read in dual-route models Glushko (1979, 1981), Marcel (1980), Kay and Marcel (1981), and Henderson (1982) have proposed versions of lexical-analogy models, in which stimulus non-words access lexically stored (or addressed) phonological information. Glushko's model might be described as one of "phonological activation and synthesis". Non-words would activate the phonology of words in the same "orthographic neighbourhood"; thus, *POG*, for example, might activate the phonology of the orthographically similar words *DOG*, *LOG*, *POT*, *POD*, *PIG*, *PEG*, etc. This lexically activated phonology would then be somehow synthesised into the pronunciation "pog". The precise computational details of how such synthesis is achieved are unclear, although Glushko argues that lexical inconsistencies (such as the phonology of the segment -EAD) would slow and/or interfere with this process.

Marcel's model, which is represented in Fig. 2, is similar in principle, but more detailed. It might be described as "orthographic segmentation and phonological assembly". Its essential features are as follows. Stimulus non-words are orthographically segmented in all possible ways (e.g. *POG* = P--, PO-, -O-, -OG, --G), and that these segments are then used to match orthographic addresses of the lexical entries (in the input lexicon in Fig. 2) of words containing the segments in equivalent positions (e.g. all words beginning with P or PO, words containing a medial O, and words ending in OG or G). This matching then activates the phonology of the words (in the output lexicon in Fig. 2). Marcel assumes that this addressed phonology is segmentable, and so the phonology corresponding to the orthographic segments (as it occurs in each activated word) becomes available. The new pronunciation ("pog") would then result from an assembly of the activated and segmented lexical phonology, although two important constraints operate in this process. First, larger segments will override smaller ones, and so will be more powerful in determining the actual pronunciation produced (if there is any conflict). Second, segments corresponding to real words and morphemes will predominate over sub-word segments, and will be retrieved from the output lexicon as whole units.

Non-word reading in lexical-analogy models is assumed to involve both the activation of orthographically similar words (or segments thereof), and the synthesis or assembly (or, in Henderson's model, "pooling") of subsections of addressed phonological knowledge.

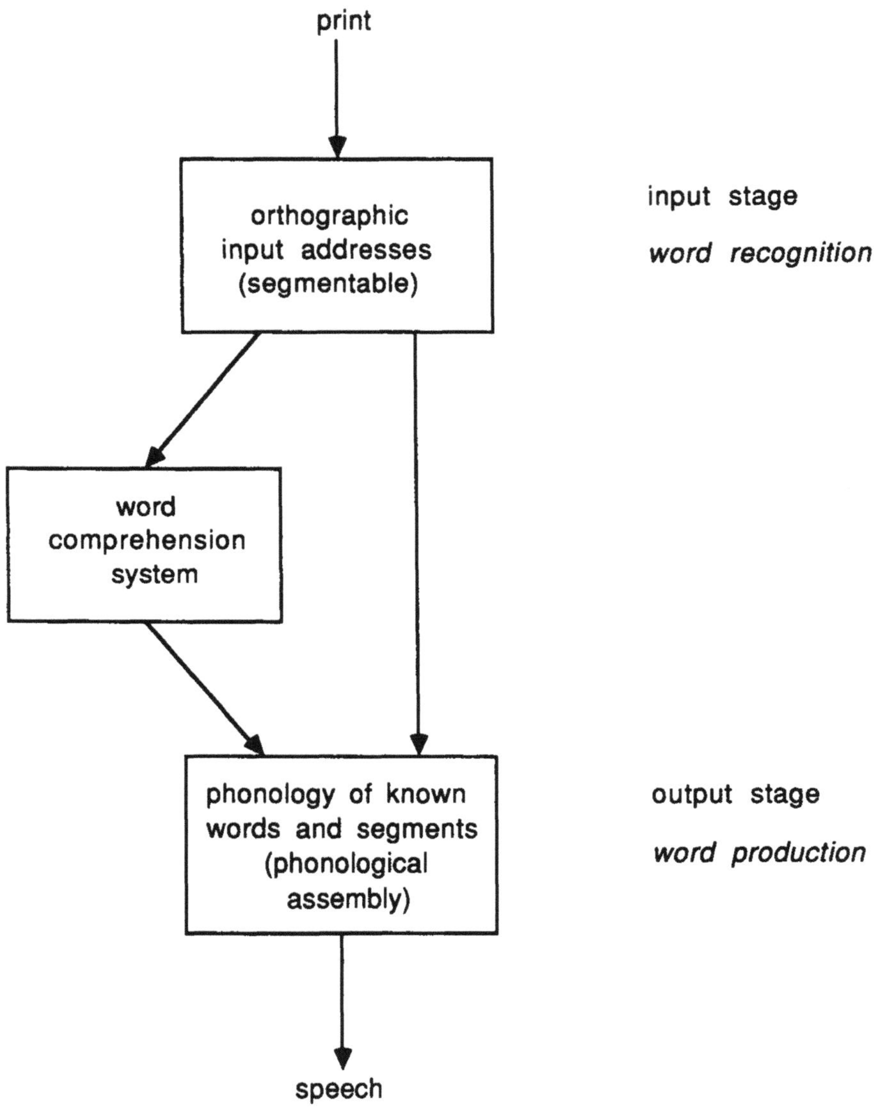

FIG 2. A lexical-analogy model of oral reading (adapted from Marcel, 1980).

THEORETICAL IMPAIRMENTS OF NON-WORD READING

It is illuminating to consider in purely theoretical terms how functional impairments to the means by which assembled phonological recoding occurs within either type of model might manifest in disturbances of non-word reading. Such an exercise serves both to clarify one's understanding of (and so fully expose one's assumptions underlying) detailed operational characteristics of the models, and to provide a conceptually derived foundation against which to compare the results from acquired dyslexic patients with specific disturbances of non-word reading. As extreme and fundamentally contrasting accounts we shall consider only the non-word-reading models of Coltheart and Marcel.

Non-word Reading by Spelling-to-Sound Conversion Rules

From the dual-route model, if the non-lexical route (i.e. the phonological recoding system) was completely abolished (and so functionally inoperative), then no non-words would be able to be read. Word-reading ability, however, should be completely unaffected, as the lexical route (which is assumed to be functionally independent) should operate normally. One would also expect that no substantive responses at all should be made to non-words, as the lexical route can only access the phonology of known words. As Coltheart (1984) has boldly stated: "The lexical procedure is *by definition* mute when confronted with a letter-string which is not a word" (p. 365, his emphasis). However, this pattern of predicted performance is predicated upon the following three assumptions:

1. The lexical and non-lexical routes operate truly independently, in that an impairment of the non-lexical route would not necessarily produce modifications to the normal operation of the lexical route.
2. The lexical route is able to work for all words; that is, phonological recoding is not an obligatory process in the recognition of known words.
3. The lexical route operates with a high degree of specificity; that is, the phonology of words that are orthographically similar to a stimulus letter-string would not be confused at the stage of response generation.

A partially impaired non-lexical phonological recoding system should also leave word reading unaffected, although non-word reading might not be totally impossible. Partial impairments of graphemic parsing, inaccuracy in the application of GPG rules (particularly, perhaps, in the application of rules requiring sensitivity to graphemic context, as in the vowel lengthening "final-E" rule, as in *HAT* v. *HATE* for example), or impairments of phonemic blending, would lead to the production of frequent errors in non-word reading. However, one should expect that such errors would generally tend to involve the production of physically similar non-words as responses to non-words.

Non-word Reading by Analogy to Lexical Phonological Knowledge

From the lexical-analogy model, there could be impairments at either the input or the output stages shown in Fig. 2.

If the input stage were totally destroyed, then there should be no reading at all, of either words or non-words, as no orthographic addresses could be accessed.

If there were only partial impairments to the input stage, then one might expect a large number of orthographic confusions to be made to both words and non-words, which might also be expected to lead to a deficit in performance in the lexical decision (word/non-word discrimination) task. One might also expect that rules governing the overriding of smaller segments to be malfunctional.

If the output stage were totally destroyed, then the system should be completely mute, although semantic and lexical decisions should be able to be made.

If there were only partial impairments to the assembly function necessary for non-word reading at the output stage, then word reading could be unaffected (as word pronunciations should be retrieved as wholes), although if one assumed that morphological analysis was an inherent feature of this model then there might be some difficulty with morphemically complex words. Non-word reading, however, should be greatly impaired, although the phonology of visually similar words, and/or segments therefore, would be activated, and might be available to influence oral responses.

A CASE OF PHONOLOGICAL DYSLEXIA IN AN ITALIAN READER

These provisional predictions will now be compared with the actual reading performance of an Italian phonological dyslexic patient. Phonological dyslexia is characterised by selectively impaired non-word reading ability coupled with fairly well-preserved word-reading ability. The received interpretation of phonological dyslexia is that it results from an impairment of assembled phonological recoding (see Beauvois & Dérouesné, 1979; Dérouesné & Beauvois, 1979; Patterson, 1982). A review of this variety of acquired dyslexia is provided by Sartori, Barry, and Job (1984).

Case Report

A.M.M. is a right-handed woman who suffered a left-hemisphere stroke at the age of 36 years. At the time of testing (three to five months post-stroke), she showed a moderate non-fluent aphasia, but no other major neurological disturbances.

Her oral repetition was tested by presenting 50 words and 50 non-words (of various lengths). She correctly repeated all 50 words and 37 of the non-words. Her errors tended to be on the longer non-words, and all involved the production of a phonetically similar non-word. Her lexical decision performance was good. Presented with 60 words and 60 structurally similar non-words, she correctly classified 58 of the words (97%) and 54 of the non-words (90%). In fact, this performance may actually underestimate her competence in this task, as her few errors tended to be made in clusters, indicative perhaps more of a wavering of attention than genuine difficulty in the process of lexical access.

Word Reading

A.M.M.'s word reading was tested on various lists of words, including concrete and abstract nouns, verbs, and function words. She correctly read 85.8% of all nouns, 57.8% of verbs (which were not, unfortunately, matched for word frequency), and 84.5% of function words. Summed over all classes of words, she correctly read 82.3%, made corrected errors to 7.2%, and made uncorrected errors to 10.5%. She never omitted any word, and only 16.9% of her initial errors involved the production of a non-word. The majority of her errors involved the production of structurally (i.e. orthographically) similar words (e.g. *PARTE*→ "padre", *INDIVIDUO* → "invidia", *MARCE* → "barca", *VOCAZIONE* → "votazione"). She also produced some "derivational" errors, involving the production of words that shared the same root morpheme as the stimulus, and these were made most frequently to verbs (e.g. *SCRIVIAMO*→ "scrivere", *USCIRE* → "uscito", *CHILOMETRO* → "chilometri", *PARTIRE*→ "partite"). Most of her errors to function words involved the production of another function word, although these tended to be visually similar also (e.g. *NE* → "me", *PERCIO'* → "perche", *CUI* → "coi", *PIU'*→ "pero").

A.M.M. was presented with 99 of the 100 nouns listed in the Italian norms for concreteness provided by Roncato (1974). She read 84 correctly, and made 9 visual errors, 4 derivational errors, and 2 other errors. There were no significant differences between the stimulus words that produced these responses on either concreteness or word frequency (values of which were taken from Bortolini, Tagliavini, & Zampolli, 1972). Length had only a small and unreliable effect on her reading success; the words to which she produced visual and derivational errors tended to be slightly longer than those she read correctly (8.6 and 9.0 v. 7.4 letters respectively).

A.M.M.'s visual errors appear to be qualitatively different from those produced by deep dyslexic patients who also have gross impairments of non-word reading. Nolan and Caramazza (1982) and Barry and Richardson (1988) found that visual errors in deep dyslexic patients tend to be made to rather abstract words, and tend to involve the production of words more concrete than the stimulus. Twenty-three of A.M.M.'s visual errors were presented to 10 independent judges to rate for both relative concreteness and relative word frequency. Only 7 of the 23 errors were rated as being more concrete than the stimulus word to which they were produced, 9/23 were rated as being less concrete, and 9/23 showed no difference. Of her 23 errors, 7 were rated as being more frequent than the stimulus word, and 14 were rated as being less frequent.

Non-word Reading

In contrast to her relatively well-preserved word reading, A.M.M. was substantially impaired when required to read aloud non-words. In a number of different tests, she was presented with a total of 176 pronounceable non-words to read aloud. She was able to read correctly only seven. However, she always produced some response, and her most common erroneous attempt was to produce a visually similar word (e.g. *FUNVO*→ "fungo"), or a string of such words. The pattern of her performance did not differ if the non-words were presented in lists (where she was told that only non-words would be presented), or if they were intermixed with words. Table 1 shows the distribution of her non-word reading attempts and some representative examples of her errors.

When A.M.M. produced a visually similar word to a stimulus non-word, she did so fairly promptly. However, when she produced an incorrect non-word as a response, she did so rather slowly and haltingly, with a laboured pronunciation. This was especially true when she produced a non-word within a string of visually similar words. Of those responses in which she produced strings containing words and non-words, she produced a word first in all but one occasion. A.M.M. clearly knew that non-words were non-words. Her lexical decision performance was very good, and she often peppered her attempts to read non-words with comments and exclamations, such as "no", "ma" (I don't know), or "niente" (nothing).

DISCUSSION

A.M.M. correctly read 82.3% of words, but only 4% of non-words. This striking dissociation clearly shows that phonological dyslexia can exist in a reader of the highly regular orthography of Italian. Italian has extremely regular spelling-to-sound relationships: There are no irregular words, only four homophone pairs (resulting from the fact that the very rare letter H is silent at the beginning of words, as in *HANNO* v. *ANNO*), and only relatively few polysyllabic words with irregular stress patterns. In principle, therefore, Italian could be read aloud with almost perfect success using

TABLE 1
The Percentage of A.M.M.'s Reading Attempts to 176 Stimulus Non-words

Response Category	%
Correct	4.0
BIMPO→ "bimpo"	
Omitted	0.0
Single visually similar word	42.0
NIETE→ "niente"	
IRONCA→ "ironica"	
CONTONARDO→ "contorno"	
Single visually dissimilar word	3.4
SICRO→ "silenzio"	
Single visually similar non-word	14.2
SILSO→ "sil-to"	
MUBRU→ "mu-ba-re"	
Single visually dissimilar non-word	5.1
RELFO→ "rol-le-to"	
Two visually similar words	11.9
CANTRA→ "capra, canta"	
VONTE→ "fonte, ponte"	
DREDO→ "credo, credere"	
Two visually similar non-words	5.7
RELSA→ "res-na, ren-sa"	
Visually similar words and non-words	13.6
CALBO→ "salvo, sam-bo"	
MERMA→ "mezza, mer-za"	
TARFO→ "tazza, tar-ra"	

assembled phonological recoding alone. A.M.M. was greatly impaired in her ability to construct non-lexical phonological codes, but did not show a total abolition of her ability to read words, which implies that assembled phonological recoding is not obligatory for reading Italian words. A.M.M. had not learned a new strategy for reading words, but relied upon her extant lexical processing system. By extension, it is likely that a lexical reading route is also available to all skilled adult Italian readers. Turvey, Feldman, and Lukatela (1984) concluded that the regular orthography of Serbo-Croatian "constrains the reader to a phonologically analytic strategy" (p. 81). The existence of phonological dyslexia in Italian suggests that the regularity of Italian orthography does *not* obligate readers to assembled phonological recoding for word reading.

A.M.M.'s impaired non-word reading cannot be attributed solely to articulatory output difficulties. Although her repetition of non-words was not perfect, it was considerably better than her non-word reading, and it was also qualitatively different, in that she never produced physically similar words when incorrectly repeating non-words. A.M.M.'s pattern of disturbed non-word reading demands the interpretation that it results from a functional impairment of the system responsible for assembled phonological recoding. Of the hypothetically derived patterns of non-word reading deficits discussed earlier, A.M.M.'s reading appears to be most similar to that resulting from damage to the phonological assembly function within Marcel's lexical-analogy model. Non-words appear to activate visually similar words, whose pronunciations are frequently available to her. Her major problem would appear to be in her inability to segment and assemble appropriately this lexically activated phonology.

However, an alternative explanation within the dual-route model may be possible. It might be argued that A.M.M. has both a grossly impaired non-lexical phonological recoding system and some disturbances within the lexical route. If one argued that the thresholds of word-detector units within the word-recognition system have been lowered (i.e. if one relaxed assumption 3 described earlier), then this may explain why visually similar words are produced to non-words. Such a proposal is not without its own difficulties, however. First, A.M.M. displays very good lexical decision performance. This indicates that any modifications to the precision of the word-recognition system would need to be restricted to those occasions when she was required to read non-words aloud. Furthermore, any lowering of word-detector thresholds would need to be implemented reasonably quickly, as she produces word responses to non-words with surprising alacrity, even when she has been informed that only non-words would be presented. Second, she often produces strings of visually similar words, which may differ from the stimulus non-word at a variety of letter positions (e.g. *NORTO*→ "morto, nosto"). This would appear to indicate either that multiple orthographic parsings had been used to address words in an input lexicon, or that the lexical-processing system may routinely produce a variety of potentially available responses. Third, she sometimes does produce non-words, although they are usually incorrect. Such responses contain phonology from word segments, and, in her strings of word and non-word responses, these segments are mainly from those very words that she produced immediately prior to her (incorrectly) assembled non-word.

Whereas these problems might be resolvable if one proposed that the lowering of word-recognition thresholds was a specific compensatory strategy used only when attempting to read non-words, the fact that A.M.M. actually produced some non-words surely suggests that a lexical activation and assembly procedure can work at least in principle. The *post hoc* and somewhat tortuous modification to the dual-route model discussed earlier is difficult to distinguish from our conceptualisation of the lexical-analogy model, although we submit that it is within the latter that

A.M.M.'s erroneous non-word reading performance can be most readily and parsimoniously explained.

Funnell (1983) has reported a phonological dyslexic patient (W.B.) with a gross impairment of non-word reading (he read none of 20 non-words) coupled with well-preserved word reading (between 86% and 9[illegible]% were read correctly). Funnell considered an explanation of W.B.'s performance within the lexical-analogy model and rejected it for the following reasons. W.B. was able both to detect and pronounce words embedded in non-words (e.g. *ALFORSUT*→"*for*"), and to pronounce separately morphemes embedded in words (e.g. *INSIDE*→"in, side" and *FATHER*→"*fat, her*"), which indicates that orthographic segmentation was intact (at least for detecting words). W.B. was also able to repeat separately morphemic components of an auditorily presented word (e.g. "forget" → "for, get"), and to pronounce only the initial phoneme of a spoken word (e.g. "cat"→"cuh"), which Funnell took as evidence that phonological assembly was also intact. Funnell concluded that this evidence "invalidates the claim that nonword reading is normally accomplished by lexical analogy procedures" (p. 172).

However, W.B. was also able to repeat spoken letter-strings that he could not read. It is possible, therefore, that Funnell's phonological assembly tasks were performed by intact auditory-to-phonological recoding processes and not necessarily by reading-specific processes of the segmentation and assembly of addressed phonology. Perhaps more appropriate tests would have involved phonological segmentation and manipulation of *printed* letter-strings that were not read aloud. Unfortunately, we were unable to follow-up A.M.M. using such tests, although if our account is correct, we would predict that she should be severely impaired segmenting and assembling such phonology.

As A.M.M. sometimes produces non-words (although usually the incorrect non-word), can we really argue that her reading reflects an impairment of the assembly of segmentable lexical phonology? Do we want to both have our cake and segment it? We think not. A.M.M.'s problems would appear to reflect an impaired but not a totally abolished phonological assembly mechanism. This would account for her rather laboured pronunciation of her rarely produced non-words. Indeed, such non-words are usually produced in a stilted, syllable-by-syllable fashion, and in a substantial number of trials, these syllables are segments of visually similar words she produced immediately before the attempted assembly of her non-word response (e.g. *TAMPO*→"tango, *tan*-po").

There remains the problem of A.M.M.'s word-reading errors. All the phonological dyslexic patients reviewed by Sartori et al. (1984), including Funnell's W.B., make visual errors to words, which is something of an embarrassment for proposed "single component" functional impairment accounts (see Shallice & Warrington, 1980) within either the dual-route or the lexical-analogy model. We have shown that for A.M.M. (and we suspect this is also true for other phonological dyslexic patients) visual errors do not appear to be sensitive to any of the psycholinguistic variables that characterise (and so render explicable within models of word recognition) visual errors in deep dyslexia. We would like to suggest tentatively that visual errors in phonological dyslexia may be slightly less difficult to explain within the lexical-analogy model, as they may be due to: (1) problems of conflict of orthographic segmentation and phonological assembly operating for long words, words containing embedded words, and morphemically complex words; and/or (2) some general perturbation in how the orthographic segmentation and phonological assembly functions interface. We would like to think that the detailed study of phonological dyslexic patients' erroneous non-word reading attempts may profitably assist the more explicit specification of such complex mechanisms.

CONCLUSIONS

To summarise, we draw two main conclusions. First, phonological dyslexia can exist in readers of the regular ("shallow" or "transparent") orthography of Italian. This suggests that Italian need not necessarily require assembled phonological recoding for word reading. To paraphrase Marshall and Newcombe's (1981) discussion of how transcriptions in the International Phonetic Alphabet might be read, the regularity of Italian orthography may *allow* successful reading solely by phonological recoding, but it does not *demand* it. Second, A.M.M.'s pattern of erroneous non-word reading attempts agrees more with our predictions derived from a lexical analogy model than with those derived from a dual-route model: She seems to activate, have available to her, and attempt to segment lexical (addressed) phonology. This suggests that it is feasible to interpret at least some cases of phonological dyslexia within lexical-analogy models of oral reading, and its existence should not be taken as unambiguous support for dual-route models. The *separability* of non-word from word reading abilities shown in phonological dyslexia should not necessarily be taken to support the view that they are functionally *independent*.

REFERENCES

Barry, C. & Richardson, J. T. E. (1988) Accounts of oral reading in deep dyslexia. In H. A. Whitaker (Ed.), *Phonological processes and brain mechanisms*. New York: Springer.

Beauvois, M.-F. & Dérouesné, J. (1979) Phonological alexia: Three dissociations. *Journal of Neurology, Neurosurgery, and Psychiatry*, *42*, 1115–1124.

Bortolini, U., Tagliavini, C., & Zampolli, A. (1972) *Lessico di frequenza della lingua italiana contemporanea*. Milan: Garzanti.

Coltheart, M. (1978) Lexical access in simple reading tasks. In G. Underwood (Ed.), *Strategies of information processing*. London: Academic Press.

Coltheart, M. (1980) Reading, phonological recoding and deep dyslexia. In M. Coltheart, K. Patterson, & J. C. Marshall (Eds.), *Deep dyslexia*. London: Routledge & Kegan Paul.

Coltheart, M. (1981) Disorders of reading and their implications for models of normal reading. *Visible Language*, *15*, 245–286.

Coltheart, M. (1984) Acquired dyslexias and normal reading. In R. N. Malatesha & H. A. Whitaker (Eds.), *Dyslexia: A global issue*. The Hague: Martinus Nijhoff.

Dérouesné, J. & Beauvois, M.-F. (1979) Phonological processing in reading: Data from alexia. *Journal of Neurology, Neurosurgery, and Psychiatry*, *42*, 1125–1132.

Funnell, E. (1983) Phonological processes in reading: New evidence from acquired dyslexia. *British Journal of Psychology*, *74*, 159–180.

Glushko, R. J. (1979) The organization and activation of lexical knowledge in reading aloud. *Journal of Experimental Psychology: Human Perception and Performance*, *5*, 674–691.

Glushko, R. J. (1981) Principles for pronouncing print: The psychology of phonography. In A. M. Lesgold & C. A. Perfetti (Eds.), *Interactive processes in reading*. Hillsdale, N.J.: Lawrence Erlbaum Associates Inc.

Henderson, L. (1982) *Orthography and word recognition in reading*. London: Academic Press.

Kay, J. & Marcel, A. (1981) One process, not two, in reading aloud: Lexical analogies do the work of non-lexical rules. *Quarterly Journal of Experimental Psychology*, *33A*, 397–413.

Marcel, A. (1980) Surface dyslexia and beginning reading: A revised hypothesis of the pronunciation of print and its impairments. In M. Coltheart, K. Patterson, & J. C. Marshall (Eds.), *Deep dyslexia*. London: Routledge & Kegan Paul.

Marshall, J. C. & Newcombe, F. (1981) Lexical access: A perspective from pathology. *Cognition*, *10*, 209–214.

Nolan, K. L. & Caramazza, A. (1982) Modality-independent impairments in word processing in a deep dyslexic patient. *Brain and Language*, *16*, 237–264.

Patterson, K. E. (1982) The relation between reading and phonological coding: Further neuropsychological observations. In A. W. Ellis (Ed.), *Normality and pathology in cognitive functions*. London: Academic Press.

Patterson, K. E. & Morton, J. C. (1985) From orthography to phonology: An attempt at an old interpretation. In K. E. Patterson, J. C. Marshall, & M. Coltheart (Eds.), *Surface dyslexia*. London: Lawrence Erlbaum Associates Ltd.

Roncato, S. (1974) Concreteness, imagery, meaningfulness and a new index: Values for 100 Italian nouns. *Italian Journal of Psychology*, *1*, 195–209.

Sartori, G., Barry, C., & Job, R. (1984) Phonological dyslexia: A review. In R. N. Malatesha & H. A. Whitaker (Eds.), *Dyslexia: A global issue*. The Hague: Martinus Nijhoff.

Shallice, T. & Warrington, E. K. (1980) Single and multiple component central dyslexic syndromes. In M. Coltheart, K. Patterson, & J. C. Marshall (Eds.), *Deep dyslexia*. London: Routledge & Kegan Paul.

Shallice, T., Warrington, E. K., & McCarthy, R. (1983) Reading without semantics. *Quarterly Journal of Experimental Psychology*, *35A*, 111–138.

Turvey, M. T., Feldman, L. B., & Lukatela, G. (1984) The Serbo-Croatian orthography constrains the reader to a phonologically analytic strategy. In L. Henderson (Ed.), *Orthographies and reading: Perspectives from cognitive psychology, neuropsychology, and linguistics*. London: Lawrence Erlbaum Associates Ltd.

Venezky, R. L. (1970) *The structure of English orthography*. The Hague: Mouton.

PART IV: FACE RECOGNITION

13 Face Perception: Underlying Processes and Hemispheric Contribution

J. Sergent
Department of Neurology and Neurosurgery, McGill University, Montreal, Canada

INTRODUCTION

Among the numerous deficits that may result from cerebral damage, impairment in face recognition is one of the least frequent, and it occurs in less than 1% of brain-damaged patients. Yet this deficit is a spectacular impairment, which may be the only disturbance that affects a patient, and, despite its rarity, it has attained considerable notoriety in the neuropsychological literature. Some authors have regarded this deficit as an indication that there exists in the brain a specific area that would be uniquely devoted to the processing of faces. This was first suggested in 1947 by the German neurologist Bodamer who coined the term "prosopagnosia" to refer to this agnosia for faces. Other researchers, on the contrary, attribute this deficit in face recognition to a disruption of neural mechanisms underlying fine perceptual discrimination of any complex visual objects. Whatever the exact nature of the deficit, the fact that some patients are selectively impaired in the processing of one particular class of visual objects has made the human face of special interest to those studying the cognitive operations mediated by the cerebral hemispheres and more essentially the perceptual mechanisms involved in pattern recognition.

I will present some aspects of the research on the perception of the human face, considering first the nature of the underlying processes as they can be inferred from findings with normal subjects. I will also discuss the results of lateral tachistoscopic experiments aimed at assessing the relative competence of the cerebral hemispheres in these processes, and I will finally come back to the problem of prosopagnosia in the conclusion.

EFFICIENCY AND LIMITATIONS OF FACE-RECOGNITION PROCESSES

One indispensable capacity that social animals must possess is the ability to discriminate between other members of the group and to recognise them, and there is no doubt that, for humans, the face has proved the most effective and reliable cue for this purpose. Of course, other physical attributes are unique to each individual and they could provide the necessary discriminative cue, but the face is obviously the most conspicuous. In a way, this is a somewhat paradoxical phenomenon, because the face is not a rigid and static object, and it can take so many different expressions and poses that its appearance is ever changing. There are many reasons why such a mobile object has become the main basis for identifying individuals, but the most important is that we are equipped with a powerful device that can encode information contained in a face, extract the physiognomic invariants, and store this information in a highly efficient and accurate manner. No computer has yet surpassed the brain in this respect, and our capacity to discriminate between faces, although it develops over time, requires no formal training and is acquired quasi-automatically. In fact, every attempt so far to increase our capacity to identify and remember the faces of other people has resulted in failure, at least for faces of our own race, and training has even sometimes reduced the subjects' capacity to recognise faces (Baddeley, 1979). This does not mean that one could not improve this skill, but two factors may prevent this improvement. One is that we still do not understand how we perceive and recognise faces, and it is therefore difficult to improve the efficiency of a function whose basic mechanisms are unknown. The second factor is that our ability to deal with faces is already at a very high level and there may be no room for improvement. As noted by Ellis (1981), our capacity for discriminating and identifying faces may represent the ultimate in our classificatory abilities, and there is practically no other class of visual objects, having such a high similarity among its members, which is dealt with as efficiently as faces.

This has contributed to the idea that faces constitute a special class of visual object, and indeed, few, if any, other categories carry with them such social, personal, communicative, and affective importance that we need pay as much attention to them as we do to faces. Identification is but one aspect of what we can do with the information contained in a face; we also make inferences about character and personality, age, mood, and feelings. As pointed out by Yin (1978), the potential uniqueness of face perception is that people derive a great deal of information from the face on the basis of very slight differences, and this is done at considerable speed. Thus, it takes less than a second to recognise a familiar face, even if the particular instance of that face has never been seen before, and one can store and identify hundreds of faces with the same efficiency. There are also examples of people capable of close to 75% accuracy in recognising faces of individuals they had not seen for more than 40 years (Bahrick, Bahrick, & Wittlinger, 1975).

Although faces represent for almost everyone the utmost in discriminating capacities, there are people who, by professional obligation or by hobby, appear to be equally competent at discriminating objects of other categories. For instance, Bateson (1977) reported the case of a person capable of identifying some 450 swans by names she had given them. In addition, our efficiency at dealing with faces prevails only under certain particular conditions, and there are a series of examples suggesting that some of our skills at processing faces have definite limitations. As shown by Patterson and Baddeley (1977), one often fails to recognise faces when they have been disguised with the addition of a beard, wig, or glasses. Our usual capacity to recognise faces despite some changes in hair style or age may in fact be partly due to our expectation to see the person and to other non-physiognomical cues. Moreover, even if we can store visual information about a great number of faces, this information is appropriate to tell whether or not we have seen a face before, but we are much less efficient at recalling these faces (Phillips, 1979), and we generally need to have frequently been exposed to a face to succeed in recalling it. In addition, although it is true that we can extract from a face its physiognomic invariant features and use them for recognition when viewed from a different angle, there are restrictions to this capacity. For example, whereas we are all familiar with the face of Mona Lisa, it is hard to imagine what she would look like in profile.

Although there may be evidence from research on brain-damaged patients and on infants and children that faces constitute a special class of object that involves specific processes (Yin, 1978), research on normal adults has so far provided equivocal findings in this respect. One of the main problems has been the lack of objective measure of stimulus complexity, familiarity, and within-class similarity, which prevents us from identifying the exact parameters that could account for differences in performance between faces and other classes of visual stimuli. In addition, the passage from casual observations to a scientific investigation into the perception and recognition of faces has been made with a great loss in realism and ecological validity to ensure a better control over the experimental variables. Most experiments have been carried out with still photographs, using only one view of each face, or with artificially made schematic line-drawing or Photofit faces presented for a brief duration. This reduces the usefulness of laboratory studies, because, for instance, our capacity to recognise faces is better when we have been exposed to several views of the same face, especially when the face is mobile. Recognition is also better the longer we have been exposed to the face (see Goldstein & Chance, 1981, for a review).

Moreover, several of the important questions that would need to be solved to reach an understanding of the processes underlying face perception and recognition have eluded us. For example, we do not know what is involved in becoming familiar with a face. What aspects of a face convey the relevant information for identification? How do we extract the invariant physiognomic features of a face and how are they stored and used for recognition of the same face under different viewing conditions? Another question that has received some elements of response concerns the basic strategy underlying facial perception, and I will now turn to this problem, along with a discussion of some of the difficulties inherent in its investigation.

PROCESSES UNDERLYING FACE PERCEPTION

How do we encode the information provided by the inspection of a face so that the information can reveal its individuality and be placed in memory? What seems to be established is that such a process does not involve a verbal encoding of the various aspects of the face. This may be suggested by the fact that speechless infants as well as monkeys can discriminate and recognise faces (Carey, 1981; Rosenfeld & Van Hoesen, 1979). More important, this is shown by research on normal adults for whom there is no correlation between the number of verbal descriptions made of a face and subsequent recognition (Goldstein, Johnson, & Chance, 1979). The availability or the use of verbal codes has little or no positive effect on face recognition.

How, then, are the component features integrated to give rise to the percept of a face, and how are they used for discriminating between different faces? Although this issue is far from settled, two main answers have been proposed. One suggests that faces are analysed in terms of their component features, which are processed sequentially and usually in a top-to-bottom order. Thus, the way we could recognise Mona Lisa would be through a serial comparison of each feature with a stored representation of her face. It is interesting to note that Leonardo da Vinci advised his students to remember faces according to such an analytic method by which each component is treated independently of the other (Gombrich, 1972). Such independent processing of each feature would be possible because we are all familiar with the particular arrangement of the features within a face. Some authors have in fact proposed that we develop a basic facial schema resulting from our frequent exposures to upright faces, and that enables us to access consistent encoding dimensions that facilitate perception and memory (Goldstein & Chance, 1980). The second suggestion is that faces are treated as a whole or a Gestalt, in terms of their configuration.

Problems Inherent in Identifying Underlying Processes

So far, most of the experimental evidence suggests that faces are analysed by a sequential process. The experimental method used in these investigations generally consists of presenting, either simultaneously or successively, two faces, and examining the time taken to decide whether the faces are the same or different. By varying the number of differences between two faces, the analysis of reaction times can reveal whether the features are compared according to an analytic strategy or to a holistic one. Typically, an analytic strategy implies that reaction times will decrease when the number of differences between faces increases, because it is faster to detect one difference when there are many differences between the faces than when there are few. On the contrary, a holistic strategy, which implies that all the features are processed simultaneously, predicts that reaction times should be constant whatever the number of differences or the number of features manipulated. In most cases, it was found that reaction times decreased as the number of differences between the faces increased, suggesting that the faces were compared analytically (e.g. Bradshaw & Wallace, 1971; Smith & Nielsen, 1970).

Although there are some exceptions to this finding, the general consensus is that faces are processed in a serial analytic manner, with each feature treated independently of the others. This seems to be a rather unsatisfactory and counter-intuitive suggestion that does not correspond to our experience of what we do when looking at faces. In fact, there are several examples that faces are better recognised when subjects are instructed to remember them according to characteristics that necessitate considering the face as a whole. For instance, when subjects are requested to examine faces in terms of honesty, personality, likeableness, these faces are better recognised than when paying attention only to the physical features. Qualities such as honesty or likeableness are not conveyed by any single feature independent of the others, and the faces must then be treated as a "unit" (e.g. Bower & Karlin, 1974; Patterson & Baddeley, 1977). This is a plausible deduction, but the exact nature of the processes mediating this evaluation remains unspecified. There are other problems with the suggestion that faces are perceived by a sequential process of feature extraction. Ellis (1981), for example, has argued that the models derived from these experiments do not reflect how faces are normally processed, because the use of artificial faces, with alterations to discrete facial features, encourages a serial-processing strategy. This is a basic difficulty that has plagued research on face perception. However, if, as noted earlier, normal individuals develop a type of schema that allows the fast processing of faces, why should such a schema be inoperative with these experimental faces?

Another problem, related to the one I just mentioned, is that one single view of each face is used, which may not require the extraction of the invariant physiognomic characteristics. Bertelson, Van Haelen, and Morais (1979) have argued that in such conditions any part of the face may be valid for comparison, in contrast to what we normally do when recognising faces. The experimental faces are static and rigid, which has led Hay and Young (1982) to suggest that in such conditions faces are treated like any other stimulus and that one is not examining the processes involved in face perception.

A third problem concerns the assumption that discrete facial features such as the eyes, the mouth, the chin, can be considered as relevant units in face perception, when we do not know what are the critical dimensions on which perception is based. What we know is that the visual system is particularly sensitive to variations in intensity, and these variations are typically concentrated in the facial features, which makes them important physical bases for processing. On the other hand, Shepherd (1977) carried out multidimensional scaling analysis on real faces, and he suggested that the internal features of a face may not be a relevant dimension when comparing faces, and that the dimensions on which processing is based are the face shape, age, hair length, and hair texture. However, this seems to be a rather unexpected finding since Ellis, Shepherd, and Davies (1979) found that the internal features are as good a clue as face shape, hair length, and hair texture to recognition of unfamiliar faces, and even a better clue to the identification of well-known faces.

Some Evidence of Configural Processing of Faces

Although these three problems should not be discarded and in fact illustrate the difficulties inherent in the investigation into face perception, there is another kind of problem that may be more critical to the understanding of the processes mediating the perception of faces. Three points may be worth considering in this respect.

The first one is that attending specifically to the facial features is not indispensable for recognising a face. One can, for example, recognise a face as far as 40 metres away and, at such a distance, the small details of the eyes, nose, mouth, which differ between faces, are no longer discernible and cannot be used to discriminate between two faces. What remains in such a case is the general configuration of the face that results from the disposition of the components within the face and that carries enough information for recognition.

This can be illustrated with the picture of Mona Lisa shown in Fig. 1, which is a coarsely quantised representation of the original face. In this face, no single part conveys enough information for identification, and it is only the interrelationship among the blurred components that allows for recognition. This suggests that a face has both component and configural properties, and a configuration becomes the most salient property of the face when the components are blurred or, in other words, when the high spatial-frequency contents of the face have been filtered out. This does not mean, however, that the configuration is removed when the components

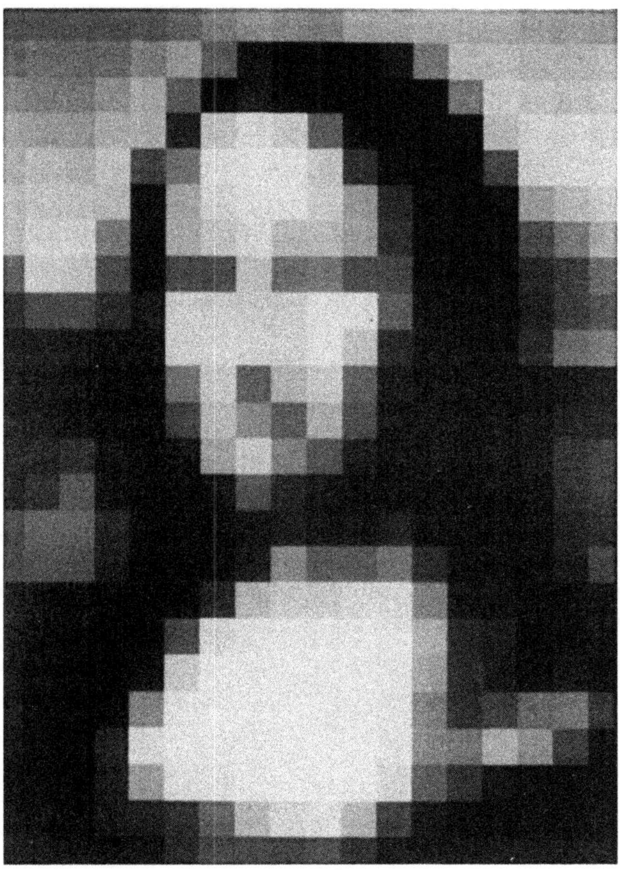

FIG 1. Block portrait of Mona Lisa (courtesy of Ed Manning).

are not blurred, and, in a normal face, component and configural properties co-exist.

As a consequence, and this is the second point, it becomes difficult to identify the relevant parameters when facial features are manipulated. Because configural properties emerge from components, and because components are the characteristics that are directly manipulated, performance in face recognition is analysed as a function of the components that are considered the critical variables, but this is not justified. Let's take a simple example. Each of the three stimuli presented in Fig. 2 is made of a circle and two spokes, and the left spoke is the only dimension to be manipulated. The normal practice is thus to consider the left spoke as the source of difference among the three stimuli and to explain any variation in performance by the objective manipulation of this dimension. Yet, it is obvious that changing a single dimension also modifies the interrelationship among the components and, therefore, the configuration of the stimuli. In this particular example, the critical variable may not be the left spoke but the spaces described by the spokes within the circle, even though these spaces are not directly manipulated. Thus changing or manipulating a feature in a visual pattern also changes its configuration, and variations in performance following manipulation of a feature is not necessarily due to processing the feature as such.

This brings us to the third point. Finding that reaction times decrease when the number of differences between faces increases does not necessarily imply an analytic mode of processing. It may as well suggest that increasing differences between faces enhances their configural dissimilarity, which in turn reduces the comparison time. The fact that this comparison time varies depending on which feature is manipulated—for example, it is usually faster to compare two faces that have different hair styles than two faces that have different noses—may thus reflect the different contribution of each feature to the configuration itself.

It is thus possible that the suggestion of an analytic processing of faces is not necessarily well-founded, and this has been examined in three different experiments, using either Photofit or schematic faces. In one experiment (Sergent, 1984a), pairs of Photofit faces were presented simultaneously,

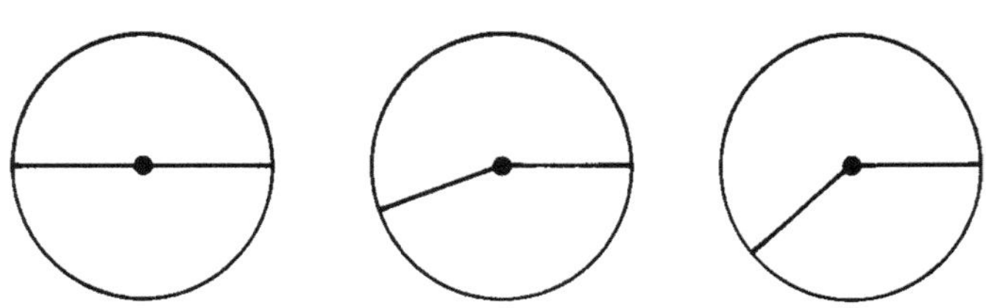

FIG 2. Three circles with two spokes each.

and subjects were required to decide whether they were the same or different. Three features were manipulated, the eyes, the inferior contour, and the internal space. The latencies to compare "same" and "different" pairs are shown in Fig. 3 as a function of the number of differences between faces and the nature of these differences. These latencies were analysed as in other experiments, and the same decrease in reaction time with increase in differences was obtained. Further analyses were carried out as a function of the nature of the differences. As is apparent in Fig. 3, the three features were not equally salient, and a difference in contour was detected faster than a difference in either the eyes or the internal space, suggesting that a decision about the contour could be made prior to a decision about the other features. If the process is purely analytic, the addition of a difference to that in contour should not result in faster reaction time because a decision that two faces are different can be made as soon as the contour has been processed, which is done before the other

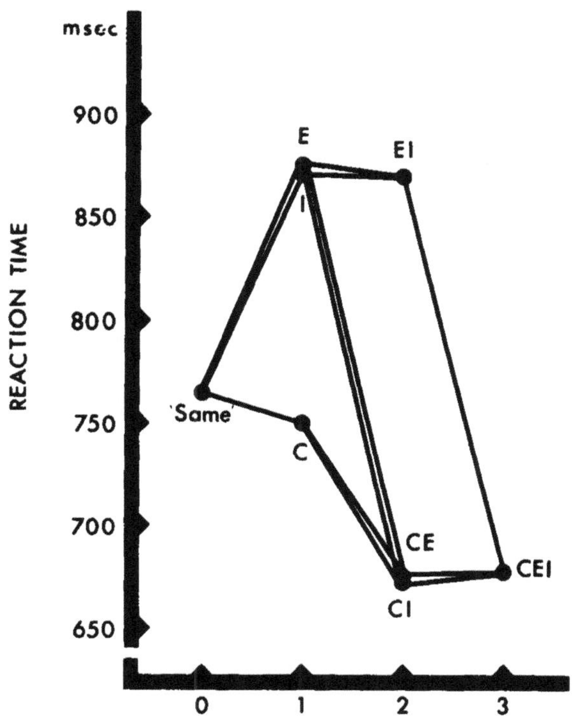

FIG 3. Latencies (in msec) to compare "same" and "different" pairs of faces, as a function of the number and the nature of the differences between faces (C: inferior contour; E: eyes; I: internal space (from Sergent, 1984a).

features. As can be seen in Fig. 3, this was not the case, and reaction time decreased with the addition of a difference to that in contour. When a regression analysis was carried out on these data, it was observed that the variations in reaction time resulted from interactions among the features and not from purely additive effects as would be predicted by an analytic mode of processing. This was taken as evidence that the interrelationship among features was operative in the comparison of these faces.

In another experiment using the same faces, subjects rated the degree of dissimilarity between each pair of "different" faces, and the results were subjected to a multidimensional scaling analysis. Figure 4 is the representation of the eight faces in the three-dimensional space resulting from the analysis. The distance between each face reflects the perceived dissimilarity between them and, as was observed in the reaction-time study, the inferior contour was the most salient dimension because faces differing in contour are farther apart than faces differing in either eyes or internal space. This holds for this particular set of faces but has no implication for feature saliency in general. What is more interesting for the present purpose, is the distortion from a perfect cube that appears in this figure. Consider, for example, the four faces at the upper corners, and specifically the two on the right and the two on the left. The two faces of each pair

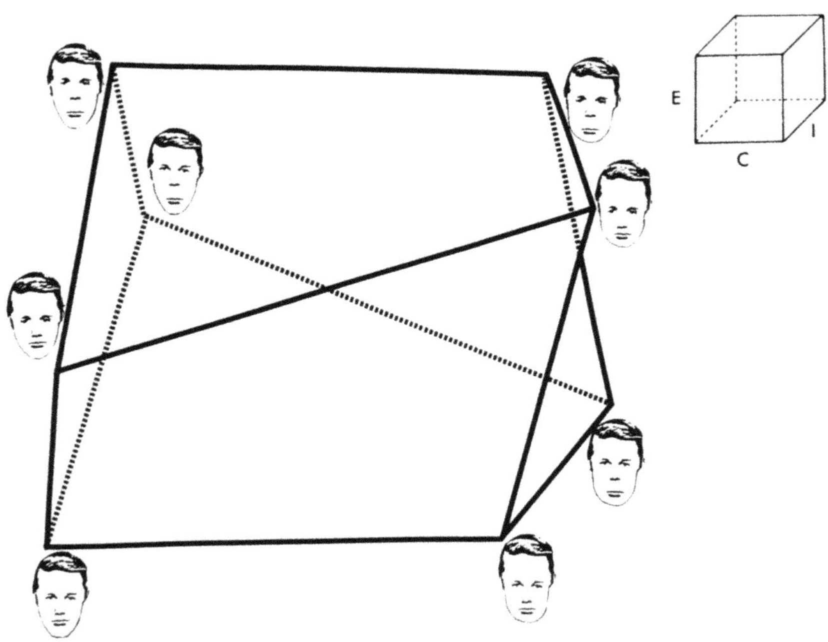

FIG 4. Derived representation of the eight faces in a three-dimensional Euclidean space (from Sergent, 1984a).

differ from one another only by the internal space, and the four faces have the same eyes. The two faces on the right have a round inferior contour, and the two on the left have a sharper contour. What is important to note here is that the same difference in internal space results in greater perceived dissimilarity when it is embedded within a sharp inferior contour than when it is embedded in a round contour, as can be seen by the difference in the distance separating the two faces of each pair. If subjects were simply considering the internal space, independent of the rest of the face, as is implied in an analytic mode of processing, the difference in internal space should be perceived similarly in the two pairs and thus yield equal distance between the two faces of each pair. This was not the case, and some parts of the face influenced how other parts were perceived, which is a clear example of interaction among the component features. This suggests that the formation of an overall impression from a face is not simply the sum of the independent sub-impressions obtained from single features, but it is determined by the reciprocal influence of the features on one another.

The third experiment combined the approach of the two previous studies and was carried out with Yoshio Takane (Takane & Sergent, 1983). We used a different set of faces, which were line drawings varying on three features, and a same–different judgement task, with two faces presented simultaneously and reaction time as the dependent variable. Thus, taking reaction time as an inverse measure of dissimilarity, i.e., the more dissimilar two faces the faster the comparison time, we analysed the results to determine the dimensions on which the faces were compared.

Figure 5 is the derived representation of the eight faces resulting from the multidimensional scaling analysis. Variations in reaction time as a function of face differences were best accounted for by a four-dimensional solution, with three dimensions describing each of the manipulated features, and the fourth dimension representing the homogeneity of the features within each face. As can be seen in this figure, interactions among features are again present, because the same difference between two faces results in different distance separating these two faces depending on the other features that compose the face. In addition, the finding of a significant fourth dimension based on the internal consistency of each face indicates that the features of a face are perceived simultaneously.

These results suggest that artificial faces do not necessarily encourage a serial-processing strategy, and the view that an analytic operation is involved in the perception and recognition of faces may then not be completely appropriate. In fact, the findings from these three experiments suggest that the component features of a face are processed in an interactive manner and are not perceived independently of the others. In other words, a face is processed in terms of its Gestalt, which may seem

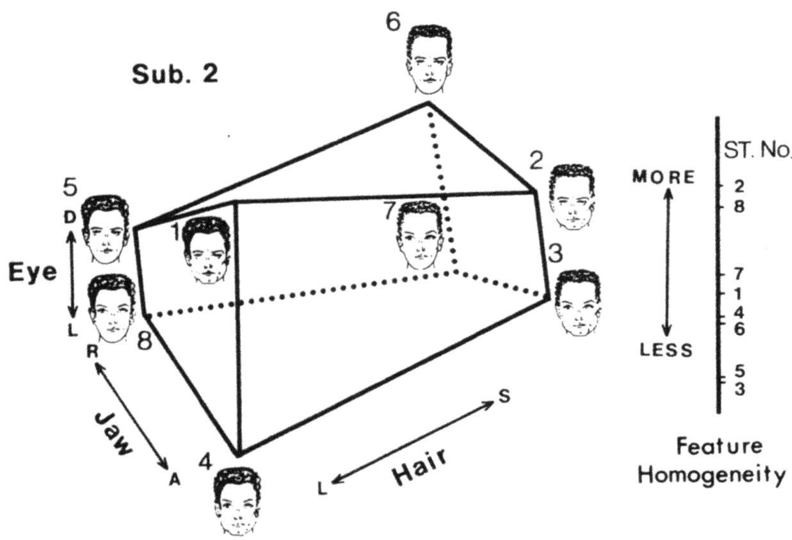

FIG 5. Derived representation of the eight faces in a three-dimensional Euclidean space. The fourth dimension is shown on the right (from Takane & Sergent, 1983).

more consistent with our subjective experience than a serial process by which we would scan each component one after the other in order to identify an individual. Such a configural processing seems to involve some kind of interplay between the face and the perceiving organism, and there is evidence that changing the orientation of the face may prevent us from implementing a configural processing. For example, in the first series of experiments I described earlier (Sergent, 1984a), the subjects were also tested with the faces presented upside-down. The analysis of latencies as a function of the nature of differences between faces revealed no interaction among features, suggesting that the configural properties could not be used when the faces were inverted, and that the inverted faces were most likely compared feature by feature. This finding concurs with the hypothesis put forward by Irvin Rock (1974) that inverting mono-oriented stimuli—that is those with a typical orientation such as faces or words—disrupts the spatial relationship of their components.

Research on the perception of inverted faces can certainly enlight us about visual perception in general and that of faces in particular. The fact that the same stimuli made exactly of the same features were subjected to different modes of processing depending on their orientation clearly suggests that it is not sufficient that faces have configural properties to be processed along these properties. If no configural processing is apparent with inverted faces, this cannot be attributed to the stimuli as such because they possess all the characteristics necessary for the emergence of configural properties, but rather to the processing organism, which finds itself unable to extract an integrated configuration of the features. In fact, the way we process upside-down faces may be either through an analytic mode of operation, as suggested by the empirical findings mentioned earlier, or through a configural mode of processing based on some type of face schema that is not quite appropriate because it is essentially adapted to upright faces. Thus, when looking at upside-down faces, we cannot get a clear idea of what it would look like upright, as has been clearly illustrated by Thompson (1980) in his montage of Margaret Thatcher's face, showing how ill-equipped we are to process inverted faces.

Leaving aside now the problem of upside-down faces, we may turn to an examination of the respective competence of the cerebral hemispheres at face perception and recognition, and try to determine whether the two hemispheres perform the same type of processing.

CONTRIBUTION OF THE CEREBRAL HEMISPHERES TO FACE PERCEPTION

Before discussing what neuropsychological investigation in normal subjects can tell us about the contribution of the cerebral hemispheres to the processing of faces, it is necessary to examine the main characteristics of lateral tachistoscopic presentation of visual information. The appropriateness of this technique is based on the anatomical property of the visual system whereby the left half of each retina projects to the left hemisphere and the right half to the right hemisphere. Thus, information can be sent initially to only one hemisphere by presenting the visual stimulus in the retinal periphery and for a duration short enough to prevent eye movements that would expose the stimulus to the two hemispheres. This creates particular viewing conditions unlike those prevailing in normal situations.

It is a truism that the visual system and the brain have not evolved to perceive and process visual information seen for such a brief duration outside the area of highest acuity. These particular viewing conditions determine the quality of the visual information that can be elaborated in the brain, and in fact they produce some form of functional sensory deficit because the stimuli cannot be resolved as well as they would be if they were presented in the fovea and for unlimited duration. One implication of this method of presentation is that the small details, or the high frequencies, contained in the stimulus will be attenuated, and this attenuation will be more pronounced when the contrast between the various components is relatively low than when it is high. This means that the small details will be more difficult to resolve in black-and-white photographs with their different levels of grey, than in schematic or line-drawing faces. It may be noted in this respect that letters and words, which are usually presented as black on a white background, and thus at very high contrast, are much less affected by a brief presentation. In the case of faces, this can be illustrated with the block portrait of Mona Lisa shown in Fig. 1. Lines can be seen at the edges of each block, resulting from the spatial quantisation of the face, and they can be greatly attenuated by defocus, or by squinting, or by looking at the face from far away. The same attenuation of the lines can be obtained by presenting such a block portrait at a very brief duration and in the retinal periphery. The net result of such a tachistoscopic presentation is that the picture loses its higher spatial-frequency components. As noted earlier, this implies, for normal photographs of faces, a reduction in the information about single facial features, but it does not affect as much the configural property of the face. This makes the capacity to discriminate between different shades of grey a critical factor for the task of face recognition, and this is quite important because Benton and Gordon (1971) have found a significant positive correlation between the ability to recognise faces and the capacity to discriminate between different patterns of shading.

Let's now turn to the experiments themselves. In the majority of studies, the finding is that faces presented in the left visual field, and thus initially projected to the right hemisphere, are processed faster and more accurately than faces presented in the right visual field. This is a frequent finding in normals, which is in agreement with results from the brain-damaged population. However, this is not always the case, and there are about 25 published studies in which a left-hemisphere superiority was found in some conditions. When one examines the particular methodological conditions that prevailed in these experiments, there are several factors that seem to be necessary for the emergence of a right-hemisphere superiority in the processing of faces. A detailed review of these experiments is beyond the scope of this presentation (see Ellis, 1983; Sergent, in press, for reviews), and Table 1 summarises the particular experimental conditions that favour the emergence of a right- or left-hemisphere superiority in tachistoscopic studies with normal subjects (see Sergent, in press).

None of the variables presented in Table 1 is by itself sufficient to determine the superiority of one hemisphere over the other, and it is their conjoint influence that makes one hemisphere more efficient. It can be safely suggested that an experiment combining the nine conditions shown on the left side of this table would with high probability result in a right-hemisphere superiority; on the other hand, an experiment combining the nine conditions on the right would likely yield a left-hemisphere superiority.

TABLE 1
Experimental Factors[a]

To a Right-Hemisphere Superiority in Face Perception	
More Favourable	*Less Favourable*
Upright faces	Inverted faces
Emotional faces	Neutral faces
Facial identity (different views of same face)	Physical identity (same view of same face)
Set of highly dissimilar faces	Set of highly similar faces
Black-and-white photographs	Schematic or line-drawing faces
Unfamiliar faces	Familiar faces
Low-stimulus energy	High-stimulus energy
Successive presentation	Simultaneous presentation
Recognition accuracy	Response latency

[a] Experimental factors contributing to the emergence of left-visual-field right-hemisphere superiority in lateral tachistoscopic studies on face perception in normal subjects.

These are primarily technical and methodological problems in such experiments, and very little investigation has yet been carried out to examine systematically the influence of such parameters. One outcome that is evident from research on normals, is that both hemispheres appear to be capable of processing faces, and the main task becomes to succeed in characterising the conditions that allow one hemisphere to be more efficient, not in terms of these experimental variables, but in terms of the effects of particular values of these variables on cerebral and neural processing.

What, then, could these nine conditions shown in the left of Table 1 have in common that would favour some special property possessed by the right hemisphere but not by the left hemisphere, at least not to the same extent?

At the outset, it may be suggested that the particular competence of the right hemisphere cannot be reduced to an exclusive specialisation of this hemisphere in the processing of faces. There are now too many studies reporting a left-hemisphere superiority under some circumstances, and with upright faces, to persist in the view that the left hemisphere has no competence in the processing of faces.

One explanation for the functional asymmetry in processing faces is concerned with the specific processing competence of the cerebral hemispheres, with the right specialised in holistic or configural operations and the left for analytic processing. This is probably the idea most often used to account for empirical data, having started with Sperry and Levy, from their research with split-brain patients, and recently supported by Bradshaw and Nettleton (1981). A quotation from Sperry (1974) may summarise this view: "The left and right hemispheres apprehend and process things in different ways. In dealing with faces, the right hemisphere seems to respond to the whole face directly as a perceptual unit, whereas the left hemisphere seems to focus on salient features and details to which labels are easily attached, and then used for discrimination and recall" (p. 14). This type of interpretation has often been successful in providing a convenient account of results, and many empirical findings seem to be quite consistent with this view.

The major problem with this approach is that such an interpretation is without objective basis in the data, and the main concepts of this dichotomy have not been defined in operational terms that would allow testable predictions. As noted by Bertelson (1982) and Marshall (1981), any finding can be made consistent with the analytic–holistic dichotomy whose explanatory successes are essentially *post hoc*.

I recently tried to examine this problem by using faces that varied on four features so that variations in performance could be analysed as a function of stimulus manipulations (Sergent, 1982). A face was first presented in the centre of the visual field, followed by the test face that appeared in either visual field. The subjects were required to decide whether the two faces were the same or different, and reaction time was the main dependent variable. The faces could differ in one dimension: hair, eyes, mouth, or jaw, or in two dimensions. Latencies are presented in Fig. 6 for each visual field, as a function of the nature of the differences between pairs of faces. The results showed that the two hemispheres were equally fast overall, i.e. the average reaction time was not significantly different in the right and the left visual fields. However, the pattern of results was significantly different in the two hemispheres, as suggested by a significant interaction between visual field and the type of difference between the faces. This interaction is clearly depicted in Fig. 6. Faces differing in hair or in eyes were compared faster in the left than in the right hemisphere, whereas faces differing in mouth or in jaw were responded to faster in the right than in the left, but not significantly so. Thus, the two hemispheres were shown to be equally competent overall, but their equal performance was the result of qualitatively different underlying processes. One conclusion to draw from this finding is that equal efficiency by the two hemispheres does not necessarily imply an absence of hemisphere difference in processing.

The results were further analysed by taking into account the particular salience of the facial features. This was done with an analysis of covariance that showed that the time taken to compare the faces in the right hemisphere was a function of the degree of similarity between the faces. By contrast, performance in the left hemisphere was not influenced by the saliency of the features, and the comparison of the faces seemed to proceed

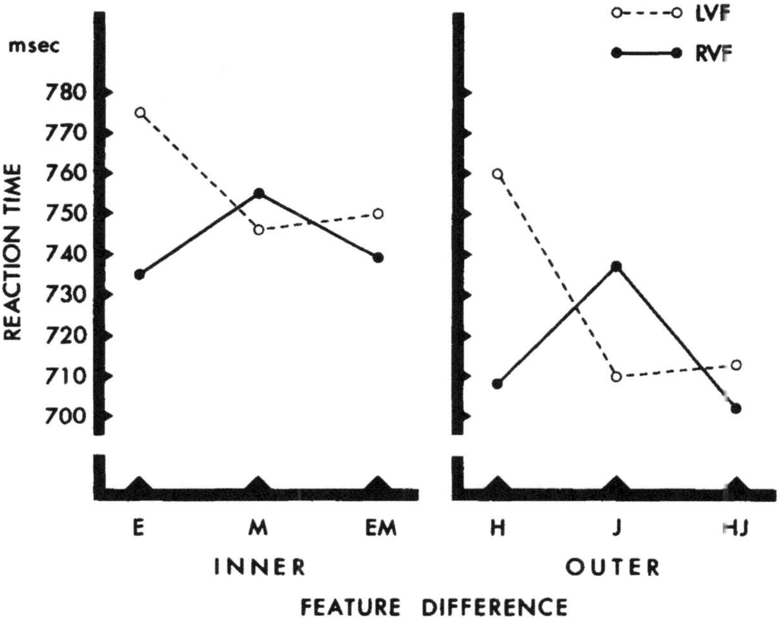

FIG 6. Latencies (in msec) to compare faces differing in one or two features as a function of visual field of presentation (LVF: left visual field; RVF: right visual field; H: hair; E: eyes; M: mouth; J: jaw (from Sergent, 1982).

in a top-to-bottom serial order. This is, therefore, in contradiction with Sperry's (1974) speculation mentioned earlier that the left hemisphere focuses on salient features. I then interpreted these findings as an indication that the left hemisphere used an analytic-processing strategy although I left the nature of the operations performed by the right hemisphere unspecified. I later came to realise that this interpretation suffered from the same deficiency as those discussed earlier. Specifically, there is nothing in the data to support unequivocally an interpretation in terms of analytic processing, and an alternative account may be that the facial features contributed differentially to the configuration, which may explain the results equally well.

To examine this possibility, a new experiment was carried out, essentially similar to the previous one although only three features were manipulated to include the comparison of all the different faces in the design (Sergent, 1984b). An analysis of variance yielded the same effects as in the previous experiment, with an interaction between visual field and type of difference between the faces. Once again the left hemisphere was faster when faces differed in hair or in eyes. Further analyses were carried out, using a maximum likelihood estimation procedure to fit the data to several models of similarity relations. This approach allows the determination of the rules by which the component dimensions of a face are combined, and four different models were tested. I will discuss only two of these models. One is the serial self-terminating model, which is the typical analytic model suggesting that two stimuli are compared in terms of their individual dimensions until a difference is detected; the other is the Euclidean distance metric model, which implies that two stimuli are compared in terms of the overall similarity or configuration that encompasses their component dimensions. The results showed a considerably better approximation of the reaction-time data by the Euclidean model in the two hemispheres of each subject, and they suggested that a purely analytic mode of comparison was too simple a process to account for the operation taking place in the left hemisphere.

This can be illustrated in Fig. 7, which shows the three-dimensional spatial representation of the eight faces for the left and the right visual field of one subject. Although the same configural process was found to underlie performance in the right and the left hemispheres, the perceived dissimilarities between the faces were none the less significantly different in the two hemispheres. The important characteristic in this figure is once again the interaction among the component features. Consider, for

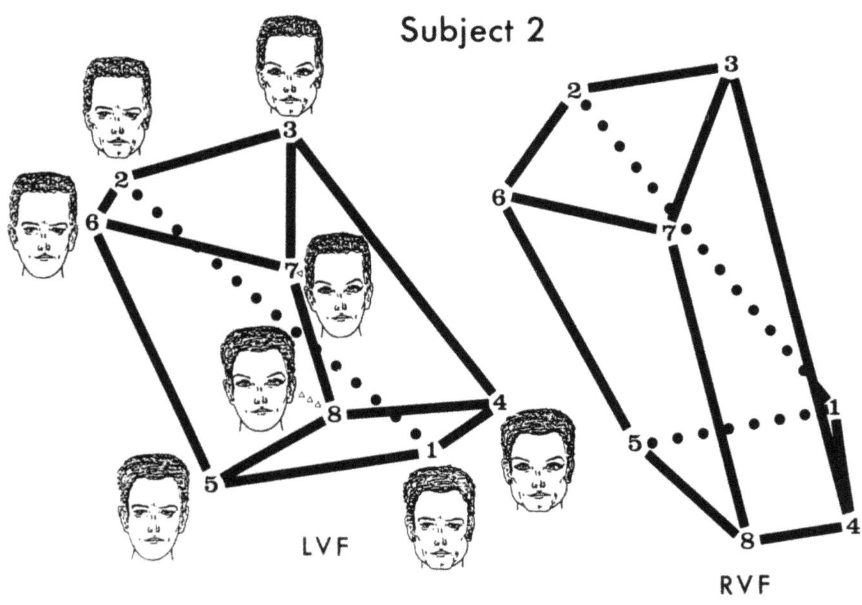

FIG 7. Derived representations, for left-visual-field (LVF) and right-visual-field (RVF) presentation, of eight faces differing on three features of two values each (from Sergent, 1984b).

again the interaction among the component features. Consider, for example, the pair 7–8 and the pair 3–4. There is only a difference in hair between the two faces of each pair, and the distance separating faces 7 and 8 is much shorter than that between faces 3 and 4. An analytic independent process would predict equal distance between the faces of these two pairs. Instead, the other features of the face influenced how the difference in hair was perceived. This implies simultaneous and interactive processing of the component dimensions, and these are typical properties of a Gestalt mode of perception, which both hemispheres are thus capable of mediating.

If the two hemispheres perform basically the same type of process, what, then, can explain the overwhelming evidence of functional hemispheric asymmetry in the perception and recognition of faces? One possible explanation may be in terms of the representation and description of visual information in the brain, which may not be similar in the two hemispheres. As noted by Marr (1982), for example, a representation is a formal system for making explicit certain entities or types of information, and how information is represented can greatly affect how easy it is to do different things with it.

This makes it necessary to consider the type of representation that can be elaborated from a lateral tachistoscopic presentation of a face. As mentioned earlier, such a tachistoscopic presentation allows only some aspects of the physical characteristics of the face to be accurately encoded, which makes the representation of information in the brain essentially in terms of low spatial-frequency components of a face. It is, therefore, the hemispheric system that is the more capable of dealing with these low frequencies that will be the more efficient at processing the incoming information in very brief tachistoscopic presentations, and there is a fair amount of evidence to suggest that the right hemisphere seems to be more sensitive than the left hemisphere to the outputs of the low spatial-frequency channels of the visual system. This is suggested by the frequent finding of right-hemisphere superiority at very brief exposure duration as well as by recent evidence reported by Keegan (1981) that faces from which the high frequencies have been removed are processed much more efficiently in the right hemisphere but not when the low frequencies are filtered out (see Sergent & Switkes, 1984).

On the other hand, conditions under which the left hemisphere proves more efficient include longer than usual exposure duration, highly contrasted faces, quite discernible facial features, and fairly similar faces that make the small details critical for discrimination. These procedural conditions allow the resolution of high spatial frequencies and may favour the left hemisphere when the task requires to process these high frequencies.

A consequence of this differential sensitivity of the cerebral hemispheres is that the representations elaborated in the brain may not emphasise the same attributes of the face in the two hemispheres. This may give the illusion that the hemispheres perform different types of processes, whereas they operate similarly on different aspects of the information.

Consider, for example, the reaction times of the last mentioned experiment as a function of the number of differences between the faces in the two visual fields shown in Fig. 8. When the faces differed in only one feature, the processing was relatively faster in the left hemisphere; when the faces differed in three features the two hemispheres were equally fast. This pattern of results might have suggested that an analytic operation was involved in the comparison of faces differing in one feature, which favoured the left hemisphere; by contrast, a holistic strategy might have become adequate when the faces differed in three features and were more dissimilar, which led to a greater improvement in performance for the right than for the left hemisphere. The analysis showed that this was not the case, and a configural mode of processing mediated the perception of faces in the two hemispheres. However, the left hemisphere seemed to be relatively more efficient than the right when the dissimilarity between two configurations were small and, thus, when a fine discrimination was called for.

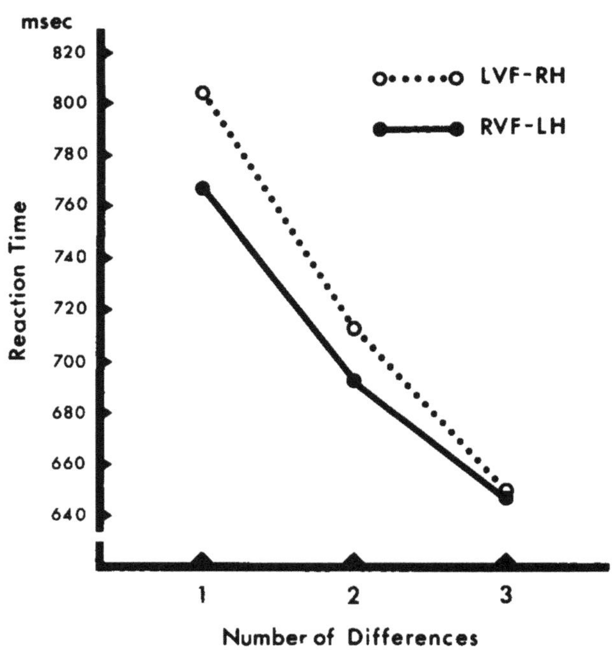

FIG 8. Latencies (in msec) to compare faces in the left visual field (LVF) and the right visual field (RVF) as a function of the number of differences between faces.

Although this is evidence that the two hemispheres can perceive and process faces using the same type of strategy, there are other findings suggesting that this may not apply to all situations. For example, research on the perception of facial emotions has yielded consistently a right-hemisphere superiority, indicating that this process, which is specific to faces and does not apply to other visual objects, may be mediated better, if not exclusively, by the right hemisphere. It is also the case that when a right-hemisphere superiority is found in the perception of upright faces, the inversion of these faces sometimes leads to the elimination of this superiority, which is not usually found for other visual objects. Although these two findings have been taken as evidence that the right hemisphere is equipped with mechanisms specialised in the processing of faces that the left hemisphere may not possess, we are far from having exhausted all the means of investigating the effects of facial expression and inversion on the performance of the two hemispheres. Recent findings from split-brain patients seem to indicate that indeed the two hemispheres are competent at processing faces, although they may not be equally efficient. As noted earlier, research with normal subjects also suggests that we perceive faces on the basis of their configural properties and that both cerebral hemispheres are equipped to carry out such processes. However, the right hemisphere may play a predominant role, not because it contains a specific face processor but because it may be more sensitive to certain physical characteristics that are critical in face perception and recognition.

CONCLUDING REMARKS

If the two hemispheres are capable of processing faces, it follows that complete disruption of face perception and recognition should result from damage to the two hemispheres and that a unilateral lesion should not be sufficient to produce a total inability to recognise faces. This seems to be the case, and all prosopagnosics for whom an autopsy could be performed have been found to suffer from damage in the two cerebral hemispheres. There is as yet not one reported case of prosopagnosia resulting from an anatomically verified unilateral lesion (Damasio, Damasio, & Van Hoesen, 1982). Although this finding is not very helpful to determine the respective contribution of the cerebral hemispheres to the processes underlying face recognition, it none the less confirms the conjoint participation of the two sides of the brain in such processes. In addition, the deficit itself may provide some information about the nature of the operations involved in face perception. It is certainly difficult for most of us to realise what it must look like to become unable to recognise familiar faces when all other cognitive functions remain normal. One prosopagnosic patient who suffered short epileptic seizures during which he was unable to recognise faces has given a very instructive description of his impairment, and the following is what he was experiencing in his own terms:

> I was sitting at the table with my father, my brother and his wife. Lunch had been served. Suddenly, I became aware of white flickering lights before the eyes. This sensation occurred rapidly, possibly lasted less than five seconds. Soon afterwards, something funny happened: I found myself unable to recognize anyone around me. They looked unfamiliar. I was aware that there were two men and a woman; I could see the different parts of their face, but I could not associate these faces with known persons. They were strangers to me. The funny thing was that at that moment I knew that these persons must have been my father, brother, and sister-in-law whom I was having lunch with just before. I realized that something was wrong and stood up. Then one of the people asked me what the matter was. I recognized my brother's voice, but the face of the man who was speaking appeared to make no sense to me (Agnetti, Carreras, Pinna, & Rosati, 1978, p. 51).

This description seems to be fairly typical of the symptom, and it illustrates the fact that the deficit occurs despite adequate vision, with an intact capacity to identify people by means other than their face, as well as the capacity to perceive the component features of the face. What seems to be defective is the capacity to integrate these component features into a whole or a configuration that would give the face its individuality. As noted earlier, this may not be due to the destruction of a processing unit that would be uniquely devoted to faces. In fact, there is evidence that some prosopagnosics are also defective in recognising other classes of visual objects that too require fine perceptual discrimination and the integration of component features to access their identity or individuality. For example, some can no longer discriminate among cars; a specialist in antiques could no longer recognise the style of his furniture; a farmer had become unable to identify his cows (Assal, personal communication; Meadows, 1974). These findings suggest that the deficit is not specific to faces, but rather to classes of visual objects that have a high level of intra-category similarity. As it turns out, for most people, the human face constitutes the only class of visual objects with such high intra-category similarity that they have to deal with. But for those people who, by hobby or professional occupation, have been led to deal with other such classes of objects, the deficit in recognition is not restricted to faces. The term prosopagnosia itself may thus be somewhat misleading because it refers only to the most conspicuous visual object that patients can no longer recognise, and for some the only one, but the deficit potentially applies to other classes, and it actually does in some patients.

Research from both normal and prosopagnosic subjects thus indicates a contribution of the two hemispheres to the processing of faces. This contribution is not the same for the right and the left hemispheres, and the right hemisphere certainly plays a critical role in face perception and recognition. There does not seem to be enough evidence at the moment to suggest that there would be a particular area of the brain uniquely devoted to the processing of faces, and it is likely the conjoint involvement of the two hemispheres that underlies the high capacity of humans at perceiving and recognising faces.

ACKNOWLEDGEMENTS

The work reported herein was supported by grants from the Natural Sciences and Engineering Research Council of Canada and the Fonds de la recherche en santé du Québec.

REFERENCES

Agnetti, V., Carreras, M., Pinna, L., & Rosati, G. (1978) Ictal prosopagnosia and epileptognic damage of the dominant hemisphere. *Cortex*, *14*, 50–57.

Baddeley, A. (1979) Applied cognitive and cognitive applied psychology: The case of face recognition. In L. G. Nilsonn (Ed.), *Perspectives on memory research*. Hillsdale, N.J.: Lawrence Erlbaum Associates Inc.

Bahrick, H. P., Bahrick, P. O., & Wittlinger, R. P. (1975) Fifty years of memory for names and faces: A cross-sectional approach. *Journal of Experimental Psychology: General*, *104*, 54–75.

Bateson, P. P. G. (1977) Testing an observer's ability to identify individual animals. *Animal Behaviour*, *25*, 247–248.

Benton, A. L. & Gordon, M. C. (1971) Correlates of facial recognition. *Transactions of the American Neurological Association*, *96*, 146–150.

Bertelson, P. (1982) Lateral differences in normal man and lateralization of brain function. *International Journal of Psychology*, *17*, 173–210.

Bertelson, P., Van Haelen, H., & Morais, J. (1979) Left-hemifield superiority and the extraction of physiognomic invariants. In S. Russell, I. Van Hof, & G. Berlucchi (Eds.), *Structures and functions of the cerebral commissures*. London: Macmillan.

Bower, G. H. & Karlin, M. B. (1974) Depth of processing pictures of faces and recognition memory. *Journal of Experimental Psychology*, *103*, 751–757.

Bradshaw, J. L. & Nettleton, N. C. (1981) The nature of hemispheric specialization in man. *Behavioral and Brain Sciences*, *4*, 51–91.

Bradshaw, J. L. & Wallace, G. (1971) Models for the processing and identification of faces. *Perception and Psychophysics*, *9*, 443–448.

Carey, S. (1981) The development of face perception. In G. Davies, H. Ellis, & J. Shepherd (Eds.), *Perceiving and remembering faces*. London: Academic Press.

Damasio, A. R., Damasio, H., & Van Hoesen, G. W. (1982) Prosopagnosia: Anatomic basis and behavioral mechanisms. *Neurology*, *32*, 331–341.

Ellis, H. (1981) Theoretical aspects of face recognition. In G. Davies, H. Ellis, & J. Shepherd (Eds.), *Perceiving and remembering faces*. London: Academic Press.

Ellis, H. (1983) The role of the right hemisphere in face perception. In A. W. Young (Ed.), *Functions of the right cerebral hemisphere*. London: Academic Press.

Ellis, H., Shepherd, J., & Davies, G. (1979) Identification of familiar and unfamiliar faces from internal and external features: Some implications for theories of face perception. *Perception*, *8*, 431–439.

Goldstein, A. G. & Chance, J. E. (1980) Memory for faces and schema theory. *Journal of Psychology*, *105*, 47–59.

Goldstein, A. G. & Chance, J. E. (1981) Laboratory studies of face recognition. In G. Davies, H. Ellis, & J. Shepherd (Eds.), *Perceiving and remembering faces*. London: Academic Press.

Goldstein, A. G., Johnson, K. S., & Chance, J. E. (1979) Does fluency of face description imply superior face recognition? *Bulletin of the Psychonomic Society*, *13*, 15–18.

Gombrich, E. H. (1972) The mask and the face: The perception of physiognomic likeness in life and art. In E. H. Gombrich, J. Hochberg, & M. Black (Eds.), *Art, perception, and reality*. Baltimore, Md: Johns Hopkins University Press.

Hay, D. C. & Young, A. W. (1982) The human face. In A. W. Ellis (Ed.), *Normality and pathology in cognitive functions*. London: Academic Press.

Keegan, J. F. (1981) *Hemispheric frequency analysis: Facial recognition*. Paper presented at the European Conference of the International Neuropsychological Society, Bergen.

Marr, D. (1982) *Vision*. San Francisco, Cal.: Freeman.

Marshall, J. C. (1981) Hemispheric specialization: What, how and why. *Behavioral and Brain Sciences*, *4*, 72–73.

Meadows, J. C. (1974) The anatomical basis of prosopagnosia. *Journal of Neurology, Neurosurgery, and Psychiatry*, *37*, 489–501.

Patterson, K. E. & Baddeley, A. D. (1977) When face recognition fails. *Journal of Experimental Psychology: Human Learning and Memory*, *3*, 406–417.

Phillips, R. J. (1979) Recognition, recall, and imagery for faces. In M. M. Gruneberg, P. E. Morris, & R. N. Sykes (Eds.), *Practical aspects of memory*. London: Academic Press.

Rock, I. (1974) The perception of disoriented figures. *Scientific American*, *230*, 78–85.

Rosenfeld, S. A. & Van Hoesen, G. W. (1979) Face recognition in the rhesus monkey. *Neuropsychologia*, *17*, 503–509.

Sergent, J. (1982) About face: Left-hemisphere involvement in processing physiognomies. *Journal of Experimental Psychology: Perception and Peformance*, *8*, 1–14.

Sergent, J. (1984a) An investigation into component and configural processes underlying face perception. *British Journal of Psychology*, *75*, 221–242.

Sergent, J. (1984b) Configural processing of faces in the left and the right cerebral hemispheres. *Journal of Experimental Psychology: Human Perception and Performance*, *10*, 554–572.

Sergent, J. (in press) Methodological constraints on neuropsychological studies of face perception in normals. In R. Bruyer (Ed.), *The neuropsychology of face perception and facial expression*. Hillsdale, N.J.: Lawrence Erlbaum Associates Inc.

Sergent, J. & Switkes, E. (1984) Differential hemispheric sensitivity to spatial-frequency components of visual patterns. *Society for Neuroscience Abstracts*, *10*, 25.

Shepherd, J. (1977) *A multidimensional scaling approach to facial recognition*. Paper presented at the annual conference of the British Psychological Society, Exeter, Devon.

Smith, E. E. & Nielsen, G. D. (1970) Representation and retrieval in short term memory: Recognition and recall of faces. *Journal of Experimental Psychology*, *85*, 397–405.

Sperry, R. W. (1974) Lateral specialization in the surgically separated hemispheres. In F. O. Schmitt & F. G. Worden (Eds.), *The neurosciences: Third study program*. Cambridge, Mass.: MIT Press.

Takane, Y. & Sergent, J. (1983) Multidimensional scaling models for reaction time and same–different judgments. *Psychometrika*, *48*, 393–423.

Thompson, P. (1980) Margaret Thatcher: A new illusion. *Perception*, *9*, 483–484.

Yin, R. K. (1978) Face perception: A review of experiments with infants, normal adults, and brain injured patients. In R. Held, H. W. Leibowitz, & H.-L. Teuber (Eds.), *Handbook of sensory physiology, Volume 8.* Berlin: Springer Verlag.

14 Prosopagnosia: A Disorder of Rapid Spatial Integration[1]

J. Davidoff
Department of Psychology, University College, Swansea, U.K.

Prosopagnosia—the supposedly specific disorder of face recognition—is usually accompanied by other visual problems. Dyschromatopsia, topographical disorientation, disturbance of body schema, constructional and dressing apraxia are reported, some of them commonly, to accompany prosopagnosia (Damasio, 1985). Most, perhaps all, of these accompanying syndromes arise from the geographical accident of the lesion disturbing nearby, but functionally distinct, areas. However, even if prosopagnosia can be easily distinguished from visual disorders not involving pattern recognition, it still remains to be shown, from investigations of brain-damaged individuals, that recognition of other classes of objects is intact.

The case for special processing for faces was first made by Bodamer (1947), who coined the word prosopagnosia, although Charcot (1883) had much earlier commented on recognition impairments that were greater for faces than for other types of objects. There are at least two problems in interpreting these clinical observations. First, faces are an extremely familiar and important class of object for which lack of recognition is likely to be commented on. Secondly, the specificity of processing is also somewhat questioned by reports of individuals familiar with other classes of object, e.g. birds (Bornstein, 1963) or cows (Bornstein, Sroka, & Munitz, 1969; Bruyer, Laterre, Seron, Feyereisen, Strypstein, Pierrard, & Rectem, 1983), who have lost the ability to discriminate within the

[1] Preparation of this chapter was supported by a twinning grant from the ETP.

particular category of their expertise. All prosopagnosic patients are to some extent unable to discriminate within other categories such as cars (Lhermitte, Chain, Escourelle, Ducarne, & Pillon, 1972), chairs (Faust, 1955), or fruit (De Renzi, Scotti, & Spinnler, 1969). Only one of the cases reported by De Renzi (1986) appears not to have another category for which recognition is difficult. The case R.B. reported below also had problems in distinguishing types of flowers and makes of cars (Davidoff, Matthews, & Newcombe, 1986).

Progress in determining specificity for faces will not be made by *ad hoc* comparisons to other classes of stimuli. Success or failure at a recognition task is only helpful to our understanding of the mechanisms underlying prosopagnosia if the procedures responsible for the failed recognition are known. Elsewhere in this volume, Rosenthal refers to the question of the modularity (Fodor, 1983) of intellectual functioning. Considerations of modularity are also relevant to face recognition if it is to be granted the status of a specific recognition disorder. Fodor contrasts vertical faculties (specific or modular input systems) to horizontal faculties (non-specific systems). If faces constitute a vertical faculty, and indeed Fodor puts them forward as a candidate, they must be informationally encapsulated (i.e. use processing that is specific), neurologically hard wired and probably innately determined.

The best evidence for neurological specification comes from neurophysiological research (Perrett, Mistlin, & Chitty, 1987). Recordings from cells in the superior temporal sulcus of monkeys while they are exposed to faces and other stimuli gives evidence for cells or groups of cells that have specific face-processing properties. The innateness of these cells has not been investigated, but they would in any case need to be modifiable by experience. It is perhaps not surprising that Perrett has found cells that respond to faces of particular individuals. However, neurological and innate qualifications for specificity are not the present concern but rather that of information encapsulation. The extent to which faces conform (or, in fact, do not conform) to the information encapsulation aspect of Fodor's definition is considered elsewhere (Davidoff, 1986b) for normal subjects, but will be considered now in the light of neuropsychological research.

Despite the double dissociation between objects and faces reported by Hecaen and Albert (1978), there is really no good evidence from neuropsychology for a process used uniquely for faces. The main problem in assessing the evidence for a dissociation is that we do not know which aspects of face and object processing are necessary for the successful accomplishment of the tasks. Let us imagine a hypothetical study in which two groups of patients were given both a face- and an object-recognition task that normals found equally difficult. On the assumption that the tasks require separate processing systems, we might predict results as shown in

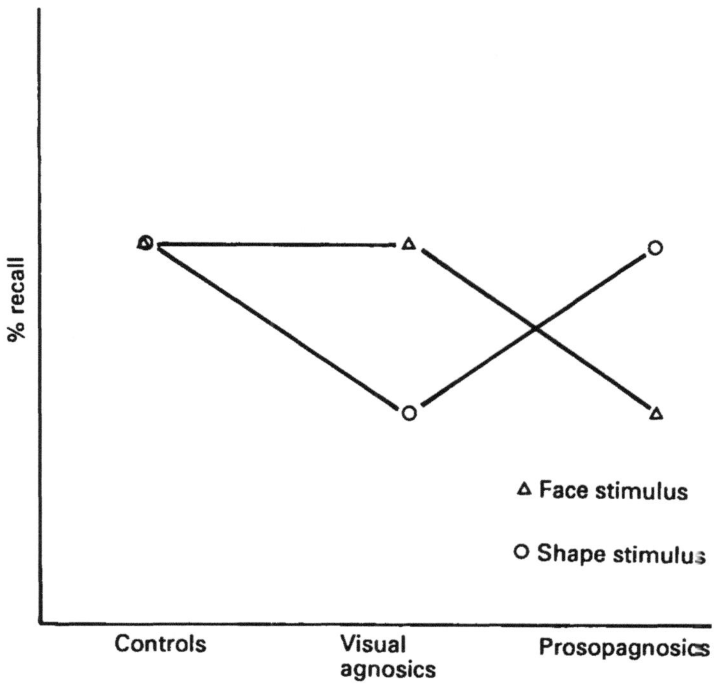

FIG 1. Differences between prosopagnosics, visual agnosics, and controls in a hypothetical recognition experiment.

Fig. 1. Empirical support would probably come for this prediction. Visually agnosic patients are very rare, but one such patient (Davidoff & Wilson, 1985) appeared to have somewhat less difficulty recognising people than recognising objects. Patients with face-recognition disorders that are worse than object-recognition problems are not infrequent, so the proposed double dissociation in Fig. 1 is certainly not impossible. However, there are other explanations of it than specific information encapsulation for faces.

As given above, the hypothetical tasks are ill-defined. In order to equate processing demands, the object task, like the face task, must require discrimination within a class of stimuli. Even then, the class of objects chosen to compare with faces may simply be discriminable by certain features not included in faces, and vice versa. Selective inabilities to make a particular discrimination could produce the double dissociation. This could occur, for example, from a selective loss for particular spatial frequencies (see Sergent, Chapter 13), though it should be pointed out that Bodis-Wollner and Diamond (1976) have found that particular spatial-frequency losses are associated with a wide range of impaired abilities.

Most recognition tasks, if not all, can be successfully accomplished in more than one way. So one other factor that would make interpretation of Fig. 1 difficult is the possibility that prosopagnosic patients, because of their lesions, adopt unusual strategies for any recognition task. There is now good evidence that prosopagnosia can arise from solely right-hemisphere lesion (Landis, Cummings, Christen, Bogen, & Imhof, 1986). If the two hemispheres have different processing modes, then the prosopagnosic could be performing a recognition task with the processing mode of the intact left hemisphere. The left hemisphere has been suggested, on not the most watertight of evidence (see Davidoff, 1982), to operate in an analytical fashion, and the right hemisphere in a holistic fashion. Prosopagnosics, it could then be argued, analyse the detail rather than the whole. Indeed, clinical evidence (Cole & Perez-Cruet, 1964) documents that prosopagnosic patients recognise individuals by exactly such a piecemeal operation, sometimes relying on apparently inconspicuous details like moles or hairline.

Taking the rather stringent condition laid down by Fodor, i.e. that unique processing procedures are required of faces to mark them as a specific type of stimulus, then a double dissociation can only be a first step towards showing specificity. A more theoretically based account is required and has not been supplied from neuropsychological research, except perhaps by Yin (1969, 1970). Yin's attempt to define faces as specific rests on the difficulty in accessing the stored representation of a face when supplied with an inverted version. Upside-down faces are very difficult to recognise, but Yin (1970) found that right-posterior patients were not particularly impaired for such faces; indeed, they performed rather better than other patient groups. This was in sharp contrast to their performance on normally oriented faces for which they scored significantly lower than other types of patients.

Face specificity is favoured by Yin; but the results do not rule out other explanations, as there was no control over the familiarity of the other stimuli used as a comparison to faces. Familiarity is an important variable to consider because face recognition from inverted faces is much improved with practice (Bradshaw & Wallace, 1971). Faces are scanned in a systematic fashion from top to bottom (Walker-Smith, 1978), and as this is an overlearned skill, disturbance of scanning patterns found in such patients (Jones, 1969) could account for a specific difficulty with upright faces. It must, therefore, be concluded that there is no good evidence for the existence of a processing mechanism used only for faces. The term prosopagnosia as used today is a clinical description rather than a strict and specific information-processing disorder.

Although the question of face specificity has not been properly addressed, there has been serious consideration (De Renzi, 1986) of whether a mnestic disorder is an essential component of prosopagnosia. Benton (1980), for example, makes the strong claim that a memory disorder is the primary cause of prosopagnosia. Any perceptual task not involving memory is regarded as being so easy that even a weakened capability for perceptual analysis would be sufficient to cope. The discrimination of unfamiliar faces is accomplished successfully by prosopagnosic patients, but the tests given use matching procedures that could be moderately well performed by comparing features or by spatial transformations of the type requiring an intact right-parietal lobe (Warrington & Taylor, 1973). These tests are not timed, and Newcombe (1979) found that although a prosopagnosic patient could match faces, this was achieved only after long and careful scrutiny. To take five seconds to match two identical faces correctly, cannot be called normal performance. It is, therefore, not correct to quote evidence of a successful match (Damasio, 1985) as showing intact performance on a non-memory task. Damasio, Damasio, and Van Hoesen (1982) suggest that the cause of prosopagnosia is the difficulty in accessing the historical context of an object—a problem that is not specific to faces. However, prosopagnosics have not lost their memory for individuals. It is standard clinical practice to make sure that the patients can identify from a verbal question the people that they cannot visually recognise.

A poor memory for faces is one of the concomitants of right temporal lobe damage (Milner, 1968), but the poor memory is shown for both familiar and unfamiliar faces as well as for shapes. There is no specific loss for familiar faces. However, other lesion studies have reported that familiar and unfamiliar faces can be differentially impaired (Warrington & James, 1967). In a similar vein, Bruyer et al. (1983) contend that, in their prosopagnosic patient, the memory for famous faces was impaired compared to that for well-known examples from other object categories. They also claim that the memory difference cannot be due to a perceptual loss. However, Bruyer et al. also point out that even when complete identification was not achieved, some partial recognition occurred. Partial recognition may arise either through partial perceptual analysis and hence poor access to the memory store or through partial damage to the store itself. The same doubt about the nature of the processing impairment applies to the observation that prosopagnosics give a covert (physiological) reaction to faces they say they cannot recognise (Bauer, 1984). One does not know what aspect of the face—it could be only a part—has caused the covert reaction.

Loss of specific neurological records cannot be necessarily assumed in prosopagnosia as it is known that, in normals, familiar and unfamiliar faces utilise different processing operations. Bruce and Valentine (1985) showed that visual similarity was relatively unimportant for recognition of famous people but was critical for unfamiliar face recognition (Bruce, 1982). Furthermore, Ellis, Shepherd, & Davies (1979) found that the recognition of familiar faces relies much more on the internal features. Access to the memory store for familiar faces will, more commonly, be achieved by a processing mechanism requiring feature integration. It is, therefore, proposed here that prosopagnosia results from an inability to process correctly spatial information that is necessary for normal face recognition; this proposal is in the tradition of De Renzi and Spinnler (1966). They stated that the basic impairment in prosopagnosia is an inability to integrate the visual input. To that is added some evidence that the spatial integration must be carried out rapidly.

Mooney (1957) noted that in normal information processing much is achieved within a very short time. His subjects were shown pictures that required what he called closure to be seen as an object or a face. Right temporal lobe damage made this closure difficult to perform (Landsell, 1968). For normal subjects, a single brief glance was as effective as prolonged inspection for closure to take place (Mooney, 1957). In a subsequent study (Mooney, 1960), this was found to generalise (to a first approximation) to recognition. Subjects were allowed either 0.07 seconds or 5.0 seconds to inspect a meaningless display of black and white patches. The improvement in recognition of a particular display after the opportunity to scan the figure, though significant, was very small. Mooney could find no convincing evidence of a processing difference that occurred as a result of long as opposed to short exposures. However, recent work has shown that long exposures can improve recognition of face parts and hence nullify the advantage of the initial integration. At short exposure durations, Homa, Haver, and Schwartz (1976) found that normal faces were recognised better than faces that had the positions of the internal face features rearranged. Using a similar paradigm, Davidoff (1986a) investigated the effect of increasing exposure duration on the recognition of the features within a face. Caricature faces such as those shown in Fig. 2 were presented at one of three exposures (350, 750, or 1000 msec). The superior recognition using Normal (N) faces rather than Jumbled (J) faces was still present at 350 msec but had disappeared by 750 msec (see Fig. 3).

A detailed investigation of the results showed that the relative accuracy with which a particular face feature (e.g. the mouth) was recognised differed for Normal and Jumbled faces despite the fact that when individually presented (Condition F, Fig. 2) the features were equally easy to recognise. Figure 4 shows that there is no difference between the ability of normal subjects to recall the eyes, nose, or mouth after a 125 msec exposure. When the single face feature was presented in the wrong position, i.e., as in the Jumbled face, then again there was no difference in recognition accuracy between the types of face features. Analysing these

FIG 2. Stimuli used for Feature (F), Normal (N), and Jumbled (J) face recognition.

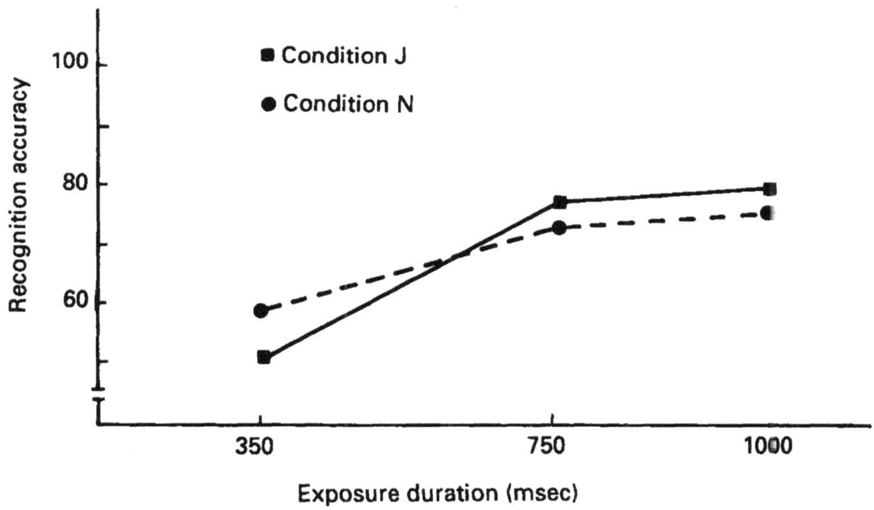

FIG 3. Recognition accuracy for features from Normal (N) or Jumbled (J) faces. Control data.

two conditions together revealed a significant interaction simply attributable to superior performance for the feature at fixation. Having shown that the features were equally easy to recognise when presented individually, differences found when features form part of a face become more interesting. When the features are put together to make a normal face, a different pattern of performance emerged. Replicating the results of Homa et al. (1976), it was found that at 350 msec the eyes and mouth were significantly better recognised than the nose. At longer exposures this difference between the features was not found (Davidoff, 1986a).

If prosopagnosia is a disorder in which spatial information cannot be rapidly integrated, one might predict that exposure duration would be of

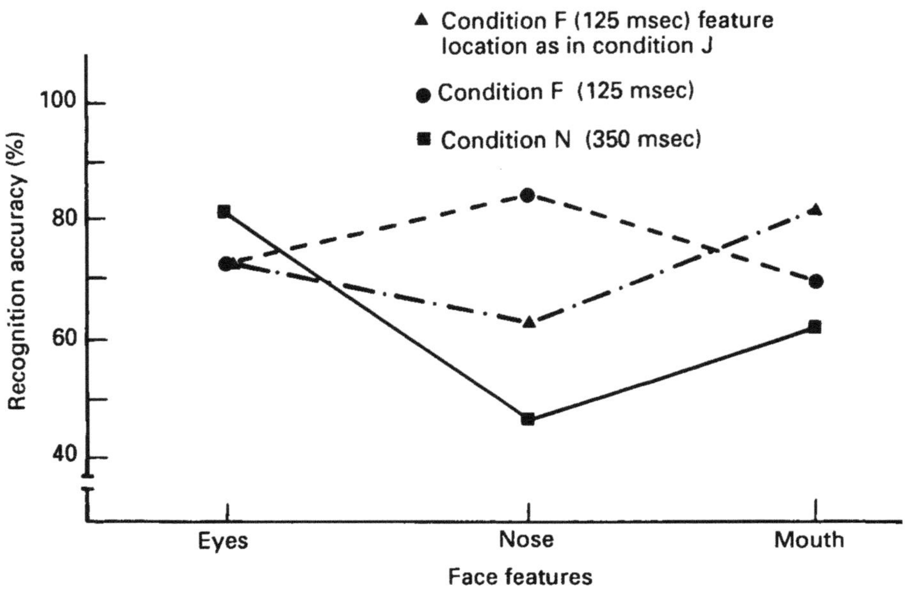

FIG 4. Recognition accuracy for features from Normal (N) faces and for two types of Feature (F) displays. Control data.

critical importance for that limited recognition that a prosopagnosic can achieve. Moreover, the processing differences that arise, for normals, at short exposures would never be obtained for the prosopagnosic. To test these ideas a prosopagnosic patient (R.B.) on whom neuropsychological data are reported elsewhere (Davidoff et al., 1986) was given face-recognition tasks.

R.B. showed a marked difficulty in perceiving the Mooney faces, performing below the average of the right posterior damaged group examined by Newcombe (1969). A similar poor performance was shown for the recognition of unknown and famous faces. The patient even reported in inability to recognise his own wife and family. These face-recognition problems were present in the presence of other well-preserved abilities (see Newcombe, 1979), especially verbal skills. There was no gross sensory loss apart from a visual field defect, and R.B. could successfully orient lines.

R.B. reported that faces were recognised by particular features. He preferred to remember the hairline, then the eyes and mouth; his behaviour showing a marked similarity to the piecemeal approach adopted by young children (Carey & Diamond, 1977) for face recognition. A systematic investigation of the effects of exposure time on face-feature recognition was carried out on R.B. using stimuli like those in Fig. 2. It is quite clear from Fig. 5 that R.B. had great difficulty with the task. Given up to three seconds to look at the Normal face, no advantage accrued over the Jumbled version. There is no trend suggesting that, given still longer exposures, R.B. would behave as control subjects do at short exposures. R.B.'s performance is more similar to that of normals when they are given a long time to inspect the face.

R.B.'s problem is that he takes a very long time to identify a single feature, perfect performance being achieved only at the sort of exposure times that are at the upper limit for configurational superiorities to be shown for faces. R.B. is thereby forced to operate on a feature-by-feature recognition procedure. An analysis of the feature recognition of R.B. shows this to be the case. Inspection of condition N (Normal face) in Fig. 6 shows that R.B. recognises the nose feature best, quite unlike the performance of normal subjects (Fig. 4) who for brief exposures do worst at remembering the nose features.

The importance of exposure time in determining the way patients deal with faces is also found in the work of Landis and co-workers (Christen, Landis, & Regard, 1985). They report three prosopagnosic patients who were able to achieve perfect performance on a face-matching task given unlimited exposure duration, but were below chance if exposure duration was reduced below one second. Landis believes that the good performance reflects slow but accurate analysis by the left hemisphere for detail. More speculatively, Landis argues that right hemisphere-damaged patients who

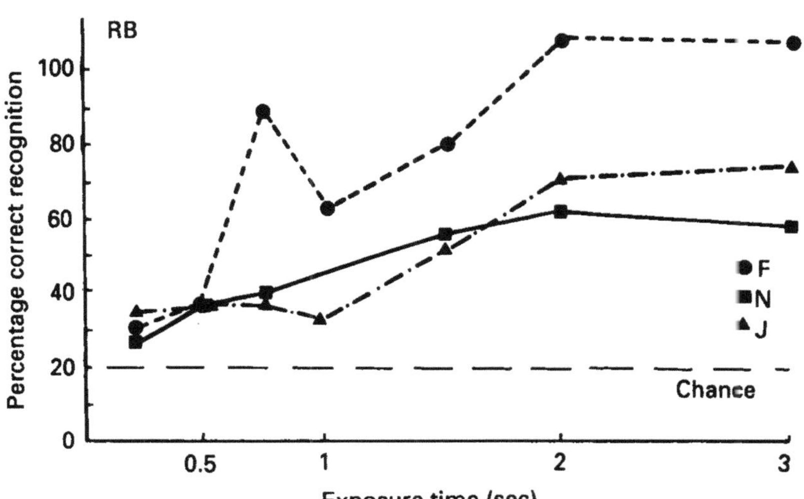

FIG 5. Effect of exposure time on recognition accuracy for R.B. using Feature (F), Normal (N), and Jumbled (J) displays.

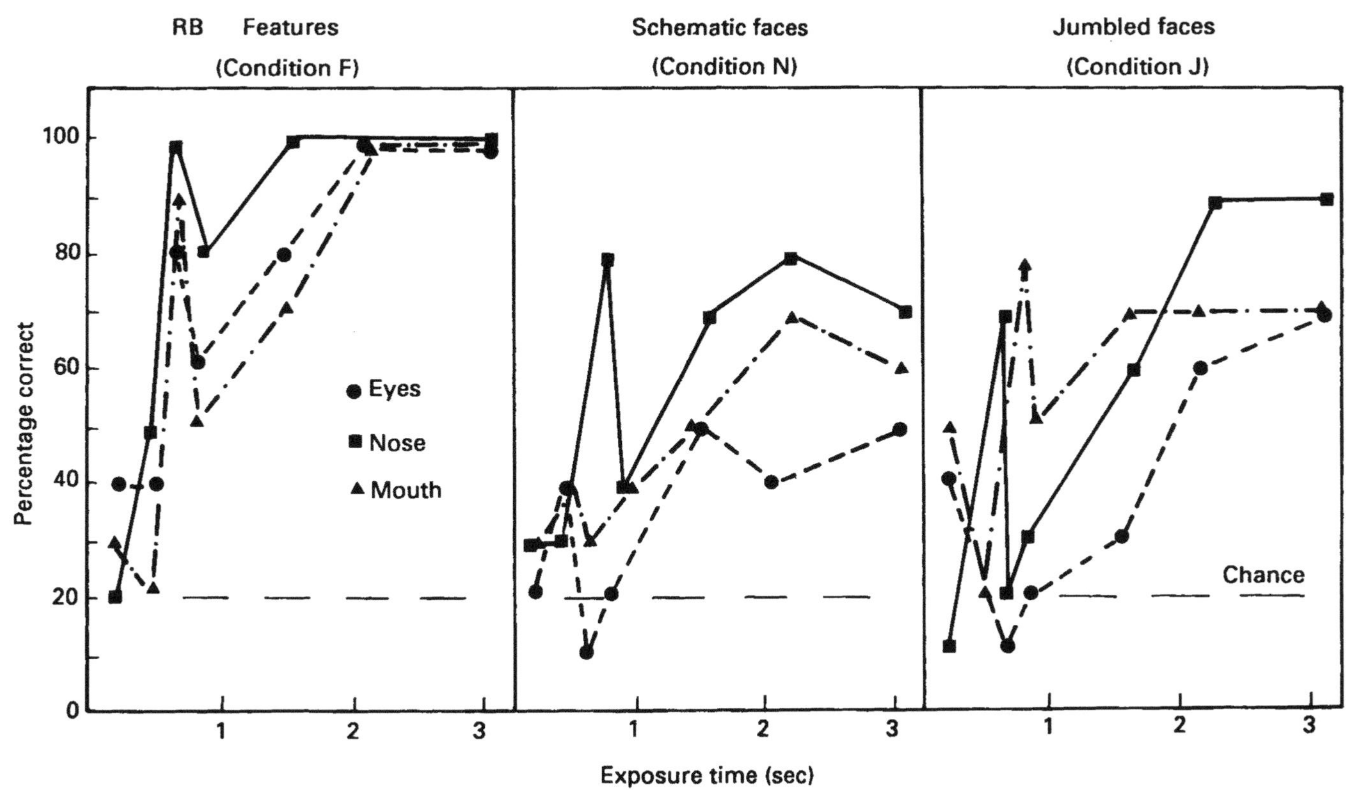

FIG 6. Effect of exposure time on the recognition of individual features for R.B.

are not prosopagnosic can show moderate recognition ability at short exposures, but do not improve given unlimited time because they continue to use their mildly impaired right hemisphere system rather than switch over to the accurate but slow intact left hemisphere.

While having given some evidence for the association of rapid information processing loss to prosopagnosia, one is not in a position to state the causal link. To do this one would require further information on the role of rapid information processing in both normals and non-prosopagnosic patients. However, some indication of its role has come from a study of Fraser and Parker (1987). They presented normal subjects with a rapid sequence of three face features and a face surround. The face surround was perceived as having been presented first almost irrespective of where in the sequence of four stimuli that it really occurred. It is, then, of some interest that R.B. tried to recognise people from the face outline. Perhaps with a faulty system for dealing with rapid spatial integration, the outline is the only aspect of the face that can be reliably processed. It should also follow that prosopagnosics should have difficulty with discriminations using other categories besides faces if a surround needs to be processed first. Accordingly, Christen et al. (1985) have found that shapes that differ only by their internal features also presented problems to the three prosopagnosic patients they studied. The range of stimuli that require the same processing as faces is not known; it might be quite limited.

Prosopagnosia viewed as a disorder of rapid spatial integration must, at present, be seen as a hypothesis. However, time-dependent processing connected with the right hemisphere has been noted in several neuropsychological reports. Difficulties with briefly presented material (Meier & French, 1965) or a slowing of reaction times to visual stimuli (Benson and Barton, 1970; De Renzi and Faglioni, 1965) have been associated with right-posterior lesions, and thus may promote a feature-recognition rather than a configurational approach to face processing. More rapid processing for the left visual field may also explain why the left half of a chimeric face dominates when it is presented to the commissurotomised patient (Levy, Trevarthem, & Sperry, 1972). It also would be reasonable for prosopagnosia to follow as a consequence of a right-hemisphere lesion.

REFERENCES

Bauer, R. M. (1984) Autonomic recognition of names and faces in prosopagnosia: A neuropsychological application of the Guilty Knowledge Test. *Neuropsychologic*, *22*, 457–469.

Benson, D. F. & Barton, M. I. (1970) Disturbances in constructional ability. *Cortex*, *6*, 19–46.

Benton, A. (1980) The neuropsychology of facial recognition. *American Psychologist*, *35*, 176–186.

Bodamer, J. (1947) Die Prosop-Agnosie. *Archiv. fur Psychiatrie und Nerven Krankheiten*, *179*, 6–53.
Bodis-Wollner, I. & Diamond, S. (1976) The measurement of spatial contrast sensitivity in cases of blurred vision associated with cerebral lesions. *Brain*, *99*, 695–710.
Bornstein, B. (1963) Prosopagnosia. In L. Halpern (Ed.), *Problems of dynamic neurology*. Jerusalem: Hadassah Medical Organisation.
Bornstein, B., Sroka, H., & Munitz, H. (1969) Prosopagnosia with animal face agnosia. *Cortex*, *5*, 793–820.
Bradshaw, J. L. & Wallace, G. (1971) Models for the processing and identification of faces. *Perception and Psychophysics*, *9*, 443–448.
Bruce, V. (1982) Changing faces: Visual and non-visual coding processes on face recognition. *British Journal of Psychology*, *73*, 105–116.
Bruce, V. & Valentine, T. (1985) Identity priming in the recognition of familiar faces. *British Journal of Psychology*, *76*, 373–383.
Bruyer, R., Laterre, C., Seron, X., Feyereisen, P., Strypstein, E., Pierrard, E., & Rectem, D. (1983) A case of prosopagnosia with some preserved covert remembrance of familiar faces. *Brain and Cognition*, *2*, 257–284.
Carey, S. & Diamond, R. (1977) From piecemeal to configurational representation of faces. *Science*, *195*, 312–314.
Charcot, J. M. (1883) Un cas de suppression brusque et isolée de la vision mentale des signes et des objets (formes et couleurs). *Progres Medical*, *11*, 568.
Christen, L., Landis, T., & Regard, M. (1985) Left hemispheric functional compensation in prosopagnosia? A tachistoscopic study with unilaterally lesioned patients. *Human Neurobiology*, *4*, 9–14.
Cole, M. & Perez-Cruet, J. (1964) Prosopagnosia. *Neuropsychologia*, *2*, 237–246.
Damasio, A. R. (1985) Prosopagnosia. *Trends in the Neurosciences*, *8*, 132–135.
Damasio, A. R., Damasio, H., & Van Hoesen, G. W. (1982) Prosopagnosia: Anatomic basis and behavioral mechanisms. *Neurology*, *32*, 331–334.
Davidoff, J. B. (1982) Information processing and hemispheric function. In A. Burton (Ed.), *The pathology and psychology of cognition*. London: Methuen.
Davidoff, J. B. (1986a) The mental representation of faces: Spatial and temporal factors. *Perception and Psychophysics*, *40*, 391–400.
Davidoff, J. B. (1986b) The specificity of face perception: Evidence from psychological investigations. In R. Bruyer (Ed.), *The neuropsychology of face perception and facial expression*. Hillsdale, N.J.: Lawrence Erlbaum Associates Inc.
Davidoff, J. B., Matthews, W. R., & Newcombe, F. (1986) Observations on a case of prosopagnosia. In H. Ellis, M. Jeeves, F. Newcombe, & A. Young (Eds.), *Aspects of face processing*. Dordrecht: Martinus Nijhoff.
Davidoff, J. B. & Wilson, B. (1985) A case of visual agnosia showing a disorder of presemantic visual classification. *Cortex*, *21*, 121–134.
De Renzi, E. (1986) Current issues on prosopagnosia. In H. Ellis, M. Jeeves, F. Newcombe, & A. Young (Eds.), *Aspects of face processing*. Dordrecht: Martinus Nijhoff.
De Renzi, E. & Faglioni, P. (1965) The comparative efficiency of intelligence and vigilance tests in detecting hemispheric cerebral damage. *Cortex*, *1*, 410–433.
De Renzi, E., Scotti, G., & Spinnler, H. (1969) Perceptual and associative disorders of visual recognition. *Neurology Minneapolis.*, *19*, 634–642.
De Renzi, E. & Spinnler, H. (1966) Facial recognition in brain-damaged patients. *Neurology*, *16*, 145–152.
Ellis, H. D., Shepherd, J. W., & Davies, G. M. (1979) Identification of familiar and unfamiliar faces from internal and external features: Some implications for theories of face recognition. *Perception*, *8*, 431–439.

Faust, C. (1955) *Die zerebralen Herdstorung bei Hinter hauptsverletzungen und ihre Beurteilung*. Stuttgart: Thieme.

Fodor, J. A. (1983) *The modularity of mind*. Cambridge, Mass.: MIT Press.

Fraser, I. H. & Parker, D. M. (1987) *Structural bias in the perception of temporally fragmented patterns*. Paper presented at the Experimental Psychology Society Oxford.

Hecaen, H. & Albert, M. L. (1978) *Human neuropsychology*. New York: John Wiley & Son.

Homa, D., Haver, B., & Schwartz, T. (1976) Perceptibility of schematic face stimuli: Evidence for a perceptual Gestalt. *Memory and Cognition*, *4*, 176–185.

Jones, A. C. (1969) Influence of mode of stimulus presentation on performance in facial recognition tasks. *Cortex*, *5*, 290–301.

Landis, T., Cummings, J. L., Christen, L., Bogen, J. E., & Imhof, H.-G. (1986) Are unilateral lesions sufficient to cause prosopagnosia? Clinical and radiological findings in six additional patents. *Cortex*, *22*, 243–252.

Landsell, H. (1968) Effect of extent of temporal lobe ablations on two lateralized deficits. *Physiology and Behavior*, *3*, 271–273.

Levy, J., Trevarthen, C., & Sperry, R. W. (1972) Perception of bilateral chimeric figures following hemispheric disconnection. *Brain*, *95*, 61–78.

Lhermitte, F., Chain, F., Escourelle, R., Ducarne, B., & Pillon, B. (1972) Etude anatomoclinique d'un cas de prosopagnosia. *Revue Neurologique*, *126*, 329–346.

Meier, M. J. & French, L. A. (1965) Lateralized deficits in complex visual discrimination and bilateral transfer of reminiscence following unilateral temporal lobectomy. *Neuropsychologia*, *3*, 261–272.

Milner, B. (1968) Visual recognition and recall after right temporal lobe excision in man. *Neuropsychologia*, *6*, 191–209.

Mooney, C. M. (1957) Closure as affected by viewing time and multiple visual fixations. *Canadian Journal of Psychology*, *11*, 21–28.

Mooney, C. M. (1960) Recognition of ambiguous and unambiguous visual configurations with short and long exposures. *British Journal of Psychology*, *51*, 119–125.

Newcombe, F. (1969) *Missile wounds of the brain*. Oxford: Oxford University Press.

Newcombe, F. (1979) The processing of visual information in prosopagnosia and acquired dyslexia: Functional versus physiological interpretation. In D. J. Oborne, M. M. Gruneberg, & J. R. Eiser (Eds.), *Research in psychology and medicine, Vol. 1*. London: Academic Press.

Perrett, D., Mistlin, A. J., & Chitty, A. J. (1987) Visual neurones responsive to faces. *Trends in the Neurosciences*, *10*, 358–364.

Walker-Smith, G. J. (1978) The effects of delay and exposure duration on a face recognition task. *Perception and Psychophysics*, *24*, 63–70.

Warrington, E. K. & James, M. (1967) An experimental investigation of facial recognition in patients with unilateral cerebral lesions. *Cortex*, *3*, 317–326.

Warrington, E. K. & Taylor, A. M. (1973) The contribution of the right parietal lobe to object recognition. *Cortex*, *9*, 152–164.

Yin, R. K. (1969) Looking at upside-down faces. *Journal of Experimental Psychology*, *81*, 141–145.

Yin, R. K. (1970) Face recognition by brain-injured patients: A dissociable ability? *Neuropsychologia*, *8*, 395–402.

PART V: MEMORY

15 Mnemonic Retraining of Organic Memory Disorders

L. S. Cermak and M. O'Connor
Psychology Service, Veterans' Administration Hospital, Boston, Massachusetts, U.S.A.

Two models of normal memory have greatly influenced amnesia research and rehabilitation during the past decade. These models include the duplex theory proposed by Atkinson and Shiffrin (1967) and the levels-of-processing hypothesis first proposed by Craik and Lockhart (1972). The former proposes that memory consists of short- and long-term storehouses that differ along several dimensions, including capacities, life-spans, and codes. Adherents of this theory tend to view memory problems as a failure in the transfer of information from the short- to the long-term store. The levels-of-processing model is a more dynamic explanation, positing that memory is a consequence of the manner in which to-be-remembered information is initially analysed. Deep (semantic) analysis is said to result in better retention than shallow (acoustic or orthographic) analysis. Memory deficits are attributed to an inability to perform, or at least to profit from, semantic analysis, coupled with a greater reliance on the shallow levels of processing information (Butters & Cermak, 1980). A third theory, the retrieval-deficit hypothesis, has also been developed by researchers in the field of amnesia (primarily Warrington and Weiskrantz). This theory proposes that memory deficits are due to an inability to retrieve that which is stored in memory. Thus, amnesia is not so much due to an inability to take in information as to an inability to get it out.

All three models have been cited as underlying rationales for memory-retraining programmes. The duplex theory describes clinical recovery as an improvement in transfer from short- to long-term memory; the levels hypothesis characterises recovery as the regained capacity to engage in elaborative or deep analysis of information; and the retrieval-deficits theory views recovery as a revived ability to retrieve information. Evidence supporting these models is beyond the scope of this report. They are mentioned simply to show that different cognitive theories have been invoked to explain memory recovery when it occurs.

More germane to this review will be the various forms of psychological intervention that have been employed to remediate memory problems. Before turning to these, however, two issues that could obscure the evaluation of these mnemonics must be noted. Most obvious is the fact that spontaneous recovery often occurs alongside therapeutically induced change. In order to distinguish between spontaneous and intervention-based recovery, one must be certain that the appropriate control groups have been included. In addition, the cause of amnesia should always be considered because therapeutic manœuvres may be successful only with specific types of amnesia. Some investigators go to great lengths to group patients according to aetiology; whereas others are less inclined to do so. Both approaches have their proponents, but one's bias ought to be included when discussing mnemonic therapy.

MNEMONICS USED TO FACILITATE RETRIEVAL

Memory retraining has almost exclusively relied on facilitation of learning and retrieval through the use of mnemonics. Although somewhat illusory, these techniques enable retention of specific information under given circumstances. The most popular therapeutic mnemonic and the most thoroughly researched method of mitigating memory problems is visual imagery. Consequently, this section will begin with a review of studies focusing on the use of imagery with memory-impaired individuals. Subsequently, it will turn to behavioural programmes, computer techniques, and some other interesting approaches to memory rehabilitation.

Imagery as a Therapeutic Mnemonic

For some time now, cognitive researchers such as Pavio (1969), Bower (1970), Atwood (1971), and professional mnemonists such as Furst (1949) and Lorayne and Lucas (1974) have all stressed the utility of imagery as a way of retaining information for subsequent recall. Their evidence comes primarily from experimental investigations demonstrating that an individual's memory capacity can be increased dramatically when to-be-remembered items are linked with an image. Attempts to apply these imagery techniques to everyday life has grown in popularity, as indicated by the increased number of books, magazine articles, and commercial schools devoted to this topic. No less important has been the application of imaging techniques to the facilitation of the memory of cognitively impaired people. Here the number of investigations is far fewer and the nature of the results much more controversial.

Pioneers in the use of imagery with brain-injured patients were primarily interested in the remediation of memory disorders in patients with unilateral brain injury. The basic premise was that patients with left-hemisphere involvement might be most likely to overcome their verbal-memory problems using visualisation, an hypothesised right-hemisphere speciality. For instance, Patten (1972) employed the "peg list" whereby patients were taught to couple visually a list of objects (e.g. a teacup or a radio) with the numbers one to ten. Each patient was then presented with the number and asked to remember the item that had been connected with number. Patten reported remarkable success with four clients who were able to use their preserved visual-memory skills to boost their poor verbal memories. One of these patients, however, showed a concurrent clearing of his expressive aphasia, which might indicate that spontaneous recovery had boosted any memory gains. The peg system was not successfully employed by three other patients who were unaware of their memory problems and consequently were unmotivated to change. These patients all had lesions in the mid-line structures of the brain, and it is likely that the degree of their amnesia was more severe than the patients with left-hemisphere lesions. Altogether, these results suggested that the peg system was only of limited value to a select group of minimally disturbed amnesics.

Jones (1974) attempted to use imagery to ameliorate the memory deficits of patients who had undergone either right or left unilateral temporal lobe excision. She taught these patients to visualise a list of paired associates in order to facilitate their verbal recall. Consonant with Patten's results, patients with left temporal lobectomies benefited from the use of imagery. Contrary to Jones's expectations, however, patients with right temporal lobectomies also improved their verbal recall when using imagery. They were, in fact, able to employ imagery as efficiently as normal control subjects.

The puzzling ability of patients with right temporal lobe excisions to profit from the use of imagery even though they lacked the supposed anatomical "site" involved in visual memory led Jones to explore this phenomenon further several years later (Jones-Gotman & Milner, 1978). This time she increased task difficulty by using a list of 60 paired associates, which were presented only one time. As expected, the left temporal lobectomy group again derived some benefits from the use of imagery (but performed well below the normals). In contrast, the right lobectomy patients group were found to be impaired on both immediate and delayed recall of high-imagery information. Quite significantly, this group's abysmal performance was correlated with the amount of hippocampus removed during surgery, thereby implicating the right hippocampus in imagery-mediated verbal learning. These findings take on added significance when contrasted with the group's performance on a subsequent task requiring *verbal* mediation between abstract paired associates. In this instance, right lobectomy patients performed normally, and no correlation could be found between the size of the hippocampal excision and memory performance.

Jones also examined the effects of imagery on the memory of two patients (H.M. and H.B.) with bilateral mesial temporal lobectomies. She found that they performed similarly to Patten's amnesics with mid-line lesions in that they were unable to recall the to-be-remembered items under any condition. Unlike Patten's patients, however, Jones reported that H.M. and H.B. were both able to form vivid visual images as per instructions. Their difficulty lay in their inability to utilise the newly formed images. They uniformly forgot that they had previously formed a visual association linking the to-be-remembered items. Furthermore, even when reminded that he had done so, H.M. was unable to retrieve his prior image and would instead conjure up an entirely new one.

Baddeley and Warrington (1973) performed one of the first imagery studies using a heterogeneous group of amnesics. They investigated these patients' ability to utilise either taxonomic or imagery clustering to facilitate their recall of a list of words. Findings revealed that taxonomic clustering was beneficial but imagery was not. Baddeley and Warrington suggested that the amnesics' failure to profit from visual imagery was due to an inability to generate a novel interactive relationship between two items. Like Jones-Gotman and Milner, they believed that the amnesics were proficient at forming single visual images, but that they could not form an image in which the two items interacted.

Lewinson, Danaher, and Kikel (1977) trained a heterogeneous group of brain-injured patients in visual imagery techniques for both paired associates and a face–name learning task. He reported that 33% of the patients in the non-imagery control condition were unable to learn the list of paired associates within the allotted 10 trials, whereas all of those trained in imagery were able to do so. However, the effects of imagery-facilitated recall persisted for only a 30-minute retention interval and they were barely noticeable after one week. Equally disappointing, imagery did not facilitate the brain-injured participants' memories on the face–name task at all.

Lewinson's finding that the face–name mnemonic technique, which had been advocated by Lorayne and Lucas (1974), might not be appropriate for use with brain-injured patients was borne out in several other investigations. Glasgow, Zeiss, Barrera, and Lewinson (1977) failed in an attempt to help a brain-injured client (Mr T.) remember to associate names and faces. Although imagery was useful when the face–name list was restricted to a small number of easily imaged names, Mr T.'s performance declined with increased task complexity. It seemed that Mr T. was unable to utilise the four-step procedure in which he had to translate a person's name into a concrete noun and then associate this image with one of the person's prominent facial features. The cognitive manipulations of this task were too complicated for a brain-injured person to use effectively.

Crovitz (1979) has stressed the importance of retrieval cues when trying to apply imagery techniques. In his procedure, a chain-type of mnemonic, the so-called Airplane List, was read to a Korsakoff and a closed-head injury patient, both of whom were experiencing memory difficulties. Crovitz found that neither of these individuals was able to recall the list freely unless provided with retrieval cues. This procedure, like one described by Jaffe and Katz (1975), focused on both encoding and retrieval aspects of information processing by encouraging organisation of incoming information and a concentrated search at time of recall.

In a detailed series of case studies, Crovitz, Harvey, and Horn (1979) described several variables that influence the efficacy of imagery mnemonics with brain-injured patients. Crovitz emphasised the importance of giving brain-injured individuals sufficient processing time when instructing them in a mnemonic technique. He rejected the traditional reverence for the formation of *bizarre* images, stating that they are actually counter-productive when used with brain-injured individuals. He believed that these patients tend to be concrete thinkers and that they need more plausible forms of mnemonics. Crovitz also cited the differential impact of experimenter-provided v. subject-generated images, stressing the superiority of the latter for brain-injured patients. Finally, Crovitz recommended that selected readings during therapy might increase the patient's chances of being able to utilise imagery.

The bulk of these reported studies has focused on patients with heterogenous aetiologies. This diversity probably limits interpretations of the predominantly negative findings because positive results may be population dependent. The consistency of Jones-Gotman's and Patten's patients with dominant hemisphere lesions would seem to suggest a certain heuristic value in concentrating on a homogeneous population of amnesics. This is not necessarily true, however, as exemplified by other studies limited to select populations of amnesics. Investigations of Korsakoff patients have attained results that are as puzzling and conflicting as those obtained with heterogenous patient groups. For instance, Cutting (1978) attempted and failed to teach Korsakoff patients the use of imagery. He attributed Korsakoff's inability to use imagery to a deficit in their capacity for active mental operations. Cutting stated that Korsakoff patients were adept only at tasks that used passive forms of meaningfulness. At odds with these results were those of Cermak (1976), who found that Korsakoff patients could benefit from imagery in both recognition and free-recall tasks. This latter success was, however, qualified by Cermak's notations that the advantages of imagery were much greater for normal subjects, and the Korsakoff patients had to be provided with imagery instructions at the time of both encoding and retrieval as previously pointed out by Crovitz (1979) and by Jafee and Katz (1975).

Undoubtedly the most optimistic report on the use of imagery with brain-injured individuals is one by Kovner, Mattis, and Goldmeier (1983a), who taught patients with severe anterograde amnesias of mixed aetiology to utilise ridiculously imaged stories to enhance their free recall of a list of words. This contrasted sharply with their inability to improve when using a selective reminding procedure (Buschke, 1973). Kovner and his associates ascribed this positive effect of the visually imaged stories to the possibility that they provided "artificial chunks" of information. The authors maintained that this explanation was consistent with the idea that the cortical processes necessary for clustering items were preserved in amnesia and that the failure of amnesic patients to encode information properly might be due to impairment in their subcortical arousal mechanism. Along these lines, imagery might be viewed as a sort of metaphorical prosthesis—enabling patients to organise information despite their natural tendency not to do so. Spurred on by this success, Kovner, Mattis, & Goldmeier (1983a) attempted to explore the learning potential of other amnesics using the ridiculously imaged stories. Remarkably, they were able to teach two amnesics up to 120 words using their method.

Despite this optimism, it must be reiterated that the practical applications of imagery are tremendously limited even for individuals with normal memory abilities. Morris (1978) suggests that imagery is only advantageous for the retention of meaningless information, which limits the value of any therapeutic application. Another problem with imagery (and, for that matter, related mnemonics such as verbal mediation, rhymes, and first-letter memorisation schemes) is its narrow focus on tasks irrelevant to everyday memory needs. Above all, the most serious drawback to the use of imagery is its concentration on encoding operations and its failure to address the retrieval component of memory deficits. This is a critical problem because elaborate encoding requires vigilance and planning, which is usually beyond the capabilities of the brain-injured individual. Research has shown that even individuals with normal memories most often elect not to use imagery, although they might try to use mental retracing of events and/or alphabetical searches (Harris, 1978). These are mnemonics that are performed at retrieval not at encoding. Given that normal individuals spurn imagery as an encoding device, it is difficult to justify it as a memory aid for the disabled. Of course, if it worked, pragmatics would dictate that it be used, but the evidence presented here certainly doesn't point to that possibility.

Behavioural Techniques

Behavioural methods have been used occasionally to improve the deficient memory skills of the brain-injured. Emphasis is directed towards the environmental influences on retention, which becomes the focus of these behavioural programmes. Research in this area is in a rather preliminary stage, and so evaluation of the absolute merits of behaviourally based programmes must await further investigations. But in the meantime, some interesting studies have been conducted.

Dolan and Norton (1977) have successfully employed an operant reinforcement schedule to facilitate the memory abilities of a mixed aetiology of patients. This success underscores the possibilities of behavioural intervention, but the study itself did not clearly indicate whether or not any other systematic regimen would have been equally beneficial in enhancing the memory capacities of these patients. Another example of behavioural conditioning comes from Seidel and Hodgkinson (1979) who designed a programme to help a Korsakoff patient (Mr T.) change his maladaptive smoking habits. Prior to this investigation, Mr T. tended to hoard cigarettes and to leave half-lit ones strewn about in ashtrays on the hospital ward. The investigators instituted a strict smoking regimen whereby cigarettes were allocated on an hourly basis and smoking behaviour was closely supervised. Within 45 days Mr T. was able to manage responsibly his own cigarette intake. This success is noteworthy, yet one wonders whether it represents a true cognitive achievement or merely reflects the Korsakoffs' well-documented facility at skill acquisition.

A behavioural regimen with Korsakoff patients has also been studied by Oscar-Berman, Heyman, Bonner, and Ryder (1980), who found far less promising outcomes than those mentioned earlier. These researchers showed that the response rate of amnesic Korsakoff patients did not conform to the reinforcement schedules in a normal manner. Oscar-Berman surmised that Korsakoff patients were basically insensitive to differences in reinforcement contingencies. If this is so, then such a limitation would certainly render them unlikely candidates for extensive behavioural training.

Other behavioural aids for memory improvement have been more directly linked to the environment than those just described. Harris (1978), who has given the name "external memory aids" to this category, includes in this group such things as shopping lists, diaries, timers, writing on one's hand, relying on another person, and leaving something in a special place. Harris proposes that more active cues are preferable to passive ones and that the specificity, temporal contiguity, and accessibility of the cue are important. One device that meets these criteria is the digital alarm chronograph. Gouvier (1982) has used the chronograph with brain-injured clients and have found it to be quite efficient when supplemented by a personal appointment calendar. The chronograph is set for hourly intervals at which times it emits a bleep reminding the person to consult her or his daily schedule book. It is convenient for amnesics to use and also allows them to be more independent in their daily routines.

Computerised Rehabilitation of Amnesia

A related area to behavioural techniques is the recent use of personal computers to meet the needs of brain-injury victims. Both the efficacy of this approach and its practical utility make it seem like a promising resource for rehabilitative interventions. Bracy, a prominent advocate of computer-based rehabilitation, gives glowing accounts of its successful clinical applications. He recently (1983) reported two case studies in which remarkable cognitive recovery was demonstrated when computer programs were used with brain-injured people. Both of his clients were evaluated three years post injury, at which time Bracy initiated a regimen of approximately 25 hours per week of home-based computer work in conjunction with weekly meetings with a neuropsychologist. Over a period of two years Bracy's patients were reported to have gained 23 and 28 points respectively in their I.Q. scores.

Often computer-based rehabilitation methods simply simulate programmes that a behavioural analyst would prescribe, but they do so in such a consistent manner that "therapy" can take place without the presence of the therapist. Many of these programs specifically address the isolated operations involved in cognition including selective attention, vigilance, discrimination, inhibition, initiation, and generalisation of responses. These tasks, referred to as "foundation skills", are inherent components of higher cognitive functions. Improvement in each area is thus important in enabling the patient to perform more complex operations.

As with so many other aspects of computer technology, however, the potential applications seem to outstrip the practical applications. Software packages written for the computer have generally been nothing more than simplistic variations of testing procedures already used with brain-injured patients, and thus merely provide a mechanised vehicle for repetitive presentation of material. Another problem is that many of the programs are written solely for a particular microprocessor, thereby mandating the purchase of an expensive device.

Two things are needed before computers can truly play a role in rehabilitation of the brain-injured patient. First, evidence must be provided to show that rehabilitation occurs at least as rapidly as that obtained in normal memory therapy. Second, a training schedule should be initiated that is more than simple repetition of randomly selected, otherwise available test instruments. The potential for the use of computers is tremendous, but the history of rehabilitation as we have traced it here has shown that no mnemonic has been very effective. To assume that the addition of computerisation to our armament of failures will result in success is not rational. Application of computers ought to be viewed sceptically so long as the software remains based within the domain of the mnemonic failures we have outlined here.

INDIVIDUAL THERAPEUTIC ATTEMPTS

During recent years, we have been involved in developing several individualised memory-retraining programmes. Most of these have been designed for alcoholic Korsakoff patients and, as might be expected, these attempts were not very successful. One problem has been that most of these patients are not aware of their own memory deficits. This has resulted in a lack of motivation to participate in the remedial programmes. Another problem has been that the severity of the patients' information-processing deficits makes the imposition of mnemonics futile. The greatest disappointment has been that even those patients who are able to learn memory aids have not employed them spontaneously.

Patients with amnesia of an aetiology other than Korsakoff's syndrome have also entered extensive individualised programmes of memory retraining at our facility. Most notable was a post-encephalitic patient with a dense anterograde and retrograde amnesia. Attempts to retrain this patient have been documented elsewhere (Cermak, 1976; Cermak & O'Connor, 1983) but can be synthesised quite simply. Basically, after many months of participating in a programme focusing on the use of imagery, verbal mediation, and rote memorisation, we found that the patient could be trained to memorise information but could not incorporate it into his knowledge base in any comprehensible fashion. For instance, he was taught to answer the question "Who broke Babe Ruth's record for lifetime runs?" by replying "Henry Aaron". But, when asked who held the record for the most home runs hit in a career, he would reply, "Babe Ruth".

Because of the parrot-like nature of his responses, we believed that this patient was not able to profit from memory aids because any new learning remained insulated from his comprehension of the information. In short, his memory (consisting of the manipulation, reconstruction, and extension of information) seemed beyond hope of recovery. This patient clearly exemplified a problem that recurrently undermines memory-retraining endeavours—namely, that specific information can be readily taught via a mnemonic device but it is rarely integrated into a patient's true comprehension of material.

A patient who was somewhat more adept at employing mnemonic strategies came to our attention after suffering an anterior communicating artery aneurysm. Following surgical intervention he displayed a dense anterograde amnesia with a retrogade amnesia extending back several years. His memory deficits were manifested in his confusion concerning his whereabouts and his difficulty learning peoples' names. Unlike the patient described previously, this patient used mnemonics spontaneously. He had, in fact, learned a series of memory aids prior to his disability. This advantage probably allowed him to rely on old knowledge in order to gain access to new information. Unfortunately, even the use of these mnemonics did not help the patient's memory in any dramatic way. He, like all others, was never able to incorporate new learning into his semantic memory. Despite adroit utilisation of mnemonics, the patient remained amnesic.

The last patient to be described was a head-injury victim whose memory problems were undoubtedly secondary to other neuropsychological disorders. These so-called secondary memory problems might well afford the greatest potential for therapy because certain cognitive functions such as attention and sequencing might lend themselves to therapy more than pure memory disorders. This patient's memory deficit (MQ = 64) was superimposed upon such difficulties. She was unable to sequence properly and had problems distinguishing a portion of a stimulus from the whole. Obviously these impairments confounded any attempts to measure her intelligence, but we suggest that she was a very bright person due to her former profession and various indices of her previous intellect. She was keenly aware of her disorders, and quite determined to learn compensatory techniques.

Most of the compensatory techniques were designed by her Occupational Therapist, and they provided the patient with ways of overcoming her perceptual and sequencing problems. Instructions that seemed too complicated for the patient to remember (such as which medication to take, when to take it, and the appropriate quantity) were sequenced and organised by placing the appropriate amounts in individual containers on a large spice rack labelled by days of the week and hours. The patient's house keys were colour coded with the locks and arrows placed above the lock to provide direction. Memory for information that did not have to be sequenced or that was not perceptually confusable (such as peoples' names) proved to be amenable to mediation. The patient enjoyed these games and, in fact, proved to be remarkably good at them. Nevertheless, her ability to put these pieces together in a comprehensive way remained poor.

It is important to note that this patient's success in memory retraining was due to the fact that her memory difficulties were secondary to other neuropsychological deficits (sequencing and perception). Her ability to grasp the nature of her difficulties was also essential to her successful outcome. Most important, it should be noted that the patient's deficit was not ultimately overcome but merely by-passed via environmental restructuring.

CONCLUSIONS

To date, rehabilitative mnemonic techniques have not successfully met the needs of the memory-impaired individual. Strategies such as the use of imagery, mnemonic devices, and external memory aids provide limited facilitation for specific memory problem areas. They do not, however, effect dramatic or generalisable changes in memory. Furthermore, they work even in these specialised instances only for patients who can be creative enough to use them and can remember to use them.

When assessing a patient's potential for recovery, the most useful perspective to take is the patient's own perspective. The cases we reviewed in the last section of this chapter provided substantial evidence for the utility of focusing on individual differences. Each person, whether brain-injured or not, has skills, deficits, feelings, and needs that are peculiar to her or his own range of experiences. Individual differences should thus weigh heavily on the evaluation of the memory capacities of the brain-injured.

One way of achieving a broader and more integrated perspective to memory therapy lies in facilitating communication between various health care professionals. The occupational therapist, nurse, neuropsychologist, neurologist, and social worker all play different roles in promoting the patient's post-injury adaptation. A team effort by these individuals would enhance their ability to view the patient in a holistic fashion. The family of the brain-injured person should also be included in this enterprise because these people are often the most sensitive to the patient's needs and abilities and are the most knowledgeable about her or his pre-injury personality and mental status.

REFERENCES

Atkinson, R. C. & Shiffrin, R. M. (1967) *Human memory: A proposed system and its control processes.* Technical Report No. 110, Stanford University.

Atwood, G. (1971) An experimental study of visual imagination and memory. *Cognitive Psychology, 2*, 290–299.

Baddeley, A. D. & Warrington, E. K. (1973) Memory coding and amnesia. *Neuropsychologia, 11*, 159–165.

Bower, G. H. (1970) Analysis of a mnemonic device. *American Scientist, 58*, 496–510.

Bracy, O. (1983) Computer based cognitive rehabilitation. *Cognitive Rehabilitation, 1 (1)*, 7.

Buschke, H. (1973) Selective reminding for analysis of memory and learning. *Journal of Verbal Learning and Verbal Behavior, 12*, 543–550.

Butters, N. & Cermak, L. S. (1980) *Alcoholic Korsakoff's syndrome: An information processing approach to amnesia.* New York: Academic Press.

Cermak, L. S. (1975) Imagery as an aid to retrieval for Korsakoff patients. *Cortex, 11,* 163–169.

Cermak, L. S. (1976) The encoding capacity of a patient with amnesia due to encephalitis. *Neuropsychologia, 19,* 311–326.

Cermak, L. S. & O'Connor, M. (1983) The anterograde and retrograde retrieval ability of a patient with amnesia to encephalitis. *Neuropsychologia, 21 (3),* 213–234.

Craik, F. I. M. & Lockhart, R. (1972) Levels of processing: A framework for memory research. *Journal of Verbal Learning and Verbal Behavior, 11,* 671–684.

Crovitz, H. F. (1979) Memory retraining in brain-damaged patients: The airplane list. *Cortex, 15,* 131–134.

Crovitz, H. F., Harvey, M. T., & Horn, R. W. (1979) Problems in the acquisition of imagery mnemonics: Three brain-damaged cases. *Cortex, 15,* 225–234.

Cutting, J. (1978) A cognitive approach to Korsakoff's syndrome. *Cortex, 14,* 485–495.

Dolan, M. & Norton, J. (1977) A programmed training technique that uses reinforcement to facilitate acquisition and retention in brain-damaged patients. *Journal of Clinical Psychology, 33,* 496–501.

Furst, B. (1949) *The practical way to a better memory.* New York: Goose & Dunlap.

Glasgow, R. E., Zeiss, R. A., Barrera, M., & Lewinson, P. M. (1977) Case studies on remediating memory deficits in brain damaged individuals. *Journal of Clinical Psychology, 33 (4),* 1049–1054.

Gouvier, W. (1982) Using the digital alarm chronograph in memory retraining. *Behavioral Engineering, 7,* 4–134.

Harris, J. (1978) External memory aids. In M. Gruneberg, P. Morris, & R. Sykes (Eds.), *Practical aspects of memory.* London: Academic Press, pp. 172–179.

Jaffe, P. G. & Katz, A. N. (1975) Attenuating anterograde amnesia in Korsakoff's psychosis. *Journal of Abnormal Psychology, 84,* 559–562.

Jones, M. K. (1974) Imagery as a mnemonic aid after left temporal lobectomy: Contrast between material specific and generalized memory disorders. *Neuropsychologia, 12,* 21–30.

Jones-Gotman, M. K. & Milner, B. (1978) Right temporal lobe contribution to image mediated verbal learning. *Neuropsychologia, 16,* 61–71.

Kovner, R., Mattis, S., & Goldmeier, F. (1983a) *Journal of Clinical Neuropsychology, 5 (1),* 65–71.

Kovner, R., Mattis, S., & Pass, K. (1983b) *Some amnesic patients can freely recall large amounts of information in new contexts.* Meeting of the International Neuropsychological Society, Mexico City.

Lewinson, P. M., Danaher B. G., & Kikel, S. (1977) Visual imagery as mnemonic aid for brain-injured persons. *Journal of Consulting and Clinical Psychology, 45,* 717–723.

Lorayne, H. & Lucas, J. (1974) *The memory book.* New York: Stein & Day.

Morris, P. E. (1978) Sense and nonsense in classical memories. In M. Gruneberg, P. Morris, & R. Sykes (Eds.), *Practical aspects in memory.* London: Academic Press, pp. 155–163.

Oscar-Berman, M., Heyman, G., Bonner, R., & Ryder, J. (1980) Human neuropsychology: Some differences between Korsakoff and normal operant performance. *Psychological Research, 41,* 235–247.

Patten, B. M. (1972) The ancient art of memory—usefulness in treatment. *Archives of Neurology, 26,* 28–31.

Pavio, A. (1969) Mental imagery in associative learning and memory. *Psychological Review, 76 (3),* 241–263.

Seidel, H. & Hodgkinson (1979) Behavior modification and long-term learning in Korsakoff's psychosis. *Nursing Times, 75,* 1855–1857.

16 The Role of Articulation in Verbal Short-term Memory

S. F. Cappa
Department of Neurology, Niguarda Hospital, Milano, Italy

G. Vallar
Istituto di Clinica Neurologica, University of Milano, Italy

INTRODUCTION

In recent years evidence has been brought forward to indicate that focal lesions involving the left hemisphere may selectively impair verbal short-term memory (STM). The main defect of the so-called STM patients is a dramatic reduction of auditory verbal span: They are unable to repeat more than two or three verbal items immediately after presentation (digits, letters, or words), the performance being consistently better when the stimuli are visually presented (Basso, Spinnler, Vallar, & Zanobio, 1982; Warrington, Logue, & Pratt, 1971; Warrington & Shallice, 1969). This auditory/visual dissociation, together with the evidence that the auditory perception of verbal items is unaffected, suggests a distinction between separate auditory and visual short-term stores, the former being selectively impaired.

These patients offer a unique opportunity to investigate the role of auditory–verbal STM in language functions. The STM patients show some impairment of speech comprehension: The defect appears confined to sentences, comprehension of individual words being spared (Caramazza, Basili, Koller, & Berndt, 1981; Saffran & Marin, 1975; Vallar & Baddeley, 1984b).

As to speech production, case K.F. had halting speech with some word-finding difficulties and circumlocutions (Warrington & Shallice, 1969). However, case J.B. had fluent spontaneous speech, with a normal amount of pausing and a normal degree of paraphasic errors (Shallice & Butterworth, 1977).

The observation of a selective impairment of the auditory–verbal short-term store, not associated with any defect of the production of speech, is not consistent with those "output" models that assume that the store is articulatory in nature, being involved in the smooth production of speech (Baddeley, Thomson & Buchanan, 1975; Ellis, 1979). Furthermore, an "output" location of the store cannot account for the auditory/visual dissociation. Conversely, Shallice and Butterworth's (1977) observation suggests an "input" locus of the auditory–verbal short-term store.

Evidence from normal subjects also argues for the existence of a non-articulatory system where phonologically coded information is stored. The phonological similarity effect (Conrad & Hull, 1964) (i.e. immediate memory span is greater for phonologically dissimilar items than for similar) is abolished by the continuous uttering of some irrelevant speech (articulatory suppression) only when the material is visually presented; when presentation is auditory the effect is not removed by suppression (Baddeley, Lewis, & Vallar, 1984; Levy, 1971; Murray, 1968; Peterson & Johnson, 1971).

A further case for a phonological non-articulatory short-term store comes from the investigation of the effects of unattended speech on immediate memory. Salamè and Baddeley (1982) showed that unattended speech impairs immediate memory for visually presented items, the disruption being related to the phonological similarity between the remembered and the disrupting items, the meaning of the unattended speech being unimportant. As the disruptive effect was found not to occur when subjects were required to suppress articulation, they concluded that by the process of subvocal rehearsal the visual items gain optional access to a phonological short-term store, which is obligatorily fed by the irrelevant spoken material (see Salamè & Baddeley, 1982, for a more detailed discussion).

Recently, Vallar and Baddeley (1984a) indicated the phonological non-articulatory short-term store as the functional locus of the deficit in a patient with a grossly defective auditory–verbal span, but normal speech (see Basso et al., 1982). Case P.V. showed the standard phonological similarity effect on verbal span with auditory presentation, but, at variance with normal individuals, she did not display any effect of similarity when presentation was visual. Furthermore, the patient, again unlike normal subjects, did not display any detrimental effect of articulatory suppression on immediate memory of visual items.

The effect of word length was also studied. In normal subjects the span for short words is greater than the span for long, an effect that appears to reflect the process of articulation being abolished by articulatory suppression (Baddeley et al., 1975, 1984). The patient did not display any effect of word length, although articulation *per se* was not impaired.

The absence of the standard effect of phonological similarity with visual material is consistent with the view that P.V.'s phonological short-term store is defective: Due to the impairment of this system, P.V. codes visually presented items in a non-phonological mode, presumably visual, as suggested by Warrington and Shallice (1972). The lack of both a detrimental effect of suppression on span and an effect of word length shows that P.V. is not using the process of subvocal rehearsal: If the phonological store is damaged, a strategy of articulatory rehearsal, which recodes visually presented material and feeds it to this store, is presumably of little value.

Vallar and Baddeley (1984a) concluded that this pattern of results provides evidence for a *phonological non-articulatory short-term store*, which is defective in P.V.'s case. Auditorily presented items have obligatory access to this store; the phonological similarity effect reflects the activity of such a system. The phonological store appears involved in short-term memory tasks such as auditory–verbal span and is useful in sentence comprehension; it does not seem to play an important role in the production of speech. Information stored in this system may be refreshed by an *articulatory rehearsal process* (see Fig. 1), which, in addition, allows *phonological recoding*[1] of visual material, for the purpose of access to the phonological store (see Vallar & Baddeley, 1984a, 1984b, for further details).

Within the frame of this working memory model, the present study aimed at assessing the role of articulation in STM performance. To investigate this issue, we took advantage of the availability of a patient who is totally inarticulate due to a brainstem lesion, but has no general cognitive impairment (see Cappa, Pirovano, & Vignolo, 1985, for a detailed description of G.F.'s performance on an extensive battery, including tests for non-verbal intelligence, for auditory language comprehension, for visuo-spatial judgement, and for reading comprehension).

THE PATIENT

G.F. was a 34-year-old male, right-handed, with five years of schooling, who, at the age of 20, suffered a stroke, presumably an infarction in the ventral pons. G.F.'s condition was stationary since the onset of the disease.

[1] The subsequent study of a patient anarthric due to bilateral cortical lesions has provided evidence for fractionating the *rehearsal process* into two subcomponents: (1) *phonological recoding*, which provides phonological conversion of visual items; (2) *articulatory rehearsal*, which feeds the output of phonological recoding to the phonological short-term store and recirculates information held in this latter storage system, preventing its decay (Vallar & Cappa, 1987).

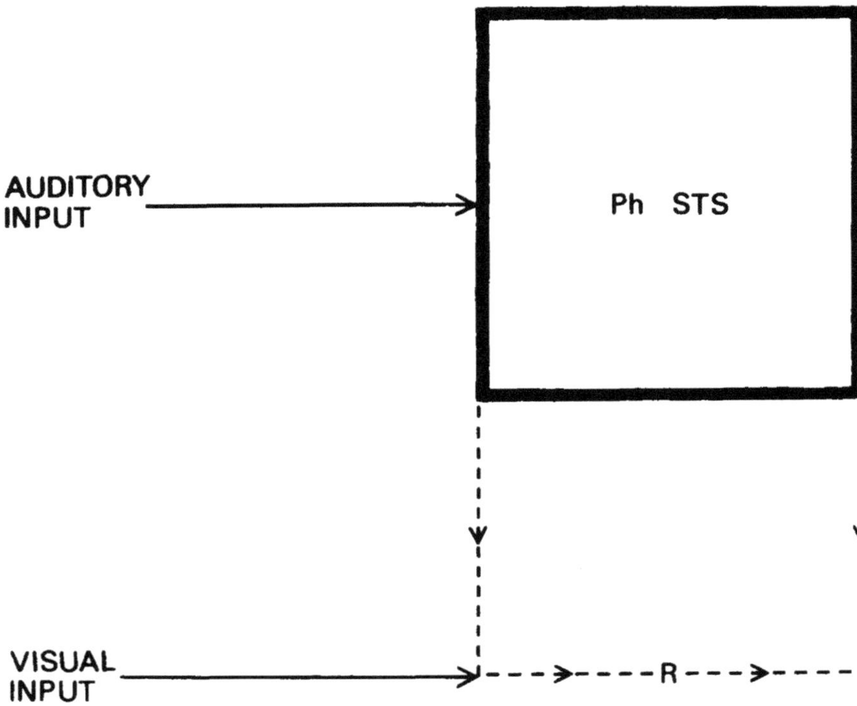

FIG 1. The phonological short-term store (Ph. STS) and the rehearsal process (R). Auditory verbal material has a direct obligatory access to the Ph. STS. Visual verbal material may enter the Ph. STS through R, which, in addition, refreshes the phonological memory trace, preventing its decay. The Ph. STS is an input storage system involved in short-term memory tasks such as span and in sentence comprehension. The flow chart shows only the components of working memory investigated by the present series of experiments (see, for further details, Salamè & Baddeley, 1982; Vallar & Baddeley, 1984a, 1984b).

He had a spastic tetraplegia, which confined him to a wheelchair. Some left/right and upward/downward movements of the head were possible. No sensory deficit was apparent, and the hearing thresholds, as assessed with a standard pure tone audiometry, were normal. Furthermore, G.F.'s performance was errorless in a phonological discrimination task, using natural consonant–vowel syllables, which comprised discrimination of voicing and place contrasts. The patient was speechless, but was able to respond to oral and written questions using vertical eye movements (downwards meant "yes", upwards "no"). In addition, G.F. was able to provide written responses by using a commercial apparatus, Possum Link, developed as a typewriting device for the severely motor disabled. The apparatus consisted of a transducer and a letter board connected to a typewriter. The patient, by means of a slight rotation of the head, pressed upon the transducer. This caused the letters printed on the board to light up one after the other. When the target letter lit up, G.F. released the pressure and the typewriter connected to the apparatus typed the letter. The production of a single letter with such a device was very laborious and took some 20 seconds. This is to be considered in evaluating G.F.'s memory performance.

THE EXPERIMENTS

Experiment 1: Auditory Digit Span

Sequences of digits were presented at the rate of one item per second. Within each particular sequence no digit was repeated. The sequences were presented in ascending order. For each length, 10 sequences were given; however, if G.F. recalled the first three sequences of a given length correctly, we assumed that this length was within his span and proceeded up to the following length. G.F. recalled the sequences by making use of the typewriting apparatus. G.F. recalled with complete accuracy sequences of two, three, and four digits. In the case of five-digit sequences, the patient recalled 60% of the sequences correctly (the proportion of correct items in the appropriate serial position was 0.78).

Experiment 2: Matching Auditory Digits

Digit sequences of increasing length were used for this matching task, which did not require the use of the typewriting device. Pairs of sequences were presented at the rate of one item per second, with a pause of two seconds between the two sequences. Each length comprised 10 pairs of sequences, in five of which one item was different, whereas in the remaining five, they were identical: for example, 3714–3714, or, alternatively, 8317–8917. G.F. had received instructions to respond "same" or "different" by vertical eye movements. G.F. matched with complete accuracy sequences comprising two, three, four, and five digits. With six-item strings he matched 80% of the pairs accurately.

Experiment 3: Phonological Similarity Effect

Two pools of letters were used. The phonologically dissimilar set (control) comprised F, K, Q, R, X, W, and Z. The similar set comprised B, C, D, G, P, V, and T. From each set, 10 sequences of either two, three, or four letters were generated at random. Within a particular sequence no letter was repeated. Both the auditory and the visual modality of presentation were tested. Auditory letters were spoken by the examiner. In the visual modality, lower case black letters were shown on white cards. Rate of presentation of the items and order of testing of the sequences were identical to those used in the auditory digit span test. G.F. provided his answers by the typewriting device. Table 1 shows the proportion of sequences recalled with complete accuracy and the proportion of items recalled in the appropriate serial position. It is apparent that G.F. displays the effect of phonological similarity with both auditory and visual presentation: The performance is better in the control condition than when the letters are phonologically similar.

Experiment 4: Word-length Effect

The effect of word length on immediate memory span was investigated using auditory presentation of sequences of words of two and five syllables. The following eight two-syllable words were used: *lupo*, *casa*, *pane*, *Aldo*, *posta*, *nave*, *libro*, *Spagna*. The eight five-syllable words were *ippopotamo*, *abitazione*, *peperonata*, *Massimiliano*, *corrispondenza*, *sommergibile*, *dattilografa*, *Cecoslovacchia*. Each pool comprised one word from each semantic category. For each word length, four sequence lengths were used, each comprising 10 strings of two, three, four, and five words. Rate of presentation and order of testing were identical to those used in the previous experiments. G.F. had received instructions to indicate recognition by pointing to the presented words, using the typewriting device. The eight words of each set were printed in a row on a board. In order to avoid spatial cues, the position of the words was changed for each trial. Table 2 shows the proportion of correct sequences and the proportion of items recalled in the appropriate serial position. It is apparent that G.F., unlike

TABLE 1
Phonological Similarity Effect[a]

	Auditory Presentation			
Sequence Length	*Control* *Sequences (items)*		*Ph. Similarity* *Sequences (items)*	
2	1.0	(1.0)	1.0	(1.0)
3	1.0	(1.0)	1.0	(1.0)
4	1.0	(1.0)	0.10	(0.40)
	Visual Presentation			
Sequence Length	*Control* *Sequences (items)*		*Ph. Similarity* *Sequences (items)*	
2	1.0	(1.0)	1.0	(1.0)
3	1.0	(1.0)	0.80	(0.90)
4	0.70	(0.77)	0.30	(0.57)

[a]Probability of correctly recalling phonologically similar and dissimilar consonant sequences with auditory and visual presentation.

TABLE 2
Word-length Effect[a]

Sequence Length	*Two-syllable Words Sequences (items)*		*Five-syllable Words Sequences (items)*	
2	1.0	(1.0)	1.0	(1.0)
3	1.0	(1.0)	1.0	(1.0)
4	0.80	(0.85)	0.80	(0.85)
5	0.10	(0.48)	0.30	(0.68)

[a] Probability of correctly recalling two- and five-syllable word sequences with auditory presentation.

normal subjects (Baddeley et al., 1975, 1984; Vallar & Baddeley, 1984a), does not show any effect of word length: Immediate memory for short words is no better than immediate memory for long.

Experiment 5: Rhyme Judgements

Previous studies, ranging from recognition of individual letters to sentence comprehension, had shown that G.F. had no dyslexic disorders (Cappa et al., 1985). In this experiment, G.F.'s ability to make rhyme judgements was investigated. Three rhyming tests were given.

(1) *Picture–Picture Rhyming Test.* In each trial of this task, two square cards were presented to the patient: In the centre of the left-hand card there was a single picture; the right-hand card was divided into four quadrants, with a picture printed into each quadrant. The name of the left-hand stimulus rhymed with the name of one of the four pictures on the right-hand card. The items were taken from the Peabody Picture Vocabulary Test (Dunn, 1965). G.F. was instructed to find out which picture rhymed with the left-hand item. The four-choice pictures were indicated by the examiner one after the other. G.F. responded by vertical eye movements. Twenty-one trials were given. In the multiple-choice display, the correct picture occurred equally often in each position in a random order. No time limit was set for responding.

(2) *Word–Picture Rhyming Test.* This test differed from the previous one in that a word was printed in upper case on the left-hand card. The 21 four-choice cards of the previous experiment were used. G.F. was required to find out the picture that had a name rhyming with the word.

(3) *Non-word–Picture Rhyming Test.* This test was identical with the Word–Picture Test except that a pronounceable non-word was printed on the left-hand card.

Control data were collected from three subjects matched for age and educational level. It is apparent that the patient has an ability to make rhyme judgements comparable to that of the three matched controls: Picture–Picture Test, G.F. 13/21, controls 12.70 (s.d. 0.58); Word–Picture Test, G.F. 18/21, controls 16.30 (s.d. 1.53); Non-word–Picture Test, G.F. 16/21, controls 18.00 (s.d. 1.73). G.F.'s unimpaired performance in the Non-word–Picture condition suggests that he is able to make rhyme judgements also without a lexical mediation.

DISCUSSION

In spite of an extremely severe defect of articulation, G.F. has an immediate memory span of five digits and is able to match six-item sequences successfully. Like normal subjects, G.F. shows the standard effect of phonological similarity in immediate auditory memory span (Conrad & Hull, 1964). Previous investigations showed that G.F.'s comprehension, both at the clinical level and as assessed by the Token Test, was unimpaired (Cappa et al., 1985). Nebes (1975) reported the case of a left-hemisphere-damaged patient who was totally unable to produce any recognisable word or syllable: She had an auditory digit span of six digits, did not display any comprehension defect at the clinical level, and had an unimpaired performance on the Token Test. Conversely, patients with a defective phonological short-term store have a grossly reduced auditory verbal span (about two, three digits) and show some impairment of speech comprehension (Saffran & Marin, 1975; Vallar & Baddeley, 1984b). G.F.'s preserved auditory digit span, the presence of the standard effect of phonological similarity with auditory presentation, and the lack of any comprehension disorder concur to suggest that the patient's phonological short-term store, to which auditory items have direct access, has been spared. Such a conclusion is consistent with the view that the phonological short-term store is non-articulatory in nature and has an "input" locus (Vallar & Baddeley, 1984a).

The presence of the phonological similarity effect with visual material suggests that a severe articulatory impairment, such as in G.F.'s case, does not prevent the phonological recoding of visually presented material for the purpose of access to the phonological short-term store. The anarthric patients described by Nebes (1975) and by Baddeley and Wilson (see Baddeley, 1983) both display the detrimental effect of phonological similarity on immediate memory for visually presented sequences of letters. These findings provide some evidence that the phonological recoding of visually presented material, provided by the process of "articulatory" rehearsal (Salamè & Baddeley, 1982; Vallar & Baddeley, 1984a) may occur in spite of a gross impairment of overt articulation.

Hence, the rehearsal process appears to be relatively independent of the actual realisation of speech.

The observation that G.F. does not show the effect of word length, which reflects the activity of the rehearsal process (Baddeley et al., 1975, 1984) suggests that the patient did not rehearse in such a task (Experiment 4). Whether this was due to a failure of the rehearsal process or was a strategy choice is unclear. However, it is worth noticing that the response modality could have prompted G.F. to adopt a visuo-spatial strategy. Furthermore, evidence has been provided that anarthric patients may display the standard detrimental effect of word length on auditory memory span performance (Baddeley, 1983; Vallar & Cappa, 1987).

G.F., like other anarthric patients (Nebes, 1975; Baddeley, 1983), is able to make rhyme judgements. This finding, together with the presence of the phonological similarity effect with visual material, corroborates the conclusion that a gross defect of overt articulation does not prevent the phonological recoding of visual material. The anarthric patients' preserved ability to make rhyme judgements is consistent with evidence from normal subjects. Baddeley and Lewis (1981) and Besner, Davies, and Daniels (1981) have shown that articulatory suppression does not disrupt the ability to make phonological judgements about words and non-words.

Finally, the present data from case G.F., together with the results of Nebes (1975) and Baddeley and Wilson (see Baddeley, 1983), may be relevant to the controversial issue (see Margolin, Griebel, & Wolford, 1982) of the interpretation of the effect of articulatory suppression. In normal individuals, suppression abolishes the effect of phonological similarity on memory span, provided that presentation is visual (e.g. Murray, 1968; Peterson & Johnson, 1971). The observation of such an effect in anarthric patients suggests that articulatory suppression does not prevent the phonological recoding of visual material for the purpose of access to the phonological short-term store by interfering with the more peripheral articulatory mechanisms, which therefore appear not to be closely involved in the rehearsal process.

REFERENCES

Baddeley, A. D. (1983) Working memory. *Philosophical Transactions of the Royal Society, London, B302*, 311–324.

Baddeley, A. D. & Lewis, V. (1981) Interactive processes in reading: The inner voice, the inner ear and the inner eye. In A. M. Lesgold & C. A. Perfetti (Eds.), *Proceedings of the Pittsburgh conference on interactive processes in reading.* Hillsdale, N.J.: Lawrence Erlbaum Associates Inc.

Baddeley, A. D., Lewis, V., & Vallar, G. (1984) Exploring the articulatory loop. *Quarterly Journal of Experimental Psychology, 36A*, 233–252.

Baddeley, A. D., Thomson, N., & Buchanan, M. (1975) Word length and the structure of short-term memory. *Journal of Verbal Learning and Verbal Behavior, 14*, 575–589.

Basso, A., Spinnler, H., Vallar, G., & Zanobio, M. E. (1982) Left hemisphere damage and selective impairment of auditory verbal short-term memory: A case study. *Neuropsychologia*, *20*, 263–274.

Besner, D., Davies, J., & Daniels, S. (1981) Reading for meaning. The effects of concurrent articulation. *Quarterly Journal of Experimental Psychology*, *33A*, 415–437.

Cappa, S. F., Pirovano, C., & Vignolo, L. A. (1985) Chronic "locked-in" syndrome: Psychological study of a case. *European Neurology*, *24*, 107–111.

Caramazza, A., Basili, A. G., Koller, J. J., & Berndt, R. S. (1981) An investigation of repetition and language processing in a case of conduction aphasia. *Brain and Language*, *14*, 235–271.

Conrad, R. & Hull, A. J. (1964) Information, acoustic confusion and memory span. *British Journal of Psychology*, *55*, 429–432.

Dunn, L. M. (1965) *Peabody Picture Vocabulary Test.* Circle Pines, Minn.: American Guidance Service Inc.

Ellis, A. W. (1979) Speech production and short-term memory. In J. Morton & J. C. Marshall (Eds.), *Psycholinguistic series 2. Structure and process.* London: Paul Elek.

Levy, B. A. (1971) The role of articulation in articulatory and visual short-term memory. *Journal of Verbal Learning and Verbal Behavior*, *10*, 123–132.

Margolin, C. M., Griebel, B., & Wolford, G. (1982) Effects of distraction on reading versus listening. *Journal of Experimental Psychology: Learning, Memory and Cognition*, *8*, 613–618.

Murray, D. J. (1968) Articulation and acoustic confusability in short-term memory. *Journal of Experimental Psychology*, *78*, 679–684.

Nebes, R. D. (1975) The nature of internal speech in a patient with aphemia. *Brain and Language*, *2*, 489–497.

Peterson, L. R. & Johnson, S. T. (1971) Some effects of minimizing articulation on short-term retention. *Journal of Verbal Learning and Verbal Behavior*, *10*, 346–354.

Saffran, E. & Marin, O. S. M. (1975) Immediate memory for word list and sentences in a patient with a deficient auditory short-term memory. *Brain and Language*, *2*, 420–433.

Salamè, P. & Baddeley, A. D. (1982) Disruption of short-term memory by unattended speech: Implications for the structure of working memory. *Journal of Verbal Learning and Verbal Behavior*, *21*, 150–164.

Shallice, T. & Butterworth, B. (1977) Short-term memory impairment and spontaneous speech. *Neuropsychologia*, *15*, 729–735.

Vallar, G. & Baddeley, A. D. (1984a) Fractionation of working memory: Neuropsychological evidence for a phonological short-term store. *Journal of Verbal Learning and Verbal Behavior*, *23*, 151–161.

Vallar, G. & Baddeley, A. D. (1984b) Phonological short-term store, phonological processing and sentence comprehension: A neuropsychological case study. *Cognitive Neuropsychology*, *1*, 121–141.

Vallar, G. & Cappa, S. F. (1987) Articulation and verbal short-term memory: Evidence from anarthria. *Cognitive Neuropsychology*, *4*, 55–78.

Warrington, E. K., Logue, V., & Pratt, R. T. C. (1971) The anatomical localisation of selective impairment of auditory verbal short-term memory. *Neuropsychologia*, *9*, 377–387.

Warrington, E. K. & Shallice, T. (1969) The selective impairment of auditory–verbal short-term memory. *Brain*, *92*, 885–896.

Warrington, E. K. & Shallice, T. (1972) Neuropsychological evidence of visual storage in short-term memory tasks. *Quarterly Journal of Experimental Psychology*, *24*, 30–40.

Author Index

Subject Index

For Product Safety Concerns and Information please contact our EU
representative GPSR@taylorandfrancis.com
Taylor & Francis Verlag GmbH, Kaufingerstraße 24, 80331 München, Germany

www.ingramcontent.com/pod-product-compliance
Ingram Content Group UK Ltd.
Pitfield, Milton Keynes, MK11 3LW, UK
UKHW021504240926
475702UK00035B/362

* 9 7 8 1 1 3 8 6 3 9 0 5 8 *